FALSE MESSIAH

Books by the same author

CRICKET
Keith Miller: A Cricketing Biography
All in a day: Great Moments in Cup Cricket
A Maidan View: The Magic of Indian Cricket
Cricket Voices (interviews)
A History of Indian Cricket

FOOTBALL
Behind Closed Doors: Dreams and Nightmares at Spurs
(Irving Scholar's years at Tottenham)

HISTORY AND BIOGRAPHY
The Lost Hero: A Biography of Subhas Bose
The Aga Khans
Michael Grade: Screening the Image
Sporting Colours: Sport and Politics in South Africa

BUSINESS
The Crash (The 1987–88 world market slump)
A New Money Crisis
Are you covered? (insurance)
Fraud – the growth industry of the 1980s
How to Invest in a Bear Market

AUTOBIOGRAPHY
The Sporting Alien

FALSE MESSIAH

The Life and Times
of Terry Venables

by

Mihir Bose

ANDRE DEUTSCH

To Hyman, Jonathan and Peter
and all the other long-suffering Tottenham and other
football supporters who deserve better.

First published in 1996 by
André Deutsch Limited
106 Great Russell Street
London WC1B 3LJ

CIP data for this title is available
from the British Library

ISBN 0 233 98998 6

Printed and bound in Great Britain by
WBC, Bridgend

Contents

Prologue	The day the Tottenham Board met at Arsenal	1
Chapter 1	The making of an institution	7
2	From Terry to El Tel	27
3	An old school friend	38
4	An eerie game	44
5	Terry's other club	57
6	Enter Alan Sugar	72
7	The untouchable	79
8	The dream comes true	86
9	Sacrifice of a dearest friend	93
10	Football's Leonardo da Vinci	106
11	The disappearing dance-floor, and other matters	117
12	Partners, but unequal	127
13	The Lazio money	143
14	The Scribes backlash	156
15	Uneasy spring	160
16	Ducking, diving and horse-trading	172
17	Undressing a transfer	180
18	The autumn of Venables' discontent	196
19	Time-bombs at Christmas	213
20	Dear Terry . . . Dear Alan	219
21	Battle lines are formed	225

22	The end game	236
23	Capturing the high ground	250
24	Bambi refuses to die	267
25	Venables' audacious coup	277
26	The war of the affidavits	283
27	The battle to save Edennote	297
28	The pictures on the wall and the screen	310
29	Of plots and conspiracies	319
30	Football and writs	345
31	The policemen and the judge	372
Postscript	Which is the real Venables?	413
Appendixes	Dates and major events in Terry Venables' life	421
	Terry Venables: companies record to 1 April 1996	427

Author's preface and acknowledgements

Terry Venables and I have one thing in common. In our youth we both fell in love with Spurs. He wanted to be their manager and more than fulfilled his ambition; I just wanted to see them repeat their feat of becoming the first team this century to win the double, and am still waiting.

Although our common love for Tottenham Hotspur does not explain this book, it explains my consuming interest in Tottenham. Even as a journalist specialising in sports and football, I was always more than interested in what was happening at Tottenham and so keenly followed Venables through his managerial career there and when he became part-owner of the club.

It was with a sense of shock and bewilderment that I saw on 'News at Ten' on the night of Thursday 13 May 1993 that the next day Venables' future as chief executive was under threat. Just over six weeks earlier I had written for my then newspaper, the *Sunday Times*, an article headlined 'Second Coming of Venables'. The article, appearing on the day Tottenham faced Arsenal in the semi-final of that year's FA Cup, explained how Venables had transformed Spurs. It went on to say that, if Tottenham beat Arsenal, 'then the fans at Tottenham's Paxton Road End would probably christen him the man with the magic wand.' I concluded the article by saying that, such was the confidence of the Tottenham team that, whatever happened against Arsenal, the future belonged to White Hart Lane and I saw this future as being shaped by Venables. In researching the article I had gone to

Tottenham's training ground and had, along with other journalists, spoken to Venables.

The Monday before ITN carried that shattering news I was at Highbury and saw Tottenham beat Arsenal, always a source of great joy, and detected no signs of any such announcement. My sense of bewilderment about what was happening to Venables increased when, after his sacking, he kept insisting that he did not know why he had been sacked. He was to repeat this theme many times on that Saturday's 'Cup Final Grandstand' on the BBC and it seemed the most obvious question for me to investigate. How could Venables, about whom such eulogies had been written on 4 April, now five weeks later be so suddenly removed and by a man whom I hardly knew, Alan Sugar? That same month I had written an article in a business magazine which was quite critical of Sugar.

My first article attempting to answer this question appeared in the *Sunday Times* the weekend of Venables' sacking and that may be said to be the starting point of this book. Since then I have discovered much about Venables, not only in relation to Sugar, but in respect of other people, many of whom date back to long before Venables became part-owner of Spurs. As I discovered more of the story I was struck by how little had emerged in the public domain and also that no attempt had been made to integrate it and present a more complete picture.

This is the main reason I have written this biography. Although no biography of Venables had appeared until that written by his father, Fred, in 1990, in the last three years there have been quite a few. Harry Harris and Steve Curry have written a joint one, *Venables: The Inside Story* (Headline, 1994), as has Guy Nathan, although his *Barcelona to Bedlam* (1994) deals almost wholly with Venables' legal problems with Sugar. Venables himself has written, with Neil Hanson, *Venables: The Autobiography* (Michael Joseph, 1994), and with Jane Nottage *Venables' England* (Box Tree, 1996). So on the face of it another book on Venables might seem superfluous. But it is not. My book is the first that aims to pull all the strands together and to present the complete man, a man of football who has also been an extraordinary man of business.

I have been spurred on in this task by the fact that Venables' autobiography seems to raise more questions than it answers – and often appears to ignore entire episodes of his life. Also, since the other books appeared, much more material on Venables, and particularly on his business activities, has emerged in court cases.

Author's preface and acknowledgements

It is these court records, transcripts and affidavits that, along with interviews, form the central basis of this book.

When I first started writing regularly on Venables in May 1993, Chris Nawrat was the Sports Editor of the *Sunday Times*. He greatly encouraged me, as did his successor, Nick Pitt. It was, as ever, a joy to work with Jeff Randall – one of the few journalists who understands both sports and business, even if his football sense is deficient, given his support for West Ham.

David Welch, the Sports Editor of the *Daily Telegraph* has been a great tower of strength and I am grateful for his support and encouragement, along with many others on the *Telegraph* sports desk, including Keith Perry, Brian Oliver, Brian Stater, Gareth David, Clive Ellis and Martin Smith – not to forget those two lovely ladies, Karen and Nicky.

I do not normally like to thank lawyers but I must record my gratitude to Arthur Wynn Davies, for I have come to appreciate Arthur's sound legal sense and steadfastness under fire.

I am grateful to Tom Rosenthal of André Deutsch for taking on this book. I have warm memories of our partnership during the publishing of my *A History of Indian Cricket*, and it was rewarding to work again with John Bright-Holmes and be reminded of his editorial skills. The partnership with André Deutsch also meant reviving an old and pleasurable link with David Hooper of Biddle & Co.

I am also immensely grateful to Wendy Wimbush who, at a very late stage, worked all hours God gave her to retype the final revised version of the book.

Many, many people helped me with information or advice during the course of my research. I cannot name them all, but I would like, in particular, to thank: Roy Ackerman, Douglas Alexiou, Martin Bashir, Ken Bates, Tony Berry, Noel Botham, Patrick Cheney, Steve Clarke, Philip Clarke, Steve Coppell, Philip Clothier, Tina Cook, Donna Cullen, Rod Dadak, Steve Davies, Hugh Dehn, David Dein, Tony Diamond, Shane Dougall, Philip Green, Gavin Hamilton, Harry Harris, Micky Hazard, Kate Hoey, James Hook, Chris Horrie, Vincent Isaacs, Frank Kane, Ash and Imran Karim, Mark Killick, Bernard Kingsley, Alan Mullery, Billy Nixon, Ron Noades, Myles Palmer, Rick Parry, Piers Pottinger, Paul Riviere, Dennis Roach, Irving Scholar, Brian Scovell, Nat Solomon, Peter Staunton, Mark Stephens, Ian Stott, David Swindlehurst, Sue Taylor, Geoffrey Van-Hay, Dee Walker, Frank

Warren, Noel White, Colin Wright, and Igal Yawetz. None of these people, named or not, is responsible for any errors or omissions in the book. Only I, as author, feature in that penalty area.

Above all I wish to thank my family – my wife Kalpana and my daughter Indira – including our extended family of Peter and Ann, who all know what this book has meant to me, and how its problems and complexities have made me face situations which I have not encountered over any of my previous books.

In one sense the account that follows in this book is incomplete because one character in the story cannot, for legal reasons, be named. 'John Brown' is a pseudonym.

The acknowledgements and thanks of the author and the publishers are due to the following for the use of copyright photographs: Popperfoto; Mirror Syndication International Ltd; Paul Riviere; Richard Young; *Daily Mirror*; Solo International Ltd.

Dramatis Personae

(The principal characters who feature in this book)

Ackerman, Roy	Executive Producer at Diverse, a television production company.
Alexiou, Douglas	Lawyer, non-executive director of Tottenham.
Allison, Malcolm	Former manager of Crystal Palace who persuaded Venables to become a coach. Boyhood hero of Venables.
Armfield, Jimmy	Former England and Blackpool captain, a head-hunter for the FA.
Ball, Ted	Head of Landhurst Leasing, a finance company now in liquidation.
Barnes, Peter	Secretary of Tottenham Hotspur Football Club.
Bashir, Martin	Journalist who researched and presented two *Panorama* programmes on Venables.
Bates, Ken	Chairman of Chelsea FC.
Berrick, Bernard	British expatriate living in Monte Carlo.
Berrick, Steven	His son, a barrister.
Berry, Tony	Director of Tottenham, now vice-chairman.
Bindman, Geoffrey	Partner of legal firm Bindman & Partners.
Bloye, Ray	Crystal Palace chairman under whom Venables worked as manager.
Bobroff, Paul	Former chairman, Tottenham Hotspur plc, the quoted company that wholly owns the football club.

Botham, Noel	An original shareholder of Scribes West.
Bowhay, Chris	Company secretary of Printdouble.
Brown, David	Former director of Transatlantic Inns. No connection with John Brown.
Brown, John	Pseudonym of a business associate of Venables who cannot be named for legal reasons.
Burridge, John	Crystal Palace player.
Burton, Ian	Partner of Burton Copeland, one of two law firms that act for Venables.
Buxton, Ted	Chief scout for England. Also chief scout at Tottenham during Venables' time at the club.
Calvino, Ivy	Former employee at Tottenham Hotspur.
Celon, Lionello	Managing director of Lazio FC.
Cheney, Patrick	Sports administrator who works with Kate Hoey, MP, and Lord Howell, former Labour Minister of Sport.
Clarke, Philip	Head of Programmes, Diverse, who produced a programme on Venables.
Clemence, Ray	Former Liverpool, Tottenham and England goalkeeper. Acted as Tottenham coach under Venables.
Clough, Brian	Former manager of Nottingham Forest.
Coomber, Richard	A director of Chris McCann Management, a Venables company.
Cooper, Sue	One of the owners of the Independent Balloon Company.
Coppell, Steve	Former Crystal Palace manager, now director of coaching at Crystal Palace and member of the three-man Premier League bungs inquiry.
Crystal, Jonathan	Barrister, former non-executive director of Tottenham Hotspur, long-time friend of Terry Venables.
Cullen, Donna	PR adviser for Venables at Good Relations (part of Lowe Bell) during his early public battles with Sugar.
Dadak, Rod	Specialist libel solicitor and Paul Riviere's lawyer.

Davies, David	Former BBC journalist, now the FA's chief press spokesman.
Davies, Steve	Organiser, with Bernard Kingsley, of Tottenham Independent Supporters' Association (TISA).
Dehn, Hugh	Producer of a *Dispatches* programme on Venables.
Dein, David	Vice-chairman of Arsenal.
Denton Hall	Lawyers for Premier League.
Docherty, Tommy	Manager of Chelsea under whom Venables played.
Dougall, Shane	Jeff Fugler's barrister during his court case against Venables and Scribes West.
Durie, Gordon	Venables' first purchase on becoming chief executive of Tottenham.
Dyer, Charlie	Former employee of Landhurst Leasing.
Ebsworth, Jonathan	Former colleague of Bryan Fugler at Fugler & Co.
Ebsworth, K. J.	Manager of NatWest Bank, Woolwich, in 1991.
Farrer, David	QC brought in by Venables during the second stage of the Fugler v. Scribes West case.
Fenton, Ronnie	Assistant manager at Nottingham Forest under Brian Clough.
Fenwick, Terry	Now Portsmouth manager, played for Venables at Crystal Palace, QPR and Tottenham.
Freedman, Edward	Former head of Tottenham's merchandising department.
Finers	Law firm which acted for Venables.
Flanagan, Mike	Crystal Palace player whom Venables bought when he moved as manager to QPR.
Fugler, Bryan	Lawyer whose firm, Fugler & Co., acted for both Tottenham and Venables.
Fugler, Jeff	PR and advertising executive. His firm acted for Tottenham and Scribes West. Brother of Bryan Fugler.
Gascoigne, Paul	England international. Played for Newcastle, Tottenham, Lazio and now Rangers.

Gilbert, Harvey	Businessman, friend of Alan Sugar.
Gillick, Larry	Businessman involved in Venables' first attempt to buy Tottenham.
Gloster, Elizabeth	QC who wrote a legal opinion for the Tottenham Board.
Gold, David	Partner of Herbert Smith, the legal firm that acts for Sugar and Tottenham.
Gregory, Jim	Former owner of Queens Park Rangers, now owner of Portsmouth.
Graham, George	Former Arsenal manager, Venables' clubmate at Chelsea.
Green, Philip	Businessman and friend of Venables.
Hall, Eric	Football agent, long-standing friend of Venables. First cousin of Bryan and Jeff Fugler.
Hamilton, Gavin Hans	Manager of Scribes West when Venables took over.
Harkouk, Rashid	Crystal Palace player when Venables was manager.
Harris, Harry	Football correspondent of the *Daily Mirror*.
Hewer, Nick	PR adviser for Sugar and Tottenham.
Hoey, Kate	Labour MP for Vauxhall, with a special interest in sport.
Holmes, John	Football agent who acts for Gary Lineker amongst other sports personalities.
Horne, Graham	DTI inspector.
Horrie, Chris	Author of *Sick as a Parrot: the inside story of the Spurs fiasco.*
Hounam, Peter	Former *Daily Mirror* investigative reporter.
Illidge, Stephen	Former financial controller of Landhurst Leasing.
Isaacs, Vincent	Businessman, shareholder in Scribes West.
Jacobs, Nick	Former accountant at Tottenham.
Jefferis, Michael	Barrister who appeared for Venables in several of his court cases, including those against Jeff Fugler and Paul Kirby.
Jolles, Bernard	Former director of merchant bankers Henry Ansbacher.
Kanter Jules Grangewoods	Law firm which acted for Venables.

Karim, Ash	Jeff Fugler's solicitor.
Karim, Imran	Son of Ash, who also works for Karim & Co.
Kelly, Graham	Former secretary of the Football League, now chief executive of the Football Association.
Killick, Mark	Producer of two *Panorama* programmes on Venables the businessman.
Kingsley, Bernard	Organiser, with Steve Davies, of Tottenham Independent Supporters' Association.
Kirby, Paul	Business associate of Venables, a former director of Transatlantic Inns.
Koumi, Iac	Works for merchant bankers Henry Ansbacher.
Lalwani, Gulu	Businessman, owner of Binatone.
Lineker, Gary	Played for Venables at Barcelona and Tottenham.
Livermore, Doug	Former coach at Tottenham.
McLintock, Frank	Former Arsenal and Scotland captain, acted as football agent, partner of Graham Smith in one of the First Wave Sports Management companies.
Mann, Martin	QC who represented Venables in his initial court battles with Sugar.
Maxwell, Robert	Controversial tycoon who at one stage owned two football clubs and wanted to buy Tottenham.
Millichip, Sir Bert	Chairman of the FA.
Mountfort, Margaret	Partner in Herbert Smith law firm.
Nayim, Mohamed Ali Amar	Former Tottenham player.
Needham, Ray	Detective Inspector of Chelsea CID.
Noades, Ron	Crystal Palace chairman.
Norfina	The company that lent Venables the money to help him buy Tottenham.
Parkinson, Stephen	DTI inspector.
Parry, Rick	Chief executive of Premier League.
Pay, Mike	Former employee at Tottenham Hotspur.
Pleat, David	Venables' predecessor as manager of Tottenham.
Pottesman, Melvyn	Lawyer with Kanter Jules Grangewoods, now deceased.

Pottinger, Piers	Director of Lowe Bell, the PR firm that acted for Venables.
Powell, Jeff	Chief sports features writer of the *Daily Mail*.
Pawlikowski, Jakob (Joe)	Business associate of Terry Venables. Later Secretary of Scribes West.
Rahman, Amin	DTI inspector.
Rahman, Anis	Former credit controller of Tottenham.
Reid, Robert, QC	Member of the three-man Premier League bungs inquiry.
Riviere, Paul	Former business associate of Venables.
Roach, Dennis	Football agent.
Rollo, Mike	Tottenham's commercial manager.
Salber, Michael	Lawyer with Kanter Jules Grangewoods.
Sandy, Colin	Former finance director of Tottenham, now non-executive director. Also administers Sugar's private companies.
Santin, Gino	Italian restaurateur, with experience of international football negotiations.
Scholar, Irving	Former chairman of Tottenham Hotspur who signed Venables as manager.
Shreeves, Peter	Had two spells as manager of Tottenham, the second during Venables' first year of co-ownership.
Silkman, Barry	Crystal Palace player when Venables was manager.
Smith, Graham	Ran two First Wave Sports Management companies, one in partnership with McLintock.
Smith, Herbert	Law firm which acts for Sugar and Tottenham.
Solomon, Nat	Former chairman of Tottenham Hotspur plc.
Stein, Mel	Adviser to Paul Gascogine.
Stephens, Mark	Partner of Stephens Innocent, a law firm which acted for Venables.
Stewart, Paul	Former Tottenham player.
Sugar, Alan	Chairman of Amstrad, and of Tottenham Hotspur.
Swindlehurst, David	Crystal Palace player when Venables was manager.
Tarvin, Robin	Former policeman and DTI investigator.

Taylor, Sue	Former secretary of First Wave Sports Management.
Theobalds, Richard	Former business associate of John Brown.
Thompson, Jimmy	Chelsea scout when Venables was young.
Trainer, Nick	Partner of John Bowden Trainer & Co., a legal firm acting for Venables.
Van-Hay, Geoffrey	Managing director of Scribes West when Venables took over.
Venables, Christine	First wife of Terry. Under her maiden name, McCann, was a director of Chris McCann Management Ltd.
Venables, Fred	Father of Terry, publican. Author of *Son of Fred*.
Venables, Myrtle	Mother of Terry, deceased.
Venables, Terence Frederick	Subject of this biography. See: 'Dates and major events in Terry Venables' life'.
Venables, Tracey	Daughter from Terry's first marriage.
Venables, Yvette	Second wife of Terry.
Wale, Sidney	Former chairman of Tottenham Hotspur FC.
Walker, Lee	Football League's television supremo.
Walsh, Paul	Former Tottenham player.
Warren, Frank	Boxing promoter.
Watts, Alan	Lawyer working for Herbert Smith.
Webb, David	Former manager of Southend and Chelsea, now manager of Brentford.
Welch, David	Sports editor of the *Daily Telegraph*.
White, Noel	Chairman of the international committee of the FA.
Williams, David	Recorder, Central London County Court.
Williams, Gordon	Writer, co-author with Terry Venables.
Wright, Colin	British businessman based in America, former business associate of Venables. Director of Transatlantic Inns.
Wynn Davies, Arthur	In-house lawyer of the *Daily Telegraph*.
Yawetz, Igal	Architect, non-executive director of Tottenham.
Yorke, Tony	Freelance journalist for the *Daily Mirror* and *The People*. Now with *Sunday Business*.

Prologue

The day the Tottenham Board met at Arsenal

At 6.35pm on Tuesday 11 May 1993, Terry Venables, then the chief executive of Tottenham, was driven by his friend and fellow director, the barrister Jonathan Crystal, to the Arsenal football ground. After Crystal had parked his car the two men separated, Venables to go to his place of work, the dressing-room where his Tottenham team were preparing to play Arsenal that evening, and Crystal up the famed marbled halls at Highbury to the Arsenal boardroom.

The fact that we know the time of Venables' arrival with such precision suggests that the match at Highbury was of historic importance, with the world's media gathered there in force. In fact, apart from the usual soccer reporters, there was no media interest and little public enthusiasm. Although this was normally one of the matches of the English season – and in recent years televised live – that evening's encounter between Arsenal and Tottenham was played only to satisfy the formalities of a season where the major decisions of the championship and relegation had been confirmed the previous Saturday.

Tottenham's season had effectively ended just over a month earlier when they lost to Arsenal in the semi-final of the FA Cup at Wembley. The defeat not only reversed the 3–1 triumph over Arsenal at the same stage of the competition two years before – one which had set up Tottenham's subsequent Wembley triumph – but it also meant that Arsenal could now aim to complete a unique Cup double. A week after their triumph over Tottenham in the FA Cup, Arsenal had returned to Wembley to win the League

1

Cup, defeating Sheffield Wednesday. And four days after this Tuesday night local derby, Arsenal were due back at Wembley for the FA Cup Final, also against Sheffield Wednesday. No team had ever won both the domestic cups in one season and even the most fervent Arsenal supporter, who likes nothing better than beating the 'Tottenham Scum' – Tottenham fans respond with 'Arse' – knew that whatever happened that day, it was what happened at Wembley on 15 May which would be much more significant.

So for the 26,393 people gathered at Highbury on this balmy summer evening the talk was about everything but the match. And there was plenty to talk about. The previous day, after feverish speculation, Liverpool had confirmed that Graeme Souness would after all stay as Liverpool manager. But that morning another football club chairman, Ken Bates of Chelsea, had parted with his manager of three months, David Webb. During that period Webb had prevented Chelsea from being relegated but his contract was up and Bates had decided to go for a new man. As Arsenal and Tottenham supporters arrived at the ground, Bates dominated the evening paper headlines and provided the lead story for the *Sun* newspaper the next day: the Tottenham-Arsenal match struggled to make the inside pages of the *Sun* – and even then it was largely about Arsenal fielding virtually a reserve side, with George Graham, their manager, making eleven changes, an all too familiar story of a manager resting his key players before a Cup Final.

But what would make this match special, and lead to the time of Venables' arrival at Highbury being recorded in an affidavit presented to the High Court four days later, were the events taking place away from the public gaze, in the Arsenal boardroom and even in the Arsenal car park. Football boardrooms are the last vestiges of an Edwardian upstairs-downstairs world. A few yards away from a director's box fans may exchange the most foulmouthed abuse with Tottenham's opponents, regularly chanting 'Kill the yids', a reference to the club's supposedly Jewish support. In the boardroom, however, there is decorum and a gentility that is almost a parody of bourgeois life, something a Luis Buñuel film might struggle to reproduce.

The Arsenal boardroom is the epitome of this. Cut-glass accents predominate, ties are mandatory – on at least one occasion a Spurs supporter arriving at the boardroom without one has been forced to wear an Arsenal tie to gain entrance – and match days mean a boardroom with a table laden with food, the choicest cuts of meat and salmon, and a bar that is always busy. There is almost an unwritten code which visiting directors must follow. They keep their support of their team well buttoned up, and there is much talk of the Corinthian spirit and 'may the best team win'.

But that evening was different. The Spurs contingent certainly behaved with impeccable outward courtesy, none of them going wild over Tottenham's convincing victory. Unlike on previous occasions when they would exchange pleasantries with their fellow Arsenal directors – relationships between the two clubs at directors' level has always been good as opposed to the violent instincts of the rival fans – they spent most of the time going into constant huddles around the boardroom. One Arsenal director watched their comings and goings in growing bemusement and wondered: what are they doing, are they holding a Board meeting, or what? But he dismissed the idea as ridiculous. Why should Tottenham hold a Board meeting at Highbury? Such a meeting would suggest an extraordinary, quite undreamt-of crisis at Spurs, and as far as the world knew nothing of the sort was in train.

It was only in June 1991 that Alan Sugar had joined with Terry Venables to buy Spurs and, while the two men could not be more different, one very much the 'cheeky chappie of football', the other proud of his hard-nosed business skills, since then no news of any disagreement had leaked out. The only hint had come the previous November when Jeff Randall, of the *Sunday Times*, had written about a boardroom row. But the story had been immediately squashed and by May forgotten. All the talk now was of how well Spurs were doing, for the team that Terry was building would, said the cognoscenti, be ready to challenge for the championship next season. Like 'Next year in Jerusalem', the famous Jewish cry, next year the championship has often been a Spurs hope; but now it seemed Venables had got the proper ingredients together.

The private reality, however, was very different. And the Arsenal director's antennae were sharp: a meeting of Tottenham directors was indeed taking place that evening in his boardroom. In fact, a minute of this meeting would be produced and, in the process, this would become the most contested and controversial Board meeting in the history of Tottenham. There would even be dispute about the time. How could it have been held at 7pm as was originally minuted? For at 7pm two of the directors had left the boardroom for the Arsenal car park where they had gone to look up a telephone number in one of the directors' cars. It turned out later that the minute was wrong on the time, the huddle in the Arsenal boardroom had actually taken place at 6.45pm.

In a few days this Tottenham Board meeting at Arsenal would take on an almost cosmic significance, at least in the Venables camp, with bitter accusations being hurled in an affidavit at Alan Sugar, the chairman. More than a year later Venables, in his *Venables: The Autobiography*, described the events that May evening as 'probably one of the darkest moments in Spurs' history, the ultimate sell-out, held at the ground of our greatest rivals'. If some of the charges hurled by the Venables camp were fanciful, they reflected the fact that Highbury was the unlikely setting for what proved to be almost the last private act before an extraordinary battle royal between Venables and Sugar for the control of the club – at times it has seemed for the soul of football itself – became public.

The apparently trivial meeting, which it turned out later Sugar need not have held, formed part of a larger, more complex story, the story of the Sugar-Venables marriage supposedly made in heaven, 'a dream-ticket' which, unknown outside the club, had been dissolving for some time. And as in all matrimonial severances, when the two sides split it was accompanied by acrimony and hatred with both sides putting the worst possible construction on each other's actions.

This did not begin for another four days, however. That evening the Tottenham supporters left Highbury in fine voice. Their team's 3–1 victory over Arsenal meant they had completed the double over the old enemy for the first time since 1974 and finished higher than Arsenal in the League. The fans sang about the joys of watching Terry Venables' blue and white army, totally unaware that their beloved Terry was preparing for another kind of battle against his nemesis, Alan Sugar.

Venables had already briefed two important Tottenham supporters, the only ones outside the immediate circle of the Tottenham boardroom to know anything of the coming clash. Their feelings at Highbury that evening, aware of what awaited Venables but unable to share it with their rejoicing colleagues, are almost indescribable. Venables was also about to engage a public relations firm to launch a pre-emptive strike, what footballers term 'getting your tackle in first'. It was in the best traditions of football, and something he had specialised in almost all his life. To an extent it was his success in pursuing this strategy that had brought him to the position he now occupied, and desperately wanted to cling to.

The lives of few men can be summed up in simple terms. Venables' is no less complex. But all through his life he had held on to one motto: to be ahead of the game, to get in first while the opposition organised and waited its turn. Alan Sugar's proposals now threatened to put him on the back foot for the first time, and he knew he had to get his retaliation in first. This he had set about doing even before he had arrived at Highbury, and the worlds of Tottenham and of football were to be convulsed by it.

Chapter 1

The making of an institution

Legend has it that the name Venables is to be found in the Domesday Book, and while this may mean little to Terry Venables himself, by the time he was forced to consider his options that day at Arsenal his name was certainly one to conjure with in English football. Commentators freely described him as an institution and these were the very words that, a few days later, his counsel would use in court.

At the age of fifty Venables had reached a position unique in English football: as a coach he had conquered a foreign country, Spain, one considered immune to English football ideas, and had gone on to become the first footballer to own a major club. In 1984, when he left the characteristically insular English football world, he not only won Barcelona the championship, ending a long drought for the club and exploding the myth that English footballing ideas could not travel, but in the process showed that Englishmen could also master another tongue.

In 1991 he emphasised his uniqueness by becoming part-owner of Spurs, bridging the most cherished English football chasm: where professionals were only allowed into the boardroom by invitation and not as of right. By the summer of 1993, with Venables as chief executive of Tottenham, one of the major clubs in the country, he could be seen as football's equivalent of the beer that could go to places which other beers could not reach. But this was hardly surprising. Almost from the beginning there was a quality which had set Terry Venables apart from his contemporaries.

His birth had been touched by the sort of luck that marks out unusual men. Had his mother been a day later with her plans, or the Luftwaffe a day earlier with theirs, he might never have seen the light of day. He was born on 6 January 1943 at his grandparents' home in Dagenham. The very night after his mother, Myrtle, heavily pregnant, had left for Dagenham, the Luftwaffe bombed the house where she had been living. The war was at its height, Terry's father Fred, a Petty Officer with the Royal Navy, was in Halifax, Nova Scotia – Fred did not set eyes on his son for months – and Terry Venables was barely six weeks old when constant bombing forced Myrtle to evacuate to Wales with her son.

From the start there were contradictory influences on young Terry. There was his father Fred's Barking background and the very different traditions of his mother Myrtle's Welsh origins. Both Fred, who published a biography of his son in 1990, and Venables' own autobiography, first published in September 1994, acknowledge what they see as the superior instincts inculcated in Terry by his mother. Fred believes that it was Myrtle's influence which made his son a 'successful businessman'.

Venables' autobiography provides a graphic early picture of the differences between his Dagenham and Welsh upbringings. His childhood was divided between Dagenham and Wales with many a summer spent in Wales. One day, when he was playing football with a group of Welsh boys, the ball went through someone's window. Venables, following the Dagenham custom, ran, only to realise he was the only boy running. He stopped and turned, to find that the others had gathered round and were trying to scrape together enough pennies to pay for Mrs Jones' window. He sheepishly returned and joined them but notes that in Dagenham 'it would never have occurred to anyone to pay for a broken window, even if caught in the act'.

Venables sees this as showing a Welsh sense of community. It would be more appropriate to see it as a Welsh sense of accountability, but whichever it was, Venables' entire life seems to mirror a struggle between the contrasting ways of Wales and Dagenham and the evidence suggests that although, on that occasion, Venables stopped to think about Mrs Jones, more often the Dagenham tendency to duck and dive has overpowered the superior Welsh spirit. So while Venables has spoken movingly of his bonds with his mother and how devastated he was when she died, in his dealings with other people his father's genes appear to have played the decisive part.

These tendencies were nurtured not only by his father, Fred – who glories in the fact that, when Terry was young, he would drive his beaten-up old van without insurance or a tax disc on the windscreen – but also by the football scout who took Terry to Chelsea: Jimmy Thompson. If the picture painted of him by Fred and Terry is accurate, then Jimmy was the ultimate ducker and diver. He was so paranoid about being discovered, particularly by another scout, that if he was sitting in Fred's home having a cup of tea and heard a knock at the door he would hide in the bathroom, saying, 'I am not here, I am not here'. Once Jimmy asked Terry to meet him at a hotel, and led him through a labyrinthine maze of corridors and pathways just to make sure that nobody was following them.

There was another occasion when he arranged to meet Venables under the four-sided clock at Waterloo. Venables, having waited twenty minutes, was about to give up when he heard someone saying, 'Psst, Psst'. He spotted Thompson behind a pillar beckoning him. When Venables wondered about the secrecy Thompson replied, 'You can't be too careful. You can't be too careful.'

Venables was all the more amused by Thompson's love of secrecy because his attire – bowler hat, pinstripe trousers and furled umbrella – would have made him stand out almost anywhere, let alone in Dagenham. Some of this mania for furtiveness may have been because Thompson knew that Venables was a prize young footballer who was wanted not only by Chelsea but by several of the top London clubs: Spurs, Arsenal, West Ham, and even Manchester United, who once flew Fred and Myrtle to Belfast to watch United play. If few other agents were quite as manic as Thompson, the world of football which Venables was introduced to was one of wheeling and dealing, the left hand often not knowing what the right was up to. This was the climate in which Venables grew up, one where Venables was soon aware that he had special gifts, but where he was also aware he had to keep his wits about him if those gifts were to be successfully exploited.

The gift Terry had for football was obvious from an early age, and with it came a determination rare in boys so young. When he was twelve a teacher, Mr Warren, tried to dissuade him by suggesting that one boy in a million might become a footballer. Terry replied, 'That's me. I'm the boy in a million.'

Spurs was the club closest to Terry's heart. He had another teacher, George Jackson, who had played for Spurs, and by the age of eleven he had written in his autograph book: Terry Venables, manager of Tottenham. In the end, the boy described as the next Duncan Edwards (who had just died in the Munich aircrash) – and who had been chased more fervently than anyone since Stanley Matthews – opted for Chelsea. Both father and son have always denied that this was due to any financial inducement, although Fred got a job as a part-time scout which gained him more money than Terry then earned as a player.

For Venables the decision to opt for Chelsea ahead of West Ham was partly because some of his friends from the England school team, for whom he played six times in all, had gone to Chelsea. But there was also a touch of cold calculation: Chelsea offered a quicker route to the top. Venables had worked out that he could replace the player occupying his midfield position and so would break into the first team earlier than at any of the other clubs.

Venables' shrewdness was soon proved sound. At Chelsea he made his first-team debut at the age of sixteen-and-a-half and, long before he had reached twenty, he was the leader of the pack, a leadership that Venables both craved and enjoyed. In his very first match Johnny Brooks, who had played for England and was a player Venables worshipped, came up to him. The young debutant expected to be reassured, instead Brooks sought Venables' reassurance about his own play. That incident convinced Venables that in football you have to be your own man.

Venables' decision was also influenced by Chelsea's glamour. In many ways, by going to Chelsea, Venables succeeded in straddling two contrasting eras. His birth as a war baby had already placed him in one, he was the last of the generation of English footballers who learnt the game by playing with a tennis ball in the streets around their home. Even the next generation in the late 1960s had few such opportunities for street football and by the time Venables became a manager it was virtually unknown, given the changes in social life.

But if he was the last of the street football generation, at Chelsea he was the first of the generation that began to taste some of the material rewards with which the game is now associated. Three years after he joined Chelsea the maximum wage was abolished, perhaps the greatest-ever change in English football, and in a further two years the Beatles had shot to fame and John F. Kennedy was assassinated in Dallas. The 'swinging sixties', as the era became dubbed, was on its way, and Chelsea quickly became the footballing symbol of the period.

Venables' Chelsea team-mate, George Graham, has rhapsodised about the delights of being in the King's Road during the swinging sixties, ogling beautiful long-limbed girls with thigh-high miniskirts and not merely looking. 'I touched and had the time of my life,' says Graham. Another Chelsea player, Ron 'Chopper' Harris, used to call girls Richard – from the rhyming slang Richard the Third, bird – and Graham's memoirs suggest that the Chelsea players of his time had their fill of Richards.

Venables' own memoir is much more reticent on this subject, preferring to mention the brief moment of glory he tasted when he was invited to Downing Street by Harold Wilson after being voted 'Young Player of the Year'. He missed the swinging sixties at Chelsea, which really started after *Time* magazine had run a cover story about 'swinging London' and after England had won the World Cup in 1966, by which time Venables was at Tottenham. In any case Venables is not convinced that the swinging sixties marked the end of deeply embedded English class distinctions. He believes the 1960s' fashion for the working class was a fad and that the upper classes resented working-class upstarts. He has never been anything but proud of his working-class origins and hates the way working-class people are still put down by the establishment, and particularly those who sneer at footballers.

Be that as it may the 1960s did open doors, did make it more possible for people from one walk of life to enter another, and Venables, a natural mould-breaker, profited from it. As a seventeen-year-old wearing his England blazer Venables had sung with the Joe Loss orchestra. Although Tommy Docherty, the Chelsea manager, soon put a stop to that, Venables, from his early Chelsea days, developed differently to his fellow footballers. Not for him wasting his afternoons after training had finished in loafing around the streets or in pubs. More often he would be found in Denmark Street in Soho, at the offices of Tony Hiller, a songwriter. It was here that he met Adam Faith, Reg Dwight, later to become more famous as Elton John, and Eric Hall, who in time became Terry's best friend, confidant and adviser.

At an age when most young people believe they are blessed with eternal youth and most footballers cannot see beyond the glories on the field, Venables appears to have sensed that his feet would not last forever, that football was a chancy business, and that he needed to secure his future. So at eighteen, advised by an accountant, he formed himself into a limited company, a move quite daring enough for almost anyone to do at such a young age, but almost unprecedented for a footballer.

An early business venture of his was called Thingummywigs, providing hats with wigs already attached so that women could hide their curlers. It proved a failure although Venables says he lost little as he did not have any great financial involvement. He was soon on to another venture, a tailoring business with George Graham, Ron Harris and the writer Ken Jones. The idea was that Chelsea supporters would like their suits to be made by the very men whose football they adored. They attracted a number of celebrity fans who went to Chelsea, but it seems they often did not pay their bills, and Venables soon discovered it was not easy to turn a footballer into a successful tailor.

These early business failures also showed another side to Venables' character. He seemed able to survive and prosper whatever the business failures. The wonders of the Teflon pan were still light years away, but none of the business debris appeared to attach to Venables, hence the popular joke of 'Teflon Tel'. He could just rinse clean, pass the whole scheme off as a joke and walk away with a smile.

About this time Venables came into contact with a writer who was to provide yet another string to his burgeoning talent. Gordon Williams, a novelist and journalist, was writing a ghosted column for Tommy Docherty and met Venables at Chelsea's training ground. Unlike other footballers Venables showed an interest in writing his own articles and, encouraged by Williams, even wrote a short story. Although this was never published the exercise spurred Venables into writing other pieces which soon were published.

Venables also decided to learn how to type and took a proper secretarial course. A photograph of the period shows him as the lone man in a class full of women, an experience he clearly enjoyed. How far the lessons helped is not clear, for he soon reverted to two-finger typing but the whole episode indicated his dedication even for matters outside his immediate purview.

By now Venables, still only twenty-two, had become something of a veteran in football terms and had good reasons to feel the football world was at his feet. In the Chelsea side he was, as George

Graham says, the orchestrator conducting from the vantage point of midfield. Graham sees him as having an almost Napoleonic air, feeding the ball through to nippy front runners with superbly delivered passes. Venables had recovered from an early setback when, in 1961–62, despite his efforts, Chelsea went down to the old second division. But from the following season he was at the heart of the many good things that happened to Chelsea: promotion in 1962–63, fifth in 1963–64, just seven points behind the champions Liverpool, who were embarking on their great period of glory under Bill Shankly. The 1964–65 season saw Chelsea win the League Cup, and this was also the season when Venables made his England debut, thereby completing a unique set of representing England at every level from schoolboy to full international.

What he did not know, however, was that he had, in effect, reached his natural heights as a footballer. He could go no further. His two caps, in October and December 1964 against Belgium and Holland, were the only ones for England. Alf Ramsey selected him for a third match but he was injured, John Byrne took his place, and Venables never got back.

His options at Chelsea were also being eliminated. The leadership quality he had hinted at from early youth and which had so impressed his father, Fred, had blossomed, first under Ted Drake, then under Tommy Docherty. Although Docherty could not be more different to the charming, elegant, Drake, in the early days Venables and he had a good working partnership. The harsh Glaswegian tones of the Doc, as he was soon to be known, blended well with the softer East End sounds of Venables. With Venables often initiating strategies for a young Chelsea side it seemed that they might become the next force in English football. But as Chelsea failed to grasp the success it aspired to, Venables' strategic vision, which was often credited with victories in the press and by the fans, began to rankle with Docherty. Venables, who had been made captain at nineteen, was proving more than a ceremonial leader – as football captains normally are. Instead, Docherty felt Venables was becoming an alternative focus of leadership to that provided by Docherty himself. Where Venables saw himself making a contribution to the new fashion for football theory, Docherty saw dangerous barrack-room insubordination. The explosion came towards the end of the 1964–65 season. Chelsea had just won the League Cup, beating Leicester, but within weeks the celebrations were soured as Venables lost the captaincy following a very public incident.

13

Docherty had taken the team to Blackpool before an important match against Burnley and, furious to find that the players had broken a curfew, decided to make an example of them. His anger was directed at Venables who, he felt, had not revealed his role in the affair. Venables' version is that Docherty had promised a night out, then cancelled it and, following a number of run-ins with him, the players decided to ignore his instructions and have a night out anyway. Venables and seven other players were sent home but, as they returned to London, the press were waiting and it made all the wrong headlines. That Friday Fred was rung by Docherty him-self and curtly told that his son was dropped for the Burnley match, both as player and captain.

The result was disastrous for Chelsea. They lost 6–2 to Burnley and with it any hopes of the championship. Venables, however, was soon back in the team and he played at Chelsea for another year. Docherty still valued Venables' advice and the following sea-son, with Chelsea back in Europe, he took him on a scouting mission to Europe. Venables was credited with masterminding the win over Roma in the first leg, scoring a hat-trick in the process and Chelsea got as far as the semi-finals. But by April 1966, after twelve months of deliberating, and with Chelsea having just lost their second successive FA Cup semi-final, Docherty decided he needed to rebuild the team. He told Joe Mears, the chairman, that Venables had to go. Mears agreed. So within weeks of his marriage to his long-standing girlfriend Christine McCann, Venables found himself on the transfer list.

Just before the play-off game with Barcelona on 25 May, both legs having finished in 2–0 victories for either side, Venables was sold to Spurs for £80,000. Docherty seemed to have cut his nose to spite his face for, in the play-off, Chelsea lost 5–0. But this was also the first time that this only child of Fred and Myrtle, who had always had his own way, had met another strong personality and had to give way.

Venables was to have his revenge over Docherty. His first season at Tottenham saw Spurs at Wembley playing Chelsea in the FA Cup Final. While Docherty squirmed in the dugout Tottenham won 2–1, Chelsea getting only a late consolation goal. Venables could not have been better pleased. Not only had he answered Docherty but whatever the result he could not have lost financially. His Tottenham win bonus was £500, but if Chelsea won he stood to pick up the same amount from the bookies. In his autobiography he writes, 'Financially that would have been a better result for me, because the winnings would have been tax-free, but I was willing to forego the extra few quid, for the pleasure of having a Cup-winner's medal. The only reason I feel safe in telling this story, even now, is because Tottenham won. If Chelsea had beaten us, I would have sent someone else to pick up the money from the bookies for me and taken the dark secret of my bet on the opposition with me to my grave.'

Venables does not say when he put the bet on, presumably just before the third round when the bigger clubs join the competition, but no passage could be more revealing of Venables the man. However, if Tottenham's victory pleased Venables it was to prove his last domestic honour as a player. At Chelsea he had been king of the castle, leading a club whose ambitions far exceeded any realistic expectations and which certainly did not have the weight of tradition and success that Spurs had. At Tottenham he came to a club which had created history, the first this century to win the double, the first British club to win European honours and a side brimful of internationals and great names: Mackay, Gilzean, Greaves, Mullery and England. Venables found everything just a touch too grand, and the manager, Bill Nicholson, and the club much more formal than Chelsea.

Venables regrets that he did not carry on his bossing traditions of Chelsea at Spurs but tried to fit in with the big names and in the process lost a lot of the drive that made him a remarkable player at Chelsea. But there was also a practical footballing problem. At Chelsea he held the ball waiting for the players to detach themselves, then passed the ball. The Spurs game was based on pass and move. Venables found it difficult to fit in with the Spurs style. His problems arose on the first day at the gym. Venables, recalls Alan Mullery, used to push his bottom out when he ran. He did so as he tackled and passed Mackay. In his autobiography Venables says that Mackay hit him in the testicles. Twice he passed Mackay, twice he got hit and, after the second time, Venables let fly with his fists. The pair soon made up, but in a sense Venables never recovered from this first-day skirmish.

In many ways Venables' footballing experience at Spurs was the odd period in his career. Unlike at Chelsea, and later at Queens Park Rangers (QPR) and Crystal Palace where he dominated the players and the supporters, he never quite got on with the Spurs fans. He was not helped by the fact that, for the critical Spurs crowd satiated by the glory of the early 1960s, he had taken the place of the much loved John White who had been tragically killed by lightning on a golf course. Try as he did, Venables never won them over.

In 1969 Nicholson sold Venables to QPR, a move that clearly indicated that his glory days were over. QPR was in the second division and this was like moving into a terraced house after living in a palace. Nevertheless Venables sees the move as the best he made in football. As player he would never play better, all things considered, and he never derived as much satisfaction as he did from his four years at QPR.

The satisfaction may derive from the fact that QPR provided some of the defining moments of his life. It meant being employed by Jim Gregory, the chairman Venables found the most endearing. The relationship blossomed so well that Gregory began to regard him almost as a son, in time calling him 'Our Tel'. Gordon Williams came back into his life and suggested they take up the idea of writing a novel they had discussed before. Most afternoons for nine months Venables drove to Williams' office in Soho and the result was *They Used To Play On Grass*, a visionary book talking of an artificial pitch, colour in newspapers, all-seater stadia, and a British Cup. Of these all but the last have either been tried – Venables, himself, introduced a plastic pitch at QPR – or realised and a British Cup is still endlessly discussed.

The novel did not get the attention it deserved, probably because of Venables' sporting associations, and was more often reviewed by sports reporters on sports pages. However this did not deter the pair. Inspired by Erich Segal's *Love Story*, then a great Hollywood success, the pair decided to embark on another novel. Their initial efforts produced a 'weepie' about two mothers and mixed-up babies which pleased neither Williams nor Venables. The character Hazell was created to try and introduce a touch of cynicism, but he took over the plot and soon the novel turned into a detective story called *Hazell Plays Solomon*.

Not quite sure how the book would be received, Venables and Williams adopted a pseudonym, P. B. Yuill. Both Venables and Williams would later claim they had an uncle of that name. Venables regretted selecting a name beginning with 'Y'. They should have chosen one starting with 'A', felt Venables; books with 'Y' tend to be stacked at the bottom right-hand corner of bookstalls. But despite this the book did well enough for Venables and

Williams to reveal their authorship. They went on to write two more Hazell books, and there was a successful television series featuring the Cockney detective played by the actor Nicholas Ball, by which time Venables had discarded his playing boots for a manager's chair.

It was QPR which first pointed him in the direction his career would take once his playing days were over. He became increasingly interested in the Professional Footballers' Association (PFA), often acting as a roving advocate on behalf of the players. And at Loftus Road he started the process of acquiring his FA coaching badge. At Chelsea he may have been an alternative fount of wisdom to Docherty, but at QPR, particularly after Les Allen (who had brought him there) was replaced by Gordon Jago, Venables began taking some of the training sessions.

Jago was not at all like Docherty, he did not resent Venables even though they had their differences on football. Venables' portrayal of him in his autobiography is not over-generous, perhaps because Venables was unhappy with the suddenness with which he was told in September 1974, just as QPR was to enjoy first-division football, that he had been transferred to Crystal Palace.

The move left Venables, momentarily, speechless. Crystal Palace were starting the season in the third division and although arthritis of the ankles meant he required a lengthy warm-up before a match, he still felt he had some years yet to give at the top level. The move also caused Jago dressing-room problems at QPR where the players were unhappy about Venables' departure. But it worked out well for Venables, as it meant linking up with an old hero, Malcolm Allison, and was an important stepping stone on his way to becoming a manager. Allison had been captain of the West Ham team when Venables was growing up in Dagenham and even as a schoolboy Venables was much taken by his flamboyant style and passion for the game.

Malcolm Allison, the Crystal Palace manager, had long coveted Venables and had vague plans for him to join the coaching staff even as he was signing him as a player. Venables played fourteen games, then, on New Year's Eve 1974, Allison called him into his office and told him he would like him to retire and become a coach. Venables shrank from the decision, a moment any player dreads, and felt he was too young, not yet thirty-two, to retire. That evening he had a drink with Frank McLintock and Bobby Moore. They were both still playing and both encouraged him to play on.

But that night, after he got home, he began thinking. Sitting with a night-cap in the darkened house he reflected on his playing life and next morning the decision was made. He was still not totally convinced about retiring but he had faith in Allison.

Venables the coach had arrived. That season, already half-over, was to bring no glory. But in 1975–76 the Allison-Venables partnership worked well, with Allison teaching Venables the usefulness of hype, not that he probably needed much tuition in this area. Their Cup travels took them to Scarborough. On the way back they heard news of the draw for the next round. As the man who appeared to have heard the news on the radio came down the train towards them Allison said, 'From the look of this bloke, we've drawn a First Division side anyway. When he tells us which team it is, get very excited, say what a lucky ground it is for you, and really give it some hype.' The words the man said were 'Leeds United', then one of the strongest teams in the land and unbeaten at home for two years. Allison leapt up in the air and punched it. Venables joined him saying how he had always played well there. Venables is convinced the bravado paid off. Palace went there and won 1–0.

Further triumphs followed and Palace were set to become the first third-division club to reach Wembley when they were beaten in the semi-finals by the eventual winners, Southampton. To compound the misery they also failed to gain promotion by just three points. As can often happen in such situations the Palace board, having seen how close they had come, felt frustrated, and they sacked Allison. Venables wanted to leave with him but was persuaded not to by Allison who had suggested to the Board that if they did not want him, Venables would make a good substitute.

Venables shook hands with Ray Bloye, the then Palace chairman, and went on holiday, only to learn while in Majorca that Arsenal wanted him as their manager. They even flew him back to London and Venables tried to get Bloye to release him from his oral agreement. Bloye refused. Venables could have just ignored it and signed for Arsenal but, as Venables tells the story, he did not want to start in management with a broken word. There was also a powerful subsidiary reason. Arsenal was a big club, an enormous challenge for a man who had never managed anything before that. Arsenal, double winners only five years previously, would be impatient for success. At Palace, in the backwater of the third division, he would have time away from the limelight to learn and develop a club which had never won anything in its seventy-four-year history.

If Venables really did not take the Arsenal job because of his agreement with Bloye, then it shows a man of character. However his confession that he also wanted to learn the job quietly shows how honour blended in sensibly with necessary caution. And Venables certainly made the right choice. Away from the spotlight he brought Palace back to the first division in three years and they won promotion in such style – 51,810 people packing Selhurst Park to see them gain victory over Burnley – that as the 1979–80 season began the talk was all about Venables and his Palace team of the 1980s. At times Palace lived up to this hype, their play suggested they might compete with the best and they even briefly topped the first-division table. There was talk of Venables being made managing director of Palace.

But amidst the promise of glory there were also problems in dealing with footballers of which, as manager, Venables was well aware. In January 1978 two of his players, Rachid Harkouk and Barry Silkman, were found guilty of possessing $25,000 knowing the notes to be forged. They were fined and Venables, who had put up bail of £2,000 for Silkman – a similar sum was put up by Arnold Warren, the Palace scout, for Harkouk – later reflected how stupid the footballers had been and how, just before all this, he had been negotiating a transfer of £150,000 involving Harkouk to a first division club. Harkouk would have earned a signing-on fee of £10,000. But this case appears to be an isolated distraction. In general Venables as manager inspired players and they responded to him.

David Swindlehurst played for Palace both under Allison and Venables and is an admirer of both. He recalls: 'Malcolm was fantastic. He put bums on seats. He was like a big film star. Malcolm was a big one for winding up the crowd. When we went for the Cup match at Leeds he went to the crowd, put his thumbs down, and began suggesting we will beat you, do this to you, do that to you. He was standing there and fruit and cans were raining down on him. Nowadays he would incite a riot. Malcolm liked you to treat the pitch as a stage. Terry was less demonstrative than Malcolm. He did all his talking on the coaching field, that's where we grew to love him. He was very thorough. Everybody had a job. He would go through the opposition. Free kicks, corners. From Thursday onwards he would work on their corners and free kicks, using the Reserves as opposition. He was terrific on set pieces and restarts. He would constantly stress: in the first ten minutes you have got to win the right to play. He stressed Positive Mental Attitude, PMA. There was a time at the Palace when Malcolm and Terry put all these big fluorescent posters up in the dressing-room saying: PMA, Be First. For the home games the dressing-room was full of posters. And there would be ghetto blasters, we did it long before Wimbledon. We didn't have rap music then, it was heavy rock, very loud. Led Zeppelin, really blasting the sound out. For a three o'clock game the ghetto blasters would be there from half one. Terry was also a great believer in first touch. He worked out all sorts of different techniques. He made me a better all-round player. He also told me to look after myself. Terry made us take out personal pensions and talked to us about those things.'

But along with these positive messages Venables was also keen to assert control, making sure that, when it came to dealing with the press, it was Venables and no-one else who spoke to the media. Under Venables, information from Palace was tightly controlled by Venables. Swindlehurst did not fully appreciate that: 'I did not even know the guy I was talking to was a member of the press. I was in the Glaziers Bar of the Palace after a game. We had been promoted to the first division and I was speaking up for Stevie Kimber. I was saying why have they left him out. Gerry Francis had come to the club and I didn't think he was fully fit. It was me spouting on after the game, a bit frustrated. It was none of my business. I did not think I was talking to anyone significant. The following day there was a piece in the paper: a first-team member of Palace is questioning Venables. That is one thing you didn't do with Terry. He had a big thing about keeping all our laundry inside, don't air your dirty linen outside. This was a constant theme, that we were a family. If you have a problem come up and see me. Following the article he held a meeting at the club. All the players were called in and we met in the dressing-room. He wanted to know: Who said it? I said it was me. I went up to his office after that. He bawled me out, he wasn't too pleased about it. I explained the situation. He said, "You know you shouldn't open your mouth." I ended up in Reserves for a couple of weeks and it wasn't long after that I was on loan to Derby.'

Swindlehurst was also not one of the 'Chosen Few', the term for the Palace players who had been signed up by Chris McCann Management Ltd. 'Soccer's Secret Agent' screamed the *Daily Star* headline in an article on 10 March 1981, investigating the existence of the agency. The reporters had discovered from Companies

House that this was a subsidiary of Terry Venables Ltd, the company that Venables had formed in 1962 to exploit his own off-the-field activities. 'McCann' came from Venables' wife's maiden name and she was a director along with Richard Andrew Coomber, a former publicity manager at Thames TV and at Penguin. The company's clients included Malcolm Allison as well as a number of Palace players.

Coomber told the journalists that he had met Venables when, at Penguin, he handled the first Hazell book. Friendship blossomed into a business relationship and, as Coomber was to put it, 'I wanted to start an agency but couldn't realise the finance and Terry agreed to fund me for a period of two years. The idea was to find a whole new generation of young footballers and to promote them. Because Terry was manager of Crystal Palace, I went there and signed the good young players on his books.'

The reporters visited Venables at his home in Loughton, Essex, and, with a touch of chutzpah that impressed the reporters, he said, 'I've heard you've been on patrol. Come in, lads.' Then sipping white wine he told them that he had sold his interest to Coomber the previous week. 'When I went to Palace I told Ray Bloye, the chairman, that we should have a commercial set-up to look after the players' interests. He wasn't keen to do it, so I did it myself, with his permission freely given. Richard Coomber was a publicity man I had met in television and he didn't have the cash to get started so I funded him. There is nothing sinister about the use of my wife's maiden name for the agency. It was a family joke. If I had really wanted to be devious I would put it in a nominee.'

True, he hadn't broadcast his connections but he did not make a secret of it and, 'Richard signed up the people in demand, Malcolm Allison, Clive Allen, Vince Hillaire, Peter Nicholas and Kenny Sansom. He went for the young players so if there was a bit of jealousy from the older players I can understand that.'

Both Venables and Coomber were keen to play down the story, with Coomber affecting quite an air of innocence. He had written to Graham Kelly, then secretary of the Football League, saying, 'I find it sad that something which started out as an act of friendship by Terry has been made to look sinister by certain people, without them being able to point to one action by Terry or myself which is improper.'

The *Daily Star* returned to the story a day later but Venables' apparent frankness had clearly disarmed the reporters. The paper had originally broken the story on 7 March 1981. By the time they did their major exposé on 10 March it had developed from a story where Venables might be under investigation into one where Venables was in the clear. Indeed their story on 10 March reported Venables as saying, 'I have done nothing wrong'. The next day the stand first – the line in bold at the top of the article – announced that, 'there was no cash reward for Venables and the McCann agency from any transfers involving Crystal Palace players.'

The story was now more of a conflict of interest, but it proved a three-day wonder. The trump card for Venables was his declaration that he had cut all ties with the agency. And the *Daily Star* began one of its stories by saying, 'Terry Venables has sold his financial interest in an agency which looks after the commercial interests of footballers at rival clubs.'

But had he? Two years later, on 22 May 1983, Christine McCann signed the final directors' report on the company for the period 1 July 1980 to 25 April 1982, after which the company was wound up. If Venables and Coomber had been correctly reported then Coomber should have been shown in these accounts as owner or having some interest. But this is what the paragraph on directors said: 'The director during the period was Richard Coomber. He had no interest in the company and at all times the company was beneficially owned by Terence Venables Limited, a company incorporated and resident in the United Kingdom.'

The accounts, which were signed by Terry Venables, show that Coomber was a paid director, receiving during that period £19,711 as salary. Indeed he was the only employee of the company. What had happened, it seems, was that Venables had resigned as director but it still remained his company. Indeed it had a loan of £6,576 from Terence Venables Ltd. Contrary to public statements Venables had not cut all ties. However, his shrewd news management of a story about a company that tried to marry his two loves, business and football, had now become one where Venables, asserting he had done nothing wrong, had distanced himself from the company. This had been a significant moment for Venables, the first attempt by him to try to combine football with business. Until then his business ventures had capitalised on his name as a footballer but were outside it.

By the time the McCann agency story broke Venables had moved from Crystal Palace to QPR. The move came during the 1980–81 season. The start of that season saw Palace lose nine of their first ten games and hit the bottom by October 1980. The previous season Venables had turned down Cosmos, who had offered £250,000 a year plus bonuses for a four-year contract to take his coaching skills to America. Bloye had responded with a four-year contract of his own, less than Cosmos but making Venables one of the best paid managers in the British game.

But with Palace at the bottom of the table Bloye and the Board held talks with Howard Kendall, then at Blackburn, and refused to give Venables the reassurance he asked for. Cosmos had not been the only ones seeking Venables. Chelsea had tried to get him a couple of years earlier and so had Jim Gregory of QPR a few months before that. Now Gregory tried again, making an early morning call, and this time Venables was an eager listener, agreeing to move westwards nearer to Chelsea and his footballing roots.

Soon after his move, he went back to Palace to buy players such as Mike Flanagan, Terry Fenwick and John Burridge. Managers raiding their former clubs are common, but it was the prices Venables paid to get these players that caused Palace heartburn. Flanagan had been bought for Palace by Venables from Charlton for £650,000. Now, ten months later with Venables at QPR, his value was set at £160,000. The transfers came a month before the boardroom changes at Palace saw Ron Noades take over from Bloye. Noades was unhappy. In his opinion Burridge was worth £170,000, not the £75,000 which Palace received for him. Flanagan was worth a lot more than £160,000 and Fenwick's value was £150,000, not £100,000. Transfer prices can be notoriously subjective and Venables insisted that his purchase of Flanagan, Fenwick and Burridge was quite above board. It was just that he had got a good bargain. The deals, he claims, merely indicated that the bottom was falling out of the market. A seller's market was becoming a buyer's market. The new regime at Palace found this hard to accept. They were well aware of the existence of the Chris McCann agency, and felt that the fact that some players belonged to it but not others caused problems in the dressing-room.

Some of the players felt the same and when news of the agency broke they voiced their feelings. Swindlehurst, interviewed by the *Daily Star* reporters at his home outside Derby, told how players like him found it very difficult to get a pay rise from Venables. 'But young lads who hadn't been at the club five minutes were getting a better deal – interest-free loans, for example. Richard Coomber was often at the practice ground talking to the youngsters and he had ready access to Terry's office but I didn't know what was going on. If I had I would have been away much quicker.'

His comments about interest-free loans are interesting. When Noades took over he found in the Palace books a loan to Venables of just over £100,000. A request to Venables to pay back the loan elicited the reply that this was a bonus due to him. Palace were faced with a tax demand and soon there were writs flying between Palace, QPR and Venables.

Harry Harris, then a young reporter on the *Evening News*, was told the story by Noades and, in great excitement, informed his editor. It was an ideal London story and the editor decided to give it a major billing. Harris rang Venables:

He said, 'I don't want you to print the story'. I replied, 'I can't do that. I have told my editor and they want to run it'. He said, 'If you run that, that is me and you finished.' I did not know what to do. It was my first year in Fleet Street and a hell of a scoop for me. Terry told me that if you print it don't expect to have any co-operation from me. But I could not stop the story now. I was prepared to live with that. But I learnt that Venables called a meeting of all the London managers and suggested that none of them should co-operate with me. I should be blanked out. By strangling me in this way he could have ended my career.

One of the managers who went to the meeting was Terry Neil. He refused to go along with Venables' suggestion. Later, when I co-wrote Neil's book with Brian Scovell he told me this story, saying, 'It has been on my conscience for a long time.'.Over the years my relationship with Venables oscillated but when he held a press conference after leaving Barcelona, organised by Jeff Powell, he leaned over and said, 'I have always wanted to get even with you.' It is interesting to contrast Venables' behaviour with that of Neil's. I did a story about Liam Brady's book that Neil did not like. A few days later Neil gave an exclusive story to the *Evening Standard* about Arsenal, then said, 'That evens the score.' But, unlike Terry Venables, he did not carry a grudge or try to strangle my journalism.

The dispute with Palace was settled out of court, without Palace or Venables saying much, a tradition that Venables continues in his autobiography where there is no mention of his court action against Palace or how it was resolved and none at all of controversy generated by his purchase of Flanagan, Fenwick and Burridge.

However there is one brief, tantalising, paragraph in his auto-biography, ventilating a grouse that Jim Gregory paid £100,000 as a transfer fee to get Venables – the first such transfer fee for managers – when Gregory should really have given him the money: according to Venables, Palace had promised the money if Venables took them back to the first division but, although he achieved his target, he did not get the money. Could this transfer have been taken as a loan and did this form part of the court action? Venables does not say.

The revelations about the McCann agency had no impact on Venables' career. As far as the football authorities were concerned this was a Venables business venture that required no special investigation. Venables maintained he had done nothing wrong or acted in any way against the rules, and that was that.

The McCann agency did not, of course, long survive and, despite reasonable payments from the *Daily Mirror* and tours to Trinidad, made little money for Venables. When the accounts for Terry Venables Ltd were prepared for 30 June 1980, the auditors reported that Chris McCann Management had ceased trading and the investment of £2,726 was being written off. By this time even this, the oldest of Venables' business ventures, was not doing brilliantly either. The fortune of Terry Venables Ltd, as the directors – Terry and his wife Christine – acknowledged depended on the popularity of Terence Venables. In June 1981 the directors' report said, 'The results reflect a downturn in the popularity of Terence Venables as a result of the decline of Crystal Palace and his subsequent move to Queens Park Rangers'. It meant no dividends and, having paid over £10,000 to directors, in 1981 just over £2,000 was available. By June 1983 the directors' report was even gloomier as it noted, 'the results reflect the decline in popularity of Terence Venables as a result of Queens Park Rangers not reaching the FA Cup Final', with turnover more than halving from just over £10,000 to just over £4,000.

In fact, Venables' managerial record at QPR was not as bleak as the figures suggested. He stayed four years at QPR and, if his first foray as a player was the most satisfying, then this second coming as a manager was in some ways the most fulfilling. His years there saw dramatic changes both on and off the field. Apart from brief periods QPR had never really been anything but a lower division club and for most of the forty years between the 1920s and the

1960s they had been in the third division. When Venables arrived they were back in the second division but a great deal of work needed to be done.

Venables set about doing this by bringing in some of his own tried and tested friends over from Palace. Apart from the players, George Graham, Allan Harris and Arnie Warren joined him on the coaching staff at QPR and soon there was another old friend, Frank McLintock. If Venables' progress was not as spectacular as at Palace, it was quite solid, taking three years to win promotion to the first division, by which time he had also taken them to the 1982 FA Cup Final where, as luck would have it, they met Spurs. Lucky to earn a replay, they were perhaps a little unlucky to lose it.

His work at QPR extended beyond the teams to such things as laying down an artificial pitch at Loftus Road and his activities were written up favourably by a sympathetic press who were dazzled by the extraordinary access he provided to some reporters. Once this included a reporter sitting next to Venables in the dugout during a match. Not surprisingly, despite the fact that QPR was hardly a power in the land, Venables' words dominated the back pages. If his team did not always win honours, his words constantly made the back page headlines.

By 1984, QPR had not only secured their place in the first division but qualified for Europe. Venables seemed ready to chart a revolutionary path in British football. Jim Gregory announced he was going to retire and there was talk of Gregory owning the ground but Venables owning the club and running it on a twenty-year contract. Venables in his autobiography blames Gregory for the deal not going through. He found the backers but Gregory bawled one of them out on the telephone, ruining a deal that Venables had been working on for months. In the end, goes this tale of woe, Venables' prospects faded so quickly that far from becoming owner, Gregory even got very difficult about the terms of a new manager's contract. Venables on £30,000 wanted much more than the £40,000 Gregory offered.

But at this stage a totally unexpected future presented itself to Venables.

Chapter 2

From Terry to El Tel

Barcelona had not tasted success for many years, and had had to suffer while their arch rivals, Real Madrid, won the honours. Their desire for a new coach was great. The Argentinian, Cesar Menotti, was leaving, and Barcelona turned to Venables.

Who suggested his name remains a mystery. Venables, in his autobiography, merely lists the various people who claimed to have recommended him: Jeff Powell, then the *Daily Mail*'s soccer writer, Dennis Roach, the soccer agent, Doug Ellis, the Aston Villa chairman, and Bobby Robson, then managing England. But whoever acted as 'agent', it was Venables in his interview at the Nou Camp stadium, on 21 May 1984, who provided what he regards as the masterstroke.

After the interview the Barcelona directors invited him for dinner and the Vice-President, Nicolau Casaus, offered cigars. But the cigar boxes proved empty and as Casaus looked embarrassed, Venables lifted up his trouser legs and took out two Monte Cristo cigars he had kept down his socks. The best place to keep them he told the astonished Barcelona directors. Venables is convinced that this one incident got him the job. Señor Casaus, a devoted cigar smoker, was 'sold on me'.

Even if this ingenuity was not quite the decisive factor, this is one of those stories you want to believe. The next morning, after another interview, Venables was given the job. When Venables asked why he had been preferred to Michael Hidalgo or Helmut Benthaus, both famous international coaches, the Barcelona directors explained they wanted a coach who was hungry. Venables returned to London to bid good-bye not merely to Gregory but also to his wife Christine, their marriage having started to unravel. Venables does not explain what led to the marriage breakdown except to suggest he was more to blame. Barcelona led to another parting, albeit brief, which in its own way is very revealing of Venables' attitude to people.

This was the parting with Paul Riviere. A few weeks before the call from Spain Venables had linked up with Riviere and Jonathan Crystal, a barrister who later joined Venables on the Tottenham Board, in forming a company called Elite Gold. Riviere was very different from the sort of fawning admirers who were now beginning to gather round Venables. A tall, soft-spoken man with a charming smile and a face that hinted at vulnerability, making him very appealing to women, his forte was marketing. He had developed these skills mainly in the field of financial services where he had headed for Abbey Life a City operation which involved employing such soccer names as Jimmy Greaves and Geoff Hurst, whom Paul recruited. After thirteen years he moved to the finance company, Cannon Lincoln, starting the London sales force for them before becoming their head of field operations. As a devoted Chelsea supporter, Riviere had seen Venables play for Chelsea back in the 1960s and over the years their friendship had developed.

The idea behind Elite Gold, promoted with the help also of Ken Jones, was that for £1,000 a person would be entitled to two best seats in any London first-division game as long as they gave forty-eight hours' notice. This meant a call by 3pm on the Thursday for a Saturday match. Deals were done with Tottenham, Arsenal, Chelsea, QPR and West Ham. Riviere recalled in an interview with me, 'The launch was at the Royal Lancaster Hotel with many football personalities and Jarvis Astaire, the promoter, the first to buy a couple of memberships. It all looked a great success. We used as an office one of the boxes at Loftus Road. Within two weeks of the launch Terry had this call from Barcelona.'

It was a Friday evening and Riviere and Venables and other friends were at the Carlton Tower, already one of Venables' favourite haunts. It was like a scene from *Minder*. Venables said to Riviere, 'Paul, have you got a minute?'

'OK, Tel,' said Riviere. They walked over to the bar.

'I am going to Barcelona,' said Venables.

'Are you going to have a break?' asked Riviere, thinking he needed a holiday.

'Confidentially, Barcelona have offered me the job,' Venables replied.

'Cesar Menotti is the manager,' said Riviere.

'No, they've got rid of him,' said Venables, 'but don't worry, because I don't think it will happen.' 'Tel,' said Riviere, 'I can't see Elite Gold without your profile and, as you know, we need to bank some £300,000 which was our commitment to the clubs.' (By this time Elite Gold had banked some £30,000 or £40,000.)

'Don't worry,' reassured Venables, 'I don't think it will happen.'

Riviere remembers Venables coming back from Spain, again saying he didn't think he would be getting the job:

He still wanted me to keep on working at Elite Gold. My memory is he made another trip to Barcelona and it was left that he would ring me at the Carlton Towers on a Wednesday. I know it was a Wednesday because an important European final was on. I met up with Malcolm Allison and we were hoping Terry would ring so we could go and see this European match on television. I said to Malcolm, thinking of the effect on Elite Gold, 'I hope he doesn't take the job'. Malcolm thought he would. He had brought Terry into management and he felt that, if Terry got the Barcelona job, then he might offer him a job with him in Barcelona. I thought Terry and Malcolm at Barcelona together would be wonderful. Then we got a phone call at the Carlton Tower. Terry was at the White Elephant Club in Curzon Street. When we got out of the cab I asked for Mr Venables and the doorman said, 'Ah, Señor Venabless', and I realised he had got the job. Venables had a large cigar and I asked him, 'Does this mean you have taken it?' 'I don't know how to tell you,' he replied, 'but I have'. He was rather embarrassed about it because he knew it meant the end of Elite Gold.

Elite Gold was eventually dissolved. Riviere recalls:

Jonathan Crystal said he would handle that, we repaid everybody their money and told the clubs we wouldn't be proceeding. I felt somewhat upset. But I wasn't too upset because the marketing of Elite Gold, which is what I was doing, hadn't taken me away from my bread and butter business job of financial services, and I knew Barcelona was a great opportunity for Terry. I was pleased for him. Looking back, the incident did not damage our friendship and when he returned from Barcelona we resumed our friendship and business association.

But we are going ahead of our story. At this stage, just before he moved to Spain, had Venables fallen under the proverbial bus, then he would have been seen as an interesting product of English football but no more. Barcelona lifted Venables above and beyond his English contemporaries. There were others who had, and still have, much better domestic records. For instance his own protégé, George Graham, has a record in England which Venables cannot match: two League championships, two League Cups, one FA Cup, one European Cup Winners Cup as opposed to a solitary FA Cup by Venables. But Graham still waits to prove himself with a European club, something he might now never do, yet suddenly Venables, in his first season in Spain, was to do just that.

Venables came to the job amidst dire predictions that he would fail and, worse still, ruin the game in Barcelona. After all, what would the English bring to the party but kick and rush? How could he manage a team of such talents as Maradona? Venables' answer was simple: he sold Maradona and bought in Steve Archibald, who proved an inspired buy. Venables also formed a working relationship with the gifted German, Bernd Schuster, who initially distrusted him but did play well for him, at least in that first season.

More importantly, having heard from Bobby Robson that Robson had turned down the Barcelona job because he could not speak Spanish, Venables learnt the local language sufficiently well to speak to the fans in Catalan on the first day of training. This, combined with his public performances in front of the demanding but generous Barcelona fans, showed how his touch for showmanship, first displayed when he sang with the Joe Loss orchestra, could be transferred to the Catalan stage.

Venables could not have had a fiercer test, the first match being against Real Madrid in the Bernabeu stadium in Madrid on 2 September 1984. Barcelona won 3–0, Archibald scored a goal, helped in the others and although, as Venables left the Bernabeu, the irate Madrid fans were besieging the coach and glass was flying everywhere, his return to Barcelona was like a Roman general coming home with the spoils. That first victory set the pattern for the year. Long before the end of the season Barcelona were champions for the first time in more than a decade and finished ten points clear of the runners-up.

The next season saw Venables try his skills in the European Cup. Had he won it his future might well have been different. But in a poor final Steua Bucharest seemed to play for penalties and after the match finished 0–0 they did go on to win the Cup on penalties. If Venables had been a hero the year before, now he was a pariah.

He had already made his plans to leave Barcelona. Peter Hill-Wood had flown out to Barcelona and a contract was signed with Arsenal which specified that he would take over at Highbury in the 1986–87 season. However, sometime in March 1986 news of this leaked out and, by this time, Venables was having second thoughts about returning to England. His marriage to Christine had not recovered, he feared a trial by tabloid, and agreed with Arsenal that they would release him from the contract. Irving Scholar, at Tottenham, was also looking for a manager to replace Peter Shreeves, and Juventus was interested, but Venables decided to carry on at Barcelona for his third and least successful season. Barcelona came second in the league and was knocked out of the UEFA cup in the quarter-final. At the start of the 1987–88 season, as Barcelona slumped to three successive defeats – two of them at home – the parting of ways became inevitable. Venables' interpreter called it half sacking, half resignation. Venables says it was very amicable, he was offered a match by match basis contract but decided to end it properly.

Even before this friends of Venables had begun to put out feelers on his behalf. In the summer of 1987 Paul Kirby, a friend, counsellor, and soon to be a business partner, had spoken to Scholar after the first rumours of David Pleat's personal problems surfaced in the *Sun*. Scholar did nothing until Pleat's difficulties resurfaced in October when, having warned him after the first occasion, the Tottenham Board decided he had to leave. He was gone by mid-October, and when Scholar set about seeking a replacement, the agent, Dennis Roach, provided Scholar with Venables' number in Florida where he had retreated to his friend Colin Wright's place and Scholar flew out to try to persuade him to come to Tottenham.

Scholar feared it might be difficult to get him, but it proved quite easy, although Venables, because of his commitments in Spain, could not start until 1 December 1987, almost six weeks after the initial contact. It does seem strange, even so, that Venables agreed to come to Spurs. He found Scholar charming but so smooth that he felt he could skate on him, and he was never sure what he really was thinking. Nor was the money the attraction. Scholar's offer was half what he had earned in Barcelona, while Juventus offered a lot more than Tottenham. So what brought Venables back to Tottenham? Was it a desire to prove that his failure to shine there as a player was an aberration? Past failure seemed to spur his present decision.

In retrospect two aspects of their talks struck Scholar. Venables was keen to get Scholar's views on football as if he needed reassurance. The other was Venables' keen eye for getting the publicity right. Once the negotiations had concluded they agreed a joint statement to be released to the press. Venables said he would speak to his friend Jeff Powell. As he went up the stairs to make the call he told Scholar, 'You get Harry Harris of the *Mirror*, I will get the *Sun*. If we get these two papers on our side, then we will be all right. We must get the press on our side, that is very important.' In the euphoria of securing Venables Scholar did not dwell too much on his remarks but, as the years rolled on, the full significance of these comments struck him with some force.

If the move to Tottenham meant Venables had fulfilled his boyhood dreams, in some ways he had gone backwards. As he left QPR for Barcelona the talk was of him owning a club. Now he was back in England but still a tracksuited manager. The chance to go to the boardroom, which must have appeared so tantalisingly close at Loftus Road, was still denied. The ultimate prize of ownership continued to elude him.

His arrival at Tottenham had been hailed as the coming of the Messiah, and it was all the more eagerly anticipated because, while they waited for Venables to arrive, the team, without a manager and in the temporary charge of Doug Livermore, suffered a succession of defeats, gaining just two points between 24 October, the day after Pleat left, and 28 November, the day when Venables took charge against Liverpool.

For the Liverpool match 47,362 people packed White Hart Lane to welcome the Messiah back, but Venables, who at that stage had never beaten Liverpool, could not work the magic. Spurs not only lost 2–0, Steve Hodge was sent off. Before he had agreed to sign for Spurs Venables had given Scholar a piece of paper marked with eleven blank positions. He wanted to know how many current players at Tottenham could fill the positions. Scholar could only think of four. Richard Gough, the man hailed as the new Dave

Mackay by Pleat just over a year previously, had gone, so had Glenn Hoddle, and some of the other players were ageing. Venables felt the team Pleat had left behind was past its sell-by-date although, when Pleat left, it was still riding high. However, the results soon indicated it needed to be rebuilt, and the need became all the greater when, on 30 January, Port Vale beat Spurs in the FA Cup, one of the most embarrassing defeats suffered by Venables. The result seemed to shake him. He declared that, next season, he would challenge Liverpool for the title and gave himself six months to shake the Kop. It is no good finishing a consolidating sixth, he said.

Venables had begun to sign players almost as soon as he arrived, although the really spectacular ones came in the 1988–89 season when he brought Paul Gascoigne and Paul Stewart to White Hart Lane. By the beginning of the 1988–89 season he was to buy nearly £5m. worth of players. But the pre-season matches, which included a 4–0 hammering by Arsenal at Wembley, suggested that, whatever Venables' new signings might do up-front, Tottenham would have their familiar defensive problems. For good measure the first match of the season at home to Coventry was cancelled just hours before the kick-off.

David Lacey in the *Guardian* wittily commented that the way he heard the news it seemed the FA had postponed the match, fearful of the punishment the Spurs defence might take. The real reason was that Tottenham's new East Stand was not ready to receive spectators and the football authorities docked Tottenham two points. Although this was recouped, their season never really recovered. At one stage Spurs slumped to the bottom, before improving to end sixth, just the position where Venables had told the *Sun* after the Port Vale match he did not want to finish.

Worse still, there were early exits from both the League Cup and the FA Cup and, to add to Venables' misery, the season saw Arsenal win the title for the first time since 1971. Venables, recalls Scholar, went into deep depression at the news that his friend and disciple, George Graham, had achieved something he had failed to do.

The 1989–90 season promised to be better. Gary Lineker and Mohamed Ali Amar, a Spanish Under-21 player, popularly known as Nayim, were signed in a package deal worth £1.5m. Venables could now plan an attacking force of Lineker, Waddle and Gascoigne, three world-class players. But these three never played together in Spurs colours. The day Lineker was being paraded at White Hart Lane, Marseille bid for Waddle and he was sold for £4.5m., a staggering sum then.

Venables was not unhappy to see Waddle go since he felt that the money would help him to buy defenders. In his autobiography Venables gives the impression that he had been promised all of that £4.5m. for new players whereas he had promised the Spurs Board at the time of the purchase of Lineker that he would try to arrange player sales to match the cost of the £1.5m. paid for Lineker and Nayim. However, Venables should have had £3m. but even that was not available.

By this time Spurs were in deep financial trouble and Scholar, himself, had to underwrite the Lineker purchase. Venables sees the sale of Waddle, and the use made of the money, as the turning-point in his relationship with Scholar. He blames Scholar for going back on his intention of buying players when in fact this was more due to the intervention of Paul Bobroff, the chairman of the public company, Tottenham Hotspur plc. Spurs had diversified into areas not connected with football hoping that it would strengthen the football club, but these diversions were now draining resources from the club and preventing it from achieving success on the field. Not that there was any guarantee that, had Venables been given the entire £3m., he would have used it shrewdly, for some of that money financed the purchase of Steve Sedgeley and Pat Van Den Hauwe, hardly the sort of defenders to render the ever leaky Spurs defence secure.

As far as the public was concerned, however, the problems at Spurs remained hidden for another year and Venables' third season in charge, 1989–90, was much like the previous two. Spurs began badly, one victory in the first six games, but finished well, ending third in the League. This was a slightly unreal position in that the winning sequence had come in March and April when there was nothing left to play for except pride: the League was long beyond Tottenham's reach and they had already gone out of both Cups fairly early – for good measure beaten at home in the FA Cup third round by Southampton. But the way the season ended, including a 4–2 away victory at Sheffield Wednesday, and a 2–1 home victory over Manchester United with both Gascoigne and Lineker scoring, held out hope for a brighter future.

However, Venables' own pride took a knock that year when, to his chagrin, he found that he was not even shortlisted for the job of managing England. The search for the man to replace Bobby Robson had narrowed to three candidates: Howard Kendall, Joe Royle and, the eventual winner, Graham Taylor.

Venables had always seen himself as an international manager. He had often spoken about managing Brazil, and the thought of harnessing his ability to organise and plan footballing tactics to Brazilian flair plainly excited him. Soon after he had joined Spurs the Welsh FA had wanted Venables as their manager on a part-time basis, but Irving Scholar had blocked that move, feeling that the managership of Tottenham was a full-time job. But not even to be considered for the England role, and to be ranked below Joe Royle who at that stage had not even managed a first-division club, rankled deeply with Venables. As he wrote at the time in *Son of Fred*, his father's biography of him:

> I now believe that only a certain sort of person gets to manage England and, unfortunately, I'm not their type of guy. I would class myself as thoughtful and serious in my attitude towards football, but with a fairly happy-go-lucky attitude to the rest of my life. I take my job seriously, but I never think I take myself seriously – and that's not good enough for the FA.

Writing this in 1990 as a concluding, thirteenth chapter in Fred's biography, Venables could not have anticipated how ironic these words would later sound. Then, convinced he had missed the England boat he predicted that his next move would be not manager of an international team but chairman of an English league club: 'I'm getting to the time in my life when I want to be my own boss. I want to work for myself, or with someone else but not for someone else.'

Venables then went on to present a riveting picture of the type of chairman he would not be – the man who appoints a manager but does not give him any real powers: 'I would probably be the same as a chairman but I wouldn't lie and give someone else the title of "manager". I'd do what they do in Spain and have a coach, someone who looks after the team and is off home by one o'clock. I'd do the rest – and I'd tell him so, not kid that he's really the man in charge.'

Venables even gave a time-scale for his move to the boardroom. With his Spurs contract expiring in 1991, that, he said, would be the time to go into ownership. He could not have known how events would hand him a wonderful opportunity to make the prediction come true. The remarks in Fred's book and Fred's overall message was to garnish the image of 'one of football's great characters', a man of many parts.

Some of these parts, of course, went beyond football and Venables' return to London from Barcelona had also meant a resumption of his business interests outside football. Paul Kirby had kept in touch with him while he was in Barcelona and their friendship had further deepened into a family one. Once, when Barcelona played in Dundee, Kirby suddenly arrived in a helicopter and organised a trip, thrilling Fred who had never been in a helicopter before. Now Kirby linked up with Venables and Colin Wright to set up Transatlantic Inns.

Incorporated on 28 April 1989, Transatlantic Inns started trading on 1 May 1989 and was designed to run pubs, one of its first being the Cock and Magpie in Epping. Venables was the principal shareholder with 300,000 ten pence shares, Kirby and Wright each having 100,000 shares. They and a fourth director, David Brown, signed, on 22 December 1989, a document which guaranteed the overdraft NatWest were prepared to give. They used NatWest's Romford branch, it being Venables' local bank, and the limit was fixed at £250,000. It was the sort of finance for a company that was seen as the centre of a growing Venables business empire. In *Son of Fred* this is how Fred Venables pictured it:

> Over the years I have expanded my own business interests with Terry, and the Royal Oak in Chingford is now just one of six pubs under our control. The company we run together is called Transatlantic Inns and we've got pubs in Epping, Marlow and Reading. Terry has great involvement in everything we do, even though the running of the pubs is meant to be down to me. He will still go round and check out the new sites and every day, no matter where he is in the world, he rings up to make sure everything is all right and asks how trade has been. He checks up on me all the time, asking if I've been up the road to Epping to see if everything is running smoothly. I've never known anyone so quick to come to a decision if something needs to be discussed.

But even as Fred was writing these words Transatlantic Inns was performing disastrously. It had always been a curious company. For a long time after its formation Terry Venables' own sole trader bank account at NatWest's Romford branch also doubled up as Transatlantic Inns' bank account and it was not until the middle of 1989 that the bank accounts were tidied up. However, nothing could tidy up Transatlantic. It was a company destined never to make money and, with rare exceptions, none of its pubs traded successfully.

The first year's accounts, ending 31 March 1990, showed a loss of £91,750 and a deficit of assets over liabilities of £31,750. Venables and Kirby, signing the directors' report, were confident that they could 'trade out of the current insolvent situation'. However, the auditors found that cash had been stolen by a manager in one of the pubs but there 'are no independent procedures to verify the extent of the theft or whether all cash sales were properly recorded.' They had been unable to obtain all the information and explanations they felt necessary, could not be satisfied that accounting records were complete or accurate and heavily qualified the accounts.

However, all this did little to dim Venables' growing business reputation. By the time the auditors signed their report on 5 April 1991 Venables had, unexpectedly, been provided with a chance to become the owner of a publicly quoted company. With the media busily projecting Venables as the saviour of a hallowed, much loved institution, nobody bothered to check how some of Venables' other businesses were doing. It was a long time before Transatlantic Inns became news and even came to haunt Venables, but by then much had changed in Venables' life.

Chapter 3

An old school friend

Paul Kirby and Colin Wright were not the only friends with whom Venables had formed a business relationship on his return from Barcelona. A major partnership had also been created with Paul Riviere, even though Elite Gold was abandoned when Venables suddenly became Señor Venabless. Two years after his return, however, he linked up with Riviere on a much more substantial enterprise. This was 'The Manager', a board game the two men jointly developed and hoped might rival 'Trivial Pursuit'.

Riviere, as head of field operations with Cannon Lincoln, the insurance company, had reached the stage in his career when he wanted a change and, in March 1989, tired of what he saw as stulti-fying corporatedom where he could earn good income but make no capital, he left to form a company called Elite First along with Joe, or Jakob, Pawlikowski, whom he had recruited to Cannon. By the end of the year Riviere employed some thirty sales people and the company was operating successfully. Despite his long involve-ment in the financial services field, Riviere, at heart, is a marketing man, and by October that year he and Terry at last began work on the board game:

> We had always talked about perhaps doing something, and Terry didn't always want to be a football coach when he got to fifty. We came up with various schemes revolving round financial services and sports agency. We went for about twenty different ideas that we thought we could do in the 1990s. One of them was the board game. Terry had mentioned

that he would like to do that. From then we worked and worked and it became rather an obsession with us. We saw each other sometimes ten hours a day for the next eighteen months. During that period I, probably, saw more of him than anyone else.

Almost every afternoon, just as soon as Venables had finished at Tottenham's training ground at Mill Hill, he would drive his Mercedes down to either the Royal Garden Hotel in Kensington or the Carlton Tower in Knightsbridge. There, in the bar with a bottle of champagne in front of them, the two men would set to work. Sometime during the afternoon Venables would say to Riviere, 'I don't want to spend all my life as a sweaty football manager', have another sip of champagne and get back to working out 'The Manager'. By this time they were working out of Riviere's Princes Gate offices, just off Exhibition Road.

The game Riviere and Venables came up with was certainly worth celebrating in champagne, and Venables repeatedly said that he felt as proud of this as anything he had achieved in football. It allowed football fans to pretend to be a manager and fantasise about the teams they would pick. Any number from two to six could play and the players went round answering questions on football, entertainment and general knowledge. Riviere thought up the football and entertainment questions, and Venables and his then girlfriend Yvette the general knowledge ones. Interestingly, the object of the exercise was to win money rather than the championship, but in every other way it was a model for Fantasy Football.

The pair knew that the Venables profile could sell the game, Riviere brought excellent marketing skills, and both spent hours devising the questions, with Riviere keeping Venables' portable phone busy as they batted the possible ones back and forth. The problem was the money needed to launch the game.

The original idea had been to assign it or have it licensed by a company like Waddington or Spears, but when Riviere went to demonstrate it to the managing director and marketing directors of both companies they proved apathetic. So Venables and Riviere decided instead to put some of their own money into it. Both men could afford the initial costs. Venables had often told Riviere of his friendship with a Spanish businessman known by his nickname Manolo, and about collateral and property in Spain probably worth a million. He never went into details, despite the fact that

Riviere was his business partner and the man whom Venables described as one of his two closest friends. Riviere, implicitly trusting Venables, did not see anything odd in that. He knew Venables liked to keep his affairs compartmentalised.

Apart from money, the Riviere-Venables partnership lacked one other vital ingredient: financial expertise. Riviere has a good understanding of finance but freely confesses that, when it comes to such matters as business plans he feels out of his depth. Venables, despite the ventures in which he had been involved since the age of seventeen, knew even less. 'Terry Venables is bright,' says Riviere, 'but he doesn't understand finance. He understands it far more than the average footballer who leaves school at fourteen, but basically in that sense he is not a business-man.' Both men therefore needed somebody who could handle the financial side of the project, prepare a business plan, monitor the accounts, and make sense of the figures. And as if on cue in walked a man who seemed to offer precisely these qualities.

This man was John Brown. His entry into Terry Venables' life is the sort of real life story that even Venables would not have dared put into one of his Hazell novels. Let Riviere tell the story:

It is March 1990 and I am waiting for Terry in the Royal Garden Hotel when this guy comes over to me. He says, 'It's Paul Riviere, isn't it?'

'Yes,' I say, not knowing what he wanted or who he was.

'Don't you recognise me?' he asks.

I nod my head still wondering what the guy wanted.

'It's John, John Brown.'

It was only then, as I looked hard at him, that I realised that it was indeed John Brown, whom I had not seen since the summer's day in 1962, twenty-eight years ago, when we both bid good-bye to our grammar school.

The two schoolmates started reminiscing. There was much to reminisce about. They had been together from the ages of eleven to seventeen, good friends in the classroom and on the playing field. Both Paul and John played in the school soccer team: John at right back, Paul at wing half. They had also played cricket, with John quite a good all-rounder. The school was proud of its Victorian traditions and insisted that the boys wear a black jacket with tie and crest.

Eventually the talk turned to what the two men were doing now, and Brown explained he was the chief executive of a clothing company. Riviere was impressed by how well his old schoolmate had done: house in the country, children at public school, Porsche outside in the drive. Riviere explained that he was involved with Terry Venables in trying to promote 'The Manager'. Soon Venables himself arrived and Riviere introduced Brown to him. No meeting was to prove more fateful for Venables. Riviere recalls: 'Brown was very impressed by Venables. Terry and I had by this time done a business plan, not a very good one, through a friend of Jonathan Crystal, a guy called Mark Citroen. This was to try and raise some money for "The Manager". Brown was very helpful in doing a proper business plan.'

Brown also said he would introduce Riviere and Venables to his bank which was down in the country. It was while he was returning from a visit to his bank manager that the first setback came. The way Brown told the story it was something that could not have been bettered by a Hollywood scriptwriter. There he is, driving his Porsche along a country road, when the car phone rings. The phone call tells him that he has just been ousted from the board of his company. Suddenly from being a man of means he finds his income has dried up. What struck Riviere was that this did not seem to worry Brown. He assured Riviere that he would get a huge compensation and everything would be all right. Riviere continues: 'He then had no income. So Terry and I decided to take him on working for us a couple of days a week as we needed someone managing the financial side of things. We paid him £2,000 a month even though we weren't making money. His wife worked for us as well, doing the accounts.'

Venables has suggested that Brown had a lot more to do with 'The Manager' than merely managing the accounts. When he came on the scene, says Venables, all he and Riviere and had to show were a plastic bag full of table mats, odd scraps of paper, cigarette packets and cardboard models of various bits and pieces. In any case the idea for 'The Manager' had originated with chats Venables had had with Gordon Williams. If Williams had indeed given Venables the idea he never told Riviere, who came to know of his connection only when he read Venables' autobiography four years later. Riviere's memory is precise: 'When we devised the scheme I had not heard of this Gordon Williams'. Indeed Riviere is so unaware of Gordon Williams that he keeps referring to him as Gordon Watson. Certainly neither Brown nor Gordon Williams featured in the publicity which would soon swamp the national media.

On 22 August 1990 Jeff Powell, in the *Daily Mail*, ran a full-page feature which showed Powell and Venables playing the game on what looked like either Powell's or Venables' living-room floor. That Powell should have been taken by the game is not surprising. Venables, according to Powell, was the 'cleverest personality' in the game. What, in retrospect, is significant is that Powell was writing this just a bare three months after Brown, by Venables' own account, had started working on the game. There is no mention of Brown, but Powell mentioned that the £180,000 costs had been funded by Venables 'equally with his partner Paul Riviere'.

This theme was emphasised in a prominent *Times* write-up of 5 December 1990 which used a photograph of Venables and Riviere playing the game at Langan's with Riviere identified as his friend, partner and the man who had helped him devise, develop and market the game. The world outside knew nothing of Brown, who was acting like a conventional accounts man, very much in the background. Riviere had wondered why he shunned the limelight and concluded he was naturally modest.

Brown was a busy backroom financial guru. What you need, he told Venables and Riviere, is a company to get 'The Manager' going. He suggested that a company called Glenhope Management be formed, and Riviere used his long-standing lawyer, Roderick Dadak, a specialist in libel, to help form the company. Dadak also helped set up Venables Ventures as a holding company for the Venables–Riviere partnership.

For Brown to be asked to form companies was a bit like a man of faith hearing the biblical call to go forth and multiply. He formed and cast off companies like others may change their socks. Two years later, in 1992, when Colin Sandy, as Financial Director of Tottenham, finally decided to look into Brown's financial background he discovered that his companies scorecard stood as follows: director of 43 companies; of these 15 had gone into receivership, 8 into liquidation and 15 were struck off. At this early stage, however, none of this was known to Riviere, who saw Brown's introduction – he became the finance director of Glenhope, and company secretary of Venables Ventures – as completing a powerful trinity:

> We had different roles within 'The Manager'. Venables did the profile with the media. I did the marketing, sales and promotion and Brown did everything to do with finance, the accounting system, invoicing. Brown was given a completely

free hand. I trusted him implicitly.

Riviere thought he had arranged everything neatly. His financial services company, Elite First, was based just off Hyde Park Square, with Joe Pawlikowski handling the day to day operations as managing director under the chairmanship of Riviere. Riviere, so increasingly involved with 'The Manager', could just about succeed in attending a sales meeting once a week. But he trusted Pawlikowski and was confident of his ability. Riviere was also keen to keep Elite First separate from Glenhope.

'The Manager' finally took off with a successful launch at Harrods in August 1990. Later, Venables was pictured with Miss World contestants providing just the right media image and by Christmas of that year there was a particularly happy Paul Riviere. His marketing projections were being fulfilled. All the big department stores were taking the game and there was talk of the ultimate prize: marketing it in America. This was meant to be done either through American football or baseball as 'The Coach' or in Hollywood as 'The Producer'. The basic ingredients could be applied to any team game: 'The Manager' was never conceived by Venables and Riviere as a pure football game; their guiding light was 'Trivial Pursuit'. They were inspired by its success but aware of the problems that it had caused for its creators.

Venables was clearly enjoying himself although, by this time, his ever active mind was focusing on another prize.

Chapter 4

An eerie game

Venables had often told Riviere about his dream of owning a football club, but his thoughts seemed to be of owning a small club. Venables was much taken by the continental virtues of management where small clubs do not create a confrontational situation with big clubs, as in Britain, but work in a much more co-operative framework, often acting as a nursery for the bigger clubs. Barcelona had opened his eyes to European club management and he was keen to import some of the continental ideas into this country.

About this time Venables was also growing disenchanted with Spurs and Irving Scholar. This appears to have grown ever since the Chris Waddle transfer and his friendship with Scholar, once much advertised, was now less evident. While Scholar continued to support and praise Venables as manager – he had defended him in the dark days of 1988, when other directors at Spurs, such as Paul Bobroff, wanted his head – Venables told Riviere that life with Scholar was not much fun.

Sometime at the beginning of the 1990–91 season he had discussed the possibility of acquiring Charlton and met Ron Noades, chairman of Crystal Palace, who were then Charlton's landlords at Selhurst Park. He had also made discreet enquiries about West Ham. But soon a bigger prize presented itself when, within weeks of the start of the season, Spurs' financial crisis exploded. The first football club to be quoted on the stock market was now paying the price for the excesses of the 1980s: diversifications into areas which bore little or no relation to football, such as computer operations and clothing. So parlous was its financial state that it did not have the money to pay the last tranche of money for Lineker and Nayim: £900,000. This was due on 1 August 1990 and Scholar, without telling the Board, approached Robert Maxwell. Scholar's initial idea was to get Maxwell's help to organise a rights issue, something the Tottenham Board had discussed but, with the Lineker time-bomb ticking away, the talks with Maxwell ended up as a loan of £1.1m., with Scholar guaranteeing the loan both with personal guarantees and a charge on his property company and a property he owned in the King's Road in Chelsea.

While Scholar's intentions may have been understandable, his choice of the man he turned to for help and the execution of the plan was less than brilliant. What one can say in Scholar's defence is that, at that stage, no one seriously doubted Maxwell's credentials. Maxwell was a name both feared and respected in the City. And while not many liked him in football, even the supporters of Derby County, one of two football clubs he owned, had not yet started singing, 'He's fat, he's round and he's never at the ground'. That came following the disillusionment resulting from the revelations of his loan to Scholar. Jeff Randall of the *Sunday Times* broke the story on 8 September 1990, ironically on the morning after Spurs had beaten Derby, and from that moment on Tottenham were in turmoil.

The partnership between Scholar and Bobroff had already cracked, and the deal with Maxwell alienated the two men further. Scholar was criticised for his handling of the loan issue – which violated City rules on public companies. Scholar left the Board of Tottenham Hotspur plc, but continued to be chairman of the football club (which the public company owned). By the turn of the year, Tottenham were forced by the Midland Bank to have a new chairman for the public company: Nat Solomon, yet another devoted supporter.

As Tottenham's debt increased – the overdraft eventually reached £11m. – the account was moved to the Midland's 'casualty unit' in Cannon Street in the City. David Buchler's accounting firm, Buchler Phillips, played an increasingly crucial role in formulating business plans in order to pacify the Midland. The situation made for endless newspaper speculation about possible rescuers.

Venables was not an early runner in the rescue stakes. Indeed, initially, he appears to have ruled himself out of the race. Frank Warren, the promoter, recollects a meeting with him, some time in

November at the Royal Garden Hotel, when Venables told him he was disillusioned with what was happening. 'Terry,' recalls Warren in an interview with me, 'said he was thinking of packing in football and going abroad. At that stage he certainly gave no indication that he wanted to bid for Spurs.'

So what changed this? Venables has provided several different versions of how and why he got involved. According to one version, it seems Scholar was the man who suggested he should try to make a bid for Spurs. In an affidavit which he swore during his court action against Alan Sugar in 1993, Venables said he had not thought of buying Spurs until Scholar put the idea in his head. Venables could not quite recall when this was but says he did not 'take it seriously until I realised quite how bad the financial situation was and that there was serious prospect of my being able to take control of the club'.

Scholar indignantly denies that he suggested to Venables he put money together to buy Spurs. The thought of turning to the man whom he had hired as manager, when he had merchant bankers and advisers forming a traffic jam in the Spurs boardroom, strikes him as risible.

A year after he had won Spurs, when he was appearing as a witness for the *Daily Mail* in the libel action brought against it by Scholar, Venables, during cross-examination by Scholar's QC, suggested he got involved with the rescue as a way of trying to prevent the sale of a key player, Paul Gascoigne.

Six months after this court appearance Venables, in an interview with Joe Lovejoy, then football correspondent of the *Independent*, described his purchase of Spurs as an emotional over-reaction. He had thought of putting in up to £500,000 to buy a club like Barnet but 'everyone got so carried away with the Tottenham thing that in the end I felt I was going to be a rotter if I didn't do it. Certain people said they would put up the money but then fell by the wayside, and I was left with the bill.'

Venables' autobiography does not clear up the confusion, many names are mentioned but no clear picture emerges. As so often, the truth is probably a mixture of these various versions, and the start of Venables' quest to buy Spurs is probably closer to how Frank Warren remembers it. 'After Terry had spoken of his unhappiness with Scholar and how he was thinking of packing it in I began to think that maybe there was a way of involving him in a bid to buy Spurs. I was working with a guy called Larry Gillick on the

London Arena, a sale and leaseback proposal. He had done something similar with Wembley and I was impressed with what Gillick had to offer. He worked from offices in Harley Street, the offices of the solicitors Kanter Jules Grangewoods, and they had provided a letter stating Gillick's worth. He seemed to know what he was talking about and I thought it might be a good idea to get Gillick and Venables together.'

So, some time in December 1990 Warren arranged a meeting at Orso, an Italian restaurant in Covent Garden. 'It was there for the time that the idea of Venables being involved in any take-over of Spurs emerged,' recalls Warren. 'The idea was that Gillick would provide the finance and Terry would be the chief executive.'

News of the plan was soon made public, inevitably by Jeff Randall in the *Sunday Times*, but even now Venables was seen as no more than fronting the show, not as the principal owner. 'He was', says Warren, 'to get 10% free and then he would have the right to buy more shares. But there would be other investors in charge of the company depending on how many put up their money.' Venables says Gillick offered 25%, but this figure may have moved up from 10% in subsequent discussions.

After his split with Alan Sugar became public Venables claimed that right from the beginning he had always wanted to have an equal partnership in the club. He never wanted to be a minority shareholder who could be at the mercy of others. It is possible he developed such convictions as he got more involved in buying Spurs, but that was not how it began. Like many things in the Venables story it started more by accident than design and, like Topsy, it grew.

Hardly surprising then that, in those early days during the autumn and winter of 1990, as would-be investors met Scholar and various members of the Tottenham Board, Venables hardly figured. Soon after the Warren story broke Scholar was approached by Tony Berry, a member of the Tottenham Board. Berry knew investors who wanted to bring money into Tottenham and this led to Scholar journeying to Sussex to meet Ted Ball, then in charge of Landhurst Leasing, a financing company. Warren was there but not Venables.

By this time, in December 1990, a letter addressed to Berry had also arrived. It was from Larry Gillick and was tabled at a Tottenham Board meeting. After some discussion it was decided that Berry should go to see Gillick, who said he was representing a company called First Security. It was after this meeting that Berry reported that they would like to do a deal, with Venables proposed as their chief executive.

Tony Berry had long been sweet on Venables. A good enough amateur himself to have had trials with Tottenham – his hero was the legendary Dave Mackay, whom he wanted to emulate as a professional until Bill Nicholson dissuaded him – Berry had become a director of Spurs just before they reached the 1987 Cup Final, the first FA Cup Final they were to lose. Soon after Scholar hired Venables, Berry was asked to help organise some additional income for Venables: 'I first met him soon after he had joined Spurs,' Berry recalls. 'I actually was asked by Scholar if I could find Terry some sponsorship to supplement the salary he wanted. I did this, it was not very much, £20,000 a year. But I got to know him fairly well really.'

Like almost everybody who meets Venables, Berry took an immediate liking to him. 'He always struck me as somebody who was likeable. He's got a certain way with people and he's quite charming.' There was one curiosity about Venables, however, that struck Berry: 'He's not as self-assured as people make him out to be. He was always asking questions on subjects where you felt he should be giving you the answers, rather than the other way around. Even on football he would ask my opinion. I had played a bit and he would say, well at least you know something about it. He didn't think many people knew a lot about football anyway, but he did like to ask people.'

Venables was now asking questions more insistently and Berry began to suggest some answers. 'When Tottenham's world collapsed with the lack of money and Maxwell came into the picture, I was very much on Terry's side.' For two years before the crisis blew up Berry had been suggesting to Scholar that perhaps Venables should be brought on to the Football Club Board. 'This was something Venables was very keen on. He was always wanting it, he felt he had more to offer than just being a football manager. He felt he had a rapport with the supporters and he thought he could get more out of the sponsors if he was there. He also had a good PR image and felt he could be useful.'

On at least three occasions Berry raised the question of bringing Venables on the Board: 'However, Irving was never a great one for that move. He felt Terry was three or four years away from that situation where he could run the business. Also there was still a certain feeling around the Board at that time that footballers don't become directors. It has started to change now with Francis Lee and people like that but in those days there was a barrier.'

However, with the club facing the gravest crisis in its nearly 110-year existence such class barriers counted for little. Berry now openly championed Venables' cause both in the boardroom and as an adviser off it. Not that there was too much to champion, not yet anyway. At this stage Venables' plans for rescue were still very nebulous and some of his possible backers were quite mysterious, ranging from a Danish bank to a sheikh. Berry attended a great many meetings but they rarely amounted to much: 'The first time was late in 1990 when Terry approached me to come to the Carlton Tower where we met with a number of people in the bar there who were friends of Terry. He had one particular runner who seemed prepared to make a move and that was the son of the ruler of the United Arab Emirates. The son was not there in the bar but his representative was.'

Venables in a television documentary made by Channel Four's *Dispatches* programme later reflected: 'All those events happened. If you wrote it, it would have been thrown out of the window because no-one would have believed it. It was quite eerie the way the whole thing went about. And this business of raising finance and nearly getting there, beaten on the line again, so many times.'

That almost fictional quality was heightened by the fact that the meetings nearly always took place in the bars of the Royal Garden or the Carlton Tower. Berry was not always sure who some of the people Venables met were. 'Some of them didn't seem right to me. The Middle Eastern one never appeared to be a serious runner in the end. The representatives would never follow it through, it seemed to me. And even Terry got a bit tired about that.'

To complicate matters, as so often with Venables, he did not always let on about all the moves he was making himself, even to someone like Berry, despite the fact that Berry was his backer on the Tottenham Board. 'Although I didn't go to that many meetings I was involved but Terry still played most of his cards close to his chest. I wasn't told who the people were for a long while even when I asked.' This did not worry Berry. 'I said I don't care about that. If you can get something together and put the money up, I'm happy to listen to it.'

One of the men Berry listened to was Jim Gregory, Venables' old mentor from Queens Park Rangers. Berry told Scholar that

Gregory might be interested in buying Tottenham. The Gregory option was also mentioned to Scholar by Venables, but when Scholar discovered that this would involve selling Gascoigne he declared he was not interested.

The runners Venables brought to the bar of the Royal Garden or the Carlton Tower were not the only possible starters. There were others emanating from the City, such as a rights issue proposed by Michael Goddard of Baltic, some proposals discussed by Stuart Lucas of Bear Stearns, although this does not seem to have gone much beyond a lunch for Scholar and Ian Gray, the then chief executive of Tottenham, and Project Tarragon, which involved Hambro Magan. On top of all this the Tottenham Board were looking at their own plan for a rights issue, with their advisers, Brown Shipley, confident they could raise between £6m. and £8m.

Through this crowded and confused field one runner did appear to be coming through, however. That was Larry Gillick and in March 1991 he made his move. On 5 March a company called Edennote had been formed, a week later Gillick and Venables became directors of the company, although at this stage most of the shares were held by Gillick through Trustees of Sky Settlement. It had a share capital of £50,000 but only £12,500 was paid, in 25p partly paid shares, a figure that had not changed by the time the company was wound up four years later.

Berry had met Gillick and felt that 'his pedigree, of course, was that he'd had a father who had played for Rangers so he was obviously taken seriously.' Riviere, too, met Gillick, but this was more by accident than design: 'I found he was OK. But he did not look like a financial consultant. When I first met him in Harley Street he was in a green cardigan. He looked like a latterday Sydney Greenstreet.'

Gillick also looked rather menacing, at least to one member of the Tottenham Board, when early in March, he, Venables and Peter Earle of Tranwood – a small merchant bank which, later that year, called in the receivers but was then acting as Venables' advisers – went to see the Board at Nat Solomon's offices in the West End. Scholar described Gillick in his book as looking like an out-of-work gangster, with his dark suit and bright fish tie not quite gelling together.

This meeting, although it led to nothing, was important for the insight it provided into Venables, the businessman operating at this level. Gillick gave the impression that he could front the purchase of Tottenham on his own. He told the Tottenham Board he would offer 90p per share, take on the debt of £12m.–£13m. and put in another £5m. which meant a total outlay of something between £25m. and £30m. Brown Shipley, advising Tottenham, were extremely dubious that Gillick could produce the money. It was a little over a year since the astonishing Michael Knighton episode when Knighton, then an unknown property man, had bought Manchester United only for it to emerge that he did not have the money to fund such a purchase.

Gillick turned out to be even more elusive than Knighton. He did not have the money, nor was his history encouraging. He had been a bankrupt and had caused the destruction of a greyhound track, although these facts were not revealed until some time later by the *Scottish Daily Record*.

Even at this stage Venables appeared to have no more than a silent walk-on part. At the meeting with the Tottenham Board Gillick was at his most expansive while Venables hardly said anything, except nod his head and occasionally murmur, 'That's right, yeah, yeah.' One or two Board members got the impression that the details were going over his head, but did the whole exercise prove too perplexing as well? Did he find Gillick drawing him into waters where he was floundering?

Gillick had started off by offering 90p per share. After some discussions, Gillick, Earle and Venables were asked to leave the room while the Tottenham Board considered their proposal. Scholar offered to have a private talk with Gillick to see if he could better the terms. How about 110p, or even the £1 at which it was floated in 1983, Scholar asked Gillick? Gillick was eventually prepared to move up by 5p per share. Scholar, Bobroff and Berry agreed to accept, they made up 44% of the shareholders, and Scholar felt sure he had a deal.

Venables, Gillick and Earle were summoned back and hands were shaken on a 95p per share deal. Scholar went up to Venables, shook his hand, patted him on the cheek and said, 'Now go and win the European Cup', a special dream of Scholar, whose fantasy was to resign as chairman the night Tottenham won the European Cup. Everyone parted on friendly terms, although nobody knew how Gillick would finance it. Within a week it was clear Gillick did not have the money and he wanted to drop the price down to 85p.

However, a year later in the libel case brought by Scholar against the *Daily Mail*, when cross-examined by Scholar's QC, Venables denied that he had shaken hands with Scholar on a 95p deal. This is how the questions from Scholar's QC and the answers from Venables went.

QC: You actually shook hands on the deal with Irving Scholar, didn't you?

Venables: Well, that is not quite accurate. May I tell my story?

QC: Please do.

Venables: It was between Tottenham directors and their solicitors and our consortium and our solicitors. There was talk about a sale at possibly 85p–90p – I wouldn't go – Gillick knew that, Scholar knew that, we wouldn't go above 90p. We were asked to leave the room. We got to the room, Gillick was behind us. We got to the room and Gillick wasn't there. He came about three or four minutes later and said that Irving had called him to one side. He looked a bit angry. He said, 'If you do it for 95p', he said, 'Irving said we have got a deal.' And I was furious because of the fact that he had slipped out and done it separately, because I was involved in the same bid as Gillick, and Gillick seemed to agree. I was very angry.

QC: I suggest that you have got that confused. There was a deal between yourself and Mr Scholar for 95p. About a week later, the money not having come up, Mr Gillick said 85p.

Venables: Gillick shook his hand, so as far as I was concerned, I was in the deal with Gillick, it was subject to contract, that deal. And also he was constantly making his job that much more difficult to raise money. In the end, after all his efforts you are quite correct, he could not come up with the money.

QC: Your understanding is that Mr Gillick, on behalf of your consortium, shook hands on the deal.

Venables: That is correct.

QC: With Mr Scholar at 95p.

Venables: Yes.

As an example of verbal wriggling this can hardly be bettered. Venables, having started by questioning he had done a deal with Scholar on 95p, ends by agreeing that, yes, he had done a deal with Scholar at 95p. Reading the testimony it seems that Venables is not denying that he had done a deal with Scholar, but that he shook Scholar's hands; in other words he seems to be questioning the physical act not the financial deal. If so, that is the sort of semantics that would disgrace a fifth former. However, that Venables should have indulged in it a year after he had taken charge at

Spurs is the best possible indication that the whole takeover was a bit misty for Venables. Often things happened of which he was only dimly aware. This is hardly surprising.

For all the street-wise sense Venables possessed and his quickness to seize opportunities on and off the football field, understanding of finance was not his forte. A takeover of a public company is a complex matter which City professionals can get wrong and it would be no shame if Venables did not master all the details. But he appears not even to have understood the broad picture. More significant is that he makes no such acknowledgement in his autobiography where details of the negotiations with Gillick are left vague. And while he rightly castigates the financial mess at Tottenham – at times so embarrassing that other clubs were threatening to sue for paltry sums – it considerably lessens his case when he does not own up to his own financial shortcomings.

In anyone else this might have been a crippling disadvantage, but Venables had one thing going for him: the huge wave of sympathy and support on the back pages of the newspapers, particularly the tabloid press. There, ever since the Warren consortium story, but more so since Spurs had begun the FA Cup run, a campaign had been going which pictured Venables as the good guy, the possible knight on a white charger who could rescue Spurs from the evil clutches of the money men, like Scholar and Bobroff, who had supposedly ruined the club.

At this stage how far the fans believed Venables could be a knight in shining armour is debatable. In the middle of February 1991, when Tottenham finally held their postponed Annual General Meeting, despite three months having elapsed since Jeff Randall had revealed the Warren consortium plan, hardly any of the fans took it seriously. The fans had plenty to say but nobody asked Venables about his plans to rescue Spurs. Venables appeared a little miffed by this.

The fans were more concerned with the embarrassment Tottenham's financial problems were causing them. For the last game of 1990 Tottenham went to Southampton for a League match only to find the club programme had printed adverse comments about their problems with Hummel, the leisure manufacturers with whom Spurs had a deal on marketing and distribution. Ken Bates had commented in the Chelsea programme about Spurs' failure to pay for the match tickets the club had bought. These were stories common to clubs in the lower reaches of the League, but not the mighty Spurs, and the press sympathised with Venables for having to plan an FA Cup campaign with the club seemingly broke.

Sympathy for Venables increased all the more because, despite the dreadful financial problems, Spurs were now enjoying their best season under him. Indeed Spurs had their best start since the Double season of 1960–61: they were unbeaten until 4 November, and although results declined after that Venables could say this was because lack of funds meant he could not replace injured players. All this provided further support to the tabloid picture of Venables holding the fragile ship of Spurs together, shielding the players from the speculation about the club's failure while performing miracles on the field, and with nothing more than his own charisma and the power and beauty of Gascoigne's footwork.

By now Paul Gascoigne had become inextricably bound up with any Spurs rescue. He had returned from the 1990 World Cup, where England had given their best ever performance away from home and the best since 1966, in reaching the semi-finals, as a major national figure who was capable of reaching beyond football. In the semi-final against Germany, which England lost on penalties, Gascoigne had shed tears, a sight that moved the nation and suggested that here, at last, was an English footballer who could play and cry, something only Latins and other strange continentals were supposed to do. Almost instantly he was converted from a fat northern oaf into a national hero, and Gazzamania swept the country.

Venables could take much credit for Gascoigne's rise to prominence. It was his decision to persuade Gascoigne to move from Newcastle to Tottenham, in preference to other clubs such as Liverpool, that had made the player. The Gascoigne he had bought in 1988 for £2m. was a youth of promise. By the time the World Cup took place in Italy he looked very much the finished product, the man who, with a bit of luck, might even have won England the World Cup.

As the Spurs crisis developed the most potent rumours swirled around Gascoigne. From fairly early on it was clear that the simplest way out of the financial mess was to sell Gascoigne, possibly to an Italian club. Doing so could fetch £7m. or £8m. and that, at a stroke, would cut the overdraft and appease the Midland Bank. Indeed Lineker had once said to Scholar, 'Why don't we sell Gazza and get on with our lives.' But Scholar, showing the schoolboy side of his character rather than the hard-headed property man who had made millions, would not hear of it and, of course, any such sale would infuriate the fans.

However, their demand to keep Gascoigne and save Spurs made little impression on the money men, and the Midland asked Tottenham to do a marketing exercise on Gascoigne, i.e. tout him around possible overseas clubs with a view to a sale. Soon after Nat Solomon took over, and just before a crucial League Cup quarter-final against Chelsea, Solomon made it clear that a Gascoigne sale was very much on the cards. Scholar reluctantly agreed to be associated with a plan to market him through the agent, Dennis Roach, but was still hopeful he could stall the deal.

But while Scholar, like Micawber, was hoping something would turn up, in the tabloid press it was Venables and his consortium, however intangible, who were seen as the real rescuers: not only would they rescue the club but they would keep Gascoigne. So as the season's FA Cup run began two events coalesced in the public mind. On the field Gascoigne, tutored by Venables, was leading Spurs to a trophy; off the field Venables looked as if he might mount a rescue that would both save the club and keep Gascoigne at Tottenham. Given Spurs' financial conditions this was totally unrealistic, like having your cake and eating it, but in the simplicities favoured by the tabloid world it did not matter.

By March Gascoigne's potency had taken Spurs to the quarter-finals of the Cup. Apart from Blackpool, in the third round, Gascoigne had scored in every round with his goals often rescuing Spurs from tricky situations, two against Oxford, two more against Portsmouth and then, on Sunday 10 March, before a live television audience, there were his heroics against Notts County in the quarter-final. After Nayim had cancelled out a Notts County half-time lead, Gascoigne, despite suffering from a double hernia that would send him to hospital immediately after the match, scored the winner. It sent Spurs to the semi-final and made talk of Spurs' name being on the Cup all the more credible.

For Venables those ten days surrounding the Notts County match were crucial, an Ides of March but in a very different way. Five days before the Notts County game, Edennote had been formed; two days after it Venables and Gillick became directors. Now, with Spurs in the semi-finals of the FA Cup Venables was in his element. This was the occasion to pit his tactical genius as a manager against George Graham and prove that the master could still teach the disciple, who had appeared to be forging ahead of him, a trick or two.

It would also be an historic match: the first time Spurs would play Arsenal at Wembley in an FA Cup tie and the first time anything other than a Cup Final was to be played at the historic stadium. For Venables it was exactly the right platform to launch his effort to buy Spurs. Scholar still could not believe Venables had the money. 'I think,' said Tony Berry, 'he genuinely believed Terry just didn't have the ability. He said he would never raise the money and he was almost proved correct in that.'

Scholar had good reason to doubt whether Venables could raise the money. About this time Venables agreed to a proposal to buy the rights to a video about himself but asked Scholar to deduct his share of the cost, £15,000, from his salary. Could a man who would prefer to pay £15,000 in instalments, suddenly mount a rescue for Tottenham that would require millions? What Scholar could not have anticipated was that Venables would use the platform the semi-final provided in masterly fashion to advance his cause.

And just before the semi-final, Venables did indeed secure a club, albeit in the West End and not in North London, and very different from White Hart Lane.

Chapter 5

Terry's other club

Four days before Tottenham Hotspur played Arsenal in the FA Cup semi-final at Wembley, Venables, in partnership with Paul Riviere, bought Scribes West. The idea of owning a club had often been discussed by the two of them. As they sipped champagne in the bar of the Royal Garden or the Carlton Tower they would muse: wouldn't it be much better if we could have our own club?

Riviere recalls that John Brown was consulted and told them that they had money in Glenhope and it would initially be £50,000 to buy into Scribes, primarily to keep the cash flow going. Riviere was not entirely convinced, thinking they were taking on too much, but was reassured by the fact that much of their hard work on 'The Manager' had been done. He also agreed because Venables insisted that he would only get involved if Riviere did the marketing.

On 10 April Venables and Riviere became 'owners' of this Kensington club. It is necessary to put 'owners' in inverted commas because the deal remained shrouded in mystery for years, so that even the Department of Trade and Industry (DTI) was puzzled over how Venables had gained control. In February 1996, during the course of the court action between Venables and Paul Kirby, there were hearings in the Court of Appeal. Kirby's counsel alleged, among other things, that Venables had misled his fellow directors at Transatlantic about the deal. The Court of Appeal judges decided that Kirby should not be allowed to bring these arguments as part of his defence against Venables. However, for the moment the world was told nothing of all this. Riviere and

Venables were partners, they were pictured outside Scribes, and there was much generally jocular media comment on Terry, at last, acquiring a club.

Venables and Riviere had 'bought' Scribes West, developed by the same duo, Geoffrey Van-Hay and Gavin Hans Hamilton, who for years had run Scribes Cellar, just off Fleet Street. As the newspapers started leaving Fleet Street, particularly the Mail Group, Van-Hay and Hamilton were approached – Hamilton believes this must have been in early 1988 – by Mail Group executives to move their club to a site in the Barkers Centre in Kensington High Street, just below the Mail's new offices. The landlords, the Al-Fayeds, had made the basement available for a wine bar.

Soon after this, Hamilton had talks with Paul Kirby and Colin Wright about an investment in the new club. Wright and Kirby wanted 54% of the company which was not acceptable to Hamilton or Van-Hay who did not want any one investor to have a majority stake.

What Hamilton and Van-Hay did not know was that Venables was involved with Paul Kirby and Colin Wright through Transatlantic Inns. They knew Terry but at this stage he was more of a friend who used to come in and drink at Scribes Cellar and who now and again bought cases of Charles Le Roi, the Luxembourg sparkling wine.

Scribes West opened in January 1990 with a number of shareholders, led by Lord Rothermere, none of them investing more than £21,000 as share capital although considerably more was provided as loan stock. The opening was performed in style by Mrs Thatcher, still Prime Minister. But whereas Scribes Cellar was just the cosy, slightly run-down but always enticing place for journalists to gather after the day's work, Scribes West decided to go upmarket and was one of those wonderful-sounding ideas which fell victim to the recession of the 1990s.

As the end of 1990 approached it had all but run out of its initial investment, and it was clear that, by April 1991, the club would be in major financial difficulties. To survive, Scribes West needed another £150,000. In October 1990, Hamilton and Van-Hay reapproached Kirby and Wright.

> They showed interest which was encouraging to us. It was
> quite a positive reaction. Paul was spending a lot of time
> there, trying to make things happen. We needed a positive

signed piece of paper saying that the money would be put in by 18 December and we were getting close to that date when everything kind-of collapsed. It collapsed in such a way that we couldn't speak to anyone. No one was available. Paul wasn't available. Colin Wright wasn't available. We realised something had gone wrong at Transatlantic Inns.

In his Court of Appeal hearing in February 1996 Kirby said he had been haggling with Van-Hay and Hamilton to get the best price. He had told Terry of the potentialities of the deal and Terry was excited. But Kirby went abroad for a holiday at Christmas and returned to find Transatlantic was no longer involved. He only came to know Venables was involved in April 1991 after the deal was done. At 2pm on 18 April 1991 he had a meeting with Venables at the Carlton Tower. However, Venables, alleged Kirby, denied he had any financial involvement but claimed that Scribes West was using his name. Kirby's allegations were made in the context of a court case brought by Venables against him. The Appeal Court judges did not give Kirby leave to amend his defence and introduced this matter in the case.

So how did Venables get involved in Scribes?

In December 1990, after negotiations with Transatlantic had collapsed, Hamilton and Van-Hay decided to approach Venables personally. 'Terry had never really been part of the negotiations. His name was mentioned during the negotiations and he had been to the club socially on a few occasions. When we approached him directly he showed positive interest on his own. He was a bit surprised that there were problems. He seemed almost to say that he didn't even know it [the negotiations with Wright and Kirby] was happening although we had been told that he knew everything that was happening. It came over from him that he didn't. That was a bit surprising to us but eventually he did sign a piece of paper saying that he, with certain reservations on points that needed clarification, would be prepared to invest money into the club.'

That was on 18 December 1990. Negotiations started between the Venables camp and Scribes West's biggest shareholder, Vincent Isaacs. These negotiations did not go as smoothly or as quickly as Hamilton and Van-Hay wished. By March 1991 they were getting low on actual capital. 'We were saying that a decision had to be made soon, otherwise we would have no cash to pay any bills, or whatever. Eventually it was decided that the whole Board structure would change. Apart from Van and myself the existing directors would resign. Three new directors would be appointed: Terry Venables, John Brown and Paul Riviere. So we had a Board of five and obviously Van and myself were in a minority position.'

But how had Venables actually got control? How much money had he put in? Whose shares did he buy? This is a subject on which Venables is very reticent. In his autobiography he merely says he bought into Scribes West because he thought it would make a good business for him after Tottenham. However, this is hardly backed up by the documents filed in Companies House. Riviere still does not know how much was invested in Scribes West as all the financial details were left to Brown.

When the accounts for August 1990 were finally filed in April 1994 – we shall see why it took nearly four years to do so – the directors' report signed by Venables states that, 'In May 1992 T. F. Venables acquired an interest in the company and has supported it through the intervening period.' So what happened between April 1991 and May 1992 which allowed Venables to assert he owned Scribes West?

'Venables,' says Hamilton, 'got control in 1991 because Isaacs gave him control over his shares. Brown and Venables had made it clear that they wanted control and Isaacs, who was then friendly with Venables, gave him that control.'

Isaacs might baulk at the phrase 'friendly with Venables'. He said to me in an interview in March 1995: 'I met Terry Venables maximum on four occasions. I was friendly with Geoffrey Van-Hay for a long time. Geoffrey asked me to subscribe to Scribes West and I did. I tried to support my old friend. Then Geoffrey came back to me and said he had found someone who would bring clientele to the club and money to the club. Would I be prepared to put up some more money? He told me it was Terry Venables. Geoffrey was a friend of mine, I am a soft touch when it comes to my friends. I met with Terry Venables, he seemed to be personally charming. He said he could do a whole variety of different things and he agreed to put a certain sum of money up. I also agreed to put up some money. But he said he would want control of the club. I said I am not interested in becoming a director under any circumstances whatsoever, I don't want control. The size of my equity was really an accident, only because of supporting Geoffrey. I was happy for Terry Venables to vote my shares for the first year until he had the option of buying many more shares. To this day I have not received the share certificates.'

In March 1995 Isaacs had not even seen the crucial 1990 accounts. But if Isaacs merely wanted to help an old friend the way he did it made the situation tailor-made for John Brown: a company in trouble and a rich man willing to invest but not keen to exercise control.

Venables and Isaacs would eventually end up in court. But for the moment, in April 1991, Venables and Riviere were pictured as the owners, with Brown as the finance man.

Venables had promised to invest £50,000. But when Van-Hay asked Hamilton if the money had come in, Hamilton replied, 'Not actually in the bank account.'

'What do you mean by that?' asked Van-Hay.

Hamilton: 'Well, another bank account has suddenly appeared and apparently the money has been paid into that.' (This was a Coutts bank account, Coutts being a bank with great significance for Brown.)

Van-Hay: 'What does that mean, "apparently"?'

Hamilton: 'Well, we don't have access to that bank account, or to any of the statements, or to the cheque book.'

The subject continued to bother Hamilton for several months after Venables had taken control. On the morning of 4 September 1990, a financial meeting of Scribes West was held with Venables, Brown, Riviere and Jonathan Crystal present, and Hamilton raised it again. The relevant minute reads: 'Mr Hans Hamilton pointed out that there was no paperwork covering the £50,000 invested in Scribes West. Mr Brown explained that Mr Isaacs and Mr Venables had loaned £150,000 to Scribes. £100,000 had been placed immediately and £50,000 remained with the solicitors. This was being used for the rent and would be shown in the next accounts.' However, the next accounts, for August 1991, were the abbreviated type allowed by law for small companies and did not have to show a profit and loss account, merely a balance sheet. By then Hamilton, Van-Hay and Riviere had left and there was nobody who could question Brown or Venables.

The DTI for a time worried about how the Venables money had been invested. 'The DTI,' says Hamilton, 'at one stage did look into the transaction but it seems the £50,000 that Venables promised to pay was used for the rent and they were satisfied it was.' But whatever was happening on the financial front, within weeks of taking control Venables was making changes. By late April 1991 there would be a new management structure: Brown would be looking after finances, Paul Riviere was the marketing man, and Venables the boss, the Mr Fix-It. 'He was,' says Hamilton, 'pretty good at it, although not very experienced. He was a good "get up and go" type. The new arrangements were quite a major strain and this affected Van very much. He found it quite difficult to accept the sort of direction which Terry wanted.'

Venables' involvement on the actual operational side was very limited. He wasn't involved at all in the day-to-day. But, says Hamilton, 'he changed the atmosphere dramatically. The whole ambience of the place changed. For example we didn't have music in the club. We didn't think that music, apart from someone playing piano in the evening, was right. The first thing they wanted to do was to race in and stick speakers up. They instantly wanted to have music, piped music, Frank Sinatra etc. It was just a nightmare to watch. Beautiful workmanship had been put into the club and then some guy hammered away resulting in botched-up speakers and loose wires hanging all over the place. I think they were trying to create the atmosphere of the piano bar of a hotel. This did not go down well with the existing members. The new people coming in were a hotchpotch of footballing people and there was a dramatic clash. It just didn't work.'

Hamilton soon realised that the ideas he and Van-Hay had for running the club were miles removed from what excited Venables: 'He had no idea what made a club like this work. The biggest room in the club is the dining-room. One day Terry said, "There's this amazing place down in Spain, a night-club, and all the walls are painted black. I think we ought to do that here. I think we ought to paint all the walls black and then there will be this incredible atmosphere."

'I asked, "Look, this is an Edwardian style interior, with dado rails, arches and whatever and you want this painted black?" I am not by nature a rude person but I thought I had better get out of this somehow. So I said to him, "Well how do you think people who come down here for lunch might accept it, during the daytime, coming into a pitch-black dining room with black walls, black ceiling, spotlights." "Oh," he said, "they'll love it, they'll love it." '

On another occasion an artist friend of Hamilton brought in three nude pictures. 'Having run art exhibitions every month for eleven years, I have seen a lot of paintings. These were bad nudes.

I even got her to admit it after a while. They were just awful. Terry loved them. He wanted them in the pride of place. "Oh, this is what we want. Let's get them up." I said, "No way, if you want to put nudes up on the wall, I will get you some nudes. These are crap and they are not going up, whatever you say, they are not going up." In fact he reacted to that quite well. If you had a legitimate crack at him, then he would listen. But he wanted these tacky nudes to go up on the wall just because they were nudes.'

Worse was to follow. One Saturday night karaoke started and Venables and his friend, the agent, Eric Hall, began to sing: 'Terry sings very well but it was very sycophantic with everyone bowing and scraping. He would sing a slimy sort of music. He does about three or four numbers. Eric Hall was there from day one, and he sang as well. But he had such a bad voice you could never understand what he was doing, some terrible old numbers.'

For Venables all this hardly mattered. The tunes he was producing on the field were so resonant that everything else seemed to be put into shade. Scribes West for him was proving a lucky purchase. Four days after the purchase he had engineered one of the great modern triumphs at Wembley. In one of the English game's greatest upsets Tottenham had beaten Arsenal 3–1 in the semi-final of the FA Cup. That season Arsenal conceded just 18 goals all season; three of them came in that match, two by Lineker. However, it was the first, from an electrifying free kick by Paul Gascoigne, within ten minutes of the start, that shaped the match. It was Gascoigne's first full match since his hernia operation and Venables had not only gambled courageously and successfully on his fitness but, for the first time that season, a manager had out-thought and out-planned George Graham.

That Wembley triumph had wider consequences for Venables. On the back pages he came triply blessed: a football genius, a potential saviour of Tottenham and, what is more, a man taking the club to their date with destiny despite the fact that Tottenham had not agreed a new contract with him; indeed Scholar had offered a lower basic salary.

The Scholar side of the story suggests that, as far as the salary negotiations went, the tabloids were painting only the Venables colours. Negotiations had been going on since the previous October but, try as he might, Scholar could never quite pin down Venables. Venables would not accept Scholar's argument that, despite the lower basic, the larger performance bonuses meant he would get nearly £400,000 if he succeeded. For Venables that was the sort of contract he had left behind at Crystal Palace. He turned down Scholar's terms but refused to name his own price.

The fact that Scholar could not agree a contract with Venables suggested that, should Venables fail to win Spurs, he would leave and it would drag Spurs into the equivalent of football's Bermuda Triangle: no cash, no manager, no team. Scholar knew that even if Venables left, there was no shortage of people in football willing to take over. He had already had contacts with people claiming to be friends of Kenny Dalglish and Graeme Souness. Dalglish had walked out of Liverpool in February saying he could not stand the pressure. Souness, then at Rangers, was feeling itchy and would soon move to Liverpool, but with such contacts not made public, Venables ruled the back pages where the emotional temperature was further raised by the news of the imminent sale of Gascoigne.

Tottenham's negotiations to sell Gascoigne to the Italian club Lazio had now progressed to the stage where a contract was ready to be signed and the player himself was keen to go – he was literally being offered millions by the Italians – although he couldn't go before the Cup Final. Venables and his friends in the press played on the theme of the double-cross. Scholar, who had gone into the sale of Gascoigne with a heavy heart, was pictured as the man doing the dirty: pretending to keep Gascoigne at the club when all along he was trying to sell him. This led to the article at the end of April 1991 in which Jeff Powell, with the help of an interview with Venables, claimed Scholar was trying to sell Gascoigne while pretending not to. Scholar sued Powell and the *Daily Mail*, obtaining £100,000 in damages. This was reduced on appeal.

While all this publicity undoubtedly played a part in undermining Scholar and the Board, it also effectively camouflaged the fact that, despite all his efforts, Venables had still not come up with the money. True, Gillick had reappeared. But having shaken hands on a 95p per share deal, he was now only interested in buying out Scholar which Scholar refused to entertain. This was, probably, the moment when Gillick began to take a back seat. Riviere recalls that, sometime in March, Brown approached Riviere. He did not much care for Gillick. 'He didn't rate him. He said to me he thought Gillick was a fucking idiot. He didn't know what he was doing. He was sure he would be able to help Terry far more. I said, "You really think so?" '

The dark side of Brown was still unknown to Riviere. 'I was still very impressed by what he had done for "The Manager". He had done the business plan, he had been instrumental in getting the company formed and was setting down accounting procedures which is something that Terry and I couldn't do. So I said to Brown, "Well, next time we see Terry, we'll speak to him." '

The next day Riviere met Venables at the Royal Lancaster Hotel. 'I said to Terry, John would like to get involved.' The die was cast. Gillick came to Scribes West and cried on Riviere's shoulders about how Brown had shoved him aside. But Gillick had had his moment and failed; Brown was ready to take over.

With Riviere's encouragement, Venables turned to Brown in March 1991 and asked him to help: 'We looked in turn at various methods of making the deal.' Venables does not specify what these deals were but one of the schemes Brown dreamt up was to try to raise half a million on the back of a company that had never traded, had no assets, but was presented as a parent company owning five other companies.

This company, supposedly at the heart of Brown's business empire, was Elite Europe, a company set up by Paul Riviere (see page 82). Brown devised a corporate structure which showed it owned six other companies with net assets of £597,752. The six companies were Wetherall Baccarat, Independent Balloon Company, Printdouble, Venables Ventures/Glenhope, Abbey Promotions and Just Football. Nothing has ever been found of the last two, but the first three were interesting. Wetherall was the company Brown was involved with when he had that accidental hotel meeting with Riviere. However, by the time he confidently listed it on this corporate structure not only had his connection ceased but the company was in receivership. Yet Brown's projected pre-tax profits were £27,000 and a turnover of £150,000.

The Independent Balloon Company was a partnership which was on the verge of receivership. It had advertised in a Sunday newspaper. Brown, who diligently read such business columns, responded and offered to invest £15,000 and take over its liabilities. Sue Cooper of the company says, 'They took our money, they took our stock, they gave us nothing in return. They just left us with the debts at the end of the day.' In Brown's corporate plan for Elite Europe, the Independent Balloon Company was shown as having pre-tax profits of £45,286 and turnover of £260,000. Riviere knew nothing of this.

The only company with any substance in this mythical empire

was Printdouble, the Essex firm which printed Riviere's and Venables' game 'The Manager'. The company had substantial assets and Brown had agreed to invest a six-figure sum to help them pay their wages. A payment of £20,000 was deposited in their bank account but subsequent payments were late and Printdouble had no time to clear cheques. The rest of the money, according to the company secretary, Chris Bowhay, was paid in half a dozen drops of about five thousand pounds in twenty-pound and fifty-pound notes. Bowhay recalls, 'They asked us to meet them at a layby just off the A10. We waited in the layby and a member of Glenhope turned up, wound down his window and handed the money over.' On one occasion Brown said he had raided Scribes West to pay Printdouble. Printdouble was shown on the corporate structure as having a turnover of £1.5m. and projected profits of £190,189.

Brown was not the only person to deal with Printdouble. While in other companies Venables' name was bandied about as being the man behind this empire, in the case of Printdouble, Venables met them himself. In the end Printdouble discovered Brown's game, cut all connections, and his paper empire collapsed.

But why should Brown, in March 1991, build this fictitious business empire? Brown's philosophy, says Riviere, was OPM, Other People's Money. Always use OPM, he used to say. And in creating a spurious Elite Europe balance sheet showing net assets of £597,752 he had ideal OPM. He could now use it to borrow against it from the NatWest Bank. On 21 March 1991 Mr K. J. Ebsworth, manager of the Woolwich branch of NatWest, wrote to Sue Cooper mentioning two telephone conversations he had with Brown, and on 25 March, Richard Theobalds wrote to Ebsworth saying, 'Mr Brown has asked me to send you the latest Balance Sheet of Elite Europe Company.'

What did Brown want this money for? Could it be seed money to finance Venables' take-over of Tottenham? Venables says he did not need money to buy the shares of Bobroff and Scholar which would give him control of Tottenham, but that he needed money to refinance Tottenham. This seems doubtful since, in the end, he had to borrow almost all the money he invested in Tottenham. It seems more likely that this scheme of Brown's was a first attempt to raise money, start-up money, to finance Venables' Tottenham ambitions.

Brown, by now, was no longer the backroom finance man. He

was quite openly visible as Venables' financial guru. Irving Scholar recalls being invited to a breakfast meeting at the Westbury Hotel with Venables, Brown and Berry. Scholar couldn't make breakfast in time but did attend the meeting which was held at Bobroff's offices. Venables did not turn up, but Brown did and, as Scholar said to me, 'I took one look at him and didn't like him. Pin-stripe suit and those turned-up shoes that look like a spiv's. He was so aggressive, saying, "Now, come, let's start talking." I made it very clear I would only talk to Venables.'

However, Brown did manage to talk to others and, although Venables still appeared to be as far from the money as ever and made cute jokes (once, asked whether he had the money he said, 'Not on me'), he was back with a new proposal.

David Garrard, a well-known property man in the West End of London, was now prepared to back Venables. It would involve a sale and leaseback of White Hart Lane. Venables signed a conditional contract to that effect. The deal would have raised £11.5m. with Tottenham paying an annual rent of around £1.5m. The moment Scholar heard about the plan he had his doubts. Paul Bloomfield, another property man, had signed the deal to purchase but, as Scholar knew, Bloomfield, while an astute property man, was not flush with funds, certainly not enough to fulfil the contract, and soon afterwards he was bankrupt.

The contract stipulated that time was of the essence and £1.1m. was meant to be deposited by a certain Wednesday morning. Soon after the deadline passed Tottenham's advisers learnt that the money had not been forthcoming. About this time Tony Berry, still very much Venables' champion on the Tottenham Board, recalls meeting 'David Garrard one Sunday morning at offices off Portland Square at the end of April. He seemed to be a serious runner. They all seemed to be serious runners but when it came to it, for some reason, they never went ahead, and I suspected that perhaps Terry couldn't put his side of it in.'

Berry had the impression that: 'Whilst Terry didn't have that sort of money required to buy Spurs, he had some money. I think we all thought he had a certain amount of business acumen over and above being a good football manager. We probably thought that he hadn't got £3m. – where does a football man get £3m. from? But we thought that the majority of the £3m. was coming from him. He'd made money in Barcelona. He used to tell me that the money wasn't the problem. He would say, "Don't worry about the money. I'm getting the money." I don't know what money he's got. He might have money overseas that we don't know about. We had no inkling that he was that stretched; that he was doing all these complicated deals.'

In trying to get the money Venables turned to many people including the architect Igal Yawetz, who had redesigned the Grand Hotel in Brighton after the IRA bombing. Yawetz, who had played football for Macabi Tel Aviv and fallen in love with Spurs when he first saw them beat Wolves, had long admired Venables. He was meant to be part of a consortium helping Venables, and one crisp Sunday morning, just before the Cup Final, found himself gathered together with others of Venables' entourage.

Berry, too, was there and recalls: 'That is when Yawetz came on the scene, before Sugar but after Gillick. There was also a solicitor present and these people all seemed interested. They felt they could raise the money to do this deal. I don't know whether they could or not. Yawetz came along as a result of that. He knew Terry. At the end of the day Yawetz was one of the people who stumped up some money to push the deal through.'

So as the Tottenham team prepared for their Wembley appearance and the fans savoured the prospect of joy in a season of such turmoil, made worse by the fact that Arsenal were winning their second championship in three seasons, Venables, guided by Brown, beavered away to secure funds and backers. Venables, as ever, was juggling several balls at the same time.

Riviere recalls a lunch on the Monday of Cup Final week. 'Just before the Cup Final Terry said to me, "I'm going to have the lads down for lunch. Let's have a few people around at lunchtime." We never usually had big lunch crowds at Scribes. I'd gone down the previous week and I'd met this girl, Nicky Tarrant, who was a friend of Frank Warren. She came down. The players had lunch. Paul Gascoigne had been doing an advertising thing up in Birmingham and came down but was behind all the others, from the point of view of not having had a drink, and got into the drink.'

Gascoigne arrived at half past four and his instant reaction, recalls Hamilton, 'was to go to the bar and he was ordering quadruple Drambuies, which I didn't realise was happening. When I did realise I was bloody angry with the guy who served him. Gascoigne had about four of these, which equals about half a bottle of Drambuie, before you could bat an eyelid and I don't think he'd eaten so of course it went straight to his head. Then the stupidity started.'

According to Riviere, 'Gascoigne said something to Nicky, which was obviously something she didn't like. She'd had a few and she went to throw her glass of champagne at him and some champagne went over his head. I said to the barman that that was the last drink Gascoigne could have. He threw some at Nicky, missed her and hit a friend of mine. The friend then went to have a go at Gazza and all hell started to break loose. Ray Clemence and the guys then took him off.'

Hamilton and the others could not help but feel that this was a disaster waiting to happen. 'It was clear there was going to be a big punch-up. Gascoigne was basically hustled out of the place by about four of them and that more or less ended the evening. It could have been ridiculous because the guy he was going to hit was a man much bigger than him anyway. He could well have found himself in a situation where he had a broken nose or whatever and in the week of the FA Cup Final.' Venables missed all this, having left half an hour before, as had Gary Lineker.

By this time it was fairly clear that Gascoigne was going to go to Lazio although Venables and his consortium kept making noises which suggested that, should their deal be accepted, he could still be kept at White Hart Lane. When the Tottenham Board met on 7 May, eleven days before the Cup Final, Berry made this point strongly. Faced by a rival proposal from Baltic, who had come up with firm proposals of a rights issue at 45p, Venables offered a rights issue at 60p, coupled with the sale and leaseback of White Hart Lane and the promise that Gascoigne could be kept. Berry was sure he could be if the Board immediately accepted the Venables proposal.

The professional advice was against the Venables plan. The sale and leaseback of White Hart Lane did not meet with the approval of Healey & Baker, the property surveyors, and Brown Shipley considered that Baltic's proposals made more commercial sense. Gascoigne's advisers informed Scholar that the player would need a package of £2m. net after tax, on top of his salary, to stay. Could Venables and his friends guarantee that? In any case did Venables have the money to complete the deal? Scholar would later write:

My problem was that I just could not see where Terry Venables was getting his money from. I had shaken hands with Gillick on 95p thinking the deal was done, and then found myself in a crazy reverse bidding situation, and now I was being offered 60p by a new Venables consortium. Even if the bidding ended here, and my solemn handshakes were translated into legally watertight agreements, what guarantee was there that Venables would produce the money? He had failed to do so in the past, and this failure had become something of a joke, even among the advisers.

The deposit payment on the sale and leaseback proposal was three weeks overdue and the comfort letter of a bank guarantee still not forthcoming. In retrospect, all these failures or near-misses on the part of Venables should have been a warning but, in the public mind, he carried the hopes of the entire club and, like a striker who keeps sniffing near an opposition goal without putting the ball in the net, there was always the hope that Venables would score.

On the Friday before the Cup Final Venables made yet another attempt. At about 4.30pm Philip Green, a businessman who had become very friendly with Venables and was also well known to Scholar – it was Green who, on a flight to Hong Kong, had introduced Tony Berry to Scholar – rang Scholar to say that Terry had finally got the money. Scholar, prepared to do the deal at 80p, offered to drop the price to 70p provided Venables agreed that he would prevent Gascoigne's transfer to Lazio.

The phone call led to a series of three-way conversations, mostly on the phone between Venables, ensconced with the Tottenham team at the Royal Lancaster Hotel, his favourite bolt-hole before an important match, Scholar in a bar in the West End, and Scholar's solicitors. By ten o'clock that evening it was clear that Venables could not deliver. Scholar wanted an unconditional deal, Venables wanted 'certain comforts from the Midland Bank'; and finally Scholar's lawyers rang to say that, if Venables could not offer it without strings, the deal was off.

Another man might have let this setback weigh him down but Venables shrugged his shoulders and, the next day, led his team out at Wembley. He had primed Gascoigne for the task but denies that he had turned the knob on too much. Indeed Venables says the normally hyperactive Gascoigne looked a bit distant and that he was not as hyped as he had been for the semi-final. Venables wonders if his transfer to Lazio – the night before he had signed personal terms, giving him an immediate £2m. and a salary of £1m. – preyed on his mind.

Whatever it was, within minutes of the start Gascoigne indicated he was over-wrought and after less than twenty minutes' play he had departed with torn cruciate ligaments following a reckless tackle. That might have been an insurmountable setback for Spurs, as the resulting free kick saw Nottingham Forest score, but Gascoigne having got them to Wembley, the remaining players made sure they kept their tryst with destiny. Despite going a goal behind Tottenham came back to win 2–1, helped by an own goal by Des Walker, a moment savoured by Tottenham's skipper, Gary Mabbutt, whose challenge led to Walker's mistake, and whose own goal had beaten Tottenham in the 1987 Final.

Venables relished the plaudits that were heaped on him: the manager who had led the club to a record eighth triumph – since equalled by Manchester United – and despite all the off-field problems would now sort out the mess in the board room. But could he achieve a double triumph? Gascoigne's shattered knee appeared to have put everything in the melting pot. The Lazio deal was in the balance; it might be rescued, but almost certainly at a lower price and would this satisfy the Midland Bank?

Also did Tottenham need rescuing any longer? Two days before the Cup Final the entire Tottenham Board had met with the Midland and for the first time the bank, having played a game of bluff and counter-bluff all season, said they were prepared to extend the sort of long-term facilities the club was looking for. Scholar now felt he could see light at the end of the tunnel.

Little did he realise, however, that what he was seeing were the lights of an oncoming express bearing Venables and a new, wholly unexpected, financial backer who would, at last, make his dreams come true. Less than forty-eight hours after Tottenham's victory at Wembley, Venables had received a telephone call that would transform his fortunes.

The caller was Alan Sugar.

Chapter 6

Enter Alan Sugar

Alan Sugar was an unlikely caller. Although a Hackney boy – and a visitor to White Hart Lane where, as a child, he used to accompany his father – he had no great interest in football, unlike his brother, Derek, who, in the last thirty-five years, had missed only two Tottenham seasons (as it happens, they were the seasons when Tottenham won the championship). Sugar has long since moved away from North London, although his first office was near White Hart Lane. He has been that rare entrepreneur who not only made money and a name during the booming 1980s, but has survived the recession and become one of the few real successes of the period. Unlike Terry Venables who is four years older, however, Sugar's public image as the creator of the electronics group, Amstrad, is that of a man who is formidable but more than a bit remote, feared rather than loved.

Sugar rang on the Monday morning following Tottenham's Wembley victory. The Tottenham switchboard told Sugar that Venables was not there and he left a message. Within minutes Venables had called back. The moment is worth dwelling on, not only because of what that call eventually led to, but because, as so often in the Venables story, we are faced with conflicting versions of what took place.

Venables does not even agree with Sugar about the first time they made contact. Since his split with Sugar in the summer of 1993 Venables has been adamant that Sugar had tried contacting him in the week leading up to the Cup Final. What is more, when he received that first phone call Venables showed little interest. In an affidavit which he filed in his court action against Sugar in the summer of 1993 Venables said, 'I did not express any great enthusiasm and said that I would revert to him. When I was told that Mr Sugar had telephoned a second time, on 20 May 1991, I discussed the matter with Mr Brown and, at Mr Brown's suggestion, decided to meet him. I certainly did not call Mr Sugar back within a few minutes, as Mr Sugar states in paragraph 4 of his Affidavit, and if Mr Sugar is trying to suggest that I was very keen to do the deal with Mr Sugar at that stage he has misunderstood me. At that time there appeared to be several possibilities.'

What these possibilities were Venables does not elaborate and, given the fiasco of his attempts to buy Tottenham with Larry Gillick and others, it seems remarkable that Venables was the reluctant bride to Sugar's eager bridegroom keen to rush him to the altar.

Also, six months before this Venables had – when making a witness statement in the unfair dismissal case brought by Ian Gray, the former Managing Director of Tottenham – said, 'following the success of Tottenham Hotspur F.C. in winning the FA Cup in May 1991 I was approached by Mr Alan Sugar, the chairman of Amstrad, with a view to making a joint bid for control of the company'. In six months 'following the Cup Final' had become 'in the week leading up to the Cup Final'.

In his autobiography Venables picks up the theme of being the reluctant bride to the rampaging Sugar who was supposed to have been 'badgering John Brown to get involved'. This, in some ways, is the most remarkable version because one quality for which Sugar is famous is his directness, a characteristic that Venables often refers to, and the thought that he would approach a minion, a man he had never heard of, in order to talk to Venables is not easy to credit.

In any case it is difficult to see why Venables makes such a mystery about this. For as he confesses in his autobiography, 'In the end he [Sugar] was the only game in town'. One explanation could be that, unlike Sugar, who readily admits he picked up the telephone and rang Venables, Venables seems to be feeling it would be demeaning to admit that on receiving the call from Sugar he couldn't believe his luck, which was the impression he gave to Sugar at that time.

On one thing both men are agreed. They met the next day, 21

May, at the Grosvenor House Hotel where Sugar was due to attend a CBI dinner. Venables came with Brown and, in the main reception area of the hotel around 6pm, the trio held a discussion about Tottenham. A curious bystander at this meeting was Tony Berry who was due to meet Venables there in pursuit of what were proving to be some rather elusive financial backers. However, when Berry asked, Venables wouldn't say. It was another couple of days before Venables told Berry about Sugar. Once Berry had recovered from his shock he was all for the deal. 'Fine, if he wants to do the deal, throw in your lot behind him.'

Sugar recalls that Venables was clearly enthusiastic about the prospect and agreed with everything he said: 'When I told him I would be Chairman of Tottenham he asked, "What would I be?" I replied by saying I don't know but he could be Chief Executive, Managing Director or something like that, but I did not know at that moment.'

Venables has another recollection. In his affidavit filed in June 1993 he said: 'This was very much a preliminary matter in which Mr Sugar wanted to demonstrate the seriousness of his intent and, beyond preliminary matters, none of the extensive discussions which Mr Sugar described in his Affidavit took place. The meeting was largely devoted to discussing Mr Scholar's and Mr Bobroff's shareholdings, the price at which they would sell and Tottenham's financial position. I told Mr Sugar that I could put up £3m. to buy out Mr Scholar and Mr Bobroff but there was still a problem with the overdraft at the Midland Bank, to which Mr Sugar's immediate response was that he could telephone the Midland Bank and offer it a guarantee. The discussions at this meeting dealt only with the machinery and feasibility of purchase. There was no discussion as to divisions of responsibility or control. Mr Sugar did not express enthusiasm for marketing as he states in paragraph 5 of his Affidavit; neither did he talk about looking on his prospective investment as a business transaction. I never asked what my position might be at Tottenham. As I have already stated, my ideas were well-defined and my plans for the acquisition of the Club long established. There was no question of my simply waiting for Mr Sugar to make suggestions about how the [*sic*] Tottenham could be run.'

The next day, as arranged, Brown travelled to Brentwood to meet Sugar's people, in particular Colin Sandy, who helps administer Sugar's private companies. Brown's mission, says Venables, was to emphasise that Venables wanted to be chief executive under a balanced Board. Sandy does not recall Brown talking about such matters, indeed it would have been a strange forum for such a discussion. The meeting was not meant for that, it was for Sugar's advisers to get details about Tottenham's financial position so that Sugar could come to a decision, and neither Sandy nor Brown had any powers to agree things on behalf of Sugar. 'If Brown had raised these issues I would have told him,' says Sandy, 'it is no use talking to me about all this, Sunshine, you will have to talk to Mr Sugar. We were there to look at the Tottenham figures and give Sugar a view as to what the company looked like. I thought the company could make a core profit of £1.7m. and it turned out to be right.'

As if these differing versions are not enough, now we have accounts of two meetings, one of which Sugar denies ever took place. According to Venables, before any approach was made to Paul Bobroff to buy his shares, he, Brown and Sugar had another meeting at Brentwood. In his affidavit of June 1993 he says: 'This was the meeting in which our respective positions on the Board of Tottenham and the Club were discussed in the most detail. At this meeting Mr Sugar and I agreed that Mr Sugar would be non-executive Chairman, I would be Chief Executive, and Nat Solomon would relinquish the Chairmanship but be allowed to remain as Deputy Chairman. We agreed that we would split the shares equally between us and that neither of us would sell our shares to any third party without the knowledge and approval of the other. Mr Sugar readily agreed to these proposals and on that basis I was content for Mr Sugar to start negotiating with Mr Scholar and Mr Bobroff on both our behalves.'

Sugar, in his affidavit, says: 'I deny that the meeting to which Mr Venables refers ever took place. I deny that it was ever agreed that I would be non-executive chairman. From the start I was an executive chairman.' It would certainly have been out of character for Sugar to agree to be non-executive chairman. At Amstrad he had at that time ducked the issue of appointing a chief executive, preferring to combine the role of chairman and chief executive – he did eventually appoint one in August 1994 – and he was also somewhat dismissive of fashionable ideas of having non-executive directors on the Board, views which would soon make him unpopular with some Amstrad shareholders.

Sugar is an impulsive man. His impulses had served him well in his chosen field of electronics. His ability to go in where a cautious man might tread warily had paid handsome dividends. His venture into Tottenham was something similar, he liked the feel of it, was taken by media reports of Venables trying to rescue the club, if necessary with his own money, and felt there were opportunities for him there. The other incentive for getting involved was that, if he did not, then Robert Maxwell, who was again sniffing around, might. Sugar had discussed this with Rupert Murdoch. Murdoch had no love for Maxwell, he even told Sugar he didn't want 'that fat cunt to get it'. But for him to agree to take a back seat would have been very unlike Sugar.

The crucial meeting took place on the evening of Saturday 8 June 1991 in a hotel near Langan's. Sugar had not yet quite made up his mind, Venables encouraged him, painting this as a good investment opportunity. Venables was confident that, despite his injury, Gascoigne could still be sold, if not to Lazio then to other clubs: Juventus and Marseille were mentioned. Venables thought Gascoigne should fetch £6m. and explained to Sugar that his injury would heal. Lazio had become difficult. They are, Venables told Sugar, trying to 'blag us' but if Sugar got on board they would realise Tottenham was in a strong financial position and they would have to come up with a sensible offer. Venables also, he believed, held out the carrot of getting £4m. for Lineker when he moved to a Japanese club.

Venables agrees that they met on 8 June but that is about as much as the memories of the two men coincide. In his affidavit he says: 'I did not seek to encourage Mr Sugar or tell him what a good business investment the joint venture would be. We discussed Paul Gascoigne but I certainly did not mention a price of £5/6m., I would not have done because the Italian club Lazio had already told the club that they would not pay more than £4.7m. for Mr Gascoigne in view of his injury at the FA Cup Final, and I believe that this figure had been more or less agreed by Nat Solomon on behalf of the club. I'm sure I did not use the word "blag" in relation to Lazio's tactics because that is not a word I ever use, but I did say that, if he was to be sold, that price certainly was not good enough and needed to be negotiated further, as indeed it was . . . I did not tell Mr Sugar about negotiations to sell Mr Gascoigne to other foreign clubs. I cannot have done so because negotiations concerning the sale of Mr Gascoigne did not really get underway until July 1991. I am certain that I did not discuss the possibility of

Gary Lineker joining a Japanese club for £4m. At that time there was no Japanese club negotiating for Mr Lineker; neither was there any negotiation at all concerning Mr Lineker at that time. Never to my knowledge has any Japanese club offered £4m. for Mr Lineker. Such a figure would have been out of the question because, although Mr Lineker had been one of the best players, he was by then thirty-one years of age.'

Venables may or may not have said that Lineker could be sold for £4m. But for him to say that no Japanese club was negotiating for him seems strange as John Holmes, Lineker's agent, had told him early in 1991 of an interest expressed on behalf of Grampus 8.* At the time he filed these affidavits in 1993 Venables was keen to establish that, right from the beginning, he had always intended to be an equal partner of Sugar, a point that his legal advisers felt was important in order to fight Sugar.

The meeting was also crucial because, the next day, the *Sunday Times* revealed Sugar's interest in Spurs. On that morning, before Sugar met Venables, he had received a call from Jeff Randall asking him about his involvement with Venables. 'Fuck me,' said Sugar, 'where did you get that story?'

Sugar's entry meant the Tottenham saga appeared to be developing into a classic triangle: apart from Sugar and Maxwell, there was the Spurs Board who were still trying to sell Gascoigne at a reduced price to Lazio, and appeared to have struck up a deal with the Midland Bank about extending the overdraft facilities. This led to even more talk from the Board that Spurs did not need to be rescued.

Interestingly, despite Venables' subsequent attempts to portray his partnership with Sugar as an equal one, right from the beginning, once Sugar had taken the decision to buy, he did almost all the negotiations with Venables hardly in the picture. Everyone agreed that Venables had at last got a man of substance. Berry had made this point emphatically, and so did Scholar although he warned Sugar that, while Venables was a good coach, that was the extent of his abilities.

The other favourable omen going for the Sugar-Venables partnership was the support of the Tottenham fans. The Tottenham Independent Supporters' Association (TISA) had been formed as a result of the financial crisis and it was a vocal and effective

---

* See below, Chapter 12, page 128.

champion of Venables. When Maxwell re-entered the fray, a poll in the *Sun* found 5,205 votes for Sugar-Venables, 236 for Maxwell.

However, while Venables at last looked like getting his Spurs, things were not going quite according to hype at his other club. At Scribes West the management figures for May had shown that the losses there had doubled.

Chapter 7

The untouchable

Money had come in to Scribes West. 'The money,' explains Hans Hamilton, 'that Terry put in wasn't as a shareholder. It was a loan to the company and this loan was to be capitalised when certain things had happened, like the licence which finished at eleven had to be made into a one o'clock licence. What he was looking for was a nightclub. He wanted it to be a night place, a sort of Kensington Tramps which it was never destined to be.'

But as quickly as the money came in it also went out. 'A lot of the money,' Hamilton goes on, 'was being spent on refurbishing the place. A massive amount of money. New furniture. A whole new outlook for the place. Flowers by the bucketful. They did look very nice, but we were not paying our suppliers. Buying flowers meant not paying the meat man. The turnover went up, not hugely, but a lot of stuff was being given away. Publicity, parties, etc., free drinks for people coming in, they were mounting up and mounting up. And then there were fees being paid to Venables and his trio. Terry paid to Glenhope Management, I think, something like three lots of approximately £15,000 as management fees. These were for Paul Riviere, Venables and Brown for their management services to the running of Scribes West. I had no knowledge that this was going to happen.'

This remained a sore point with both Hamilton and Van-Hay and they raised it at a Scribes Board meeting on 15 August 1991. Brown explained that it had been agreed with Vincent Isaacs and, in any case, some of the invoices had not been paid and the hourly rate charged was well below the commercial value of the services.

What was worrying Hamilton and Van-Hay was that, following the Venables take-over, they were suddenly getting solicitors' letters on behalf of creditors demanding payment. 'We had sailed pretty close to the wind but we'd never had a solicitor's letter. We might have had a phone call saying, "Come on, boys, it's about time you paid the bloody rent." But after the Venables take-over we'd got ourselves into a situation where we were six or nine months late. It just got worse and worse.' So bad that in late May 1991 Hamilton had to confront Venables about a non-payment which threatened to leave Scribes West without electricity. 'I knew that Terry was in the bar of the Royal Garden and I went over to see him and said, "Terry, we've got all these financial problems at the moment." And he said, "Yes?" I said, "Well, why have we just been given a writ for £25,000 and two hours to pay the electricity bill, otherwise they will cut the electricity off." Terry went white and he got the phone and rang Tottenham up. Brown was there already. He was squatting in an office there and doing work for Terry, before the take-over. Terry was shouting down the phone, "I don't care what he thinks, get him on the phone now!" And then he went absolutely ape-shit on the phone. "You were supposed . . . I don't give a fuck what you've done . . . I want this money paid now." '

Venables' anger was all the greater because, says Hamilton, 'he was a very good delegator because that's the way he's always worked. It was quite a well-structured team at Scribes. From him to Riviere, to Brown, then down to Van and me. So there was a reasonable chain of command that worked quite sensibly.'

The incident with Hamilton reveals Venables reacting to a situation which put him on the spot. 'He doesn't like being put on the spot,' explained Hamilton. 'I suppose none of us does, but Terry especially doesn't. So he never liked getting himself into a position where people could do what I had done, which was to belittle him like that. Terry hated being isolated. He always surrounded himself with friends. If he knew that Van and I had a problem, or wanted to discuss something businesswise or what was going on, he would never be alone. You'd probably say, "Look can we have a chat, we want to talk about price structure", or whatever. He'd say, "OK, OK, about ten minutes?" Ten minutes would go by and then there would be some of his people there with him. So he would never take anything on by himself. I don't think he was that sure of how the business was run. I never had the impression, if you went through a profit and loss account with him or a balance sheet, that he was totally aware what it was all about.'

The flash of Venables' anger meant that the writ was then paid. But, as Hamilton was to discover, this was 'the Brown game, the last-minute game. He was moving money all over the place. Into here, out of there.'

Outwardly the trio seemed to be working smoothly: Venables and Brown busy trying to buy Tottenham, Riviere working from ten o'clock in the morning to one o'clock at night at Scribes building up the business and trying to establish a bigger client base. Even here there was one curiosity. Although Riviere was not involved, Venables often used Riviere as his spokesman in the Tottenham affair. In many ways, given that Brown was doing the deal, it would have made more sense to use him but Riviere found Brown very reluctant to be the front man. He made it clear he did not want to brief the press or be in the limelight. Riviere did not mind. Terry was fighting the greatest battle of his life and Riviere was eager to help him. On Crystal's advice he appeared on *Hard News*, a television programme dealing with the media, to argue Venables' case.

By this time Riviere was having some business problems of his own because he spent so much time on 'The Manager'. 'I took my eye off my own company,' he told me, 'and I left Pawlikowski to manage things. But I lost six of my top salesmen who left to form another company. At that stage we had been going very well and the company was making six-figure sums. Without these people Elite First could not operate and I had to close down my Hyde Park Square offices. I moved Pawlikowski to Exhibition Road where he was involved in winding up Elite First. This meant he was in the same office as Brown but they were supposed to be totally separate components of my life and there should have been no reason for them to have any business deals.'

However, this move by Riviere, innocent as it was, proved fatal and on Friday 17 May Riviere was suddenly confronted with a situation he could not have dreamt of. He recalled: 'Everything on the accounting side of Scribes West and "The Manager" had been left to Brown and I, initially, had total confidence in him. Then we were having problems paying bills at Scribes. So I went over to Exhibition Road. When I got there I heard a hell of a row going on between Brown and a guy called Theobalds. I had only met Theobalds once before. Brown had given him a little office to work in and told me he was helping him with the accounts. Brown was really swearing and shouting at him, calling him everything under the sun. I said to Theobalds, "What is this about, Theobalds?" and he said, "I think there are things you should know." I said, "Come down to Scribes with me." He did so, and told me money had gone out of Scribes to pay the print company. Printdouble, which printed "The Manager", had some problems, and as I understood it we had agreed to pay them some amounts of money. What I didn't know until Theobalds pointed it out was that we were paying them money virtually to buy their company.'

It is now that Brown's strange goings-on with Elite Europe began to percolate to Riviere, although he didn't get the full picture until some years later. To Riviere, talk of Brown and Elite Europe was mystifying. This was a shell company Riviere had started with Pawlikowski. 'We had never traded. The idea behind Elite Europe was Eastern Europe falling to pieces in 1990. Pawlikowski was Polish, we had two or three Poles working for us, we decided to form it because Elite Europe Company Ltd, whose initials make EEC, could come in useful in case we could get into Poland. The other thing was, our offices were above the Polish Club in Exhibition Road. But as far as I was concerned it had never traded.'

Riviere now began to learn about the schemes Brown had hatched using Elite Europe and how this supposedly dormant company had been very busy. Far from Pawlikowski and Brown being totally separate they had actually come together, and Brown's plan had been to build a business empire on the back of Elite Europe of which he was not even a director.

Riviere learnt of business plans drawn up for Elite Europe to buy into three companies. In addition to his plans for the Independent Balloon Company and Printdouble Ltd, which formed part of his scheme, Brown wanted to use Elite to have 90% of another company called Scale Link which made fine-scale cast metal 1914–1918 war military models for the model railway enthusiasts and architectural models for government departments.

Following the Scribes meeting, on Monday 20 May 1991, Theobalds wrote a five-page letter to Riviere. He laid out the basis for the business empire which Brown was planning. Theobalds explained that he had known Brown for a long time, and they had a mutual defence regarding actions brought against them by the clothing company. 'At that time,' wrote Theobalds, 'it was agreed that I should come to work for Elite Europe Ltd, receiving no payment but reimbursement of expenses. John told me he had determined that Elite should become an investment company holding shares in a wide range of investee situations. Elite, of course, had no cash, and no line of funding, but I was told that Blundell of Coutts had already been told about Elite, and overdrafts etc. would be no problem. Consequently, Elite invested in three companies, all of which you are now familiar with [Scale Link, Printdouble, and Independent Balloon Company]. In the case of Printdouble, Elite guaranteed substantial HP contracts for the take-over of plant and machinery from the Receiver; in the case of Balloon, Elite has guaranteed a bank loan, circa £30,000, and contracted to provide £14,000 for immediate working capital and so on. Elite had still no funds or access to funds.'

Theobalds' projections showed that Elite would require £90,000 in the initial months. 'Because there were no overdraft facilities for any of these companies, or indeed Elite, sums were drawn from Glenhope, and later from Scribes to keep Printdouble going.' As Theobalds pointed out, 'It was wholly evident that what Elite had contracted to do, it could not do.' Theobalds was worried that 'without any source of finance all the Elite companies would fail, and that Elite would be in clear breach of contract, and might be entering into agreements it clearly could not keep.'

Theobalds had worked for four months without pay on the understanding that he could claim expenses; but when he did so he incurred the wrath of Brown. Riviere arrived at Exhibition Road in the middle of his row. But despite the high and mighty tone which Brown took, Theobalds could point to the grave danger he faced. 'John,' he wrote to Riviere, 'has failed in his attempts to obtain a voluntary arrangement with those creditors he has incurred prior to the last failure, "Wetherall". This means that he will inevitably be bankrupted.'

News of this had reached NatWest and also Blundell at Coutts, to whom Theobalds had gone to raise finance for Elite but who 'felt that he had been deceived by John, since he had no knowledge of this matter, and had of course provided Glenhope with banking facilities and John with a substantial personal overdraft'.

Later Blundell would come to lunch at Scribes and tell Theobalds that he could not keep any of the accounts with Coutts and that included Glenhope and Scribes. He wanted them out within a month. Brown had constantly assured Theobalds that Glenhope had overdraft facilities of £30,000. It turned out that it had nothing.

Brown now had to prevent his financial fictions being revealed.

On the Friday when Riviere had summoned him to Scribes West Brown had assumed the air of the financial highbrow and dismissed Riviere's fears.

'Money is going out of the company that I know nothing about. Surely this shouldn't be done?' Riviere asked.

'It's OK, inter-company loan, that's nothing,' Brown replied.

'What is Theobalds doing?' asked Riviere.

'Oh, he's doing some work for me,' said Brown.

Riviere then confronted Pawlikowski and asked, 'What are you and Brown doing together?' But, as Riviere recalls, 'they both denied working together and Pawlikowski said Brown was "just helping me out".'

Riviere now says, 'Venables and I were so busy then and he was involved in trying to get Tottenham, and because we totally trusted Brown, we had signed a dozen, maybe fifteen, blank cheques. One of these cheques, Theobalds told me (now it appears there were two), was for £5,000 cash. Pawlikowski had taken it to the bank and then he had gone off to the print company. Later, very white-faced, he admitted to me he had done that, working with Brown behind my back. He had gone to the print company with the money.' He was the courier in the lay-by off the A10 whom Chris Bowhay, the company secretary, had mentioned.

In a further letter to Riviere on 23 May, Theobalds explained how the Scribes blank cheques were used. 'Inevitably the Elite companies had to have cash to meet direct wages. I was told not to discuss this with you, and was aware that this meant you had no idea that Scribes had paid the direct wages of Printdouble using a spare signed cheque. Doing this was against the interests of the shareholders of Scribes and this is why I carefully noted full details on the cheque stub.'

Yet even now it is a measure of Brown's status as a financial craftsman, a magician of figures, that even those who were wounded by him, some mortally, refused to castigate him. Theobalds, who had been lured to working for him with the promise that he would have a career with Riviere and Venables, wrote to Brown more in sorrow than in anger, still declaring, 'My respect for your talents remains undiminished'.

Riviere is a mild man but his response to all this was an anger that was fierce. 'I had a major row with Brown and we nearly came to blows. I do not get angry but when I do people know.' Brown knew this time.

Riviere had to get away from a situation not of his own making and one he knew nothing about. On 23 May he resigned from Elite and, in a letter addressed to Brown and Pawlikowski, said that, 'I have no reason to doubt at this stage either of your integrities'. He was still not fully aware of all that Brown and Pawlikowski had done. Brown had sought to beguile him with talk of intercompany loans and also spoke of taking legal advice when confronted with the Theobalds letter.

But where in all this did Venables stand? We know he met Printdouble but was he aware of all the other things his financial adviser was up to? Interestingly Theobalds had told Riviere he intended sending a copy of his letter to Venables and his 23 May letter to Riviere was marked 'copy Terry Venables, held back pending a meeting with you next week'. Theobalds also told Riviere that certain people, into whose company the name of Venables had been taken, would inform Venables of the situation. Whether they did so or not we don't know, but Riviere showed Theobalds' letter to Venables. Riviere was aware how busy Venables was with the Tottenham take-over but he felt he ought to know. 'I told him,' says Riviere, 'what had happened and what Brown was up to.'

'Have a word with Jonathan,' responded Venables. Riviere did, and Jonathan Crystal saw both Riviere and Theobalds. He also saw Theobalds' letters but nothing came of that. Brown was too important for Venables to rock the boat now. The prize he had sought was so tantalisingly close.

There was, though, another cloud on the horizon. Brown could not escape being made a bankrupt and he was declared one at 11.19 on the morning of 6 June 1991. The bankruptcy was enforced by the Commissioners of the Inland Revenue, who had presented the petition on 18 September 1990. Brown had not been present but he managed to keep his bankruptcy secret.

On Friday 21 June, therefore, as Brown arrived at the offices of the merchant bankers, Henry Ansbacher, to complete the Tottenham deal on behalf of Venables, his financial past was not known to anyone there. On a night of high drama it was to prove the best kept secret of the evening. As far as the outside world was concerned he was the shrewd financial adviser helping Venables, his financial skills matching Venables' footballing ones. Indeed Sandy was so impressed that for some time afterwards he could be heard telling anybody who would listen, 'That John Brown, he is a true professional.'

Chapter 8

The dream comes true

Venables had played little part in the negotiations and was not even at Ansbacher's when the meeting began early on the afternoon of Friday 21 June 1991. Nor was Alan Sugar planning to be there. He felt he had done enough: he had spoken to Bobroff and to Scholar on the phone, and had met Bobroff. Despite the bluster and noise being made by Robert Maxwell, Bobroff assured Sugar that he and Scholar would sell to the Venables-Sugar team.

Then at 4pm Sugar received a call from Colin Sandy. There had been a hitch, could he come? Maxwell had rung Ansbacher's, and told them he was going to buy all of Bobroff's shares and part of Scholar's. Unknown to Sugar, Scholar, who by this time had left London for his Monte Carlo apartment, was changing his mind and returning to Maxwell. That day's *Daily Mirror* had carried the news that Maxwell was withdrawing but this was a smokescreen. Soon Maxwell was on the phone offering Scholar a deal. Scholar feared that the Sugar-Venables deal would not mean any new money for the club, nor had he ever liked the idea of Venables moving from the 'dugout' to the boardroom. On that Friday afternoon Maxwell, seeking to put pressure on the Tottenham Board, even told Solomon that he had bought Scholar's shares. This was a lie, but it caused Solomon to go white with anger.

As Sugar made his way to the City others were arriving at Ansbacher's, not all of them welcome. Maxwell's bankers, Hill Samuel, had somehow got past Ansbacher's security. As they did so, Bernard Jolles of Ansbacher received a call from Maxwell demanding that Hill Samuel be let into the meeting. If Jolles did not allow this, then Maxwell, in that classic bullying style, threatened that the Maxwell-Ansbacher relations might be jeopardised. Maxwell was a 9% shareholder in Ansbacher.

Jolles refused to be threatened. He put the Hill Samuel men in a room and placed on guard a so-called baby banker, a 6' 2" New Zealander called David Glenn. Tony Berry, there as part of the consortium, found a shaft of humour in all this. 'It was rather funny really. They phoned up and said they wanted to come as Maxwell's representatives. They turned up outside and I think they left them in a room downstairs. I don't think they actually locked the door but it was the next best thing to it. They couldn't gain access to any of the floors, including the second floor where the meeting was taking place.'

Soon afterwards, Maxwell's lawyers, Titmuss Sainer, arrived in a black Ford Scorpio. But Ansbacher had learnt their lesson. Titmuss Sainer were not allowed in and remained outside the building peering in. In other rooms were the other protagonists: Tottenham sprawled out in one room, Midland in a smaller room at the end of the corridor, and Sugar's team in the main conference room.

As Sugar's Rolls drew up everyone stiffened. If past experience was any guide he would be in a storming mood, shouting and cursing. Instead he gently ambled into the conference room, shaking his head, and said, 'That Maxwell is a monkey, a real monkey.'

At that moment Maxwell was on the phone to Jolles who told him, 'Mr Sugar has just arrived, do you want to speak to him?' Sugar took the phone, saying, 'Alan Sugar'. The next few minutes there was silence from him as he listened to Maxwell. Then he slowly put the phone down. 'The rudeness of that man,' said Sugar. 'You know what Maxwell has done? He's just put the phone down on me. Just like that.'

A few minutes later the phone rang again. It was Maxwell. 'Sorry, old chap, had some people with me, wanted to clear the room so we could have a private chat, just the two of us. I think you and I can do a deal on this. I am buying Irving's shares and Tottenham will have two Sugar Daddies, you and me.'

'This is my deal,' interjected Sugar. 'If you want to invest in Spurs, buy the shares on the open market. But leave my deal alone.' And with that Sugar put down the phone.

Sugar's initial anger was directed at Bobroff. 'Bobroff,' recalls

Berry, 'was talking about changing his mind. He'd been on the phone to Scholar and he thought that perhaps he shouldn't do the deal. Sugar went absolutely berserk at him. He gave him everything really. He said, "You can't fucking welsh on me", that sort of thing.'

The image Bobroff presented left an indelible imprint on Nick Hewer, Sugar's PR man: 'A small, roly-poly man in a dark suit, with black-framed glasses, sweating openly, standing in the door to the Sugar conference room, looking absolutely terrified. He did not have a friend in the place, and all eyes swivelled on him, and he reacted by swaying from one foot to another. "Well I've always stuck with Irving, and I don't want to act without him." It was a bit like a kid at school caught off guard in the playground with a rival gang, without his bigger, stronger, and more well-known protector. He was ushered into another room so he could contact Scholar, and eventually left the building to use his car phone.'

Scholar's lawyers were initially absent. When they arrived in their Armani-style suits, with slim Cartier watches, they all seemed to effect a rolling gait. Hewer thought they moved their shoulders in a Miami sort of way and seemed to have Mont Blanc President fountain pens.

The contrast between them and Richard Godden, Sugar's lawyer from Linklater and Paines, could not be greater. Godden was one of the old school, a man who seemed to be from the age of the Parker 51, and possibly thought Armani was an Italian hairdresser. He spoke softly but made sharp observations. Venables' lawyers, Kanter Jules Grangewoods, were not very prominent and looked ill-at-ease.

In Monte Carlo Scholar had gone out for the evening leaving his solicitor, John Bennett, with a phone number. And there was no Venables. Sugar asked Brown to summon him and he arrived looking somewhat incongruous in a sports jacket. With him was Jonathan Crystal. Hewer recalls: 'Venables was clearly confused as to what was going on and who was doing what to whom. Crystal was there to hold his hand. In the palm of his hand Crystal held a cigarette, held behind him as Sam Kydd had done in so many war films playing a sentry having a crafty smoke. Crystal followed Venables quickly around the conference room where the signing ceremony was in full swing. Whenever Venables was asked a question, Crystal would immediately step in front of Terry and quietly advise, "Don't answer that, Terry, could be an implied warranty."

Then raising his voice a little he would tell the questioner, "Speaking as a barrister, are we sure that this matter conforms to . . ." and he would mention some section of the Companies Act. He would conclude by saying, "I'm a barrister, you see", and you could feel this last was added with real pleasure.'

Crystal's interventions led to an exchange with Richard Godden. Sitting on the boardroom table, Crystal lit another cigarette and, with a leg swinging carelessly, he interrupted Godden, who was discussing some arcane points of the law. 'Surely,' said Crystal, 'I speak as a barrister, that could be misconstrued as in the famous case of . . .' and he mentioned a case. Godden, without looking up from his papers said, 'Thank you very much, Mr Crystal, but I think we are managing quite well. Now Amanda, as I was saying, you will find the document under the yellow tag, if you would be so kind.'

Brown looked the part but his problem seemed to be a reluctance to meet the Midland Bank. The bank was crucial to the deal, of course. Scholar wanted immediate repayment of the loan he had given to Tottenham to safeguard the Lineker deal. He was not going to let it remain in the company once Sugar and Venables were in charge. But Tottenham didn't have the money to pay, so Sugar would have to pay it. That was fine in principle, but with the overdraft at £11m., if Sugar paid £1.2m. into the account the bank could just use it to offset the overdraft. Midland had to be persuaded not to do so if the deal with Scholar was to go through.

Sugar, Sandy and some others huddled into the room being used by Midland to discuss this, but when Sandy looked round he could not see Brown. Funny, thought Sandy, he was beside me a moment ago, I thought he was coming behind, where did he get to? It did not mean much to Sandy then. It was months later he understood why Brown had no desire to come face to face with the people who had just forced him into bankruptcy.

Eventually, after tense negotiations with Midland, there was an agreement whereby Sugar gave Midland an assurance that either Midland's money would be repaid by November 1991, or, alternatively, Tottenham would be in a position where Midland would be happy and satisfied to continue to provide banking facilities. Sugar made it clear to the bank that he would not pour money into the company, but as soon as he was in a position to do so he would involve various financial people who would take control of Tottenham's finances and ensure that Midland was provided with regular information. So an in-out arrangement was made. Sugar provided Tottenham with £1.27m., and this money was immediately used to repay Scholar.

Bobroff had signed at midnight. Scholar telephoned Ansbacher's and confirmed he was selling. Soon after this Maxwell telephoned to congratulate Sugar. The telephones in Sugar's conference room were occupied, and he had to take the call in the kitchen. There, knee deep in McDonald's hamburger wrappings, Sugar spoke to Maxwell and, as Maxwell conceded defeat, Sugar, the new owner of Tottenham, absentmindedly kicked the polystyrene boxes into a heap in the corner of the room.

But there were still some wrinkles to be ironed out. One such had shown the contrast between Sugar and Venables. Sugar had had his banker, John Mackenzie of Lloyds, present through the night with Mackenzie armed with the necessary banker's draft. But when it came to Venables' turn to produce his money there was no response. Brown sidled up to Sugar and said, 'There's been a hitch.' He explained that Venables' money hadn't come through. But he promised it would the next day or the day after. Mackenzie wrote out the additional banker's draft and the next day or two stretched to ten before Venables' money arrived.

What Sugar did not know was that Venables was in the middle of his mighty struggle to raise the money. When Venables got involved in the Spurs take-over the common assumption was, as Tony Berry had surmised, that he might not have all the £3m. for the deal but at least most of it. Berry recalls: 'He would say, "Don't worry about the money. I'm getting the money." We had no inkling that he was that stretched, that he was doing all these complicated deals.'

Brown had been at the heart of these deals but it all required time and was not quite ready by 21 June. Sugar's financing of Venables on the night the deal was done remained a secret for almost two years. Berry, despite being a member of the Venables consortium, didn't know Venables hadn't put his money on the table: 'We knew there was some sort of hiccough,' he told me, 'but Sugar was covering things anyway, so it didn't matter. Some months later I knew indirectly from Ansbacher when they indicated to me that it hadn't been paid. But it was only when all of this came out [after Sugar fell out with Venables] that I realised Sugar actually paid the whole thing: all of it on Day One and that did surprise me.'

In his autobiography Venables devotes almost three pages to describing the night's activities but he does not mention that he had to rely on Sugar's help to complete the deal. It seems that, such is his bitterness for Sugar now, he cannot acknowledge that, without Sugar's banker, the deal would not have gone through.

There was one further wrinkle, although few people seemed to pay any attention to this. Sometime during the meeting a draft shareholders' agreement between Edennote and Sugar was given to Sandy by Brown. Sandy revised it, made amendments, and asked Brown what it was for. Brown said it was not urgent and it should be left. It was not mentioned again. The proposed agreement was to prevent both Sugar and Venables from buying and selling shares in Tottenham without the other's consent. Sugar got the impression that Venables had changed his mind and did not want Sugar to have any control over his shares.

Two years later, when Venables decided to take Sugar to court, this piece of paper, almost unnoticed in the hurly-burly of that Friday in June 1991, would assume tremendous significance. Then Venables would affirm, in an affidavit in his action against Sugar in 1993, that the draft agreement was actually prepared by the solicitors, Linklater and Paines, on the joint instructions given to them by Brown, acting on his behalf, and Sandy acting on Sugar's behalf.

It simply is not true that I did not want to sign the first draft because I did not want to let Mr Sugar have any control over my shares or any restriction on my ability to sell shares. The reason why the draft was not signed was because it was only a first draft; it was incomplete; Clause 2 had yet to be completed, there had been no legal advice tendered. There did not appear to be good reason for rushing into signing a first draft. Neither party wanted to do so. For my part, I was not worried about my position because the overall understanding between myself and Mr Sugar was clear and was backed by the circumstances in which we were acquiring the shares from Mr Bobroff and Mr Scholar, that is '50/50'. Any concerns which I might otherwise have had were further alleviated when I was appointed Chief Executive at the Board Meeting dated 28 June, 1991.

That Venables was reassured about being appointed Chief Executive is significant because that was a vital clause in the getting of his money together, a process which proved much more bothersome than anyone realised. The fall-out from that would haunt Venables for a long time.

That same Tottenham Board meeting also made Sugar Chairman. City rules required that Sugar and Venables now make an offer to every shareholder for all their shares and this was not very convenient as some of the shareholders, despite pleas from Sugar and Venables, were inclined to accept the offer, thereby reducing the new money available for the club. But it was part of the baggage of the take-over and, in the euphoria of the moment, of little consequence. Hewer, too, was happy. On the Friday night he had been annoyed to find that Lowe Bell Financial, acting as Tottenham's PR advisers, had made an early press release. On the Saturday, as the actions of the night before were announced to the world, Hewer made sure that Lowe Bell were put in their place.

On that Saturday everything in the Tottenham garden appeared to be rosy. The fans had already acclaimed the Venables-Sugar partnership. Like new managers they were paraded at White Hart Lane holding aloft the FA Cup as a symbol of the riches and success they would bring to the club. Having suffered for almost a year, fearing their club might well be in the hands of the Receiver, the fans were ecstatic about this dream team: Venables' undoubted footballing expertise matching Sugar's financial knowhow.

'Terry will look after the eleven players on the field, I will look after the £11m. in the bank,' said Sugar, and it seemed to sum up the new mood.

Chapter 9

Sacrifice of a dearest friend

If there was a new broom at Tottenham the successful take-over had also changed the Venables-Riviere partnership. 'Up to the time of the Tottenham take-over I had always been the principal partner of Venables,' says Paul Riviere. 'We were the ones who had taken the financial pressure of our companies and Brown was in charge of the finance. Over the two or three weeks when he finally did the deal with Alan Sugar, Brown took on a new mantle. Brown had helped Venables to secure Tottenham. Now he was Terry's principal adviser. Brown's attitude was different towards me as well. He doesn't say a lot and he's not arrogant in a *prima facie* way, but his attitude to people if he doesn't want to answer them is that he kind of dismisses them. He then knew he had the backing of Venables and was very, very tough with people.'

Riviere had been in the United States, working on 'The Manager', when the Tottenham deal went through. 'When I came back I missed Brown because he had gone off on a family holiday to Jamaica. I didn't see him for about three or four weeks. This was the first time he had been away from the financial reins, and I had hardly seen anything of him or Terry for the two months preceding the take-over of Tottenham. That was one of the problems we had. I would do all the marketing at Scribes, then I would see we had to pay these bills and Brown would say, we have got to wait till the eleventh hour. He never wanted to pay bills, never. He waited till the last minute for everything – the kind of guy who would always wait for the red reminder. His eleventh hour became the thirteenth hour, I don't think he knows the meaning of denouement.

'While he was away Angela Edwards [Riviere's assistant] and I went over to Exhibition Road. I looked at the accounts for the first time and saw that they were in a total mess. I then learnt we had two judgements against us. There were three writs of summonses against us. I spoke to Terry about this and that is when I realised Brown was of paramount importance to Terry. He said, speak to Jonathan Crystal. I spoke to Jonathan. Jonathan said, it is serious, get Brown back. I faxed him in Jamaica saying we need to talk about this. He did not interrupt his holiday. He came back in due time. When he came back he was very aggressive with me. "What are you trying to do, are you trying to fuck me?" he asked.'

But Brown had already been undermined by the bankruptcy order and his secret was about to emerge. One day in July 1991, not long after the Tottenham take-over, the fax machine at Scribes started humming. Hamilton and Van-Hay were there. 'A facsimile came in on the machine,' recalls Van-Hay. 'A single sheet, no covering letter. I couldn't even read it. My eyesight is not very good and I said to Gavin, "What the hell is this?" '

Hamilton, who was cashing up at the time, took the fax and his jaw dropped. 'Shit.'

'What's it about?' asked Van-Hay.

'Brown is bankrupt,' said Hamilton, almost unable to believe his own words. The fax that had been sent without any covering letter was Brown's Bankruptcy Order.

'Christ Almighty,' said Van-Hay.

'We don't know who sent it,' says Hamilton. 'There were ideas but nobody has actually owned up to who did it. I think it was a solicitor friend of his because Paul Riviere's involvement was getting very shaky as he was losing money from Brown making a balls-up of his business side. Paul wasn't there but he came in a bit later on and Van showed it to him. Paul was deeply shocked, he was absolutely devastated. Paul was so angry and so hurt he just disappeared.'

The fax, says Riviere, 'had been sent to Scribes by Rod Dadak, my lawyer. I had told him about my worries about Brown, and asked him to keep his eyes open, which he obviously did. When I got there Van-Hay said, "There is a fax. I think it is for you." I was totally surprised because he was our finance director. Rod told me later what this meant in respect of any financial activity by Brown.'

This is when things about Brown began to gel for Riviere.

Van-Hay rang his lawyers – Scribes' old solicitors who had been replaced by Venables' lawyers after he took over Scribes West – and they confirmed Brown could no longer be the finance director of the company. That was breaking the law. He also spoke to Roger Gilbert of Associated Newspapers, a prominent shareholder, and some other people. 'I then waited for Mr Venables to arrive. He came through the back door, as he normally did, after parking his car. I approached Terry in a very friendly way. I said, "By the way, Terry, I need to speak to you very urgently, it is very important." He said, "What's it about?" I said, "I have got some pretty bad news for you. Do you know Mr Brown is a bankrupt? And the law is quite clear, I have spoken to my lawyers, I have also spoken to Associated Newspapers and I have spoken to a couple of other people. This man cannot stay on the board of this company and I cannot allow it." Terry reacted very angrily. He was ashen-faced and said, "Mind your own fucking business, this is fucking nothing to do with you." He raised his fists at me and although he didn't touch me I got the impression he might hit me. I said, "Terry, are you going to hit me? If you want to, take me outside. But I know what the law is, we can't have this man here." Terry was furious. He said, "Mind your own fucking business. It's nothing to do with you. John Brown is my future." '

'The next day,' says Hamilton, 'Paul came and there was an enormous row between Paul and Brown in one of the rooms, which ended up with Paul going out in tears, tears of anger rather than anything else. He then resigned.'

The logical move at this stage would have been for Venables to distance himself from Brown but, as he had told Van-Hay, he saw Brown as the man protecting his future, the man who had delivered Tottenham to him, and he could not do that. However, a situation like this calls for a sacrifice and the one who was sacrificed was Riviere. Riviere had been one of Venables' dearest friends – 'I don't think there is a nicer man than Paul,' Venables had once told Scholar – but now, for the sake of the promised land that the new friend had apparently delivered, Riviere had to go. Venables had always said how he rates loyalty as one of the most cherished virtues. Riviere, a friend of fifteen years, was to experience anything but that from Venables. Riviere wrote anguished letters to John Brown and Pawlikowski describing how their actions had ruined him. By the third week of July Riviere knew that he would probably go bankrupt himself. He had been advised to do so by his lawyer and accountant, both of whom had urged him to cut his losses. 'The way Brown was dealing with things, companies I hadn't heard of, the use of a shell company, of money going out, I was advised both by my lawyers and my accountants at whatever cost to come away from the companies as I was now on the verge of a nervous breakdown.'

There was to be one final confrontation for him with Brown and it came at the Scribes West Board meeting in July: 'Because of what had happened to me on different companies,' Riviere explains, 'I needed to get some money. I always thought there was £34,000 in Glenhope, that was the figure Terry Venables and I had looked at. I then asked Brown to explain where the money had gone and he went into a long story about it. I said, "I don't understand this, John, at all." So he said, "Well, the trouble is, Paul, you didn't understand maths at school." I replied, "I know, but you did." He said, "What do you mean?" I said, "You know what I mean." We were all in this small room at Scribes. Gavin and Van will tell you that I'm a very quiet man until I get angry, but I was in a difficult position there and I was angry. When I accused Brown he denied it. I turned to Jonathan Crystal, who I'd told the full facts after Theobalds had told me everything, and Jonathan said, "Well, Paul, I'm a lawyer, I can't be involved." I said, "Well, having known you for fifteen years, I don't think you are just a lawyer, Jonathan. I think it's terrible you're not getting involved. You know the story, this man is wrong." I looked at Venables and said, "Well, what do you think, Terry?" He just shrugged his shoulders, put his arms in the air and said, "I just want us all to be friends." That was when I realised Brown had become Mr Untouchable, and I resigned my directorships.'

Venables has since claimed in his autobiography that Riviere is wrong in saying there was no money in Glenhope. Venables has bank statements which show 'in excess of £100,000 on deposit' in the bank. Riviere says, 'If there was £100,000 why should I have left and why should I have made myself, quite voluntarily, a bankrupt? I was not forced into it like Brown. And if there was £100,000 I am entitled to half because I was Venables' partner at that time. So where is my share?'

Venables' statement of £100,000 being in the bank account of Glenhope is all the more remarkable because, on 31 July 1991, just before he went off on holiday, Bryan Fugler, whose law firm was acting for Venables, wrote him a letter, with copies to Crystal, Brown and Riviere. It made very bleak reading.

A number of creditors had obtained judgement against Glenhope but Dadak, after setting up the companies, had, as instructed, passed the papers back and it seemed documents appointing Venables and Riviere as directors had not been filed with Companies House. One creditor had claimed that it was unlawful to trade without a director or secretary. This meant there could be a risk of personal liability on Venables, Riviere or anyone claiming to be a director or secretary.

Alan Roberts of Printdouble, part of Brown's paper financial empire, had refused to release 'The Manager' games he had in stock, and Fugler was convinced that 'unless a satisfactory arrangement can be made for the release of the games the Company will not be able to continue and you should not inject any further money or give any personal guarantees.'

The bank was prepared to issue a further facility of £30,000, but this would require Venables' personal guarantee. It is quite clear from Fugler's letter that Venables would have to invest more money into the company in order that it could trade, but even then Fugler wondered if Venables should not resign as it might damage his reputation. So if there was £100,000 in the Glenhope bank why should Fugler write in this way?

Riviere resigned from Scribes and from Glenhope Management. His financial services company, which Pawlikowski had been supposed to look after while Riviere devoted himself to 'The Manager', had also gone down. Through that company, Elite First, he had lost nearly £200,000 and his only hope was Glenhope and/or Scribes. In September 1991 Riviere declared himself voluntarily bankrupt. 'Yes, I took my eye off the Elite First business but that was in order to make "The Manager" a success and I blame what happened, because of my association with Venables, on Brown and Pawlikowski.' So devastating were their actions that, for almost two years after that, Riviere was still learning some of the things they had done.

What about Venables? 'No, I feel Venables should have seen through Brown as I did. Terry always said I was one of his two very best friends but he did nothing to help. Brown became more and more influential and I could never understand why. Terry and me falling out was purely over Brown.'

Even at this stage Brown tried to brazen it out. He was off the

Board because of his bankruptcy but he tried to assure Hamilton that it was all nonsense. 'He was coming to me,' Hamilton said, 'and taking me quietly to one side and saying, "Look, you don't know what it's like, the pressure I've been under. I find myself being pilloried by all these people. It's just not fair. I'm owed hundreds of thousands of pounds by companies that have screwed me up. I think you ought to think more carefully about how you treat me." To me it was like a fingers-down-the-throat job, it was so nauseating. Listening to him I said, "Look there isn't any argument. You are a bankrupt and under those circumstances, it is statutory that your directorships go. What do you want me to say? It doesn't make any difference whether I feel sorry for you. The situation is, within the company you are no longer financial director or a director of any sort." '

But where did Venables stand in all this? Hamilton has mixed feelings about how much Venables knew: 'Some people have said to me that he did know but he preferred to keep quiet about it. But I think perhaps he didn't know, or maybe he did know but didn't think it was going to come out in such a way that was to cause embarrassment.'

Had Hamilton and Van-Hay been smarter they could have caused Venables greater embarrassment, perhaps, indeed, regained control of Scribes West. With Riviere off the Board, and Brown thrown off, Hamilton and Van-Hay had the power to vote Venables off. As Hamilton now says: 'If we'd had our heads screwed on the right way, we could have actually ousted Venables. We didn't think of it until it was too late. In the long term, would it have been the right thing to do anyway? It wouldn't necessarily have been the right thing for us.'

But they didn't act, and this allowed Venables and his friends to regroup. On 4 September 1991 they organised a meeting. The minutes record that Terry Venables called the meeting to nominate a new director but Hamilton recalls that 'at a Board meeting Jonathan Crystal said, "Right, firstly I want to propose Mr Fred Venables as a director of the company." Crystal wasn't a member of the Board but he was there as an adviser. Basically he stood in for Terry Venables, when Venables was not present. Then Crystal said he would act for Fred.'

Here the Scribes West story, already complicated, took another turn. When the directors' appointments were finally filed with Companies House, more than a year afterwards, they showed that

Fred Venables was appointed director on 11 April 1991, the same day as his son, while there was no mention of Brown ever being a director – despite much Board discussion, which was clearly minuted, about his resignation following his bankruptcy. As for Riviere he was a non-person, as if he had never existed.

The arrival of Fred Venables was, in some ways, the last straw for the men who had created Scribes. The changes Venables had made were already grating on Hamilton: 'We always seemed to have meetings. Venables, Brown and others would disappear into private rooms and have meeting after meeting. Members coming into the club used to get angry about it. They would say, what is this place, you can never go into rooms, there are always meetings going on. The telephone was in constant use. People found it difficult even to get through to book tables.'

But worse was to follow when Fred arrived. 'I did not like him at all,' Hamilton went on. 'He is, as he states he is, an East End docker. I remember him whistling in the dining-room. He was so out of place there. He just sat in the dining-room waiting for his food to arrive and he started to whistle. He was pretty abrupt. He didn't like Van and I don't think he liked me particularly. His relationship with his son was very good. He called Van stuck-up. We were in different leagues. It was chalk and cheese and it didn't gel at all. He reacted to it because I think he found it odd. Terry was fine. It didn't worry him but I could see it was something that bothered Fred. He thought it was no good. These pair of stuck-up twits and what did they know? He's run a pub for many years. It is a pub and that's it. It's not an upmarket West End club, which is what we were, and that's why it didn't work with him.'

Hamilton and Van-Hay were also to suffer from what they saw as 'Terry's attitude is to divide and conquer'. 'They don't like groups, or two people who are very strong working together. Without question they tried to break Van and me up. Van was earning more salary than I was and I remember being asked, "Why does Van have more salary than you? You do a lot more work. You are more involved. It's ridiculous. You ought to do something about it." And the same sort of thing would be said to Van. They would go to him and say, "What's Gavin doing here? Why do you let him do this . . .? This was Venables and Brown and in the early days Paul was part of that, too, part of Venables. It was only when everything started to change, and Paul's position became difficult, that they split into two different camps. You had Crystal, Brown and Venables on one side and Paul, Van and myself on the other. Paul resigned as a director but stayed on, in a slightly lesser capacity, doing just as he was before: fixing things, getting parties organised, bringing people in and trying to up the business. But he was a very different person. He felt he had been very badly let down. So he came on to our side, which of course caused no end of problems for Terry because that wasn't supposed to happen at all.'

But try as they might to sort out the problems, Hamilton and Van-Hay were always finding themselves having to cope with new plans. One of these was a greater flexibility on closing times which soon led to the Kensington police summoning Hamilton and Van-Hay who, in almost twenty years of club management, had never been in such a position. 'When we got to the station we were told we were not being cautioned but even then we were questioned and it was a frightening experience.'

Things came to a head in August 1991 when, says Hamilton, 'we were running out of cash again. We had bills going back to May, suppliers' bills that hadn't been paid. That was when the recession was at its deepest, and suppliers were not as happy as they were five or ten years ago to let things slip. We worked on thirty days' credit. May bills should have been paid in the middle of June at the latest, not remain unpaid getting into August. So one after the other our suppliers were putting us on Stop. We couldn't get wine supplies, we couldn't get food supplies. It was a constant, hourly battle. At the end, over three-quarters of the suppliers were not supplying us. The attitude of Brown, who was still basically acting as financial boss, was, well go and buy them from the cash and carry.'

Hamilton and Van-Hay's position, after so long in the business, was being eroded. At two Board meetings Hamilton raised the question of Scribes' solvency: 'I said, and had it minuted, "I want a straight answer; is the company solvent? Are we in a position to continue trading because if we are not then we ought to be consulting our shareholders." But I was fobbed off with, "What do you know about it? Absolute nonsense. We can continue running. There's no problem at all." I said, "Well, I don't believe it. I believe that we are in a position where we are not able to pay our bills. We don't have any reserves. We don't have any overdraft facilities. We are in a bad state." '

After much arguing it was decided to review the whole of the trading side and cut everything. 'The paper came across from Crystal. It was just a scrappy piece of paper. Our overhead at that stage was between £35,000/£40,000 a month and they wanted to cut it to £25,000. Their argument was, "We are going to have to cut staff. We are going to have to cut all the expenditure down." I looked at the figures which were put on the table, and said, "With the way the operation is running, that is impossible. We'd lose half the kitchen staff." We were on a pretty thin staff anyway.'

But the cutback proposals were even worse. If accepted it meant neither Van-Hay nor Hamilton would get paid, they would have to work without wages. 'I said, "I'm an employee of the company. If we were talking about directors' remuneration being slashed, I would say fine. I know the rest of the directors are not being paid although Glenhope Management money would appear to be going out towards directors, but you are seriously expecting me, as an employee, not to take any salary for three months. How am I supposed to pay my mortgage? How am I supposed to eat and feed my child and wife?" The answer was, "That's one of the problems with working in senior management." I said, "Well, it's not a problem for me, because I'm not going to do it!" '

Extraordinary as the request may seem it is interesting to consider the reasoning put forward by the Venables camp. 'Their line,' says Hamilton, 'was, "You've made these people put all this money into this company. (We were up to about three-quarters of a million pounds.) You've got to take some of the come-back on it. You've asked these people; why should they suffer?" '

Not surprisingly Hamilton did not see it that way. 'I said, "That's not the way I look at it. These people have made an investment, which is always a risk. I'm doing the work to run the operation to the best of my ability and for that I shall be paid because it says so quite clearly in my contract." It was put to a vote on the Board and, of course, Van and I were outvoted and we said, "Well, that is not acceptable." So they said they would reconvene the meeting in two days' time.'

Hamilton now believes the whole exercise was preplanned to get rid of him and Van-Hay. 'Basically, with the combination of Van's and my salaries, it was in the interest of Terry and Brown to get us out. Van was on £36,000 and I was on £24,000, making £50,000 a year. It was quite a lot of money but you can't run the place without someone to run it.'

Hamilton left on Friday 13 September not having received his

101

August salary. He had given an ultimatum of that Friday to receive the money. 'Friday came. We didn't get paid. They all disappeared. They were not available. When it came to five o'clock I left. Van stayed on, unfortunately for him. He got into a terrible row with Venables, Brown and Crystal. All of the *Daily Mail* people knew there was trouble. It was getting to the end point. They had rallied and were in the bar. I had gone. Van was very emotional and went in and confronted them in the little bar.'

It was, recalls Van-Hay, on 22 September that 'in the main bar were Christopher Morgan, Jeff Powell, Mr Wooldridge. I was suddenly summoned by Mr Crystal to the little bar and was told to hand over my keys. He said, "You are no longer required by the company." I handed him my keys and I said, "What about money? I need money, I can't even get home tonight. I've had no salary, I need some money." '

Then looking at Venables, Van-Hay said, 'You have brought this on yourself, Terry. I don't necessarily think you are a rotten man, but I think that you are going to end up a rotten man if you don't mend your ways.'

As Van-Hay finished speaking, with another plea for money, Venables put his hand in his pocket, and pulled out a wad of notes. 'Ten pound notes. They were sealed, brand spanking new as if they had just come from the bank and threw it at me. It was £500. I took the money and ran out of the club. Jeff Powell and Christopher Morgan ran after me, wrestled me down in the street and brought me back; but as I stood at the bar Crystal and Venables came out from the small bar, saw me, and walked out.'

Van-Hay, very distraught, was eventually put on a train home. That evening, at about eight o'clock, Hamilton rang and asked what was going on. 'Crystal spoke to me and told me to be at the Royal Garden at one o'clock on Tuesday and I could collect my salary cheque. I told him to get stuffed. "You can bloody well send it to me. I shall be in the club tomorrow. Oh, and by the way, I presume you don't want me to work out my notice?" This stunned him slightly. He said, "Well, you've resigned, so you are not at the place any more." I said, "I see." I did get my cheque in the post. I got paid for August, but not September, and Van also.'

But the matter did not, could not, end there. Hamilton was still owed money. 'I wrote to Terry three times and actually went down to the club on two or three occasions. I met him at a couple of parties and spoke to him. There was no animosity at all. He bought me a drink at the bar on one occasion when I went down there. I remember him saying, "Why are you writing me all these letters?" I said, "Because I want my money. It's not unreasonable." He asked why he owed me money. I said, "Because I worked for two weeks and I should be paid. I'm an employee. In theory you should pay me for my notice." "Ah, well, we'll sort it out, we'll sort it out." Anyway it got from the sublime to the ridiculous and nothing happened. Eventually I went to some solicitors. I was owed about £1,000 in pay and holiday pay. It should have been more than that really because I was on three months' notice. I didn't want to get into a big fight about the payment of notice but I was very certain I wanted to be paid for the work I'd done.'

At one stage Crystal came in on the act. 'He wrote to me very early on saying, basically, how dare I ask for money, I'd been paid everything that was due to me. Then he went on to say what about Van being paid the £500 out of Terry Venables' pocket. Don't you think that is a full and final settlement?'

Hamilton eventually decided to consult lawyers about his outstanding amount. 'I was going to take out a Small Claims against Venables which, with hindsight, is probably what I should have done. Instead I went to the solicitors, which is bloody expensive. The Brown and Venables attitude, and I've seen it from the other side when we were fighting off creditors, is to delay. They work on the basis of "let's wear them down to the point where they'll either shut up and go away or we'll settle on the Court steps". I was now on the receiving end of that. There were ridiculous counterclaims being pushed against me about things that were absolute nonsense like chairs that they were saying had been sold. We had chairs that we were buying on lease over five years, so theoretically you can't actually sell something which is on a lease like that. But we hadn't sold them, we'd lent them. We had too many chairs to store on the premises. There was never any argument about the fact that these were on loan. They could have come back at any time if we'd asked for them back. As it happened, when Terry found out that these chairs were on loan to the French House [where Hamilton now works] he wasn't at all happy about that and he insisted they be paid for. It came up at a number of Management meetings and it was to be sorted by Van. He was to sort out a price for the chairs and it is minuted. Money was paid for the chairs and received by Scribes. All this was instigated by Terry. But when I claimed for my back pay he turned round saying that as General Manager I sold off chairs which were on leasehold. This was ridiculous. He sold them off. It seemed to me a stalling tactic, to make it costly for me to pursue the action. In the end, I spent more money than I was owed and decided to forget about it.'

Even after Hamilton had gone, Scribes West would keep turning up like a bad penny. 'There was a big dispute about car parking space underneath the club. After we left, the *Daily Mail*, who owned the car park, put in quite a big bill. We heard back that Venables had written saying we know nothing of this car parking and we refuse to pay this bill, it's nothing to do with us at all. Only I've got documents showing that this was openly discussed in management meetings: car parking and what we were going to do with the car parking space, going right back to the beginning when they first came in. But that's the way they treat any demand for money.'

But could all this be that damning of Venables? Is this just the gripe that may be expected of an ex-employee who was unhappy about leaving the club he had created? Venables, as the owner, might have a very different version. The only problem with that is, Venables does not provide any view. In Venables' 468-page auto-biography, Hamilton, Van-Hay, let alone Isaacs, do not get a mention. None of these events we have heard about figure there, the references to Scribes are cursory, and Riviere is dismissed as the man down on his luck, deserted by his wife of a couple of weeks, who was employed by Venables at Scribes.

Not surprisingly Hamilton's assessment of Venables and his entourage is bleak.

'I don't think Terry is all good. Sometimes I think about him and I think he's not stupid. He's very streetwise. I don't think he is hugely talented on the financial side to the extent that I believe that Brown has got him tied in knots. Brown is not very good, he can't be very good to have all those bankrupt companies in his name, but he's sharp. He talks a good line. I don't think Terry is fully con-versant with the sort of upper strata of high technical finance. But then you might turn round and say why should he be, he's not an accountant. I'm certain this is why he's so tied to Brown.'

What puzzles Hamilton is why Venables has defended Brown so stoutly: 'It just strikes me as odd that he hasn't known Brown very long, probably no more than a few years, and yet you'd think he would give his life away rather than get Brown into trouble. The covering he's done for him.'

In some ways Hamilton's most interesting assessment is of a Jekyll and Hyde character in Venables: 'I think Terry wears two hats. Socially he is very good company, he's generous, he's one of the boys, good value. That's one side of him. On the other side, when he comes into business, I don't think he's nearly as clever as he thinks he is. So you come up against a kind of arrogance. He does believe he's smart. He thinks he's a big wheeler-dealer, ducking and diving and making money. He certainly has made money. He certainly is a very hard worker. He puts a lot of hours in. He's working basically from dawn to dusk. He is hyperactive. He's got a grasshopper mind and can be very careless. I've come across papers left around on the top of the bar, right at the height of the Tottenham deal, which journalists could have got hold of. There were all the plans and profiles of people and the Board. That was not once, but more than once. This was a club stuffed full of journalists. If it hadn't been me who had found them, it could have been anybody. When I gave them back to him he was very embarrassed.'

Despite the departures of Hamilton, Van-Hay and the sacrifice of Riviere, Venables' problems at Scribes were not over. But with Brown to guide and advise him there was always a solution, although nobody could have anticipated that one of these solutions would involve so presenting Scribes' accounts and information on the company that both Brown and Riviere would become non-persons. When the Scribes accounts were finally lodged at Companies House, three years later, it is as if all that had happened which reduced Riviere to tears had never taken place.

Chapter 10

Football's Leonardo da Vinci

On Friday 28 June 1991 *The Times* ran a feature on Venables. The writer, Kate Muir, described him as 'football's renaissance man, the Leonardo da Vinci of the League'. The rhetoric, if overblown, was understandable, for the public man was riding high. That day a Board meeting was held at White Hart Lane which confirmed Venables as chief executive and Sugar as chairman of Spurs. However, such public actions camouflaged private ones.

Far from the public gaze two other events took place on that day which have a crucial bearing on Venables' story. Venables' company, Edennote, received a payment of more than half a million pounds from Norfina, £533,500 to be precise. The same day it was put on overnight deposit in a call account. Also on that day Venables resigned as director from Transatlantic Inns (although this was not filed with Companies House until the following February). The two events were curiously related and went to the heart of how Venables had raised the money to finance his purchase of Spurs, a financing that is now one of the charges brought against him by the DTI in a civil action which seeks to ban him as a company director.

At that stage, eight days after the events at Ansbacher's offices, Venables had not yet put any money into buying Spurs. Sugar had bailed him out on the night of completion and it was the first week of July before Venables paid him back. Venables has never publicly acknowledged Sugar's help, nor fully discussed how he raised the money and when evidence of some of his intricate dealings began to emerge in the media he has provided contradictory public explanations. Two *Panorama* programmes and innumerable press articles have since been devoted to resolving the apparent contradictions.

To understand it all we need to look at how Venables bought Spurs. Both Venables and Sugar had promised to invest £3m. each. For Sugar the money was no problem. Venables, in contrast, had to negotiate complicated deals.

Two million pounds of the three million he required was borrowed from Norfina, a little-known finance house based in Southwark close to London Bridge.

Norfina wanted security for the £2m. it was lending to Venables. This was given in the form of a mortgage over Venables' Spurs shares. However, Norfina thought this was such a high-risk proposition that they also wanted some additional security. They insisted that Venables take out an insurance policy with Pan Financial, a company which was then selling innovative insurance policies and was 49% owned by Skandia. The insurance policy meant that, if anything went wrong, Norfina could always get its money back.

In essence this was similar to the mortgage into which most house-buyers enter, except that, with mortgages, failure to pay the interest and capital can mean repossession and the home buyer might find himself on the street. In this case Venables stood to lose the shares. In other words he was buying Spurs by, in effect, using the shares he was purchasing as his security.

Brown was at the centre of these deals. While dabbling in Printdouble he had met a broker, David Bedford, director of Legal Trade, then a member of the British Insurers and Investments Brokers Association, who turned out to be a fanatical Spurs supporter. Bedford put him in touch with Pan Financial and may also have introduced Venables to Norfina, whose offices were not far from Bedford's then offices in Borough High Street.

The arrangement did not come cheap. Edennote had to pay a commitment fee of £7,000, there was a premium of £100,000 prior to the issue of the insurance guarantee and other costs, charges and expenses. Venables also had to agree to a number of Pan Financial conditions: not to underwrite any rights issue for Spurs without its approval and the whole deal would be off if Venables were sacked as chief executive. This last condition would provide a wholly unexpected twist, forcing Venables to apologise in court two years later. Venables promised not to buy shares in Spurs unless Sugar agreed to buy a similar amount and to get Sugar to agree to a shareholders' agreement, a certified copy of which had to be provided to Pan Financial. It was this condition which was forcing Brown to come up with draft shareholders' agreements, some of which would still be circulating for many months after Sugar and Venables had bought Spurs.

The Norfina deal intrigued many. But unusual as it was it was neither illegal nor dubious. It was the rest of the money needed by Venables to buy Spurs that brought him to the attention of the DTI investigators.

The Norfina-Pan Financial loan of £2m. was not enough. It was enough to allow Venables, with the help of Sugar, to get control of Tottenham, but much of that money had gone to pay for the shares of Scholar and Bobroff. If this had been all that was necessary in taking over Tottenham, then the Norfina loan would have been enough. But this was a take-over of a publicly quoted company and, in taking control, Sugar and Venables had also acquired more than 30% of Tottenham. So under the City Code on take-overs they were required to make the same offer they had made to Scholar and Bobroff to all the other Tottenham shareholders.

On 3 July 1991, in a detailed 31-page document called a Mandatory Cash Offer, Venables and Sugar did just that, explaining how they were going to complete their take-over of Spurs. In a joint letter Venables and Sugar said they had approximately £7.5m. to invest in Tottenham. £2.7m. had already been paid to buy out Scholar and Bobroff. They wanted to put the remaining money into Tottenham but they could only do that if all the other shareholders refused to accept their offer and kept their shares. They appealed to them to do so, hoping they could appeal to them as football fans who would appreciate the need to use the money to strengthen the team and recreate the glory days of the club. But they could not be sure that the shareholders – who had seen their shares decline in value – would listen to their pleas. So Sugar and Venables had to have more money available to pay shareholders who might want to accept their offer. Again, for Sugar, with his mountain of money, this was no problem. But where could Venables find the extra million?

Yawetz had come up with a loan of £250,000, becoming a director of the football club. Although this was not a condition of the loan it was described in a letter as a gesture of the respect and generosity Brown felt for Yawetz. For a time Yawetz also became director of Edennote. But that still left Venables to find another three-quarters of a million. How did Venables secure this money?

In the Mandatory Cash Offer document Venables said this three-quarters of a million came from his own resources (in his autobiography he repeats this phrase, but by this time the figure for own resources had gone up to £1.3m.). The offer document also said Edennote had no borrowings other than one bank loan.

Two *Panorama* programmes, one in September 1993, the other in October 1994, have since produced powerful evidence to suggest that Venables was being more than economical with the truth when he made those statements. Both of those statements could not be true. According to *Panorama*, he borrowed a million by pledging assets he did not own and one of which did not even exist.

The money was borrowed from Landhurst Leasing. Run by Ted Ball, the company, amongst other things, specialised in lending money to high-profile sporting celebrities. It was one of those finance companies that mushroomed in the booming 1980s, which lent on anything from Ferraris and Lamborghinis to dental equipment and, in one case, a mobile telephone.

Venables borrowed two lots of money from Landhurst. The first lot was for half a million pounds. It was borrowed with the help of Philip Green. On Thursday 20 June, about twenty-four hours before Venables was due to complete his take-over of Tottenham, Green got a call from Brown. Brown had hit a problem. In order to buy Tottenham, Venables needed to show that he had £3m. But he was half a million pounds short. There had been talk in the Venables camp that Green, himself, might be a possible investor. Brown wanted to know whether Green could help raise the last half million? Green offered to help.

He turned to Ted Ball and it was agreed that an unsecured loan of half a million pounds would be provided by Landhurst to Edennote, Venables' company. However, the money was sent not to Edennote or Edennote lawyers, but to Green's London solicitors, who kept it in their client account. Stephen Illidge, Landhurst's financial controller, tried to ensure that while the money was at Green's solicitor it would be kept to Landhurst's order. But Ball told him not to worry on this score. The feeling was that Venables would never have to call on the money as not enough Tottenham shareholders would sell their shares. It is not known if there were any conditions attached to the loan; if there were, then Venables could not have claimed as he did that he had the £3m. needed to buy Spurs. In any event the half million pounds was not used, and some weeks after the take-over was completed the loan was returned to Landhurst by Green's solicitors along with interest it had earned during the period they held the money.

On 7 August, Stephen Illidge wrote to Green saying, 'Dear Philip, I am pleased to confirm that the £500,000 advance in respect of Edennote plc has been returned to us.' He also enclosed an invoice for a fee of £22,500 for arranging the loan.

Green was not best pleased. There had been no discussion of paying a fee to Landhurst for the loan. The letter made it seem as if he was a middleman when he had just done a favour to Venables and got no gain from it. However, he suggested to Illidge that Landhurst might be able to earn a fee when they provided another advance, this time for the £1m. that Venables needed. Green had already discussed this advance with Ball.

A couple of months later, therefore, Venables borrowed £1m. from Landhurst. According to evidence presented in the two *Panorama* programmes, he pledged assets to secure the loan. He also gave Landhurst Leasing a personal guarantee.

The assets he is alleged to have pledged belonged to Transatlantic Inns. A schedule to the lease agreement he is said to have signed with Landhurst said: 'all structural fixtures and fittings, bars, kitchen equipment, audio equipment, furniture and carpeting at the following premises: Maceys, 32 Duke Street, London; Cock and Magpie, Epping North, Epping, Essex; The Granby Tavern, 12 London Road, Reading, Berks; Miners, Claremount Road, Cardiff.'

Venables was in effect selling the fixtures for £1m. and then leasing them back in return for regular interest payments to Landhurst.

Panorama has produced other evidence to support its allegation. In addition to the lease agreement, Illidge sent a letter to directors of Edennote on 2 September 1991, confirming a credit line of £1m. had been agreed, one of the terms being 'the refinancing of the fixtures and fittings of various public houses, details of which are to be advised to us'. This letter was countersigned by Venables.

This letter also had another interesting clause. Item 5 of the letter spoke of Venables providing a personal guarantee. Before its collapse in 1992 Landhurst lent £100m. to various individuals and always insisted that the borrower give a personal guarantee. Ball's philosophy was that he lent to high-profile people and they would not default because they had given a personal guarantee.

Soon after Illidge sent the letter, Charlie Dyer, a senior employee of Landhurst Leasing, was at the Spurs training ground in Mill Hill. Venables, he claims, signed a number of documents including a personal guarantee. The scene was curious. Outside Venables' office that day, as he was signing the documents, waited Ray Clemence and Paul Walsh. The latter, in a fit of pique at being substituted had hit Clemence, and the pair were there to receive Venables' verdict. Whether they knew anything of the quite different drama in Venables office, we don't know. Alan Sugar recalls a meeting with Venables, sometime after Landhurst had gone into receivership, when, claims Sugar, Venables said that he had given a personal guarantee.

Panorama also discovered that one of the pubs mentioned in the documents, the fourth pub, the Miners, did not exist and there is no 'Claremount Road' in Cardiff. When *Panorama*'s researcher reported back to the producer that no such pub existed, the producer bawled her out. Eventually the Geographers' Company confirmed to *Panorama* that there was no Claremount Road in Cardiff.

There is also the question of the valuation. Were the fixtures and fittings of the pubs really worth £1m.? One valuer would rate them as worth no more than £100,000. Given that Landhurst is once said to have lent £100,000 against the security of a mobile telephone, lending a million against fixtures, probably worth £100,000, is not strange. However, the higher figure placed on the pub fixtures and fittings was crucial to the million Venables needed to buy Spurs.

If the evidence produced by *Panorama*, and now the subject of the DTI case against Venables, is true then it appears compelling. So what does Venables say in his defence?

He does not deny he borrowed money from Landhurst, but regarding the £1m. he borrowed he denies he pledged the assets of Transatlantic Inns to do so. Confronted by *Panorama*'s evidence of Landhurst leases bearing his signature he states his signature is a forgery. Venables does admit he signed a Landhurst document entitled Equipment Lease Agreement but says he signed a blank form.

Venables is quite insistent that he never signed a personal guarantee. Soon after Landhurst collapsed a number of personal guarantees went missing. Arthur Andersen, Landhurst's receivers, in a report dated 24 February 1994, said, 'You may recall that Mr Venables' original personal guarantee was one of those we believe was removed from Landhurst's files prior to receivership.' If such a document does exist, it has never surfaced.

Venables says Ted Ball gave the loan without asking for anything in return, it was a 'no-strings loan'. The picture he presents of Ball is a man so keen to lend the million pounds he almost forces it on Venables. In his autobiography he recalls how Ball asked him, 'Do you want it, or don't you want it?' Brown and Ball's man are soon put in touch and the deal is done. In another version Venables has elaborated on this describing how he had met Ball quite accidentally at Langan's Brasserie, in the company of Tony Berry. Venables told him of his need for a million. He met Ball again at Harry's Bar and it was here that Ball told him, 'Do you want a fucking million, or not?'

But why should Ball lend him a million without any security or even a personal guarantee? In his autobiography Venables makes light of this, saying it was Ball's duty as lender, not his as borrower, to 'satisfy himself that he will get his money back'. Nobody can doubt that, but it does tell us something about the kind of borrower Venables is that he can be so cavalier.

Venables is also vehement in asserting that the million he borrowed from Landhurst was for him personally. This is despite the fact that the leasing documents make it very clear that the loan was to Edennote. This was the company named on the Leasing agreement and the letter from Illidge of 2 September 1991 was addressed to Edennote. Finally when the cheques came from Landhurst they were made out to Edennote and banked by the company.

But perhaps the most compelling evidence that this was a sale and leaseback deal with Edennote was that in September 1991 Brown sent an invoice on Edennote paper to Landhurst Leasing. This invoice was for £1.05m (£50,000 was the fixing fee for Landhurst) and refers to the sale of furniture, fixtures and fittings as per an attached schedule. The schedule lists the four pubs. The invoice also promised to send a VAT invoice although this was never done.

In spite of such apparently overwhelming evidence Venables has continued to deny it was a sale leaseback agreement between Landhurst and Edennote. On some occasions he claimed it was to Venables Venture Capital Ltd, yet another of his companies now dissolved. At other times he has said the loan was to him personally.

Venables' other denial is that he used the million to buy Tottenham shares. This is, perhaps, his most puzzling denial. He has never quite explained what use he had for this money although in one explanation he has suggested he wanted it for other business ventures at Scribes West. No details have ever been given as to what these business ventures might be.

Again the evidence seems to point the other way. Landhurst, in making the £1m. loan to Edennote, issued three cheques: on 2 September, 9 September and 10 September 1991. They were received by Edennote on 3 September, 10 September and 11 September. The first two cheques were for £250,000 each, the third for £500,000 making up the million.

Six days after the last tranche of money was received from Landhurst, on 17 September 1991, Edennote made a loan of £800,000 to Tottenham. This matched a loan of exactly the same amount that Sugar made at the same time.

Tottenham was heavily strapped for funds and needed the money and Venables had pledged to invest £3m. in the offer document. Five days before Venables lent the £800,000 to Tottenham, on 12 September, the Tottenham Board had decided to go for a rights issue. Although this did not take place until December, when it did, both the Sugar and the Venables loans were converted into shares.

Despite this, when he came to write his autobiography, he insisted, 'The money was not used to purchase Tottenham shares – they had already been bought by the time the loan was made'. Given that the loan was converted into shares in the rights issue and the loan came as a cheque from Edennote after it had received the million from Landhurst, this seems an odd statement.

Venables further makes the point that the Serious Fraud Office was satisfied there was no fraud on his part. This is not really the point. The SFO is investigating the collapse of Landhurst and a couple of the directors have been charged with fraud. Venables was interviewed as a witness in the case, not as a potential suspect as far as Landhurst was concerned. Landhurst may have been foolish in lending him the money but that is the responsibility of Landhurst directors.

If there has been any wrongdoing on the part of Venables then it is in relation to Transatlantic and the way Venables is alleged to have used its assets. The SFO has never investigated Transatlantic because the amount involved, £1m., is well below their investigation threshold of £5m. And it is how Venables is alleged to have behaved with Transatlantic that is most fascinating.

If, as *Panorama* and the DTI allege, Venables used the assets of Transatlantic Inns, then he clearly acted unlawfully. He had no authority to pledge the assets of the pubs. The agreement with Landhurst was signed on 30 August 1991, two months after Venables had ceased to be a Transatlantic Inns director. It means Venables was acting as a director of Transatlantic, despite the fact that he had resigned two months earlier. The other three directors have told *Panorama* that they knew nothing about this transaction and it had not been authorised by the Board of Transatlantic.

Colin Wright went on the second *Panorama* programme in October 1994 and recalled his shock and dismay when sometime in 1993 – two and a half years after Landhurst lent the money – he discovered what Venables had done. The discovery came about because by then Transatlantic Inns had gone into liquidation and the Official Receiver had come across the Landhurst leases which Venables had signed. On 16 March 1993 Paul Kirby was summoned by the Official Receiver and asked about the deal which, says Kirby, is the first he learnt of it and he was dumbfounded to know what had happened to the fixtures and fittings of the pubs.

Well, Venables might say: they would say that, wouldn't they? Both Kirby and Wright are in bitter dispute with him and he clearly sees them as enemies. So we have an impasse. In any event, notwithstanding evidence apparently to the contrary, Venables vehemently denies pledging the pubs to obtain the £1m.

However, is it possible that, back in the summer and autumn of 1991, when the deal was done, Venables felt he owned the pubs in any event and so, probably, felt he had a right to pledge them?

To answer this question we need to look at the almost parallel developments that were going on in Transatlantic Inns at that time. In February 1996, as part of the court action between Venables and Kirby, a great deal of material emerged about Transatlantic and from that it is possible to build up a picture of what was happening between Venables, Transatlantic, its pubs and Kirby and Wright.

In essence the version of the Venables camp goes as follows. By April 1991 Venables had got very worried about the continuing losses of Transatlantic. That month he was given the draft accounts which showed the overdraft had reached £286,675 and total net liabilities of £127,000. He consulted Brown who expressed concern.

Meetings followed with Transatlantic's accountants and in mid-June Brown advised Venables to resign. He did so on 28 June 1991.

But resignation did not mean he walked away from Transatlantic. He wanted to run the pubs, was keen to put money in to restructure the company, and says he wanted to protect the remaining creditors. This resulted in a series of meetings in the summer of 1991, almost paralleling the ones Venables was having in his attempt to take over Tottenham. Although events in both companies were sometimes similar, those at Tottenham were often in the full glare of publicity, while the ones at Transatlantic Inns were private. So in May 1991, as Tottenham was worrying about its bank overdraft with Midland, over at NatWest in Romford there was worry about Transatlantic's overdraft. The only difference was that, whilst Midland worried about an £11m. overdraft, NatWest Romford were concerned about an overdraft approaching £300,000. It is one of the curiosities of the Venables story that the man who was a director of a private company with a near £300,000 overdraft was somehow presented in the media as capable of rescuing a public company with an £11m. overdraft.

Venables initially wanted to take over Macey's but this was rejected by Kirby. However, with Brown playing a leading role, by August 1991 a deal was agreed in principle. According to the Venables camp, on 9 August Venables and Brown met Kirby, his wife Sue and Peter Davies, who was acting for Kirby. It was agreed that Venables would purchase the Cock and Magpie and the Granby Tavern. He would do this through a new Venables company, Recall City. The previous day Terry and Fred Venables had become directors of this company. Joe Pawlikowski had been a director of this company since 22 March 1991.

On 12 August Venables and Brown met the manager of NatWest's Romford branch at Scribes to tell him about the deal. NatWest agreed to give Recall City an overdraft of £185,000 which would fund this deal, and release Venables from the guarantee he had given on the Transatlantic overdraft, provided Kirby and Wright could provide alternative security.

It is within two weeks of this date that Venables is alleged to have signed the lease with Landhurst, pledging the assets of the pubs in order to get his million-pound loan. The agreement also mentioned Macey's (and the non-existent Miners in Cardiff) but Venables might have felt he was owner of these properties or soon would be. Indeed, for some months afterwards he kept on trying to get hold of Macey's. So is it possible that in his mind in September 1991 he saw himself as owning these three pubs and therefore used their fixtures and fittings in the Landhurst lease to secure the loan? It would be an unusual way of doing business, to say the least, but in the Venables business world that is hardly surprising.

A glimpse of how the Venables business world operated is provided by Paul Riviere. Sometime in June 1991 he recalls being in Scribes. 'I had brought some clients when John Brown approached me and said, "Have you a minute, Paul?" He took me to the Scribes boardroom where I found David Brown [the fourth director of Transatlantic Inns and no connection of John Brown]. John Brown said, "Paul will buy your shares." Then, turning to me, he said, "Terry wants you to do that." I was astonished. It emerged that Venables was keen to buy out David Brown from Transatlantic and I was supposed to buy his shares. I knew nothing about it. I had no intention of buying shares in Transatlantic and I said, "I don't care what Terry wants. I am not going to do it." I could see John Brown was not pleased.'

All this clearly reveals the terrifyingly casual way the Venables camp ran their businesses, seemingly improvising on the spur of the moment. In such circumstances, is it not possible that, having agreed in principle in August to buy the pubs, and still keen to buy Macey's, Venables felt that while the agreement was not yet signed and sealed he had the moral right to claim them? After all he would end up paying £185,000 for them by November and some more in a few months' time.

It is a reasonable question to put forward but impossible to answer. Only Venables knows the answer and he is not telling. While he fulminates in his autobiography against Kirby and the alleged mess he made of Transatlantic Inns, the details of the various deals are not discussed, let alone the chronology of events in a way that would enable us to assess their wider impact on Venables' life.

Chapter 11

The disappearing dance-floor, and other matters

Venables was always going to be an unusual chief executive of a public company. In the early days of the take-over much was made of the fact that he had exchanged a track suit for a pin-striped one. But not only did he never wear a pin-striped suit, he must have been unique in being a chief executive who only rarely, if ever, attended the company's principal place of business, White Hart Lane.

Throughout his football life Venables had always seen the training ground as his office. As a player he went to the stadium on match days, as manager on the odd other days. As chief executive he did not vary this routine. In that first season, with Peter Shreeves in charge of the football side, Venables did not even feel the need to visit the training ground much either. Tony Berry, as chairman of the football club, often had to speak to him and found his style of dashing from meeting to meeting, and his approach, somewhat disorganised. Berry did not doubt Venables' capacity for hard work but he was never sure where he would find him. 'I believe that he visited the training ground only once or twice during each week. Indeed I am not sure where he was,' says Berry. With Venables seldom visiting White Hart Lane, Berry often had to go to Scribes, the Royal Lancaster or the Royal Garden to meet him.

Also Venables' attitude was, as Berry puts it, 'that the take-over had happened because of him, not because of Alan's money. Therefore he had some sort of pole position as a result of it. And he started doing things really off his own bat which he felt he was entitled to.'

During his two years in charge as chief executive the Board of the football club never met, except for an initial meeting just after Venables took over. With most but not all members of the football club also on the main Tottenham plc Board, Venables probably felt there was no need to hold any such meetings, but it did make for a situation where, on football matters, he made all the decisions which left Sugar panting after him to catch up with some of them. For example, Sugar was unaware that Venables would appoint Peter Shreeves as coach – or that his title was later changed to manager.

Venables had discussed with Berry the idea of appointing a coach, an idea that surprised Berry. 'But that's what you are for,' he said. Berry did dissuade him from appointing Don Howe, on the grounds that a man who had previously been a manager of Arsenal would not go down too well with the fans. However, Venables' choice of Shreeves was ironic because, when he came to Tottenham in 1987, his was the name suggested as assistant by Scholar, but Venables then had shown no interest.

Although Sugar was surprised not to be told about Shreeves' appointment, he did not much mind that. 'To be fair to Venables,' says Sugar, 'he did say at the beginning that he would be having a manager. But what he did say also was that he would spend all his time directing and helping the manager. Peter Shreeves was the man who was supposed to do the donkey work and he would be doing all the tactics and strategy. But that's not how it worked out. In that first year he hardly got involved and left everything, near enough one hundred per cent, to Shreeves.'

This began to change towards the end of the season and in quite a dramatic way. Then, with Shreeves increasingly under strain and Tottenham in some danger of relegation, Venables bought players that Shreeves did not want. Towards the end of the year Venables purchased Andy Gray, days after Shreeves had told Steve Coppell, Gray's manager at Crystal Palace, that there was no way he would want Gray at Tottenham. He had worked with him before and thought he was a problem. But Venables liked the player.

In the 1992–93 season Venables did go more regularly to the training ground but his priorities remained clear. In the large room at the training ground where he had his offices he had installed a fax machine. The pre-selected dialling numbers on the machine went: 1 Scribes, 2 Royal Garden, 3 Crystal, 4 Brown, 5 Sugar, 6 secretaries. Wherever he was Venables remained loyal to his old friends and to his old world.

The result of this was that, at White Hart Lane, John Brown was seen as the rising star of Tottenham from the moment the take-over was complete, except that he was a star who never wanted to shine in public. On the day Sugar and Venables had been presented as the dream team to the adoring supporters at White Hart Lane, the one person missing was Brown. 'Poor old John,' Hewer thought, 'pity him missing out on this day after all that he has done.' Of course Hewer did not know that Brown had every reason to shun the limelight.

'No, no, no,' Brown kept telling Sandy, 'I am a backroom boy.' When Berry inquired, Brown made his desire to remain out of the public glare very clear. But for a man who wanted to be in the shadows, the power he had at Tottenham in the new Venables regime was considerable.

This became evident once Brown returned from his family holiday in Jamaica. For, still in his pomp, he was ready to exercise what he saw as his right and proper role by Venables' side. Venables took over the office Scholar had as chairman, Brown moved into Venables' old office. Spurs staff were encouraged to call him 'general manager' although he was never formally given that title. Curiously he gave the impression of a man perpetually on the move. Whenever Hewer saw Brown he seemed to be carrying a couple of suits on a coat hanger, as though moving from one home to another. Hewer's remark, 'Moving, John?', became something of a joke between the two men. Brown was always ready with a smile and this only increased Hewer's liking for him.

With Brown being known as the general manager, the switchboard often referred to him as such and he signed letters, which described him as general manager, granting staff salary increases. Venables says in his autobiography that Brown 'worked alongside me as my personal assistant throughout my time as chief executive at Tottenham. He was under my control and direction and would never make decisions without checking with me first.' However, very few people at Tottenham knew he was a bankrupt, and most received the impression that he was more than his master's voice.

Everyone was soon made aware that, if they wanted to get to Terry they would first have to deal with Brown. Brown, states Sandy in an affidavit, behaved 'as if he owned the place. Everyone was led to believe that there was nothing Mr Brown did which did not have the express authority of Mr Venables. On every occasion when asked, and sometimes without asking, Mr Brown would state that Mr Venables' approval had been obtained.' Sandy has his doubts how often Venables was consulted, but with Brown given the right to hire and fire staff everyone was in awe of him.

Even in his second year as chief executive, when Venables visited the training ground more often, he was rarely there after 12.30pm, and he was happy to let Brown run the public company. Sandy, who found Venables' day 'somewhat unpredictable and varied', was told to copy all correspondence to Brown. Venables had two stamps with his signature. As time went by, Sandy got the impression that Brown had control of these and was the author of many of Venables' memoranda.

Under Scholar, Ian Gray was managing director but, now that Venables was chief executive, what role should he perform? In an early meeting with Gray, Venables said that Gray should add 'finance' in brackets after his title of managing director, clarifying that Gray was answerable to Venables. Gray appeared to agree, attended the first meeting of the new Board but then, much to Venables' surprise, he went off on a pre-arranged holiday.

This proved a mistake, for Brown had taken a dislike to him and to his assistant, a Miss Baily, and when in late July there was an informal meeting of the Tottenham Board at Scribes with Sugar, Venables, Berry and Crystal all present, Brown made his feelings very clear. Gray was being obstructive, wanted more money and clarification of his job title, and was he really worth £50,000? I can do the job better than that, declared Brown. Sugar, totally unaware of the complexities of Venables' business deals or anything about Brown, had no feelings either way on Gray. His initial view, encouraged by Sandy, was that Gray knew what he was talking about and he could remain there to monitor the financial situation. But with Brown denouncing him, and Sugar keen to start on the right foot with Venables, he agreed to tackle Gray and speak to him on his return from holiday.

The telephone conversation did not go very well. What exactly was said between the two men is not clear but at the end of it a somewhat bemused Sugar came and told Sandy, 'Ian Gray says he has been constructively dismissed'. Gray eventually decided to go to court claiming £223,106.80. The initial advice from Fuglers, the lawyers whom Venables had brought in to act for Tottenham, was that the claim could be resisted, although there was danger of litigation. Tottenham soon realised how great a danger. The matter dragged on for more than a year, and as late as October 1992 Venables was providing affidavits in connection with the case. Berry was asked to intercede and came back with a settlement. 'When I came back and said what Ian Gray wanted, it was far too much for Alan and for Terry, particularly Alan. So we found ourselves in court and we lost. We had to pay a lot more, three times more than what I offered him.'

The whole affair left a bitter taste in the mouth both for Venables and Sugar, each thinking the other could have handled it better. Sugar felt particularly sore about Crystal. But by then this was the least of the matters dividing Sugar and Venables.

One result of Gray's departure was there was now nobody left in management positions from the old Scholar regime and Brown had a virgin field in which to work. Sugar, too, had to rethink his strategy. Initially there had been no thought of bringing Sandy to Tottenham but with Gray gone he wanted his own man as finance director. This gave Venables the opportunity to propose that Crystal be appointed to the Board, as a sort of 'you have got your man in Sandy, I want mine in Crystal' bargain, although nothing was ever expressed quite so crudely. Sandy and Crystal's appointments were confirmed on 7 August 1991.

Brown had said he could do the financial job better than Ian Gray. However that may be, he was a lot more expensive. Tottenham paid him £6,500 a month. In addition, Brown could claim expenses each month of £450, the first expense payment being backdated to the start of his employment. In his first year Brown's fees plus expenses would cost over £80,000, more than £30,000 above Gray's basic salary. The two years 1991–93 would see Tottenham spend a total of £152,000 for Brown's services. Tottenham did not pay him directly but initially through a firm called Penfolds Consultants – which later became part of Gearbury Ltd, a company Brown said was managed by his wife and his then twenty-year-old son. In September 1994, at a public hearing on Brown's bankruptcy, Brown claimed that he lived on £100 a week paid to him by his wife.

Brown was not the only one who found the new Venables regime friendly. So did many of the players. Paul Stewart, wanting for family reasons to return north, was given a new contract at a much higher salary. Venables was particularly fond of Stewart. As manager, Venables had signed the letter which gave Stewart a very generous loan, £75,000, more than anyone else, and on which

Tottenham had to pay a lot of tax. Venables let Brown negotiate a new contract for Vinny Samways, a midfield player, which resulted in Samways getting more money than even his agent, Eric Hall, had demanded. Samways was later to say that one of the things he liked best was negotiating with Terry Venables, a remark that did not please Venables.

One of the most significant features of his take-over of Scribes West had been how quickly Venables' friends and associates moved in. Something similar happened after Venables took over Spurs. The people he had known for a long time gathered at the club. Terry was in charge and they wanted to be part of the action. 'Terry,' says Berry, 'used his own people for everything. He used his own contacts for travel trips. He brought in Brown, he brought in everyone he felt comfortable with around him. His daughter Tracey was on the marketing side. Then she got into shirt-sponsorship. He was certainly not running Tottenham as a public company should be run. But that only became apparent afterwards.'

Soon, too, Eric Hall became prominent at Spurs, getting his own car-parking space and being given the title Vice-President. Hall's relationship with Venables has the touch of gooey romance to which Barbara Cartland might perhaps do justice. Eric Hall's greeting card on his answerphone says 'Monster, monster'. The calling card that drew the attention of the Spurs accounting office was an invoice addressed to John Brown. This arrived just over two months after Venables had taken charge. Dated 29 August 1991, it seemed a simple enough invoice: a fee for £15,000 in relation to 'commercial and public relations activities'. The oddity was what these activities related to. They were meant to have been provided during the FA Cup Final. Hall was well known at Spurs and many of the club's players used him as an agent. But lest anyone misunderstood what this was, someone at Tottenham had written in hand, 'This is a club expense – nothing to do with players pool'. Venables signed the invoice and the account was paid.

Twelve days after the Hall invoice there was another invoice which, like the earlier Hall one, became the source of much hectic investigation later. This came from Frank McLintock Sports Management, was marked for the attention of Venables, and claimed to be 'in respect of commercial consultancy carried out on behalf of Tottenham Hotspur FC season 1990/91'. The consultancy was in relation to 'brand merchandising and the exploitation of all commercial opportunities at the club'. The invoice was numbered 0001 and, like Hall's, was paid.

At this stage no one thought twice about it, but two years later, when Tottenham began to look through their records, it struck them that both invoices were for work done before Venables had taken charge but paid after he had assumed control. So they approached Gray, Scholar, Berry and Douglas Alexiou, all of whom had been directors in the previous regime, and some other members of the old management team. None of them could remember any work that could have resulted in these payments. In court Venables' QC promised an explanation but it has never been forthcoming.

For all the controversy, there may well be a satisfactory explanation. Hall, after all, had been paid £25,000 in October 1990, an invoice addressed to Ian Gray as a two-year retainer for 'commercial and promotional activity including public relations on behalf of the club'. Hall, in an interview with the *People* (26 November 1995) claimed that the £25,000 payment was for negotiating a new five-year contract for David Howells. He also alleged that the wording of the invoice – which he admits was misleading – was at Scholar's behest for he had offered him the money in the first place. Scholar disputes this. 'Hall's version of who said what,' he says, 'is pure fantasy.'

There is a thin, but distinct, line between management of a private company and a public one. In a private company where there are no outside shareholders, the directors can treat a company's property as their own. A bottle of whisky bought on the company credit card can be taken home. A public company rightly demands higher standards. Venables behaved as if he owned Spurs, as if Tottenham Hotspur plc was his own private estate.

Venables later declared that, 'I never took as much as a bag of crisps from the social club'. Undoubtedly he did not, but Tottenham's accounts office became increasingly concerned with the expenses, some of which appeared to be his own personal expenses. They ranged from the serious to the trivial, one of them being quite farcical, what became known as the affair of the missing dance-floor.

Tottenham, as was only to be expected, had a suite named after its greatest manager, Bill Nicholson. The suite had a dance-floor that could be screwed down when dances were held there and was particularly popular with Tottenham fans. They were keen to hold their functions in a room which honoured the manager who had won the Double in 1960–61, the first club to achieve that feat this century. Some two months after Venables had taken over, White Hart Lane received a message: would the dance-floor kindly be taken to Scribes? Since Tottenham had a second dance-floor, this was adequate to meet most demands.

That is until Christmas 1992, when it was decided to hold the staff Christmas party there. With the only available dance-floor being used, Mike Rollo, the Tottenham commercial manager, started making enquiries about the other one and realised it was missing. He spoke to Brown, who told him to hire another. Sandy wondered what had happened to the old dance-floor. Rollo discovered it had gone to Scribes, but when he rang Scribes the answer came: it has been concreted to the floor. A replacement dance-floor had to be bought and Tottenham were quoted £1,500 for it.

Sandy tried to collect the money and in a tart memo Venables rebuked him. 'Your assertion that I should be charged for this invoice in the light of Scribes obtaining some old derelict dance-floor sections almost eighteen months ago is not acceptable. My understanding of what Scribes acquired was that it was, in any event, Letherby and Christopher's property and they no longer required these sections as they were unwilling to invest £3,000 in refurbishment and replacement. These parts were incompatible with the Spurs dance-floor. Would you please therefore process and pay the invoice.'

A week later the invoice was paid. Again Venables may be quite right. These were useless dance-floor sections, nobody wanted them – although before Venables nobody had thought of discarding them – and he just took them. If Tottenham was his own private business such matters would hardly have mattered but, in a public company, a chief executive, like Caesar's wife, must be above suspicion and Venables was behaving more like an imperial Caesar, with Brown and Crystal the commanders of his Praetorian guard.

In addition to his salary of £225,000 per annum Venables was entitled to the sort of perks common for chief executives: medical expenses, reimbursement of cost of telephones, travelling in connection with work, etc. However, tax laws are strict on what a person can claim in such situations. They must, as Section 198 of the Income Tax Act 1988 makes clear, be expenses 'wholly, exclusively and necessarily in performance of those duties'.

Venables, however, went further. Tottenham did not just reimburse him for telephone calls he made on Tottenham work, his home telephone bills were addressed to the club. Venables had three telephones listed at his home, all of them in his then girlfriend Yvette Bazire's name. And all of them were marked: 'Y. Bazire, c/o Accounts Department, Tottenham Hotspur Football Club, 748 High Road, Tottenham.'

From almost his first day as chief executive Venables took the attitude that if he wanted to travel he just asked Spurs Travel, a travel agency at 762 High Road, Tottenham, to book it and the accounts department to pay it. At his first Board meeting on 28 June, Venables had informed his fellow directors that those who became directors of Spurs Travel could get a 25% discount. Scholar and Gray had been directors of the travel company and Venables advised the members of the new Board: let us all become directors of Spurs Travel, we can also get this concession.

In theory, as long as he reimbursed Spurs for his travels there should have been no problem, but as Colin Sandy was soon to find out, the invoices, although relating to personal travel by Venables and his family, were addressed to Tottenham. The result, as Sandy later testified in a court affidavit, was, 'My accounts team have had to determine whether the invoices related to business or personal use (Mr Venables provided no assistance).' Attempts would be made to collect money from Venables but this was either 'difficult or only successful after some delay'.

The first of Venables' trips was on 29 July 1991, a month after he had taken over. He returned to his old hunting ground, Barcelona, staying at the Princess Sofia hotel. By August he was travelling again, this time to Amsterdam. October saw him back in Spain, this time Valencia where he also hired a car. November saw Venables on a trip to Porto. The purpose of his trip could not be doubted. Tottenham were playing Porto in the second leg of the European Cup Winners Cup, but it was striking that his entourage included not only his daughter, Tracey, who worked at Spurs, but also his father, Fred. It would not be the last time Tottenham paid for Fred Venables and, in time, medical expenses incurred by Venables' father-in-law and Venables' honeymoon and holiday expenses would all find their way to the accounts department at Tottenham.

However, at this stage, in the autumn of 1991, none of this

mattered. The Sugar camp was in the middle of its honeymoon with Venables. Sandy was still feeling the ecstasy he had experienced when he had driven through the gates for the first time after Sugar had taken over: 'I was a supporter, always have been. To drive through and to be told by the security man you have got car parking was like heaven. I cannot describe the feeling. Tottenham had won the Cup, we were in Europe, and we were all still in a euphoric state. Terry can be charming and captivating and it was wonderful to feel that glow.'

Sandy had also taken a liking to Scribes West. To mark Tottenham's return to Europe, the preliminary match against Sparkasse Stockerau of Austria had seen a dinner organised.

Scribes had won the contract to hold the dinner for the visiting team and officials. Sandy had been part of the Tottenham party and had often returned after that to Scribes, taking part in Terry's karaoke evening. 'Yes,' he recalls, 'it was nice, great atmosphere. Terry has the ability to make things happen. When he talks to you he can make you feel you are the most important person in the world, and I enjoyed it.'

That season, as Tottenham progressed to the quarter-final of the Cup Winners Cup, every European feast was held at Scribes. These were legitimate expenses paid for by Tottenham, although for some reason Venables in his autobiography says that Scribes charged much less for it than they really did. More significantly, and unnoticed until much later, the party that had been held at Scribes before the Cup Final, when Gascoigne had nearly been assaulted, also got through the Tottenham accounting system.

At this period Sugar seemed happy to let Venables call the shots. Occasionally he would pull him up. At the first Board meeting Venables had been very critical of the catering at Spurs and the way it was handled by Letherby and Christopher. 'I am sure I can do it much better,' he had said. Sugar smiled and then told the story of how a man had once approached him about making boxes. He offered to make them cheaper, Sugar accepted, but since Sugar knew nothing about boxes it ended up costing him a lot more. So let us leave it, Terry, Sugar advised, almost paternal in his concern, let the experts handle it. But he was soon to discover that Venables could not be that easily restrained.

Chapter 12

Partners, but unequal

With the 1991–92 season about to start, affairs at Tottenham were not very different from those under the former regime. The overdraft was still huge and the Midland was becoming increasingly restless. The bank was almost apoplectic when, in early August, they found that Tottenham were going to buy Gordon Durie from Chelsea. Sugar had assured the bank that, until Tottenham's finances were sorted out, no players would be bought. Now Tottenham was not only buying one, but paying a club record transfer fee of £2.2m. Some years earlier, before his move from his native Scotland, Durie had been offered to Tottenham for a fraction of the price. Then Tottenham had rejected him. There was another footballing curiosity about the deal. Just before signing Durie, Venables had been keen to sign Paul Parker, a right back at Queens Park Rangers. Parker went to Manchester United and suddenly Venables' choice of player switched from defender to attacker.

Sugar was on holiday in Italy when he received the call from Sandy.

'Terry wants a bank draft for £1.1m.' (Half the money for Durie due immediately.)

'What for?' asked Sugar. When Sandy explained, Sugar thought, 'That's a bit funny.'

However, when he rang Venables, he was quick to charm his way out of it.

'Don't worry,' said Venables, 'John has done the sums and we do need somebody up front.'

'Terry,' remonstrated Sugar, 'the bank will go mad. You know we promised them not to buy any new players, while we still owe them all this money.'

But Venables reassured Sugar he would speak to the Midland. Durie's purchase would be balanced by the sale of Lineker and another player. 'It is all a matter of timing, Alan,' he added. Sugar, reluctantly, agreed but he was soon to realise how wrong Venables could be on his timing. He was already getting used to hearing of Venables' moves long after they were made, sometimes from the press.

To be fair, this was how Venables behaved with everyone. Tony Berry knew as much about the Durie purchase as Sugar. 'I was told at a meeting that we needed some players. But in general terms, with Alan you had to be more precise: what, when, how and how much. So you have a situation where Terry said he needed someone of Durie's type. I think Durie's name was mentioned in early August in a general discussion. Alan was there but it possibly didn't mean much to him. He wouldn't know the name. It went through at a fairly expensive price really, more than we all thought, fairly quickly. Terry wanted to go ahead and do it. I suppose he felt he was the Managing Director now and that it was his decision to make. He could make all the decisions. As far as he was concerned, Sugar was really a non-executive.'

Sugar was even more mortified when he learnt that the Lineker deal, meant to balance Durie, was not quite what he had been led to expect. Sugar was under the impression that Lineker would be sold for £4m. When Sugar mentioned the figure to Venables, Venables laughed and said, 'No, no, the deal is worth £4m. to Gary but there's never been any question of receiving more than £1m. for him. He is thirty-one, you don't get that sort of money for a player of his age.'

To add insult to the sense of injury Sugar carried, the actual payment was just £850,000. When Venables, John Holmes, who was Lineker's agent, and Sugar met the Grampus 8 agent, Sugar asked for direct access to the people in Japan as he had had dealings with them during Amstrad work. The Grampus 8 agent did not agree and Sugar concluded in one of his affidavits that 'the reluctance of the Grampus 8 agent to allow me to negotiate directly with Japan was that the full value of what Grampus 8 was actually paying for Mr Lineker was not being disclosed.'

Venables has consistently denied that he ever told Sugar Lineker would fetch £4m. and he has been backed up in this by Holmes who, in an affidavit, described how the deal came about. In the early part of 1991 Holmes was approached by two Japanese organ-isations representing a Japanese football corporation which expressed interest in Lineker. The organisations represented Toyota and were backing Grampus 8. Lineker met Grampus 8 and Holmes informed Venables. Holmes disputes putting a figure on the transfer, certainly not £4m. Holmes also disagrees with Sugar's view that Grampus 8 would have paid a lot more. Venables, says Holmes, fought aggressively in favour of the deal and the deal could only take place with Lineker's consent. As for Sugar's alle-gation that the full amount had not been disclosed, Holmes finds it 'ludicrous and offensive to me and my client. The whole trans-action is above board and above reproach.'

But whatever the dispute about the price for Lineker, he was cer-tainly not sold according to the timetable Venables had promised the Midland. As Venables had pictured it to the bank it would be Durie in, Lineker out. The Lineker deal did not go through for sev-eral months after the Durie purchase and seriously damaged what little goodwill the new regime had built up with the Midland. Tottenham were in a very difficult position, the shares were still suspended, and with Venables having got his timing wrong, the club was indeed, in Sugar's words, 'in a very awkward position with the bank'.

The only thing that could get Tottenham out of it would be new money and this new money meant a rights issue. Anybody with even a limited knowledge of finance should have understood this. Indeed talk of a rights issue had dominated Tottenham Board meetings for over a year. The old Board had sought to have one and Sugar and Venables had promised such a rights issue in their mandatory cash offer, Rule 9, document. When the Tottenham Board met on 12 September it agreed that the rights issue was the way forward. Venables voted in favour, evidently willing to live with the fact that Sugar might end up with more shares than he had himself.

It is worth stressing that, right at the beginning of the so-called 'dream' marriage, at the stage when the Rule 9 document was being issued, and for all the talk of theirs being an equal partner-ship, Sugar was providing more money than Venables. Venables accepted that. The Rule 9 document mentioned that £7.5m. was available to invest in Tottenham, £2.7m. having been used to buy out Scholar and Bobroff, the remaining £4.8m. to pay off shareholders who decided to sell their shares. However, Edennote specified that there was a ceiling for this beyond which it could not go: £1.7m. Sugar would provide the rest of the money. So if all the shareholders had decided to ignore the advice and accept the offer, then, even as early as July 1991, Sugar would have ended up as the more powerful shareholder.

This is of importance because of the fuss which Venables made when, some months later, this is what happened as a result of the rights issue. For all Venables' subsequent protestations that Sugar used the rights issue to wrest control from him, right from the very early days of this partnership Venables accepted that he was the junior partner, except when it came to presenting his image to the media.

In theory a rights issue need not have adversely affected Venables, who was starting off with the same shareholding as Sugar. The problem was that nobody wanted to underwrite the issue. In a normal rights issue financial institutions are all too eager to act as underwriters. For them it is almost money for old rope. They agree to take up the shares if the existing shareholders do not, in return for which they are given a commission. In all but the most exceptional cases most issues 'get away', in other words the rights are taken up and the underwriters pocket their fee.

But Spurs was not a normal public company, it was a football club, its shares were still suspended, and nobody wished to underwrite the issue. Bernard Jolles of Ansbacher soon made this clear to Sugar. The only way the rights issue could proceed was if Sugar agreed to underwrite it himself. This would mean that, as Venables could not afford to take up all the shares that would be due to him, Sugar would have to buy his portion of the rights as well. In many ways Sugar would be really acting as the Sugar Daddy he had been pictured as at the time of the take-over.

At first it appears Venables did not quite understand how a rights issue worked, but as that realisation dawned on him – or was made to dawn by Brown? – he began to fear that it would turn the dream partnership into a nightmare. He knew Sugar's financial muscle would always outweigh his. So he began to come up with alternative ways in which Tottenham could raise money, the favoured Brown one being a mortgage on the stadium and a further increase of the overdraft. This scheme was one of the dafter proposals ever to emerge from any company. With base rates then at 10.5%, and Tottenham paying interest to Midland at 12.5%, the need to service an overdraft as well as the mortgage would mean that all the money which the club earned would go in paying the interest, and nothing would be left to make capital repayments, let alone profits. All Brown's scheme would have accomplished was to transfer the debt, when what Tottenham required was new money to cancel the debt. This is what the rights issue was meant to do.

By the autumn and with the bank pressing, Sugar decided to explain his thinking behind the rights issue. He recalls going to Scribes to meet Venables and Crystal. (As is typical of the Venables story, Venables does not agree with some of Sugar's recollections and the differences tend to become more pronounced when crucial events are recalled. As far as this meeting is concerned Venables believes it came later, sometime in November). Venables made it clear he could not take up all his rights and that would mean that Sugar would be a higher shareholder than he was. It clearly worried him. Venables wanted to explore other ways of getting money, therefore, particularly the mortgage option. Crystal wondered whether Sugar would be prepared to sign an agreement whereby he agreed not to vote against Venables. Since this would mean creating non-voting shares, it made no sense to Sugar. If he was going to put his money up, he had a right to the power the money gave him.

On 5 November 1991 Sugar went to see Midland. The previous day he wrote a memo to Brown and Sandy which neatly summarised Tottenham's financial options:

The prime objective is that the bank agrees to give us facilities until December 1992. If they give us those facilities we can then produce a working capital statement and get the re-listing of the shares back. I would suggest the following strategy is adopted. We have shown them our cash flow, which they will not be happy with. Our attitude should be that this cash flow is the worst case and things are going to be better, and that really we should be out of the woods by May of next year because two things will happen:

a) the Gascoigne money will definitely be in, either from Lazio, or from the insurance policy, and

b) a successful rights issue would have been received.

The Lazio/Gascoigne matter was complicated, of course, and Sugar wanted to hold out the rights issue as the carrot to bait the bank to agree to extend facilities until December 1992, which was vital to get the listing back. His memorandum continues:

One of their worries and concerns would be a rights issue, what would happen if the shares were not taken up. My immediate answer to that is we would be arranging an underwritten rights issue. Their next reply to that would be how can you be sure that you will get an underwriter. I would say if I cannot get normal commercial underwriters in the marketplace, that I personally (A. M. Sugar) will underwrite the rights issue. The ramifications of this statement need to be discussed deeply between Terry Venables and John Brown, because if in the worst case I do have to be the underwriter, it will mean that at the end of the rights issue I will end up with a much larger percentage of the company than Terry. Before I make such a suggestion to the bank, please clear this in your minds and if you are against it then I will not put it forward. However, I feel without putting such a proposal forward we are going to have a very tough meeting.

Sugar was keen to make sure that Venables both understood what he was proposing and was happy with it. In one of their previous decisions, when he had mentioned 'variable shareholdings', Venables had agreed to go along with it if it was 'for the benefit of the company'. In the memo Sugar emphasised that Brown should make the ramifications very clear to Venables: 'However, I would like John to point this matter out again to him clearly so that when we go into the meeting, if I have to use this trump card (which I do not want to) I can do it without having to worry at a later stage.'

If the worst came to worst and Sugar had to act as an underwriter, he was prepared at a later stage to arrange placings 'for me to get rid of some of those shares to other potential shareholders who could not have taken up the offer of the rights issue because they were not existing shareholders.'

Sugar heard nothing from Brown or Venables, and the next day Sugar and Sandy met the Midland Bank. They would have wanted Brown to come along but for the reasons we know, which Sugar and Sandy didn't then, he wouldn't come. The meeting proved very frosty.

In tones that were polite but icy Brian Clare and Fred Miller of Midland made no bones of their unhappiness with the way Venables had bought Durie and failed to balance it by the sale of Lineker. Surely, said Clare and Miller, this new Sugar-Venables team was no different from the old regime? The Midland men felt the old Board made promises that were not kept, so did this one, so what's new? In June Midland had allowed the take-over to go through in the hope things would change. But now six months later the borrowings still had not come down.

Sugar, required to wear the hairshirt, did so, apologising for Venables' optimistic forecasts and, in his view, the rash buying. 'I first apologised for the delay in the Lineker transaction and was embarrassed to have to explain why the Durie transaction had taken place, in their eyes, in blatant disregard of the assurances I had given at the completion meeting.' Sugar also painted a bleak picture of the mess he and Venables had inherited, how they were tightening up in all areas and reducing costs. True, Venables had told the bank the Durie purchase and Lineker sale would be back-to-back but while the Lineker sale was taking longer it would earn a lot of money for Tottenham. Sugar pleaded with the bank to continue to support the club and promised to 'put money into the business until the rights issue could raise enough money to reduce Tottenham's indebtedness'.

Clare was very doubtful that in Tottenham's present condition they could get a rights issue away. Who would underwrite it? Sugar thought that if he offered an extra 1% commission someone in the City might, but failing that, he was prepared to do it himself. But even if the rights issue did take place Sugar did not want to do it until February. By then the half-year results would show a profit and provide the right platform for a rights issue and at a price much higher than the one which might be possible in November. Sugar thought the rights issue would raise £7.5m. This would actually mean £4.5m. of new money, £3m. being conversion of the loans Sugar and Venables had already given into shares.

Clare, keen not to miss a trick, immediately suggested: 'Mr Sugar, while we are waiting for the rights issue perhaps you could deposit a cheque of £4.5m. now as a guarantee of that?'

Sugar's reply was brief, 'Of course not.' But he was prepared to give a letter saying there would be a rights issue by February, he would act as the underwriter if need be, and that a net sum of £4m. would enter the club somehow or other by April or May.

Midland were not entirely convinced but, after much discussion, agreed that Tottenham could still have an overdraft of £9.2m. By 30 May 1992 this would have come down to £5m. and by 30 June it had to be reduced to zero or £2m. However, Clare was quick to point out that agreeing to an overdraft of £9.2m. did not mean they could go out and buy new players. He had been deeply scarred by Venables' purchase of Durie and was determined to prevent a repeat. If the overdraft fell below £9.25m., say to £7m., then that did not mean Tottenham had £2.5m. for a new player.

What if we sold a player for £1m., could we buy another for £1m.? asked Sugar. Surely that could be an in-and-out transaction. No, said Clare, the bank would look at every case on its merit and it would want to see the money coming in first. In other words the player had to be sold before another could be bought. Midland were no longer prepared to buy promissory notes like the ones Venables had given. Clare also wanted Tottenham to delay payments on the Durie transfer to Chelsea. Sugar later suggested to Venables that perhaps there could be a delay even at the price of additional interest. Douglas Alexiou was asked to see if Ken Bates would agree to a delay. Bates, rightly, insisted on his due.

Midland, of course, were being handsomely paid for the overdraft, £40,000 a month, and Sugar got them to agree to take a one-time fee of £50,000. This, as Sandy's memo to the Tottenham Board says, 'was finally agreed after much bitching. On top of this Mr Sugar asked them to reconfirm that we would be charged no more than 2% above the base rate.'

On 7 November Sugar wrote to Fred Miller of Midland confirming the details of their meeting. Would the bank now give the 'comfort letter' so that Tottenham's share suspension could be lifted? But although the bank felt quite reassured by Sugar, he had not quite done the trick. Two weeks later Sugar was back at the bank. The club's position was now quite desperate. Getting the money from Gascoigne's sale was still being haggled over with Lazio and it needed someone to write out a large cheque. That someone could hardly be Venables, who was in any case still fighting the idea of a rights issue.

Venables returned to the theme of the mortgage on 21 November when, accompanied by Brown, he met Sugar at the Grosvenor House Hotel. Exactly six months earlier to the very day, and at the same place, their partnership had begun but now the mood was somewhat different. Brown recalls a quite heated meeting although Sugar remembers a polite, breakfast meeting where he found himself having to deflect arguments against a rights issue. But something had to give in Tottenham's search for money. Venables, egged on by Brown, still spoke of the mortgage route and although Sugar could see little sense in it he agreed that Brown should be allowed to explore it.

Sometime during the Grosvenor House meeting Brown took some sheets of paper and wrote out a letter from Venables to Sugar. The 'Dear Alan' letter read:

I confirm the context of our agreement this morning, concerning the refinancing of Tottenham.

We adopt a strategy as follows:

a) Gascoigne monies received from Lazio;

b) You provide a commercial mortgage/loan of £4m. against the stadium;

c) We secure bank overdraft facilities of £2m.;

d) If by 31 July 1992, you are unable to realise your mortgage/loan plus the Scholar loan, I will fully support a rights issue by Tottenham at your discretion.

Venables signed the letter, so did Sugar. Brown's recollection is that, as they were preparing to sign the letter, Sugar said, 'Trust me, even if I pick up all of the shares, we have a shareholders' agreement'. Sugar has no recall of the remark. Not that the mortgage plan was ever proceeded with. How successful Brown might have been in arranging it is doubtful. He made a cock-up with the broker even as he was getting started. The broker, Summit Finance, wanted a guaranteed up-front commission for organising such a mortgage. It was agreed that Sandy would sign the cheque and give it to Venables. Venables was to sign it only if Tottenham went ahead with the mortgage. Brown was meant to explain all this to Summit.

Then suddenly Sandy got a frantic call from the accounts department. Summit had the cheque and had asked for special clearance. Sandy put a stop on the cheque but Summit sued and, since a cheque represents a promise to pay, Tottenham had to pay £33,000. 'Terry was not supposed to have signed,' recalls Sandy, 'unless we went ahead. And even when the cheque was presented Brown was supposed to have explained all this to the mortgage broker. But he didn't and it was very incompetent.'

The fact is, as even the 'Dear Alan' letter implicitly accepted, there was no genuine alternative of mortgage lending from a third party. Even here Sugar would have to be the lender, in other words the money man, something both he and the bank were beginning to realise.

Within days of the Grosvenor House meeting the rights issue

was back to the top of the agenda. Sugar had gone to the meeting by no means certain that the rights issue could go ahead. However, soon after he returned to his Brentwood office Bernard Jolles of Ansbacher rang to say that a rights issue could be priced at £1.25 a share. This started Tottenham on the road to making a rights issue and on 6 December, three weeks after the Grosvenor House meeting which seemed to have put it on ice for six months, Tottenham announced their rights issue. Why did things change?

Venables' answer is simple. He consented to a rights issue because Sugar came back with a proposal for a new shareholders' agreement which removed 'my worries about him acquiring extra shares and using their voting powers to unseat me'. Venables and Brown have given two potentially damaging pieces of 'evidence' to support their version of events.

According to Brown, soon after Sugar's call with Jolles, he rang Brown, telling him the news and asking him to suggest a plan whereby Venables could live with the fact that Sugar would have a much larger shareholding. Brown says he rang back to propose that a) either Sugar sell his additional shares or b) since that would be difficult, he agree not to vote the additional shares. Brown even gave it a name, calling it the Sugar surplus shares.

Sugar, says Brown, agreed with b) and the next morning, 22 November, Brown rang Michael Salber of Kanter Jules Grangewoods and asked them to draft a shareholders' agreement along these lines.

Sugar denies there was any such contact with Brown, and there are oddities about the Brown version. The note of the telephone conversation with Kanter Jules, which was subsequently produced during the Sugar-Venables court battle, shows Brown saying that Sugar would end up with 47% and Venables with 23%. Yet this presupposed that the rights issue would be 6 shares for every 11 shares. However, at that stage that was only one of the ratios being considered.

Three days later Iac Koumi of Ansbacher sent a memo to Sandy, with copy to Brown, which showed that this was only one of three options being considered. The others were a 1 for 2 rights issue and one at 4 for 7, which was eventually accepted. So how was Brown so sure on 22 November that 6 for 11 would be the option that would be accepted? Could he accurately predict what was going to happen?

Venables in his autobiography argues that he accepted the rights issue because, at a meeting at Scribes on 26 November between himself, Crystal and Sugar, a shareholders' agreement was thrashed out. Just before the meeting Brown handed Crystal the draft shareholders' agreement which Kanter Jules Grangewoods had prepared. As Venables tells the story, Crystal presented this draft to Sugar who assured him that nothing would disturb the equal partnership that existed. And relying on his assurance Venables generously waived the Grosvenor House agreement of 21 November and the rights issue went ahead.

There is only one thing wrong with this version. Sugar does not agree that any such meeting took place. On the morning of that day he met a Robin Crossley of Video Plus and in the afternoon went to the offices of Sam Chisholm, head of Sky Television. He was, he says, never at Scribes that day.

Once the Sugar-Venables row reached the court, Venables made much of this alleged 26 November meeting. And the Venables camp did try to find people who could provide independent witness of such a meeting. In June 1993, with the High Court hearing the Sugar-Venables case, Paul Riviere took a call at about 8.30 in the morning from Crystal:

> I was then living in a hotel in the Cromwell Road – having lost all I had. Crystal said, 'Terry is in trouble. You have got to help.' He then asked me if I was able to swear an affidavit saying I had been at Scribes on 26 November 1991 and had seen Alan Sugar there. It was the last day of the court hearings and Crystal wanted me to go immediately to Venables' lawyers and swear the affidavit. I did not understand why Crystal was making such a request. I had no idea of the significance of the date, I was no longer involved, if anything I had been ostracised by the Venables camp, and in any event, I remembered I wasn't at Scribes on 26 November, so I could not provide the affidavit.

(Interestingly, the previous day, on 25 November 1991, Venables did have a meeting at Scribes with Paul Kirby, Colin Wright and John Brown where an agreement on Transatlantic Inns' future was signed by Kirby and Wright but not by Venables. When Venables' case against Kirby came to the courts in February 1996 the judge ruled that this agreement, which would have indemnified Venables against the NatWest guarantee, had not been concluded. Venables, by this time had, through an overdraft on Recall City, paid £185,000 into Transatlantic Inns.)

The date 26 November was to prove a crucial day in this story. Venables and Sugar may not agree on what happened but it was the day when Sugar knew that he would have to put money in if Midland were to be kept at bay. Both Brian Clare and Fred Miller of Midland had made it clear that unless the money became available or Sugar gave the bank £4m. come 31 December, they would have to 'review' Tottenham's overdraft. The Gascoigne transfer was still proving so difficult that it had led to the first spat between Sandy and Brown. Sandy was in the offices of Bernard Jolles when he heard that the bank was threatening to cut back the overdraft facilities. Sandy rang Brown, 'What's happening with the Gascoigne money, can't we hurry up this insurance thing?'

'Don't be such a naive prat,' retorted Brown, and for the first time the scales began to fall.

So on the day when Venables claims he and Crystal met Sugar, a meeting for which there is no evidence, we have firm evidence that Sugar wrote out a cheque to Tottenham for £4,056,000. On the same day Fred Miller of Midland wrote to Tottenham providing the letter setting out the basis for the agreement that Sugar and Sandy had sought. Now there was no point in delaying the rights issue and it was decided to proceed and instruct Ansbacher.

Jolles, in his rounds of the City seeking an underwriter, had met with polite laughter: the shares were suspended and this was a football club, so Sugar had to be the underwriter, helped by Frank Sinclair, the former director whose family company, Viewthorpe, had lent Tottenham £350,000 back in March and April 1990. However, Sugar as underwriter waived the usual commission.

The rights issue, launched on 6 December, confirmed that Sugar and Venables were now unequal partners. Venables did not take up the rights, just converting the £800,000 he had lent into shares. Sugar took up most of the rest and it meant he ended up with 48%, Venables with 23%.

Even after the rights issue had taken place Venables, along with Crystal and Brown, appears to have tried to get Sugar to agree to a shareholders' agreement. Venables says he did so before a football match; Brown claims to have attempted if after one (neither says which match); and since Crystal also says he did so, he probably did so at half-time in this same unspecified match. But the answer was the same: No, with Sugar, it seems, going a bit further when Brown approached him, by saying, 'Fuck off. I am sorting it out.'

Sugar denies saying any such thing or having any discussions with Venables, Brown or Crystal about a shareholders' agreement. His memory is that after the rights issue Brown brought a draft agreement to Sandy who told Sugar it was 'ludicrous'. Sugar agreed and instructed Sandy to tell Brown that there was no way he would agree to it. Sugar might have agreed not to buy or sell any shares he had in Tottenham without Venables' consent, provided he got a similar undertaking from Venables. No such agreement was ever made.

By the time Venables came to launch his court battles with Sugar, and write his autobiography, he would present the rights issue as the first real breach between them, the moment when Sugar made his bid for power. Sugar, says Venables, lured him with the promise of agreeing to a shareholders' agreement, then went back on his word and used his greater financial muscle to make Venables a minority shareholder. But there is little contemporary evidence to suggest that Venables was at all perturbed after the rights issue. If anything, the evidence is that he was happy, he had had the best of both worlds: Sugar had put the money in, Venables was still firmly in charge.

Some time after the rights issue Venables met Berry. Berry wondered if Venables realised that Sugar had nearly twice as many shares as he did? Yes, said Venables, he knew that but any worries he felt on that was more than made up by the fact that the rights issue had meant he was now sitting on a profit. He had bought at 75p, the rights issue had been priced at £1.25 and this meant he had improved the value of his shares without having done anything.

At the time of the take-over Sugar had talked of Tottenham shares being worth £2 and if the optimistic noises coming after the rights issue were confirmed then Venables could have sold half his shareholding, made a profit, and still be in charge of Tottenham. 'At that time,' recalls Berry, 'there was no suggestion whatsoever made to me by Mr Venables that there had been any discussion or agreement between Mr Sugar and him to the effect that there were to be any differential voting rights, so that Mr Sugar would not be able to take advantage of his greater shareholding for that purpose.' Indeed Venables had told Berry that Sugar would not agree to any such thing and Sugar confirmed this to Berry.

And if Venables, Crystal and Brown felt aggrieved then it does seem strange that on 28 November, the day the Tottenham Board approved the rights issue, Crystal proposed a resolution from the non-executive directors appreciating the work of the executive directors and Brown. Venables was pictured as both making money for himself and Spurs and at the heart of a successful partnership with Sugar.

In fact at this stage all the public noise from the Venables camp was that the situation could not be better. On 31 December the Spurs shares were relisted and the price, after climbing to £1.05, settled in at £1.00. The *Sun* ran a story declaring that Venables had made a 'cool £455,500 in four hours' which was presented as a sign of his cleverness. If Venables and his entourage had indeed begun to feel Sugar had a hidden agenda – as they have since said they did – they kept this feeling very much to themselves. On the contrary, Sugar began to feel that he was being treated as irrelevant to the whole show. The Venables camp behaved as if to say: We have had your money, Alan, now we don't need you. Sugar said in a later interview: 'I got the feeling that I was being treated with a little bit of contempt. Well, we have had your money and we really don't want you for anything else.' The Durie purchase had made Sugar doubt the way Venables operated. 'I was surprised pretty quickly into the relationship that a person would do things the way he did. He didn't feel he had to ask my permission for things such as large expenditure on a player like Durie. At the Charity Shield [the curtain raiser for the season when Tottenham, as Cup holders, played Arsenal, the champions, and drew 0–0], it was there is only one Alan Sugar, it was well done, Alan, and you are marvellous and all that. But thirty minutes into the match they had forgotten me and that was the end of Alan. They never mentioned my name again. It was all Terry, Terry, Terry, Terry.'

It began to hurt Sugar that, while he continued to heap praise on Venables and would continue to do so for nearly another two years, 'In all those years that I was associated with Terry Venables in all the press articles that have been written there was never any acknowledgement at all of me, as if I didn't exist, as if I wasn't there. He felt he had found some kind of rich lunatic, rich nutter who had put his money in. Just you sit over there and mind your business. Give him a few seats in the Directors' box and he'll be happy.'

Berry noticed Sugar's resentment: 'Alan did not know enough about football and I think he resented the fact that even the ground or the coaching staff, all the security people, they didn't really recognise Alan for what he was, as the Chairman, I think he resented that. They would never ask who he was but they wouldn't actually particularly acknowledge him. Alan also is quite shy really. If you speak to him, he'll speak back to you, but he would just walk past anybody and they took that the wrong way. I tried to tell him that that wasn't the way to go about it. Terry even tried to say to him, "if you speak to them, they'll speak to you". I think he was probably a bit irritated that he had actually put the money in to help Terry in the first instance. Not only did he put his own bit in, on the night of completion he put Terry's bit in as well. Alan as the majority shareholder stuck in a lot more money but it was seen as Terry's club. Understandably, he didn't like that.'

But if Sugar was being sensitive, couldn't Venables have done something to make him feel more welcome? 'All Terry had to do really,' says Berry, 'was to try and placate him a little bit. Terry doesn't give anything, ever, on anything. He is not a giver. He's a charmer but he won't give ground on anything because he will see it as a sign of weakness. He'll ask for advice and listen to it about certain things, but there are areas where he wouldn't particularly want to acknowledge Alan because it would be a sign of weakness for him.'

Sugar could never have hoped to match Venables in the image department but to an extent Sugar allowed Venables to make the image by saying from the beginning that he saw his investment as 'a business. And I was attracted to it as a business in the beginning. It was very, very important to me that it was going to be profitable and run correctly.'

Such an attitude has its dangers. English football is both highly romantic and deeply suspicious. It trains its most ferocious scepticism on people who, it feels, have come into the game to make money. The people it loves are those like Venables who are believed to be in love with the game and claim to be devoting their life to it. Sugar, as an outsider, would be accepted if he did a Jack Walker, the benefactor of Blackburn Rovers, and came with an open cheque book and declared he was doing it to fulfil a childhood fantasy. Such an approach would have been anathema to Sugar who did not even mind admitting that he was unaware of certain aspects of precious Tottenham history.

Just before the Charity Shield, on the very day Sandy and Crystal joined the Board, I interviewed Alan Sugar for an article in the *Sunday Times*. When I asked him if he had fallen in love with

Tottenham the year they won the Double – a landmark every Tottenham supporter knows – he asked, 'Double, was that something in the fifties?' He felt no qualms about showing such ignorance. Curiously, the remark was made in front of Crystal, who was introduced to me by Sugar and who later, and incorrectly, told me that Sugar was not pleased with the article.

Two years later, after Venables had broken with Sugar, the Sugar self-confessions played right into Venables' hands. Venables cited that interview to portray Sugar as a footballing ignoramus and helped to paint him as a man who had come into the game to make money when Sugar, while not in the Jack Walker class, has proved to be perhaps the greatest benefactor Tottenham has ever known.

However, with Sugar desperate not to display his generosity, if anything keen to portray himself as the exact opposite, his investment of £8.1m. by November 1991 hardly caused a ripple. The result, when Sugar and Venables split, was that Venables could convincingly portray the rights issue as a naked power play by Sugar to gain control of the club. In contrast his own attempt to fight the rights issue, fuelled by justifiable fears that he would lose control of Tottenham, was presented as one of high moral principle. Preposterous as this argument was, it showed how Venables could turn even the most hopeless case in his favour.

Sugar has since said that Venables deserves an Emmy for the way he manipulated the press. Perhaps; but the opportunity was provided by Sugar's tactics, which matched the self-confessed naiveté, or candour, he had displayed in rushing into the deal with Venables.

Chapter 13

The Lazio money

Nothing illustrated the Venables business style more vividly than the deal which finally took Gascoigne to Lazio. Such a transfer was always going to be difficult to effect, for when Venables' name was first linked to the take-over of Spurs, the expectation amongst the fans, and in the media, was that any Venables-fronted rescue would mean not only saving the club from the clutches of Maxwell but also keeping Gascoigne at Tottenham. By the time Sugar came on the scene, Venables knew there could be no alternative. At a meeting at Brentwood, when they finalised the terms for the take-over, Venables made his feelings about Gascoigne very plain. As Sandy recalls:

> Terry was there and John. We were all sitting in Alan's office round the long table he has. Alan had said Gascoigne had to be sold and Terry said, 'Yeh, yeh, I agree'. I was interested because, being a fan and having heard he wanted Gazza to stay, I wanted to know what Terry thought. Terry said he had become disillusioned with Gascoigne on the night before the Cup Final when he learnt that he had agreed terms with Lazio. 'That's when I gave up on him', said Terry. 'In any case you can't have £10 million of assets walking around on those legs, controlled by that brain. You never know what he is going to do.'

On 6 June the formal letter Sugar and Venables presented to the Tottenham Board outlining their offer was equally clear. 'The proposals are subject to completion of the sale of Mr Paul Gascoigne to Lazio for net proposals of not less than £4.5 million'. So far the story seems simple. Venables had started off by wanting to keep Gascoigne at Spurs but then realised he must bow to the inevitable and accept that saving Spurs and keeping Gascoigne was imposs-ible. The first problem starts here. A year after this 6 June letter Venables went to court to give evidence in the libel action brought by Scholar against the *Daily Mail* and said he had agreed to no such deal and that even after the take-over he was still interested in pre-venting the sale of Gascoigne.

Under cross-examination, furiously trying to distance himself from that letter, he said of the letter 'it was within my knowledge' but that he hadn't seen it, that the letter 'went with my knowledge but without any agreement', that there were two other letters fol-lowing that which said something else. He went on to tell the court that, despite what had been said in the letter, he was still con-vinced he could make Alan Sugar see the 'value for keeping Paul Gascoigne'. And while the club may have done a deal, 'I always believed that we could [undo the deal].'

However, by the time he came to write his autobiography, two years after that court appearance, it seems he had returned to the position he had outlined to Sandy and Sugar that day at their meeting in Brentwood. Once Lazio had confirmed an interest in Gascoigne, even after the Cup Final and his horrific injury, Venables knew he could not keep Gascoigne. 'Any hopes that I had harboured of keeping Paul at White Hart Lane evaporated.'

Of course, if consistency is the province of fools then Venables is the wisest of men. The point is that these different versions, each given in response to a different circumstance, means that it is very difficult to know what Venables is thinking at any particular time, and to understand the Gascoigne transfer we need to be sure of the lines which the principal actor was speaking as the events unfolded. Before the take-over the general impression was that his victory would mean Gascoigne staying at Tottenham, as Venables would undoubtedly have wished, all things being equal, to keep him. In June 1992, when giving evidence for his friend Jeff Powell and the *Daily Mail* against Scholar, it was understandable for Venables to suggest that, even after he took over Spurs, he was try-ing to keep Gascoigne at the club. By the time he came to write his autobiography, in 1994, his recollections were different. Now he wanted to answer *Panorama*'s allegations about the deal and the role of Gino Santin. Like Harold Wilson, the master of tactical political battles, Venables has always had an eye for the tabloid headlines. Unfortunately, the Gascoigne deal cannot be understood in such terms.

For a start it was a deal that should have died when Gascoigne got injured in the Cup Final. Other football deals have been scuppered for far less. But Lazio were still interested – which amazed Scholar – and Gianmarco Calleri, the Lazio man, turned up at Gascoigne's hospital with an early birthday present of a £7,000 wrist watch. By the time Venables and Sugar won Spurs, the previous regime of Nat Solomon had gone a long way towards reviving the Gascoigne deal. Gascoigne had already signed the relevant papers for the transfer. It was no longer a case of whether Gascoigne would go. As Venables, himself, says, 'all that remained in question was the price that Lazio would now be prepared to pay'. Even the price was not much in dispute, there was an offer on the table, albeit conditional. The real question was what hoops Tottenham would have to jump through to get its hands on the Lazio money and how long the money would take to reach the Midland Bank.

Gascoigne's injury meant that Lazio's price had dropped from £7.5m. to £4.8m. At one of the first Board meetings of the new regime Venables confirmed this. 'He advised the Board,' recalls Sugar, 'that the money on the table at the moment from Lazio was in the region of £4.8m. and the difficulties were in getting them to pay it considering that Gascoigne was at the time injured and like anybody with half a brain is not going to part with money unless they're sure that the goods they're buying are in first-class condition. That was our understanding of the situation.'

On 28 June Venables met Lazio at Hyde Park Hotel. Apart from Berry and Brown, Venables also took along his friend, Gino Santin, an Italian restaurant owner. At the meeting three figures were discussed: £6.7m. on the condition that Gascoigne was capable of playing 40 games in a season; £5.5m. with warranties about fitness; and £4.8m. where Lazio could have Gascoigne almost immediately. Venables wanted £6.7m., Lazio would not agree and the meeting ended with Venables, Berry and Santin arguing on the pavement outside the Hyde Park Hotel with Santin saying he could do better.

Venables, interviewed by *Dispatches* for their programme broadcast in September 1993, said that he used Santin because he would be useful in talking to the Italians. Santin had played football, acted as an agent, was well known in certain London society circles, but at the Hyde Park Hotel meeting he was merely helping Terry as an interpreter, no more.

Quite why Venables felt the need for an interpreter is not clear. In all the discussions with Lazio that the previous Board had organised there had been no interpreter because, as the agent Dennis Roach told me, 'Communications were made extremely easy because Lazio had a general manager, Mancini, who spoke perfect English, having originally worked for British Airways.'

Perhaps Venables felt more comfortable having his own Italian in the negotiations. In any case, within twelve days Santin had moved from translator to become a central figure in the transfer, taking over as agent. In his autobiography Venables says, 'Santin was originally involved purely as a translator in the Gascoigne transfer but when we reached the impasse I called him in to broker a deal.' According to Venables, until then Santin was working for nothing, now he said he wanted a fee and proper authorisation to act for Tottenham. Santin's association and the fee paid to him eventually led him to figure prominently in the two television documentaries, one of which, the *Panorama* one, also led to a successful libel action by Santin against the BBC. Santin collected £20,000 in damages in an out-of-court settlement where the BBC accepted that he had been libelled when it was falsely suggested he had done nothing to deserve his fee.

However, the most important question to ask is: why did Venables want to upgrade Santin from translator to agent for the deal? He already had an agent in Dennis Roach. He had been working on the deal for months, had found Lazio in the first place, finalised the deal on Gascoigne just before the Cup Final, and had been involved in reviving the negotiations which Venables inherited after the take-over. Why not carry on with him?

Venables gives no answer in his autobiography. In the section dealing with the transfer there is no mention of Roach. He pops up 82 pages later on page 399 and is presented as a double agent whom Venables, with Tottenham and football's interest at heart, is trying to get rid of but is thwarted by Sugar.

Let us follow through how Venables presents Roach's departure from the scene. He quotes what he calls a Spurs document: 'It would appear that Mr Roach has been on the payroll of the club, unknown to Mr Solomon and Mr Berry, having been paid £64,400 in the year ending 31 May 1991. It would also appear that Lazio may also be paying Mr Roach in connection with the Gascoigne sale – this is forbidden both under Football League and FIFA regulations.'

This sounds both damning and conclusive. What he does not say is that this Spurs document is part of the legal report which Jonathan Crystal had presented to the Board on 7 August 1991, the first meeting Crystal attended as director. As it happened, Crystal had got some of his facts slightly wrong. Roach had never been on the Tottenham payroll, his company had a retainer to provide first options on tours and the amount Crystal gave to the Board was not quite correct. Roach's company had earned no more than £5,000 to 31 May 1991, nor was he getting paid by Lazio from the deal. Roach learnt of the Crystal report years later, when it was leaked to the *People* newspaper, and took it up with Tottenham, whose lawyers, Herbert Smith, sent him a letter confirming that the wrong figures had been given to the Board.

In some ways more significant is that Venables' autobiography omits crucial details about Crystal's report on Roach. Before he gave the report to the Board on 7 August, Crystal had told the Board that on the Gascoigne deal Roach was claiming 1% on the first £7m., 1.5% on the excess, all of which would amount to £55,000 of which he had already received £10,000. The Board, impressed by what Crystal said, 'instructed Mr Crystal to continue his investigations into Mr Roach's involvement with the Club and to report to Mr Venables on an ongoing basis and the Board at the next meeting'. The clear impression from the minute is that Roach was a man Tottenham should be well rid of.

Another omission in Venables' autobiography concerns the contacts which he and Crystal had with Roach. We have to turn to Roach to find out what these contacts were. He says in a letter to me: 'Sometime in late July [1991] I was contacted by Jonathan Crystal who, having submitted my invoice to Tottenham Hotspur, informed me that Tottenham Hotspur would not be paying the invoice, the club were in serious financial problems and suggested a meeting with him and Venables. This meeting took place at the Royal Garden Hotel in August where both Venables and Crystal put heavy pressure on me. They again stated that Tottenham were not prepared to pay my invoice, I did not conclude the negotiations, the club were short of money etc, etc and offered me a settlement.'

The offer was £25,000 plus £2,500 for expenses. At one stage

Crystal sent a letter to Roach asking him to accept this in full and final settlement but, if the Gascoigne deal fell through, Roach would have to return £15,000. Roach indignantly rejected his final condition but reluctantly agreed to the original offer. He was not to know until much later that he would be replaced by Santin, let alone that Santin would be paid £200,000.

Venables does tell us Roach was paid off with a £27,500 payment but he puts the words 'paid off' in inverted commas, which seems to imply that Roach's contract was terminated not by himself and Crystal but by somebody else. The Tottenham Board were also told about the Roach payoff in Crystal's legal report at the meeting on 12 September and, since they had been previously told Roach could be due £55,000, they felt Crystal and Venables had done a good job.

It was after this, and at the same meeting, that the Board discussed Santin's fee. He wanted 5%, £275,000, and the Board wondered whether this could be reduced to £150,000. Here we have a mystery: why did the Board – and the meeting was attended by Solomon and Berry who were both members of the previous Board – not ask how come Roach's fee was 1–1.5% but Santin wants 5%? How is it Roach can be happy with a payoff of £27,500 but Santin is asking to be paid ten times that amount? These would have been valid questions to ask, and there could well have been valid answers, but it seems nobody at Board level asked these questions, or if they did they were not minuted.

Roach finds it extremely difficult to understand, 'particularly as members of the existing Board were aware of the amount of work that I put into the transfer and presumably were made aware of the amount of work that Santin had done'.

What was minuted certainly gives the impression that the payment to Roach was seen as an introduction fee, and indeed Crystal described it as such. The minutes do not record any discussion about Santin's role, merely his fee, so it is impossible to know what the Board were told about Santin's role or whether any explanation was asked as to how or even if Santin's role compared with that of Roach.

Another question arises: why, when Venables came to write his autobiography three years after these events, did he minimise his role in replacing Roach? And why does he make the charge that Tottenham, meaning Sugar, concealed Roach's involvement in the deal from the football authorities and that 'The wild allegations against Gino Santin have provided a convenient smokescreen to conceal this.'

Surely, if there was any concealment, then Venables, as chief executive, must be held responsible? While Crystal was presenting monthly legal reports the two of them had been charged by the Board to deal with Roach. Did not Crystal report to Venables on 'an ongoing basis' as the Board had directed? If not, what did Venables do about it? We do not know because Venables appears not to acknowledge in his autobiography that such questions exist.

Roach concludes, 'I have come to the conclusion that the smoke screen was in fact the reverse, so that my clear and professional involvement was blurred.'

This does not mean, of course, that there was anything wrong with the deal, nor is the fact that Venables should have hired Santin in this way any reflection on Santin. There can be little doubt that Santin is a well-regarded businessman and he had been involved in some high-profile football transfers. So let us try to follow how in this deal Santin came as translator and left as agent.

Soon after the Hyde Park Hotel meeting, where Santin appears for the first time as translator, Venables went on holiday to Bermuda. Before he did so he told Sugar he could get Olympic Marseille to pay £5.5m. for Gascoigne. Sugar says Venables even arranged for Len Lazarus, Gascoigne's financial adviser, to meet Olympic Marseille. This came as news to Mel Stein, Gascoigne's solicitor and agent, who said his client did not want to go to Marseille but was looking forward to Italy. Venables says he raised Marseille as a bait to get Lazio to pay more.

Venables also asked Sugar to keep an eye on the Gascoigne deal and on 5 July 1991 Sugar spoke to Lazio's general manager, Manzini. Sugar also sent a fax to Lazio indicating he wanted to finalise the whole deal by 10 July. 'The price, as far as I was going,' Sugar has since said, 'was cast in concrete. I was told and we were told very convincingly by Venables that the price was £4.8m.'

Sugar's discussions with Lazio were about devising a scheme whereby Tottenham could get this money even before Gascoigne's fitness had been proved. Then if Gascoigne failed there had to be mechanism for Lazio to have the money back. It was imperative for Tottenham to lay its hands on the Gascoigne money. Midland were becoming increasingly restless and Sugar felt that, if they could get the money even on a conditional basis, it would be of immense help in placating the bank and convincing them that the new Board at Tottenham really had abandoned the spendthrift ways of the old one.

Lazio seemed to be slow to respond and, on 8 July, Sugar faxed them again threatening to pull out unless Lazio met the terms. Sugar has since said this did not mean talks were breaking down but was part of his negotiating stance. He was sure the deal was going through.

The next day Venables rang from Bermuda. Venables says he had angry words and got Sugar to leave the negotiations to Santin. According to Sugar, whose memory of the call is vivid, this is the first time he had heard of Santin:

'Who is this bloke?' asked Sugar.

'Well,' said Venables, 'he's an Italian, he's done a lot of work, he knows football clubs, he's done a lot of transfers before, he knows Milan, he's a very well-known restaurateur and entrepreneur.'

Sugar, not mixing in such circles, had never heard his name.

'What's in it for this Santin guy?' asked Sugar.

'Look,' said Venables, 'you've come out of the computer business, you don't know anything about the football business. People who are associated with football do funny things. They, believe me, they do things just to be associated. I mean they like to be associated with the high life, with the Gascoignes and Tottenham and this stuff. You won't believe it, I know you're cynical, but people do things for no money. Jonathan, for example, is giving us all this legal advice and charging us nothing.'

Sugar remained sceptical but Venables reassured him that all that Santin might want was a drink. It was less than a month since Sugar had been in the football business and he naturally accepted that Venables knew more about it. Sugar is definite that, in the beginning, he was told by Venables that Santin did not want a fee.

The next day, 10 July 1991, Lazio faxed their commitment to buy Gascoigne along with their terms. But when Sugar rang Venables in Bermuda with this he was told to reject Lazio's request and contact Santin who was in Italy by this time. Sugar sent a fax along these lines to Lazio with a copy to Venables.

Santin's position as Tottenham's agent was formalised ten days later. On 20 July Sugar was at home when he had a call from Crystal who was at the Tottenham training ground. He had been speaking to Berry, who in turn had spoken to Venables, still in Bermuda. Lazio were trying to play one Tottenham director against another, said Crystal, and Venables now wanted Santin to deal with all the negotiations. Sugar, reassured that Venables would be back on Monday, agreed and Crystal dictated the fax. Sugar took it down by hand and sent it, with a copy to Venables in Bermuda. To Sugar it made sense to have someone like Santin. He would certainly be more comfortable with the language and Santin would know what made them tick but he still wondered what Santin wanted.

He was soon to discover. Within days of Venables' return he rang Sugar to tell him that Lazio was now offering £5.5m., with less stringent performance warranties, but that Santin wanted paying. According to Sugar, Venables said, 'You won't believe this, he wants 5%, £275,000'. Venables seemed to be as surprised by this demand of Santin as was Sugar. 'Yeh, I know,' he told Sugar and some other board members, 'it came to me as a shock also. I know I told you that, I mean he didn't tell me nothing. He didn't say anything to me, didn't say he wanted paying. He said nothing, he just came along, he said, I thought we were just going to give him a drink.'

Sugar sent a memo to Venables saying 5% was out of the question and this unexpected increase in the price of a drink resulted in a three-way conference on the phone between Sugar, Venables and Santin. 'I was speaking to this Gino for the first time myself personally,' says Sugar in an interview on the Diverse programme on Channel Four, 'and his attitude was very abrupt, he was like, "Don't even start, don't even discuss with me about I'm not getting a fee. Don't talk to me about all this bullshit," were his words. I mean, you know people do nothing for nothing basically, which is justified realistic comment, I suppose, but I said to Terry, "You told me that you didn't discuss the fee with him", and Venables said, "Well, I didn't". Gino starts to get aerated on the phone and basically says, "Look, this is nonsense. I can just as well walk away from this transaction and scupper the deal as to make it go through", and I could see this guy had a bit of a violent temper, typical Latin, and I said, "Look, Terry, you better sort it out with him".'

However, Sugar and Santin did not quite fall out. Sugar later met Santin while both were on holiday in Sardinia. Santin, aware Sugar was going to be there, asked Sugar to ring him when he got there. Sugar did, then, quite accidentally, they found themselves in the same restaurant and Santin sent over a bottle of champagne.

It is possible that in the beginning Santin may well have thought he was doing no more than a favour for a friend. But friendship appeared to have turned to business when he got involved in what he told Channel 4 was the second Gascoigne deal. Santin's argument is that Sugar's fax of 8 July 'agree or we go away' meant the deal was off. He had to restart the talks which would involve a great deal of his time and effort. It even cut into his holiday that summer in Italy and he spent so much time on the telephone his wife got quite annoyed. For Santin selling a 'broken' player like Gascoigne involved many twists and turns and he would tell Channel 4 that it was his intervention that was decisive. He would claim that the price of £4.8m. was increased, and arranged for Tottenham to play Lazio in two games. Venables would claim that Santin also helped in arranging the televising of the games.

Perhaps Santin did bring something special and Italian to the negotiations but did he actually increase the fee from £4.8m. to the eventual £5.5m.? In September 1993 both *Panorama* and Channel 4 were to unearth a document which questioned this assumption. This showed that at 12.26pm on 20 June 1991, little over twenty-four hours before Sugar and Venables completed their take-over, a fax arrived in the offices of Ashurst, Morris and Crisp, Tottenham's lawyers in this deal.

It was from Allen and Overy, lawyers for Lazio. It said: 'In view of difficulty in achieving satisfactory insurance arrangements, our client requires that the fitness test to be taken by the player will be along the lines of the draft perforance [sic] warranty which had previously been faxed to you. On this basis the client would be prepared to pay a price of £5.5m. I should be grateful if you could obtain your client's instructions on this proposal.'

The next day Sugar and Venables took over at Tottenham and it appears that this fax was mislaid. Scholar received a copy, so did Solomon, but despite this it did not surface until September 1993. Scholar had left for Monte Carlo the day after the fax was sent, then went on a world tour, but, at Crystal's request, he did send back his files relating to Tottenham. It was in these files in September 1993 that Tottenham found this fax. When the fax first surfaced there was some suggestion that it was a hoax, allegedly produced to embarrass Venables. But Lazio confirmed that the fax was genuine, Lazio finance director, Gian Carlo Gurra, saying so. A month before this fax was sent, Lazio had also agreed to play the two friendly matches against Tottenham and the television fee was the work more of Sugar and Sam Chisholm, head of Sky TV, striking a deal.

That Santin paid an important role in the negotiations cannot be denied. The Lazio managing director, Lionello Celon, would tell the Channel 4 programme, 'When Mr Santin got involved, many, many points were cleared up and this was an essential role played by Mr Santin during these negotiations. Without his involvement the whole thing could have fallen through: jeopardised and the whole transfer falling through, because of these misunderstandings. I'd say that from the point on where Mr Santin got involved, many things were cleared up and solved.'

But whether this justified the fee of £200,000, given that Roach's work only merited £27,500, is open to debate. Not that this can concern Santin. He had done a job and had got paid and like anybody wanted to get paid as much as he could – he can hardly be blamed for that. If Tottenham overpaid then the question must be directed at Tottenham and Venables. Why was Santin's work worth quite so much more than Roach's?

This question was never discussed at Board level, although the Board was not overjoyed by Santin's demands. Having asked Venables to settle at £150,000 they accepted that the best deal was £200,000. It was another year before Tottenham actually wrote out a cheque for Santin. There was nothing sinister in this delay since the transfer was conditional on Gascoigne being passed fit by the doctors, which they did on 1 June 1992.

However, there was an oddity about the payment to Santin. The invoice was dated 2 September 1992 and did not mention Santin's name. It required Tottenham to pay the money to a Post Office Box number in Zurich and came from a company called Anglo-European Market Research and Consulting. The invoice claimed that the work had also involved providing 'legal advice' on the transfer.

In retrospect the invoice appeared worse than it did at that time, although the misspelling of Gascoigne's name, spelt with C instead of G, and Lazio spelt Latio, was odd. Interestingly the invoice was not signed off by anybody at Tottenham, that is, it was not authorised for payment. 'Normally Terry would do that,' says Sandy, 'it was a football matter. But in this case it didn't happen. The invoice had come through the post and Brown delivered it to the accounts department, saying it was Gino Santin's invoice.'

Tottenham's procedure was that all cheques over £100,000 had to be signed by Sugar and Venables jointly but, with Venables not available, Sandy and Sugar signed. When Tottenham got their cheque back, it having been cleared through the Zurich company, they found that it had been signed on the back for cash guaranteed by Credit Suisse. However, all this did not concern Tottenham at that time. The payment may have been to a foreign firm, but how Santin arranged his affairs was his business. This was a legitimate payment for services rendered. It is only when the storm broke over Sugar and Venables that the invoice acquired a sinister meaning. Santin has told the *Daily Express*, 'I was advised by my accountant to set it up to allow me to do similar deals.'

The invoice attracted attention when the television producers handed Sugar the fax from Lazio of 20 June saying they were all along prepared to pay £5.5m. Then Sugar felt like a mug and thought his wife was right: sometimes I can't see beyond my nose. Venables, too, was surprised when shown the fax.

One reason why Santin's demands did not excite too much interest at the time was that, once the Gascoigne deal was done, everybody at Tottenham was concerned about getting the money from Lazio to a UK bank even before the medical. Venables had signed the main deal on 1 August 1991. Sandy signed a supplemental regarding procedures for medical examinations on 16 August. After that date the numerous Sugar-Venables discussions were not about what Santin was demanding but what was going to happen to the Lazio money. The Gascoigne medical was not due until 31 May 1992 and the energies of both Sugar and Venables were devoted to devising a plan whereby the money Lazio were prepared to pay could somehow be made available to Spurs before Gascoigne proved his fitness.

Between September 1991 when the Board first discussed Santin's fee, and September 1992, when the Board learnt that Santin had been paid his cheque for £200,000, there are two references in Board minutes to Santin's payment. But almost every Tottenham Board meeting had some discussion about Lazio and how to get the money released earlier. Lazio were reluctant to put the money in escrow in Midland, fearing that Midland might keep hold of the money even if Lazio should want to withdraw it. Eventually Lazio agreed that the money could go to Midland.

Sugar thought it might be possible to persuade Lazio to release the money earlier through a guarantee or a second charge on the stadium. Brown had an alternative plan: how about obtaining an insurance policy? When Venables brought this up at a Board meeting Sugar reacted sharply, 'You must be dreaming if you think you will find an insurance company that will do anything like this.'

The chances of finding such a policy deteriorated even further when, in the autumn of 1991, Gascoigne, emerging from a night-club in his native Newcastle, broke his kneecap. For Sugar this seemed to prove the impossibility of getting an insurance policy. What if he was injured again or run over by a bus? Would the insurance cover that?

Don't worry said Venables, leave it to me, and with Brown ferreting away he spent many weeks and months trying to figure out a policy which would persuade Lazio to release the money earlier. Sugar thought this was a waste of time and, even more, was running up the costs. Ashurst, Morris and Crisp were charging legal fees for examining the policies being produced at Venables' and Brown's prompting. At one time Sandy did see a policy that appeared to be acceptable but Ashurst, Morris and Crisp reported that it would not provide cast-iron guarantees. One policy with a premium of £475,000 was put forward by Venables, but it had so many provisions that it was practically worthless. Even then Venables was very keen to take on the policy and only a forceful Sugar intervention stopped him.

The Lazio money only arrived when Gascoigne had passed his fitness test, but the search for a policy made Sugar aware for the first time of 'Venables' lack of business acumen and lack of common sense'. Sugar, says Sandy, expected 'Terry as chief executive to be on top of his job. The Gascoigne affair became complicated because Terry was not. Maybe he had a hidden agenda, I don't know.' At this stage this was not yet a problem, but Sugar was beginning to think that Terry Venables was a good football coach but did not have the grasp of affairs other than football.

Chapter 14

The Scribes backlash

For the moment, however, nobody could question Venables' mastery of Spurs, but there now arose an unexpected problem at his other club, Scribes West. The shareholders who had put in a total of a million pounds before Venables took over began to show signs of rebellion.

The revolt was lead by Noel Botham, a former journalist who had turned to writing books. He had invested some £25,000. He had welcomed Venables' arrival at Scribes, seeing him as a breath of fresh air. He liked the man, found him entertaining and a desirable companion, but as Geoffrey Van-Hay and Gavin Hamilton left he began to get worried. His worries were increased by the realisation that the new Venables management did not seem to bring prosperity. On one occasion when dining at Scribes he was enthusiastically welcomed by a relieved maitre d'hotel who told him that it was specially nice to see him as he was the only paying customer that night – the rest in the packed dining-room were all on freebies.

Botham – and Riviere – had been asking Venables and Brown to convene a shareholders' meeting for some months but they had been fobbing him off. By December 1991 they had done nothing, neither had accounts been produced. Botham wrote to Venables calling for an emergency meeting of the shareholders. The meeting was put off until after Christmas and finally held in January 1992. Venables, Brown and Crystal were there but the meeting did little to placate Botham: 'The meeting was a joke, really. They had no minute books, no accounts. They scribbled some figures on a piece of paper saying they thought £100,000 was owed to suppliers. John Chalk, Brian Basham's wife and Vincent Isaacs were among the shareholders present. John Chalk got very angry and he said, "This is rubbish, gobbledegook. You are trying to pull the wool over our eyes and I am not going to stay here any more." He then walked out.'

The following month another meeting was held. This time Bryan Fugler was present as the lawyer along with Venables and Brown. Botham soon discovered that they had come with a strategy to deal with the existing shareholders of Scribes West:

They passed a paper round which said that there had been a meeting of the directors the previous year and this had issued new shares. The result of this share issue was that Venables and Isaacs owned more than 75% of Scribes, and all the other shareholders owned less than 25%. Brown said, 'As far as we are concerned, the rest of you can be in Scotland or somewhere with your shares'. The paper went round the table, the lawyer representing Associated Newspapers said, 'Well, that's it, we are finished'. I took the paper and said, 'This is rubbish. You can't do that. You can't treat shareholders like this. This piece of paper does not refer to the shares we are talking about. It refers to other shares. This does not give you any powers to issue new shares. You are trying to con us.'

Botham threatened to call a press conference and reveal what was going on, saying, 'I am going to put this company into liquidation.'

Venables, getting increasingly flustered, said, 'I'm not going to sit here and listen to all of this,' and got up and walked out. Brown followed him. But five minutes later they came back and suggested that there be an amicable resolution. Botham said, 'The only basis we can talk on is if you admit that this bit of paper had nothing to do with any shares being issued. You have no right to issue any voting shares.'

Venables agreed, saying, 'OK, we will stop this attempt.'

'You cannot issue shares,' said Botham, 'unless it has been ratified by the existing shareholders. No company can do that. The directors cannot just issue 10,000 or 20,000 or a million shares and deprive the existing shareholders unless the existing shareholders agree. That is company law. If you say there has been a directors' meeting about this, where is the minute book? Show me the minute book.'

This demand of Botham caused renewed consternation in the Venables camp. The answer came back that the minute book was not there. Botham reminded them, 'The law says the minute book should be at the registered premises of the company.'

At this stage, Botham thinks it was Fugler who said that the minute book was with the lawyers.

'Ring the lawyers,' demanded Botham.

Botham believes either Brown or Fugler went out and came back to say they did not have it but it could be in another one of their offices.

'In other words,' said Botham, 'you are not going to produce the minute book.'

'We can't,' said someone from the Venables camp.

'Well, you don't want to,' retorted Botham.

By this time there had been another revelation. Four of five sheets of paper had been circulated around the table as the new PR programme for Scribes West. Botham was not impressed. It was badly typed, and he was aghast when he realised it was a copy of a programme that had already been done. 'It turned out they had paid £40,000 for a copy of what we had. Vincent Isaacs, who knows a bit about PR, wanted to know who had done it. Fugler said it was done by his brother. Isaacs asked what PR work he had done. There was an embarrassed silence, and then Fugler said, "I can't remember".'

Botham, in a truculent mood, was determined to prevent what he felt was an attempt by 'Venables and Brown at grabbing the company'. They had to be bought out. Isaacs decided to stick with Venables, hoping to be able to influence him from the inside but the rest wanted to be paid out. 'In the end Terry agreed to pay us 16p in the pound,' Botham said. 'He was getting it cheap, but had I not intervened we would have got nothing. However, I insisted on a personal guarantee from Terry to back his promise to pay us.'

A few weeks later at the end of February or early in March there was another meeting. When Botham got to Scribes, however, there was no Venables, only Brown and no personal guarantee. 'I am not going to sign it,' said Botham, 'unless I get the personal guarantee.' 'Terry is at Tottenham,' said Brown. ' "Get in touch with him, I'm not leaving here until I get that personal guarantee." Then they faxed Terry's personal guarantee and we had our first cheque which was about 20% of the amount we were to get. The remaining 80% was to be paid a year later. And remember we were only getting 16p for every £1 we had invested.'

But as the year passed Botham waited in vain for his cheque. Eventually he rang Scribes and was told he would be paid. He was, the cheque arriving a day or two before the court case between Sugar and Venables opened in June 1993. The cheque drawn on Edennote bounced. Venables' lawyers were telling the court that Edennote was to be the vehicle of a plan to buy out Sugar which would cost millions but it seemed the company could not meet a payment of £2,600. The *Daily Mirror* heard about it and on the day Sugar-Venables went to court reprinted the bounced cheque. 'Terry certainly got his timing wrong,' says Botham. 'He eventually paid me but the tragedy of this was I liked the guy, genuinely liked him and enjoyed talking to him. He is very pleasant, very affable. I used to go to Scribes on a karaoke night and we would get up and sing, have quite a jolly evening. He went wrong by using Brown. Brown is an odious, unpleasant man.'

Now, in the spring of 1992, Brown's business methods were about to become unhinged as his secrets at last started tumbling out.

Chapter 15

Uneasy spring

On 15 January 1992 an Edennote cheque to Landhurst Leasing for £55,812.50 bounced. This was the interest due on the £1m. loan. Edennote had to pay bank charges on an unpaid item of £25 and Venables knew he had a problem. The payments to Landhurst had to be renegotiated.

On 3 February Venables, Brown, Ted Ball and Charles Dyer of Landhurst, and the racing driver Johnny Herbert met at Grosvenor House. It turned out to be a riotous meeting with bread rolls being thrown at one stage. Nevertheless a decision was arrived at. There would now be a second lease. The first lease had four payments, the second one provided for a pause. In return Edennote made a payment of £10,000, in cash. On 24 February Brown wrote to Landhurst enclosing the cash payment and asking for a copy of the letter to be signed as acknowledgement. The money was never deposited in Landhurst Leasing's account and next to the Edennote working papers a note would duly appear, 'what for?' No answer is recorded and the payment remains a mystery. Venables acknowledges that such a payment was made but denies he signed the second lease, or for that matter the first, claiming the signature was forged. This was his defence when *Panorama* made the allegation and later when the DTI began investigating it.

All this activity with Landhurst made Brown, already valuable, now virtually indispensable; he knew too many secrets, he could not be tossed away – however dubious his record. The problem was that his record was about to be exposed to Sugar and to the Tottenham Board.

Venables had, of course, told Sugar about Brown's bankruptcy. It is not known exactly when he did that. He says he told Sugar within twenty-four hours of finding out in the first week of August 1991. Given that the fax about Brown's bankruptcy arrived at Scribes on 30 July, it is hard to see how he could have told Sugar within twenty-four hours, and Sugar's memory is that he was told several months later. But whenever Sugar learned about Brown he did not make anything of it. Venables presented it as the sort of mistake any man can make, once. Nothing was said of his remarkable list of business failures, nor the impact Brown had had at Scribes or on Riviere. Sugar, not knowing the history of the man, felt that one bankruptcy could be a misfortune and did not see it as a hanging offence. However, it was clear that Brown could not now be appointed to the Tottenham Board, of which there had been some talk.

Apart from Sugar, not many at Tottenham knew Brown was a bankrupt and his stock remained high. It was only after the rights issue and the wounds this inflicted on Colin Sandy that the situation began to change. In helping to get rid of Ian Gray, Venables and Brown may have felt the last obstacles were removed. But now Sandy was to turn into a major roadblock on the way to complete control of the accounts. Sandy had continued to have two jobs, retaining his finance directorship at Amsprop, a private Sugar company, while being finance director of Tottenham. This meant dividing his time between Brentwood and White Hart Lane and clocking up forty hours or more a week on Tottenham work.

For Venables and Brown, Sandy was too much Sugar's man, too much their enemy. Realising that he had no accounting qualifications they had begun to take a condescending attitude towards him. Venables spoke to Berry about Sandy: are you impressed by him? I am not. Berry agreed, he didn't think much of him, he seemed to be cautious, he was not very experienced. But Berry felt he might grow into it. Venables was convinced he would not.

Venables mistook his man. Sandy, with his ginger hair and a certain scholastic look, can be easily caricatured but there is both pride and professional determination in him. He may not have been a qualified accountant but he was a well-qualified tax expert and had worked as an investigator specialising in tax for Touche Ross. He had been 'at the coal face' and, as Brown sought to extend his domain and became more obstreperous, Sandy began to see Brown in a different light. There was less talk now about how professional John could be, more of how difficult Brown was.

Sandy, as the finance director and member of the Board, saw himself as the man who was responsible for any money coming in and going out of the club. If money was involved Sandy wanted to make sure that it was being handled properly. In theory this should have caused no problem with Brown, who apparently answered to Venables.

But Brown saw his domain in such extensive terms that it threatened to leave Sandy with almost nothing to do. Unlike most other football clubs Tottenham was not only a club but also a public company. The public company wholly owned the football club. Brown felt that everything that happened in the football club, including accounts, should be his responsibility. He persuaded Venables that this was the only way Venables could control things, and tried to impose this on Sandy. But since the public company's main, if not only, business was football, for Sandy to accept this would be reducing himself to the man who just consolidated the accounts and prepared them for presentation to the outside world. In other words, despite his title as financial director, he would have no real control over the finances of the football club.

In January 1992 Brown called a meeting to discuss his plan. Sandy readily agreed to attend, and alongside him were the various accountants of the club. Brown did not mince his words. Tom Allen was responsible for the club's accounts. Brown told Sandy that he would have to give Allen a list of things he wanted him to do. As long as he does what is on the list fine, but if you want him to do anything outside this list then he will have to get my permission, said Brown. Sandy could hardly believe his ears. He had never heard of a finance director and Board member of a public company not being able to tell an accountant supposedly working for him what he could do, that he had to seek someone else's approval.

'There is no way I am going to accept this proposal,' retorted Sandy.

The meeting had been held on a Thursday. On the Saturday, as Sandy and Brown met during a home match, Brown returned to the theme and Sandy was just as forceful.

'You will be sorry,' warned Brown, 'I am not going to leave this. I shall take it up with Alan and Terry.'

'Do what you like,' said Sandy.

The warning shots had been fired. Battle between Sandy and Brown was now joined.

Sandy decided to do some digging into Brown's background and contacted an old colleague of his at Touche Ross to make some enquiries. Sandy discovered that not only was Brown a bankrupt but he had been associated with a number of companies. While Sandy was digging into Brown's past, Brown had his own target: the merchandising division. With a turnover of £2m. this was an important division of Tottenham plc. Edward Freedman was the merchandising manager and by all accounts he had done a good job. However, the Venables camp was distrustful of Freedman because he was a Scholar appointee, one of the few from the old regime still left in a powerful position. Freedman was also a friend of Scholar and the Venables camp suspected he kept in touch with the king over the water in Monte Carlo.

These suspicions turned into real distaste when they learnt that Freedman was going to arrange tickets for a European Cup Winners Cup match for Scholar. In March 1992 Freedman suddenly found that Mike Pay had been appointed as sales manager. He had not been consulted and Pay, Freedman felt, was not up to the job. His arrival left little for Freedman to do. On 18 March a formal meeting took place between Freedman and Brown with two other Tottenham staff members present, Janice O'Callaghan and Audrey Zolnierowicz, who acted as Brown's assistant.

Brown made minutes of the meeting and, what is striking in them is how Brown saw himself as the man in charge of Tottenham. The minutes note Brown talking of 'the company was prepared to put in resources to develop merchandising and achieve the business plan'. Nobody reading the minute can be unaware of Brown's commanding role. The meeting achieved little, however. Brown denied there was any intention of removing Freedman, but within weeks Freedman had gone, considering himself to have been constructively dismissed. It was a grievous loss for Tottenham. He went to Manchester United where he effected a merchandising revolution, pushing up its merchandising turnover from under £2m. to its present £24m.

Venables later gave contradictory explanations of why Freedman left. He told David Dein of Arsenal that Freedman had left under a cloud, yet when he came to file his wrongful dismissal case he stated that Freedman left because he would not receive a

£10,000 bonus. Only after this, he says, was Mike Pay engaged. How he could make such a statement in the face of Brown's minutes of 18 March 1992 is a mystery. As it happens, the minutes record Brown discussing the bonus of £10,000. He was prepared to pay £5,000 immediately but provided Freedman agreed to commit himself long-term to Tottenham. Freedman clearly could not.

Freedman's departure was to produce a little vignette of its own. Inevitably in such situations Crystal, as the in-house lawyer, was called in. Sugar wanted him and Brown to sort it out. After one evening match Crystal walked into the VIP lounge at Tottenham and assured the Board, and in particular Sugar, that they had dealt with the matter and Freedman was no longer a problem. But soon Sugar discovered that the matter had not been properly dealt with. Freedman came back with a demand for £20,000. He had to be paid a substantial sum to drop his threatened legal action.

Freedman's departure sounded the alarm bells for Sandy. He already knew Brown was a bankrupt who had dealt with a number of companies. Now he initiated enquiries with a firm called Pridie Brewster into Brown's financial background. With Freedman gone, Sandy had nobody on the merchandising side who could tell him what was going on except for Mark Burton, the accountant. But Brown had designs on him as well. This became clear on Easter Saturday, 18 April. The occasion was another home match.

Home matches that season were not something to look forward to for Tottenham. Shreeves had always been good at producing sides that could win away from home. In 1984–85 he had taken Tottenham close to the championship but lost to Everton because Tottenham could not win at home. Now Tottenham were in the middle of establishing their worst ever home record and that Easter Saturday, with Wimbledon as the visitors who provided both muscular and difficult opposition, few looked forward to any relief from a depressing series of defeats and draws.

But to the delight of the Tottenham fans the team suddenly came alive, Lineker scored twice, Hendry added another and Tottenham won 3–2 in a pulsating game. During the match, as Sandy relaxed in the Directors' box, relishing this rare home triumph, only the third in almost four months, Brown leaned over and said, 'Could we talk about Mark Burton after the match?'

At the end of the match Sandy and Brown walked through the Oak Room, heavy with memories of previous Tottenham triumphs, to the VIP Room. Sandy had no sooner entered than Brown pulled him towards the loo near the entrance to the room and said, 'I am very displeased with Burton. He has been very disloyal.'

'What you mean?' asked Sandy.

'He has been slagging me and Tottenham off. I can't allow that sort of behaviour.'

'What are you talking about?' asked Sandy.

Brown explained that Tracey Venables had overheard a conversation that Burton had had with Peter Bensted, the man who ran the Spurs shop in Birmingham. Burton had spoken scathingly about the 'big man', meaning Brown, and how fed up he was with his behaviour.

'So I am afraid he has to go and I have summarily dismissed him,' declared Brown.

'You what!' exclaimed Sandy.

'Indeed I have changed the locks in his office and told the security people that he is not to be allowed in. He has gone.'

Sandy could barely contain himself. 'What do you think you are doing? He works for me, not you, and you have no right to take such a decision. I am going to pursue this and I am not going to let it rest.'

That weekend Sandy worked feverishly in the study of his home trying to determine what had happened and giving vent to his outraged feelings. Faxes flew thick and fast from the study, including several to Sugar who was holidaying in his Florida retreat. All this activity finally brought Venables into the picture. On Easter Monday evening Venables rang Sandy: 'What are you doing sending all these faxes?' After Sandy had explained what Brown had done Venables said, 'I want to see you and John in my office tomorrow.' As it happened the meeting took place the day after, on the Wednesday, and Sandy demanded that Tracey Venables and the others produce statements to describe exactly what Burton was supposed to have said that could merit such a drastic punishment. Venables promised to look into the matter and give what he called his executive decision. But the statements were not forthcoming and a day later Venables confirmed Brown's decision.

By this time Pridie Brewster, urged on by Sandy, had produced their report on Brown. It was a damning document. His bankruptcy was no accident. This was a man who courted financial disaster. The eleven-page report was a terrifying exposé of

Brown's financial incompetence, one that showed Brown as having been a director of 43 companies, 16 of which were in receiverships, 8 in liquidation and 15 struck off. Company after company was sent to its grave. In two cases assets had been transferred prior to the appointment of a receiver.

On 23 April Sandy faxed Sugar with the letter from Pridie Brewster which had accompanied their detailed report. The details were so copious that Sandy and his staff spent the weekend collating it. Sugar could hardly believe what he was reading. When Venables told Sugar about Brown's bankruptcy he had treated it as an accident. But this was no accident. As it happened Berry was also on holiday in Florida at that time and Sugar faxed him a copy of the letter. Berry, who quite liked Brown, was aghast. Brown was someone he had come across in the past, he didn't know much about him and promised Sugar that he would find out. In fact Brown had worked for Michael Ashcroft (Brown had told Riviere it was the other way round), a great friend of Berry. Ashcroft painted a bleak picture of Brown: incompetent, keep well out of reach of him. Clearly Brown had to go and Sugar told Sandy to go and see Crystal.

Sandy recalls the occasion vividly: 'I went to see Crystal at his chambers in the Cloisters. While I was there showing him the files Alan rang. Alan was screaming down the phone. Although Crystal had the receiver pressed to his ear I could hear Alan saying, "Get rid of him. I want him fucking out of there, now." Crystal was saying, "I've just got the file. We will get to the bottom of this. But you must realise, Alan, it is a very difficult time for Terry. We will need to look into this carefully." Alan was saying, "I don't care, just get rid of him. We can't have a man like that at Tottenham." '

The contents of the file may have come as a surprise to Crystal but the fact that Brown was a bankrupt and that he and his business methods caused ruin should have come as no surprise, not after what Riviere had told him almost a year earlier. Sugar looked to Crystal to sort it out. But what Crystal appears to have done is to show the file to Brown. This meant that Brown now knew that Sandy was his public enemy number one, and the relationship between the two men, already bad, deteriorated further.

Sugar returned from Florida to take up the matter with Venables but the idea of being without Brown was unthinkable for Venables, particularly at that moment. Apart from the Landhurst Leasing problems, some of his other business problems had begun to catch up with him. Transatlantic Inns had gone under, failure to pay rates to Westminster Council being the last straw. And Grand Metropolitan were taking him to court over a dispute about the control of the Cock and Magpie pub, and unpaid rent at Macey's, the wine bar. Inntrepreneur Estate Ltd, a Grand Met offshoot, had been upset by the way Venables had transferred tenancy to Recall City. They were also claiming that Venables owed £45,000 in unpaid rent on Macey's. This was not the time to lose John Brown.

So as the season ended Brown was still at Tottenham. However, his bankruptcy could no longer be kept secret from the outside world. On 31 May the *Independent on Sunday* ran a story revealing that Brown was a bankrupt. The article did not give details of his business disasters and the Pridie Brewster report was still a closely guarded secret.

Nick Gilbert, who wrote the story for the newspaper, would have liked a reaction from Venables. He contacted Nick Hewer, Sugar's PR man, who in turn asked Venables. Venables told Hewer he was not interested in talking to Gilbert and the very fact that such a story was emerging raised his hackles. Venables was keen to find the mole and soon stories were circulating in the Venables camp that Riviere had leaked it. In fact he had not, but the rumours became so persistent that Riviere was forced to get Rod Dadak to write to Fugler denying he had any hand in the story. Some in the Venables camp even suspected Hewer. He had not leaked it and tried his best to defend Brown. He told Gilbert that if the Tottenham switchboard had described him as general manager they must have made a mistake. Brown did not have anything to do with finance. 'He plays a role in things like personnel, property and merchandising.' And Hewer could not let on about Brown's business record or that it had led to the dangerous Brown-Sandy stand-off, because he had yet to be told about those revelations.

Here again Sugar showed a certain naiveté. Had he really wanted to undermine Venables he could have fed Gilbert or some other journalist Pridie Brewster's report. Such a public disclosure could have had a devastating impact. But at this stage Sugar still believed he could work with Venables and, in any event, he had not mastered the media game as well as Venables had.

Curiously, Gilbert's revelations did not lead to anybody investigating Brown. The fact that a bankrupt was close to power at Tottenham and had even been involved in the Gascoigne transfer was brushed aside as 'just one of those things'. One of the reasons for this was that the story emerged at the moment when the football world was still recovering from the way in which Sky Television had won the right to televise the new Premier League, a decision heavily influenced by Sugar and where the Sugar-Venables partnership was seen to be leading Tottenham in a new direction.

Just two weeks before Brown was 'outed', the Premier League had met in the Royal Lancaster Hotel, to discuss television rights. ITV had been showing live televised football since the late 1980s and wanted to do the same with the Premier League. Sky, keen to muscle in, saw the new League as a golden chance for it to sell more dishes on the back of live football. Sam Chisholm had rung Sugar and asked: 'Who do you think I should talk to about television rights for the Premier League?' 'Talk to Terry,' advised Sugar.

Soon Chisholm, Sugar, Crystal and Venables met at Scribes West and the meeting could not have been more amicable. The simmering rows at Tottenham remained firmly hidden. The talk was about the new league and how much more money television could provide. Sky's concern was that ITV had secured its exclusive rights to live television by its close connection with the so-called big five of soccer: Arsenal, Manchester United, Liverpool, Everton and Tottenham. Could Chisholm tempt Spurs to defect? He knew that many of the smaller clubs, like Wimbledon, were unhappy with ITV; if Spurs came on board it could break ITV's hold. Sugar was clearly sympathetic to the Sky proposal.

Not that Sugar was Sky's only advocate. Rupert Murdoch also intervened and promoted his company's offer by meeting with some of the football club chairmen including Ron Noades and Ken Bates. However, after the Scribes meeting Sugar appears to have played little or no part in the negotiations except to agree to attend the Royal Lancaster Hotel meeting on 18 May.

There, just as the football club chairmen were preparing to enter the room, ITV put in a final bid seeking to trump Sky. Sugar decided to ring Chisholm and tell him about the offer. Sugar, Venables and Crystal repaired to a telephone booth outside the conference hall. And, while Crystal held open the ITV letter, Sugar read it out and then barked at Chisholm, 'Blow them out of the water'.

During the meeting David Dein tried to prevent Sugar helping Sky to blow ITV out. Sugar had readily confessed he would benefit from the Sky deal (soccer for Sky would mean more satellite dish sales for Amstrad) and this represented a conflict of interest. Sugar offered to abstain, but the other chairmen accepted he could vote, and Sky did blow ITV out of the water.

That weekend newspapers debated the morality of the whole affair and its effect on television and sports. Nobody watching that scene would have had any suspicions of the friction at Spurs. Crystal seemed as enthusiastic about Sky as Sugar and ended the meeting being rebuked by Peter Robinson of Liverpool. After the vote Crystal warned the clubs not to violate the agreement and make individual deals. This was intended as a reference to Liverpool which, during that season's European ties, had gone with the BBC as against the preference for ITV shown by other clubs. Robinson, incensed by this, said, 'I shall not have a director of Tottenham Hotspur lecture Liverpool Football Club about ethics'.

Some observers did detect a touch of friction between Sugar and Venables. The meeting had begun with Venables sitting in the front seat, Sugar behind him. However, once the discussions started on the television contract Sugar moved to the front seat. Venables had received disturbing words from the training ground about Gascoigne's fitness and rushed there. Sugar then proceeded to hold something like a seminar on television and what it had to offer. As Sugar had rarely, if ever, attended football meetings, did his public switch of chairs suggest he had taken charge?

As we know, it did not. Indeed the last weeks of the 1991–92 season had confirmed Venables' dominance at Tottenham. True, on the field Spurs had done little that season, but then the fans had expected little. Gascoigne was gone, Lineker was going and while relegation was a threat almost until April, when a 3–0 home victory over West Ham eased the fears, there had been some encouraging Cup runs: semi-final of the League Cup, third round of the Cup Winners Cup, which meant that, until the beginning of March, the fans had something to cheer about.

For much of the season Venables had been insulated from the playing side. Tony Berry had wondered if Venables' desire to appoint a manager was to make sure he was not vulnerable to the vagaries of form on the football field. So it turned out to be. The fans' discontent was targeted at Shreeves, Venables confessed that he might have made a mistake in appointing him and, for the second time in his Spurs career, Shreeves was sacked, the pay-off costing £15,000. News of Shreeves' sacking was revealed by Joe

Lovejoy in the *Independent*, and this did not please Venables who, for a day or two, hunted unsuccessfully for the mole.

Venables toyed with the idea of appointing David Webb, an old friend and a man with whom he had done business. As manager, Venables had bought players from Southend when Webb was manager there. More than three years later Webb revealed how he had been kept waiting at Scribes one evening for almost four hours before Venables decided not to give him the job. Webb was so upset he thought of hitting Venables, and went to consult his friend Jack Petchey, chairman of Watford. Then Venables, as if in compensation, asked him to do some scouting.

Soon an invoice from David Webb Management Ltd was winging its way to Tottenham. Dated 1 August 1992, it was for £10,000 and said: 'Scouting Duties . . . Europe (Portugal) (Sweden). To and including games in European Nations Finals.' Webb's use of the words European Nations Finals was odd since that term had gone out of use many years before; it was now known as the European Championships. The invoice was paid.

How serious Venables was about appointing Webb we do not know. Towards the end of the Shreeves regime he had himself taken a more active role in team management. He had bought Andy Gray from Crystal Palace over Shreeves' head. Frank McLintock was the agent on the deal and Spurs were invoiced £10,000 plus VAT on 2 March 1992. But McLintock was also Gray's agent and three weeks later Gray's wife Karen withdrew £6,000 from the Halifax Building Society in Croydon, kept £1,000 for spending money and Gray himself paid £5,000 to McLintock at the Mill Hill training ground.

Jason Cundy was also bought as a defender, initially on loan from Chelsea, but with a promise that he would be signed, and he impressed Bobby Moore. Commentating on radio on Tottenham's 3–0 victory over his old club, West Ham, he made appreciative noises about Tottenham's shrewd acquisition of Cundy.

Tottenham won five of their last ten League matches; Berry complimented Venables on that, so it was not surprising that the 1992–93 season began with Venables much more involved. It was made clear that Doug Livermore and Ray Clemence would be in charge of the first team, providing a dual management team, but Venables would be looking after the team and providing guidance and advice and would be much more active than he had been the previous season. The decision had the effect of pleasing almost everybody at Tottenham. Whatever was said about Venables as chief executive, nothing could be said against his football ability. Berry liked his decision and Sugar felt Venables could now concentrate on what he knew and did best.

Not that the Brown issue had gone away. Sandy went on hammering and at one stage Crystal suggested that he was overdoing it: 'It's finished, why go on?' All this may have lulled the Sugar camp into thinking they had neutralised Brown. They had not. In retrospect Sugar should have sacked Brown. But much as Sugar wanted Brown to go, he wanted to carry everyone in the decision. Venables was still his partner, he still wanted the partnership to work, and he was looking to Crystal and Berry, as non-executive directors, to help sort it out. It has often been said that Sugar's bark is worse than his bite. In this case it was true.

So as the 1992–93 season opened, the public at large was presented with the image of Venables in contented charge of Tottenham with Sugar as his sleeping, but happy, partner. The reality, of course, was different and Venables, himself, was to suffer from the heat of the summer of 1992, a heat produced by renewed worries about money.

Chapter 16

Ducking, diving and horse-trading

Soon after the start of the 1992–93 season, Venables' purchases and sales of players meant he was £1.3m. over budget. He reassured Sugar that it would all work out. All he wanted was time to 'duck and dive' and 'horse-trade' so that in a couple of months' time the budget would balance out. As it happened those very phrases could have accurately reflected his own private finances.

Venables faced two major financial problems: interest payments on the loans he had taken to buy Tottenham and the unresolved problems with Transatlantic. Although the Tottenham problems were much the bigger headache, in a sense, Transatlantic was nearer home. The company's bank account was at his local NatWest branch at Romford – and at one stage Transatlantic's bank account was part of his own sole trading account at the branch – and Venables was under pressure to sort it out. Transatlantic, as we have seen, had collapsed – although the last rites, a compulsory winding-up order, came the following year. By 17 March 1992 the bank overdraft was £140,485.86 and the bank made a formal demand for repayment of this sum to all the guarantors. Venables requested payment from his other co-guarantors of the overdraft but by this time he had fallen out with them, and on 1 June 1992 Venables cleared the overdraft of £144,359.64 himself.

Venables has presented this as the act of a honourable business-man who always meets his obligations, but there was a pressing business need. Apart from wishing to keep his local branch manager sweet, he was trying to acquire the properties of Transatlantic.

He had formed a company called Recall City to acquire the Cock and Magpie and the Granby Tavern. It had cost him £185,000 for which NatWest Romford had provided an overdraft of £185,000. On 17 June 1992 another Venables company was born, Thurston Barnett; its purpose was to take over Macey's. Taking over these pubs proved a messy business; there were many problems with leases and Venables' then lawyer spent some time trying to sort it out. Venables eventually got hold of the pubs and paid out more money. But let us leave the lawyers to try to sort out who had what lease of which pub.

At the same time Venables was juggling other financial balls. Here the amounts were much larger, millions instead of hundreds of thousands, and Venables was soon involved in negotiations not with British banks but banks as far afield as Liechtenstein and Hungary. His main problem was to pay the interest on the money he had borrowed from Norfina to buy Tottenham. The debt burden was heavy and on 9 July 1992 he refinanced the loan, mortgaging another 2.6m. of his Tottenham shares.

However, some important items were left dangling in the air. Norfina had been promised a statement of Venables' net worth in two weeks. It was on this promise that they had completed the deal on 9 July. On 28 July 1992 lawyers Norton Rose, acting for Norfina, wrote in some exasperation to Venables' lawyers saying, 'Failure to produce such statement is, of course, a breach of the Financial Facility Insurance Guarantee Letter. Accordingly my clients are requiring Mr Venables to produce a statement of his net worth as a matter of urgency.'

A sort of Venables' statement of net worth had been floating around for some time. In 1991, when the original deal was done, an informal statement had been produced. But for Norfina's purposes this was nowhere near precise enough. It showed Venables having properties in Kensington and Chelsea, and owning pubs and a villa in Spain. Norton Rose wanted to know the addresses of each of the Venables properties, the address of his villa in Spain and details of his other assets.

John Brown had drafted another statement of net worth and was showing it around. About this time plans began to be made to replace Norfina with another bank and there was talk of Chubb taking over the Pan Financial guarantee. David Bedford, who had helped organise the first deal, got involved in replacing Pan Financial, who were also due their money, £3,625 by the end of

July. On 30 July Venables was reminded by his advisers of his obligations to pay this amount. All this financial juggling meant a lot of work for Brown. On 6 August Brown, accompanied by John Mackenzie, a director of Avil Group Ltd and Avil Finance, flew to Amsterdam. There they saw a Dutch firm called Ficq Finance, which in Holland acts as a representative branch of Dresdner Bank, one of Germany's largest banks.

This trip would become controversial nine months later when the Sugar-Venables row reached the courts. Then the Sugar camp, trawling through Tottenham books, found that Spurs Travel had booked the tickets, Spurs had paid the bill, which was signed for by Venables, and on the bill was marked 'scouting'. This implied that Brown had gone to Amsterdam to look at players Tottenham might buy. Whatever his financial skills, nobody had previously ascribed such footballing skills to him. But when, as part of the Sugar-Venables court battle, Sandy, in an affidavit, expressed the view that the trip was really a trawling exercise meant to secure finance for Venables, the Venables camp vigorously denied it. An affidavit from Mackenzie said the purpose of the trip was to bring Ficq and Tottenham together to discuss the possibility of a loan for Tottenham against the security of the stadium at White Hart Lane. Why, in August 1992, Tottenham should be looking for more cash is a mystery, the more so as it had its major cash injection the previous December through the rights issue and was just about to unveil very good year-end financial results which were trumpeted as a triumph of Venables' business skills.

But for whatever reason Brown went to Amsterdam he was certainly busy elsewhere trying to get new financial backers for Venables. He was talking to other possible financiers including the Hungarian International Bank. Riviere has described Brown's business methods: OPM, use other people's money, always pay a bill on the thirteenth-hour principle, wait not only for the red bill but also the writ. But there were grave dangers in following this approach with Norfina. Here the clock was set and ticking away.

Norfina was due interest of £36,301.37 on 28 August 1992. Failure to pay would mean that there would be an additional default interest of £976.31 per day to be paid. Norfina made it clear that if interest was not met by 3 September then the whole of the loan plus the interest would be due and payable immediately. Something had to be done. In addition to the interest, Norfina was

Terry Venables *(left)* portrayed by Bob Thomas in his Chelsea days. *(Right)* He leads out the Chelsea team as captain at the age of eighteen. *(Below)* He is playing for Queens Park Rangers against Portsmouth on 24 October 1970.

(Left) Here, bearded and moustached, Venables is playing for QPR in February 1973.
(Right) Malcolm Allison, an early hero of Venables. As manager of Crystal Palace he
persuaded Venables to become a manager.

(Below) UEFA Under-21 Final, 1982: West Germany 3, England 2; England win on
aggregate. Bert Millichip, FA Chairman, on the right, and Ted Croker, FA Secretary, on
the left; with the managerial team of Dave Sexton and Terry Venables.

(*Above*) Jim Gregory, almost a father figure to Venables at QPR, was Venables' favourite chairman. Here they are visiting the FA to discuss QPR's artificial pitch in November 1981. (*Right*) QPR top the Second Division in 1983, and are promoted.

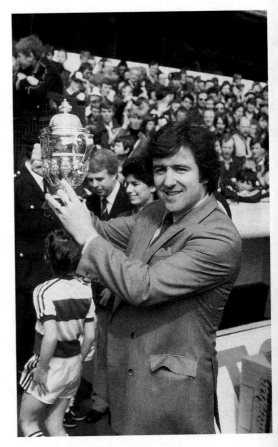

'Señor Venabless' speaks to 35,000 fans as manager of Barcelona, having first taken the pains to learn Spanish.

(Left) Venables pondering his moves as his Barcelona side prepares to play Juventus in the European Cup, 1986.

Terry Venables and Paul Riviere devised their game 'The Manager'
together. Here they are launching the game and *(below)*
demonstrating how to play it.

(Above) Irving Scholar and Venables on the latter's appointment as manager of Tottenham Hotspur 23 November 1987.

(Left) Venables vigorously encourages his new team against Liverpool a few days later, although The Reds won 2-0.

Venables and George Graham, old colleagues from Chelsea days in the 1960s, meet as rival managers in 1989.

(Right) Venables and Paul Riviere outside Scribes West in Kensington after their take-over of the club in April 1991.

FA Cup Final, 1991. Brian Clough and Terry Venables lead out their teams at Wembley. *(Below)* Support during the match for Venables to buy Spurs.

owed £30,000 as arrangement fee for organising the refinancing. This was due on 9 September.

On 21 August Norfina warned that if they did not receive their arrangement fee this would also be a default under the terms of the refinancing. Four days later, on 25 August, Venables' then lawyers wrote to him setting out his pressing financial commitments. Norfina: £30,000 arrangement fee, £36,301.37 as interest. Pan Financial: £3,625. One can imagine how Venables must have felt as these letters and faxes came thudding in. But there was little he could do.

Late on Friday 28 August Norfina wrote saying they had not received the money and warned that £36,301.37, plus interest accruing at the rate of £976.31, must be paid by 3 September. On 1 September his lawyers wrote to him setting out the dire consequences if Norfina was not paid. 'This would involve the enforcing of the charge over the shares held by Edennote in Tottenham Hotspur plc, making demands under your personal guarantee or calling upon the insurance bond issued to Norfina by Pan Financial.'

What could Venables do? Brown's talks with the Hungarian International Bank were going well, well enough for the Hungarians to send an offer letter. But this contained a few errors. Also they were only offering a one-year loan, when Venables wanted two, and in order to get it he would have to fork out money: an arrangement fee of £70,000. Moreover, like Norfina, they wanted a statement of net worth and the last two years' accounts of Edennote.

This was Venables' biggest headache. Edennote was a nothing company. Its only income was the money Venables earned from Spurs. When its accounts for 31 March 1992 were finally filed with Companies House – on 31 July 1993, two months after Venables was sacked – it showed that its income for the year was £8,511. The detailed trading profit and loss account showed an operating loss of £398,769 after providing £199,528 interest for the Norfina loan, £26,185 for interest on the Yawetz loan (which never had to be paid) and £167,000 'commitment fees, arrangement fees and premiums'. Its expenditure was interest and other fees – including legal and professional fees of £40,000 – incurred in an attempt to raise the money Venables needed to buy Spurs.

Venables had to do something to inject more into Edennote and he turned to his only source: Tottenham.

On 7 September he did a quick shuffle of his Tottenham contract. The five-year contract with an income of £225,000 a year, which he had entered into in July 1991, was now split into two. He would be paid £75,000 for which he signed a 'supplemental agreement'. The remaining £150,000 would be paid to Edennote through a management agreement. In reality it made no difference to the work Venables did for Spurs but it meant that Edennote now got a yearly income of £150,000. So desperate was Venables' need for money that there was not even time to discuss the new contract and have it approved by the Board, as would be normal practice.

Before this Crystal had spoken to Sugar. Terry, he said, was embarrassed to talk about it but he did need money and wanted to change the way he was paid. Sugar agreed and so the entire £150,000 due to Edennote was paid on 7 September which meant Venables received three-quarters of his Spurs salary almost a year in advance.

It was only on 29 October 1992, seven weeks after the money had been paid to Edennote, that the Tottenham Board approved. The minutes for that Board meeting, under the innocuous subject of Group Finance, had an item which read: 'The contractual arrangement for Mr Venables was considered and the Board confirmed approval for Mr Sandy to sign on its behalf.' Sugar would later tell Venables how Sandy had done this 'to protect us', as otherwise Venables' actions might possibly have been seen as an infringement of the Companies Act. For several months the contracts remained a mystery, for as late as January 1993 Tony Berry had no idea what they were for.

The day after he signed the new contracts at Spurs and got Spurs to pay Edennote £150,000, Venables also repaid a loan of £50,000 that Tottenham had given him. In 1987, when he had accepted Scholar's offer to become Tottenham manager, he had, in addition to his salary, got an interest-free loan. Such loans were then common at Tottenham. Many players got them along with Venables. The players' loans were not disclosed to the football authorities and Tottenham have since been heavily punished for this failing of the Scholar regime.

Venables' loan had nothing to do with League regulations since he was not a player but by September 1992 it had to be resolved. Until that stage not one of the many documents Tottenham had put out – the mandatory cash offer, the rights issue, or even the accounts for year ended 31 May 1991, which were issued in

December 1991 – had mentioned that Venables had had a loan. The reason was these documents did not have to mention the loan.

Now, for the first time since Venables had become chief executive, this information had to be disclosed. Tottenham were about to issue their first accounts of the Venables-Sugar regime. So Venables repaid the loan, but as he did so Tottenham paid Edennote £50,000 as a sort of signing-on fee for Venables. In other words Venables received £50,000 in one hand and paid it back in another.

A week later, when the Tottenham accounts were signed off, all this remained obscure. The world was only told in a three-line item in the directors' report that a £50,000 loan which Venables had been given before he became director and which bore no interest had been repaid. No mention of the signing-on fee or, of course, of the way Venables had rearranged his contract. Those unfamiliar with the intricacies of the arrangement would have made nothing of the disclosure in the accounts. Venables, seemingly so open with the press when it came to those quick chats about football, could, it appeared, be somewhat secretive about his own personal dealings, disclosing only what the law forced him to disclose, nothing more.

The transactions showed another side of Venables' character. Just as Venables had found it embarrassing to talk about his financial problems, he would always find it difficult to be open about his deeds even when they were disclosed to the world. So when all this was revealed in court during his battle with Sugar, Venables would try to put an entirely novel spin on it. He stated that the reordering of his Edennote contract and the payment in advance was not due to his financial difficulties but justified by a change in share capital of Spurs. This made it sound awesome, as if Venables as chief executive had done something spectacular. In fact all that happened was that Tottenham had written off the money accumulated in the share premium account (the difference between the nominal value and the issue price of a share). This is a purely notional accounting entry which could be done by an accounts clerk.

Venables' argument that this was a major capital change suggested he either did not understand or chose not to. In some ways it put him on a par with some of the supporters who, in the really comical twist to the story, saw these notional millions in the share premium account as real money which could be made available to buy players. When they raised this point in the Annual General

Meeting Sugar got irritated by their suggestions and made his feelings plain. The ultimate twist was that when the Sugar-Venables marriage broke up, Crystal pointed to Sugar's behaviour as proof of his dictatorial tendencies.

The rearrangement of his Tottenham contract meant some temporary respite for Venables on the Norfina front. Three days after the new contract for Edennote, on 10 September 1992, Venables pledged a further 800,000 Spurs shares to Norfina.

But even this was not enough. Venables needed another backer. On 2 October he found a new lender: the Bank of Liechtenstein. For Venables, it was almost a bank of last resort, his negotiations with the Hungarian International Bank having fallen through. The insurance policy was provided by Chubb which had the right to take any dividends paid and any of Venables' income paid into Edennote.

Not that Venables could breathe a sigh of relief at having sorted out Norfina. In that summer of 1992 Norfina was not the only finance house Venables was 'ducking and diving' from. There was also Landhurst, his undisclosed financier. Venables' relationship with this company was known only to a select few in his circle. However, its name kept popping up. It figured as an item of query by the Tottenham auditors when they went through the books. They were concerned about the lack of any formal documentation regarding the letting of Box 44 in the West Stand to Landhurst Leasing. By this time, with Landhurst in financial difficulties, there was no question of claiming anything from the company even if Tottenham could prove they were owed money. It was yet another of the things that had to be written off. The minutes of the Board meeting, where this was discussed, do not record Venables saying anything about his connection with Landhurst. But since then, in his wrongful dismissal case against Tottenham, he has explained the use of the box as one of the perks of office. Box 44, he claims, was a box for his use as chief executive and he did not require permission to invite people.

However, Venables could not deal quite so easily with his own financial involvement with Landhurst. As we have seen the documentation of the Landhurst loan to Venables was all in the name of Edennote. However, on 5 August, a draft leasing agreement between Landhurst and Venables Venture Capital (VVC) was sent out to Edennote. Why? By this time it was clear to Landhurst that things were not going well and the company would soon be in the hands of receivers. That would mean they would start asking for loans to be repaid. It seems likely that this information was passed on to some of the borrowers and it is possible that Venables and his advisers, on becoming aware of Landhurst's plight, decided to transfer the loan to VVC. Had the change been made the effect would have been very significant, for it would mean the Landhurst loan of a million pounds would be transferred from Edennote, a company vital for Venables, to VVC, whose demise would have little impact on him. VVC had not traded and has since been dissolved.

On 14 August the receivers walked into Landhurst. They discovered that the previous day the personal guarantees given by various borrowers, including allegedly Venables, had apparently gone walkabout. The guarantees have never reappeared.

On 11 September Brown, along with Pawlikowski, turned up at Landhurst offices with the VVC lease, the one Landhurst had sent out on 5 August. Most of the form was not filled in but nevertheless Brown hoped to have it substituted for the two other leases in the name of Edennote. Stephen Illidge was later to tell *Panorama* what happened:

I met Mr Brown for the first time probably a month after Landhurst had gone into receivership. I had been retained by the administrative receivers after the receivership and he approached the receivers with a view that the loan should have been in the name of Venables Venture Capital. The Landhurst documentation was all annotated Edennote, the invoices were from Edennote and the funds had been paid to Edennote, so I didn't believe that that was the case.

Illidge got the impression that Pawlikowski was Brown's lawyer. Of course he wasn't and the attempt at substitution failed. Venables could only now wait and hope that somehow the Landhurst problem would be sorted out.

Chapter 17

Undressing a transfer

On 28 August Venables defaulted on the Norfina loan. But that was a private agony. The day before, 27 August, Venables was involved in a deal which has produced much more public agony. That was the day Venables approved Teddy Sheringham's transfer to Tottenham.

Now more intimately involved in team matters, Venables had been quite busy that pre-season buying a forward and a defender and selling a striker turned midfield player. The forward was Darren Anderton, bought from his old mentor Jim Gregory of Portsmouth, the defender was Neil Ruddock, whom he was buying back after having sold him, and the midfield player he sold was Paul Stewart. All these deals were very shrewd and emphasised his fine footballing instincts.

But they were a prelude to the deal of the summer which has proved to be Venables' most astute football signing, giving Tottenham one of their most valued players. However, the way it was organised, involving a cash payment of £50,000, which has never been fully explained, has since made it the most talked about signing in English soccer history.

Venables had decided that he needed a striker to replace Gary Lineker. The previous year he had broken the then Tottenham club record to buy Durie, but that had not quite worked out as he hoped and Venables was, initially, keen on Dean Saunders. However, Liverpool's price was, he felt, a quarter of a million too high. His thoughts turned to Teddy Sheringham, then playing for

Nottingham Forest. Venables was put in touch with Sheringham through First Wave Sports Management run by Graham Smith and Frank McLintock. McLintock says he was contacted by Ronnie Fenton, Brian Clough's assistant at Forest, and told that Forest were not keen on Sheringham, news that considerably surprised McLintock.

The Forest side of this story, as narrated by Clough in his autobiography, is somewhat different. According to Clough it was Fenton who was surprised when, on a pre-season tour of Ireland, Sheringham came up to him and said he had heard a rumour that Spurs had made a bid for him. Then Sheringham said he did not want to play against Shamrock Rovers that night. Soon, says Clough, Graham Smith had offered £2m. for Sheringham but Clough told Fenton to reject it.

Not that Tottenham were the only club interested. Chelsea were also in the hunt. This was sorted out when Venables spoke to Ken Bates. Both Chelsea and Tottenham had also been linked with Robert Fleck of Norwich and Venables suggested to Bates that they should not allow Robert Chase, chairman of Norwich, to get the two clubs to bid against each other. Chelsea's then manager, Ian Porterfield, decided he preferred Fleck – although he later wanted to change his mind – and so it was decided that Bates would go for Fleck and Venables would be free to pursue Sheringham.

Sometime during the 1992–93 pre-season, Sheringham arrived in London and met Venables at the Royal Garden Hotel. Forest, he said, were prepared to let him go, the only question was the fee. Venables has given more than one version of how much Forest wanted and who wanted it. In his affidavit, filed as part of his court action against Sugar, he said that Fenton mooted a minimum figure of £2m. But the figure was then increased by £100,000 as Forest realised they had paid Sheringham's signing-on fee and wanted to recoup this (Sheringham was due £100,000 for each year of his three-year contract). However, in his autobiography Venables said that Ronnie Fenton 'came back with a price of £2.1m.' Then Fred Reacher, the Forest chairman, tried to get an extra £100,000 on top of £2.1m. The autobiographical memory seems suspect for the affidavit version is supported by McLintock.

But whatever the starting figure there was a lot of haggling. The haggling was such that by the time the season started Sheringham was still a Forest player. Indeed he scored in Forest's opening game which resulted in a misleading victory over Liverpool, so misleading that after this Forest were tipped as possible champions when, in fact, that season they were relegated.

The Sheringham transfer gathered pace in the first week of the season. Spurs began badly. Venables had said this was another transitional year but the early games suggested it could be a doomed year, an away draw followed by a home defeat.

Just after this, on Thursday 20 August, Venables met Tony Berry. According to Berry they had lunch at Langan's during which a call came for Venables. It could not be put through to the table, so Berry suggested the caller ring Berry's mobile phone. The caller was Ted Buxton, the Tottenham coach, who was involved in the Sheringham negotiations.

After Venables had finished the call he told Berry that the deal was done but that Fenton wanted more money. Fifteen minutes later the phone rang again, again it was for Venables. The price for Sheringham had increased again, Venables told Berry, but did not want to discuss it further.

However, for a long time Venables would not even accept that he had lunch with Berry, let alone his description of what happened during the meal. Venables' original contention was that it was not lunch but dinner and it was not at Langan's but at Scribes. Berry then submitted receipts from Langan's. On balance it seems Venables no longer denies the lunch but he still denies receiving the phone calls.

That Saturday Tottenham played Crystal Palace at home and earned their first home point of the season. White Hart Lane was agog with the fact that Tottenham's equaliser was a last-gasp effort which, according to Ray Clemence, the joint coach, had left the players feeling like they had won the Cup. However, before the match had even started an even more significant scene may have taken place at the offices of the club. Or at least that is the contention of Alan Sugar.

Sugar claims he saw a door closing on what appeared to be a private meeting in Venables' office at Tottenham attended by Venables, Brown, Frank McLintock and someone else he could not identify. When Sugar asked Venables, his reply was that it was a meeting to do with the transfer of Sheringham. However, in his affidavit, Venables denied that any such meeting with McLintock ever took place.

On 25 August Tottenham played a midweek match at Leeds where, with Cantona rampant, Tottenham were beaten 5–0. Sugar did not travel to Leeds but watched it on the big screen at White Hart Lane and left before the match was over, not happy with his team.

After the match Peter Barnes, who as club secretary travelled to Leeds with the team, took a short holiday. Barnes recalls: 'I had not taken any holiday that year and Terry was very keen I take one. He seemed particularly keen for me to go and kept telling me you look knackered, you are looking peaky, take a holiday. Jonathan Crystal was acting as a counsel for the Pakistan cricket team then touring England and he said, "You like cricket. They are playing at Scarborough." Tottenham had played at Leeds on the Tuesday night, the match was in the area, so I went for a few days. As it happened it rained.'

A few weeks earlier Venables and Barnes had had an altercation about the transfer of Paul Stewart. After Stewart was sold to Liverpool for £2.25m., it was discovered that Tottenham would not receive the full fee as they had to pay 10% of any fee in excess of £2m. to Manchester City which meant handing over £225,000. When Sugar discovered this, Venables blamed it on Barnes, claiming he had not kept him informed of this aspect of Stewart's contract. Barnes says that Venables had not told him he was planning to sell Stewart, he only knew after Stewart had been sold. Barnes tackled Venables: 'I said straightaway, "You know there is a sell-on". He got very upset, saying, "Why didn't you tell me?" "How could I?" I replied. "I did not know you were planning to sell him." '

Given that Venables had signed Stewart from Manchester City, and had been involved in giving him loans, the explanation that Barnes was at fault did not go down well with Sugar. It suggested that Venables was ready to blame subordinates for his own failings.

The effect of the Barnes holiday was that when, two days later, Sheringham was signed, Barnes, who would normally have been involved in drawing up the contract, was not there. It was also on 25 August that an invoice was issued which, on the face of it, seems to have no connection with the Sheringham transfer but has since assumed great significance in this context. The invoice was from a company calling itself Silver Rose International Ltd (Export). The invoice seems innocuous enough. It has a long-stemmed rose imprinted on it, an address in the Finchley Road and no clue as to what the company does. The invoice, addressed to

Brown at Tottenham, asked for £50,000 for the following work: 'For the assistance in arranging distribution and merchandising network on behalf of T.H.F.C. in the U.S.A. to include travel and all consultancy work involved in the project'.

It was two days after this, 27 August 1992, that the most crucial moves in the Sheringham transfer took place. If 28 June 1991 is a day of tremendous significance for Venables, then 27 August is a day that could yet haunt him.

Here we need to pause and remind ourselves of the principal actors in this drama and where they were that day. As ever Venables was at Tottenham's training ground at Mill Hill. Sandy, as he did so often, began the day at his tenth-floor office at Brentwood just down the corridor from Sugar. He was due at Tottenham later that day but this was very much part of his normal day, generally the morning at Brentwood, the afternoon at White Hart Lane. Brown was at Mill Hill, but went to Tottenham later. McLintock was also at Mill Hill before going to Tottenham in the evening.

According to Venables the deal was finally done when he rang Fred Reacher direct, told him now or never, he came back within an hour and the deal was on. The only thing to be decided was Sheringham's personal terms. McLintock and Sheringham came to the training ground and his personal terms were quickly agreed.

Brown was also there. With Barnes on holiday he was involved in drawing up the contract for Sheringham along with Venables and Crystal, with the assistance of one of the girls from Barnes' office. But there must have been aspects of the contract where they needed clarification, for at one stage Crystal even rang Barnes about a point on the Sheringham contract.

Brown made handwritten notes about the contract and a page of it has survived. It contains cryptic words like: 'Player – s/o £100k, further £100k, £30k car not £20k, invoice by 1.00pm, check last regd time, medical 1.00pm, Premier 7th Sept' and a mobile phone number: 0836-353980. In the bottom right-hand corner of the page '£25k' was circled.

At some stage Brown phoned Anis Rahman, Tottenham's then credit controller. Rahman's recollection is that Brown told him that Venables had authorised a payment of £50,000 to McLintock. It had to be cash and he ordered him to organise that.

Rahman, unnerved that such a large amount of money was wanted in cash, rang Sandy at Brentwood. Sandy knew the money was for the Sheringham deal. But that the money had to be paid in cash raised Sandy's hackles. For Brown to demand it was like a red rag to the bull and Sandy stormed into Sugar's office.

'Talk to Terry,' said Sugar, quite calm about it, or at least much calmer than Sandy.

'I telephoned Mr Venables,' Sandy says in his affidavit, 'and asked for an explanation. He told me that no other method of payment, not even a bank draft, would do and if we did not do it this way, the Sheringham deal would fail. I said I would arrange for the cash but that I would not authorise its release unless I received a VAT invoice.'

Venables' recall of that phone conversation is very different. In his affidavit he said: 'Frank McLintock insisted on having the money before he would let Mr Sheringham sign the contract. He wanted the money that evening or the contract would go off. Accordingly, I told Mr Sandy that Frank McLintock had to have the money that night, but I never said that it must be in cash. Mr Sandy did not query the request and I certainly never told him to mind his own business. Mr Sandy knew that the money was in connection with the Sheringham transfer, and that Frank McLintock wanted it that night but if he did not get it that night the deal would be off. Mr Sandy did not query why a banker's draft would not be sufficient and I never specifically requested cash. What I believe must have happened is that Mr Sandy must have discovered that a banker's draft could not be made available in time. I cannot recall whether Mr Sandy mentioned a VAT invoice.'

McLintock has said that his firm had done a lot of work for Tottenham and he used the Sheringham transfer as a lever to get paid.

Sandy rang Rahman asking him to collect £58,750 in cash, £8,750 being the VAT on £50,000, but not to hand over the money without Sandy's authority. It was in some fury that Sandy got into his car and drove to Tottenham. He arrived to find that Rahman had not yet returned from the bank.

The cheque Rahman took to the bank was signed by Sandy and Sugar, although a similar bank authorisation was also signed by Venables but it took longer to get to the bank from the Tottenham training ground. By the time it did the Tottenham accounts department had already acted on the Sugar authorisation.

Rahman did not find it easy to cash the cheque. Tottenham's

local Midland Bank did not have such a large sum in cash and Rahman had to go to Midland's Aldwych offices. He returned accompanied by a security guard. When he got back Sandy was not in his office. Rahman put the money in the cupboard in his office and left.

Meanwhile Brown had returned from Mill Hill to White Hart Lane. The Tottenham security log says he arrived at 3.30 in the afternoon. Here we must introduce another character who played no part in the transfer but who claims to have heard and seen things in Brown's office that day which would be the subject of sensational revelations in court more than three years after the events we are describing. This character is Jeff Fugler.

He had been involved in doing design and marketing work for both Tottenham and Scribes. He made the revelations in the context of a case he had brought against Scribes West asking for nearly £20,000 of unpaid fees. The Venables camp vigorously contested the action and denied Fugler's statements. The judge, Mr Recorder Williams, found in Fugler's favour and accepted his version of what took place in Brown's office on that day. This put an entirely new light on the whole affair.

Fugler is a life-long Tottenham fan and had good reason to feel excited that he was at his favourite ground when they signed such an important player as Sheringham. In his court evidence he says he came to Brown's office to discuss payments due to him from Scribes. The Tottenham log records him arriving at 6.13 and going to see John Brown. Brown sat behind his desk, Fugler to one side of the desk and he spread his papers on the desk. In the course of his conversation, Brown showed him several invoices. They were all addressed to Brown at Tottenham, they were all for the same amount, £50,000, and the wording was identical. However, they were from different companies.

One of the invoices was the Silver Rose invoice of 25 August (which we have already discussed). There was more than one copy of this invoice on Brown's desk. One had been faxed addressed to Brown at Tottenham on that very day at 11.56 am. Another had been faxed, again addressed to Brown at Tottenham, from Monaco bearing the name and fax number and initials of a B. S. Berrick. That was timed at 18.13 that day. Assuming that it was faxed from Monaco and, given that French time was an hour ahead, it means it was faxed at 5.13pm British time.

My subsequent investigations revealed that B. S. Berrick was

Bernard Berrick, a British expatriate who lives in Monte Carlo. He is a fervent Tottenham supporter and his son Steven, a barrister, is married to the daughter of Jeffrey Silver, the owner of Silver Rose. Bernard Berrick, when asked, could not work out why and how his fax number appeared on a copy of the invoice.

The invoice from Silver Rose International Ltd (Export) raises a number of questions. The company claimed to be a member of the British Chamber of Commerce, something no firm can claim to be since it is a parent chamber bringing together other local chambers; but a company can belong to a local chamber like the London Chamber. Also no listing for such a company has been found in this country or the Channel Islands. It could be a trade name and it is certainly odd to find words coming after Ltd on a company invoice. The invoice shows no company number, no VAT number.

A company with a similar name has been in liquidation since 1987. When I spoke to Jeffrey Silver, who is again trading under the name Silver Rose in Finchley Road but a few hundred yards from the address on the invoice, he said he knew nothing about the invoice but could not be sure if he had ever traded under that name.

Fugler was also shown an invoice from First Wave. This was identical to the Silver Rose invoice. It asked for the same amount, £50,000, had the same wording, claiming to assist in arranging distribution and merchandising network on behalf of Tottenham in the States. There were two extremely minor differences in the wording of the Silver Rose and First Wave invoices. In the First Wave invoice Tottenham's name and the USA were spelt out in full. And it was dated two days after the Silver Rose invoice, 27 August. In other words the same day as the events we are describing.

The mystery is what these two identically worded invoices were doing in Brown's offices at Tottenham. Was the Silver Rose invoice a first draft of which the First Wave was the final version? And what did arranging distribution and merchandising network on behalf of Tottenham have to do with the Sheringham transfer?

The answer came more than three years later when Jeff Fugler presented his evidence in the case he had brought against Scribes West. Brown, he claimed, was using these invoices to raise £50,000 in 'cash in connection with the transfer/purchase of Teddy Sheringham'. Fugler testified that he had no doubt in his mind that these invoices 'were all bogus'. To convince him further that something wrong and improper was going on, sometime during their meeting Brown took a call from Venables, who told him that David Webb should be paid £20,000 for his marketing services. This infuriated Fugler who felt others were being paid when he was not, and all the more so as Brown gave Fugler to understand 'that Mr Webb's marketing consultancy was actually something to do with the earlier sale of two players by Southend United Football Club [where Webb had been manager] to Tottenham Hotspur'.

For Fugler this picture of what he saw as financial impropriety was completed when Brown told him that 'Venables wanted me to overcharge Tottenham Hotspur Football Club on jobs to offset my fees due from Scribes. I was shocked at this suggestion from someone who is after all the chief executive of a Public Limited Company. I said that I would not even begin to consider this. I repeated my request for payments as promised by Venables.'

Fugler's meeting with Brown was not very long, at most fifteen minutes. Brown denied Fugler was there, even when presented with the evidence of Tottenham's security logs. Also Brown's counsel suggested that if it was accepted that the meeting took place, Brown and Fugler couldn't possibly have discussed all this in fifteen or so minutes. However, the judge, Mr Recorder Williams, held that while Brown 'was anxious to deal with more important matters, particularly the transfer of a player and the payment in cash to Mr McLintock, it could well be said, in language more appropriate to the East End of London, that things were done "on the 'urry up" but, translated into our language, it was a fairly quick meeting. I accept, on the balance of probabilities, that there was such a meeting, and that it is more or less as described by Mr Fugler in his written statement and his oral evidence.'

One reason for the hurry was that, as the Tottenham log records, at 6.28pm McLintock arrived. Fugler saw him come into the ground. His position in Brown's office gave him a vantage point. He could see out of the window on to the Tottenham car park and saw McLintock drive in. Soon the security buzzed Brown of his arrival. Brown asked Fugler to leave and he left. In the hurry it seems Fugler accidentally picked up some of Brown's papers including copies of the First Wave and Silver Rose invoice and also part of Brown's handwritten notes on the Sheringham transfer which had got mixed up with his papers. Back in his office, when he discovered the error, he got his secretary to return them but unknown to him she kept copies which he discovered only in June 1995 – almost three years later. When this emerged in court the

Venables camp tried hard to discredit Fugler's version but Mr Recorder Williams accepted that Fugler had picked the papers up from Brown's desk.

Sometime after this, with Fugler gone, the money that Rahman had collected and put in Sandy's cupboard was given to Brown and McLintock. The handover took place in Sandy's office with Brown and McLintock there. Sandy was intrigued that McLintock separated the money in two piles, one for £50,000, another for £8,750 which was the VAT amount. McLintock's action struck Sandy as a bit odd. As soon as Brown and McLintock got the money they left Sandy's room.

Sandy, keen to get his invoice, followed them to Brown's office where he was given a First Wave invoice. This was the second version of the First Wave invoice. It was identical to the first version of First Wave and even had the same invoice number: 0053. It was also, of course, identical to the Silver Rose invoice, except for the way it spelt Tottenham and USA. The only difference was that unlike the Silver Rose and the first version of the First Wave invoice this second version had VAT added to the £50,000, making a total of £58,750.

It is worth stressing that, although this transfer generated three invoices, this First Wave invoice with VAT added to it was the only one Tottenham paid in this transaction. The other two invoices did not surface until more than three years after the transfer took place. At this time Sandy and Tottenham only saw the First Wave invoice with VAT, and this was the only one that was in the public domain, until September 1995 when I revealed in the *Daily Telegraph* the existence of the other two invoices.

Sandy got McLintock to sign this First Wave VAT invoice. He also wanted Venables' signature on this. Brown, says Sandy, promised to get it. Sandy left the original with Brown and took a copy for his records, waiting for Venables to sign and return the original.

McLintock left White Hart Lane at 6.45. The money was in a cardboard box and bank bags and McLintock has said he felt uncomfortable as he drove away with the cash from the ground. He was happier when it was stored away. He does not say where it was stored but after leaving Tottenham, McLintock picked up Sheringham and they drove to the Post House Hotel in Luton where they met Ronnie Fenton.

Why did they meet Fenton? Sheringham has said he does not

know as he never left the car. McLintock has said to the Premier League enquiry that he went to meet Fenton, not to give him anything, but to receive an envelope containing the transfer forms. Why Fenton should drive some one hundred miles to Luton from Nottingham to hand over transfer forms is a mystery. It is an almost unheard-of procedure in a transfer for forms to be given by an assistant manager of one club to an agent who has acted for another club. More so to drive over a hundred miles to do so. It would be more usual for such forms to be faxed between the clubs concerned.

A few days later, says Sandy, the original invoice signed by Venables was given to Tottenham's accountants. But there was an oddity about the way this invoice was filed at Tottenham. For some reason a strip of paper was put over the bottom part of the invoice which read: 'Received cash with thanks' followed by McLintock's signature. When this invoice became part of the court documents in the Sugar-Venables case it was photocopied in this fashion, although from the photocopy it is evident that there is something that is being obscured, squiggles of writing are just visible. The unvarnished original with Venables' and McLintock's signatures has since been produced, although why anybody should want to obscure McLintock's signature is a mystery. It might have been a mistake, we don't know. In any case it does not matter because McLintock has never denied signing the invoice.

However, three and a half years after the deal was done, Venables – who had said nothing about his signature on this invoice, despite the fact that he had mentioned this transaction at various times, including in court affidavits, to the police, in his autobiography, and to the Premier League inquiry – suddenly spoke about it. In the last week of November 1995, he told the *News of the World* that his signature was a forgery.

Venables claimed he had never seen the invoice, did not know how his signature got there; it would have been physically impossible for him to sign since he was at Mill Hill and the invoice was never faxed to him at the training ground. It is hard to see what difference it makes, since he authorised the payment – indeed in his autobiography he says he asked for the payment.

It is puzzling that Venables says he did not see the invoice because two days after the deal was signed he appears to have realised that McLintock was paid VAT on top of the £50,000. In his autobiography Venables says Brown reported to him that

McLintock had been overpaid. Could this reporting have taken place when Brown brought the original invoice for Venables' signature? It is very likely that that was when Venables realised that the VAT was added to the £50,000 payment.

What happened after Venables found out is not in dispute. He rang McLintock in some fury saying the deal was for £50,000 inclusive of VAT. McLintock apologised and the same day, 29 August, he drove back to White Hart Lane. McLintock saw Peter Barnes, who by then was back from his brief holiday. Barnes counted the money, put it in an envelope and locked it in his safe, giving McLintock a receipt. Barnes has said that Venables had given him instructions to keep the money in the safe and he did just that. Sugar, Sandy and Tottenham did not know the VAT had been returned, let alone it was locked up in the safe. They only found out when they read about it in McLintock's affidavit filed during the court action between Sugar and Venables in June 1993.

By the time this happened the Sheringham transfer was front-page news. This had happened when, in his first affidavit, detailing what he saw as Venables' misdeeds, Sugar blew open this transfer, blasting wide the door to the long suspected, but never openly discussed, soccer world of 'bungs'. In the wake of Sugar's allegations all sorts of matters came tumbling out, making it the most notorious transfer in English football history.

In his affidavit dated 21 May 1993 Sugar alleged how in the days leading up to the transfer he had had a couple of conversations with Venables which made him very concerned over where some of the money in the transfer was going.

In one of these conversations Venables told him that Brian Clough 'likes a bung':

> He explained that Mr Clough wished to receive a payment personally for selling Mr Sheringham. I told Mr Venables that it was absolutely out of the question and that I have never heard anything like this before and it was certainly not the way Tottenham Hotspur or I would conduct business.

A few days later, says Sugar, Venables returned to the subject. Now there was more detail about how Clough liked receiving the money.

> What usually happened in these cases was that people would meet Mr Clough in a motorway cafe and Mr Clough would be handed a bag full of money. At this I told Mr Venables I don't want to discuss this matter again and that he should not even mention it to me again.

After the transfer was complete Sugar raised the matter with Venables. In his affidavit he says:

> I strongly protested to Mr Venables. He told me that it was all above board and that we had a VAT invoice. I effectively told him not to undermine my intelligence and that this whole affair stank and that I wanted nothing whatsoever to do with it, if it ever came out. He said that it was all above board and that it was Mr McLintock's commission for putting the deal together. I told him again that it stinks and that he knew damn well where some of that money is going.

Although Sugar did not explicitly say Clough had received a bung from the transfer the clear inference of his court allegations was that some of the £50,000 in cash was a bung. Clough indignantly denied it. Immediately Sugar made the bungs allegations he asked Sugar to repeat these allegations outside the privilege of the court room so that his lawyer could deal with them. In his autobiography he said:

> I still cannot understand why my name should have been thrown into a squabble which was Tottenham business and nobody else's . . . What I do know is it was not paid to me – not in fivers, not in a plastic carrier bag, not in a lay-by or a motorway service station. Not in any shape or form. Not at all.

For him the allegations were preposterous. 'A bung? Isn't that something you get from a plumber to stop up the bath?'

Venables, in his affidavit dated 2 June 1993, not only denied Sugar's allegations, but denied he ever had any contact with Clough on the Sheringham transfer:

> I tried to speak to Brian Clough but he would never take my calls . . . I had no direct contact with Brian Clough, since all my negotiations at that time were conducted with Mr Fred Reacher, the Chairman of Nottingham Forest . . . The allegation that I told Mr Sugar that Brian Clough 'liked a bung' is untrue. I never used that expression and I've never used those words or words to that effect to Mr Sugar. As to what I am alleged to have said to Mr Sugar about Mr Clough meeting people in motorway cafes to collect his bags of money, it really is a lot of nonsense. I certainly never said any of that to Mr Sugar, he is either making it up or he is repeating something he heard from some other source.

Just as vehemently McLintock and his partner Graham Swift denied that they were acting as bag carriers for Clough. McLintock told the *Evening Standard* on 21 September 1993, 'This was money we earned. Why should I give some of it to someone else?' Smith and McLintock claimed the money had gone into their company. Although Smith has a limited company called First Wave Sports Management, this money supposedly went into the partnership of the same name he had with McLintock. The First Wave VAT invoice that Tottenham paid, and the one without VAT that Fugler saw on Brown's desk, had the word limited crossed out.

However, when the Premier League inquiry, set up in the wake of Sugar's allegations to look into this transfer and other transfer irregularities, tried to follow where the £50,000 went, they discovered some interesting inconsistencies. The £50,000 was paid into First Wave partnership's accounts as McLintock and Smith claimed but this did not happen until after the affair had been made public by Sugar. The company also submitted a late VAT return. This seems very odd and suggests that the money went into First Wave only after the balloon went up. So what happened to the £50,000 that Tottenham paid on 27 August 1992?

It is interesting to note that, in his affidavit, Sugar never claimed that the money went to Clough. That was more the impression created. Clough, as we have seen, has always denied he received any of it and, while in general Clough's public personality evokes many emotions but rarely sympathy, in this situation one does feel that he was put in an invidious position, being dragged into the internal feuding of Tottenham.

On 26 November 1995 in an article in the *News of the World*, where he denied he had signed the invoice, Venables said:

That invoice was used as a stick to beat me with because my detractors claimed it was proof that I had engineered a bung for Forest manager Brian Clough and was looking for a cut out of the deal myself.

Venables has also pointed to the return of the VAT as proof that he had no designs on the money. He wrote in his autobiography:

If I had wanted to steal that money I would have said, 'Bring it back to me'. Instead I told him [McLintock] to go to the club and give it back . . . I thought no more about it until my court action against Tottenham a year later when I was told that the £8,750 was apparently still in the safe. I have no idea why Barnes did not pass it directly to the accounts department.

So the mystery remains unsolved. A public company made a cash payment; a whole series of invoices, one from a naughty nighties company, was raised, all of them having the same wording and for the same amount, yet people associated with it disclaim knowledge. More than two and a half years after the Premier League inquiry started its work it has still to report. Leaks have indicated that the problem has been a mass of contradictory stories with some people, at a second or subsequent interview, recalling details they had not discussed in the first interview.

For instance, the meeting that McLintock and Sheringham had with Fenton on the day of the transfer, only emerged when they were recalled for a second interview. When asked why they had not mentioned it earlier they said they were not asked. Similarly, at first Graham Smith, justifying his assertion that £50,000 was for his company, said he had used part of the money to pay his builder. The builder when contacted said he had received some money but this was in July, more than a month before Tottenham had paid.

Venables and his associates insist that nothing untoward happened in the transfer; that the fuss about it was all due to Sugar seeking retrospectively to justify his decision to sack Venables. But they admit that the wording on the invoice was misleading. Both Venables and McLintock made the admission in the witness box during the Fugler case. Their defence was that these were antiquated FA rules about not making payments to agents and, in any case, they were following past practice.

It is interesting to note how reactions have changed following fresh disclosures on this issue. In court Jeff Fugler submitted the documents he had picked up from Brown's desk on 27 August 1992. Fugler had picked up four documents: two copies of the Silver Rose invoice, a copy of a First Wave invoice without VAT, and the handwritten note. During the court hearings Brown admitted the handwritten note was his, part, he claimed, of a larger document which, after his return from Mill Hill, he had given to the Tottenham playing department to help prepare the Sheringham contract. He suggested Tottenham had loaned or gifted to Fugler. As we have seen, the judge rejected that Fugler had received this from Tottenham. We also know that Barnes was on holiday then, so why should Brown give this document to the playing department?

Furthermore, McLintock in his witness statement in the case claimed that there were always two First Wave invoices. He said:

> There is no mystery regarding these invoices and I have already
> explained the connection with the other proceedings how these

invoices came to be brought into existence. I asked my then secretary, Sue Taylor, to prepare and send an invoice for £50,000 to Tottenham Hotspur which she indeed did . . . Unbeknownst to me at the time, someone from Tottenham Hotspur rang my office and pointed out that her invoice should have VAT. As a result of this my secretary, without first consulting me, prepared a further invoice . . . which was for the sum of £50,000 plus £8,750 VAT. That was faxed to Tottenham Hotspur. I did not prepare it nor did I see it at the time.

The reference to the other proceedings is the case between Sugar and Venables in the summer of 1993 when McLintock gave an affidavit about this affair. However, in that affidavit there is no mention of there being two invoices. When he gave his 'full and frank' interview to the *Evening Standard* on 21 September 1993 he did not mention there were two invoices.

Also, when I spoke to Sue Taylor and read this statement out she laughed, and said she had only ever done anything at First Wave on the instructions of Graham Smith. It is possible that McLintock's memory, more than three years after the event, was playing tricks. For instance he says Venables rang him about 5 September 1992 regarding the overcharging of VAT. Yet his *Standard* article clearly says it was two days after the Sheringham transfer, 29 August. Such mistakes in memory are always possible but when a person makes definite assertions as McLintock does, which are not borne out, it does not inspire confidence.

There are other loose ends in this story. Venables has not only tried very hard to prove the Silver Rose invoice was a forgery but that there was no connection whatsoever with them. That may well be so. However, there is evidence to show that there is a connection between Steven Berrick, son-in-law of Jeffrey Silver of Silver Rose, and Graham Smith. They clearly know each other. The Berricks – father, son and mother – run a Panama-based company called International Sports Investment Inc.

What all this means is that not all the ramifications of this extraordinary transfer have emerged. This may even remain the case after the Premier League inquiry has reported.

Chapter 18

The autumn of Venables' discontent

Even at this stage Sugar saw Venables as a man he could work with. He wanted Brown to go but he still felt he could assist Venables in understanding the finer points involved in being a director of a public company. It was in this spirit that he had used the Tottenham Board meeting on 5 September 1992, which approved the accounts, to get the auditors Touche Ross to hold something like a seminar on how directors should behave. Sugar had realised that, whatever he did, Venables would always have his outside interests, his Scribes and various other business relationships. Perhaps the seminar, he felt, could make him realise that being a chief executive of a publicly quoted company involved different and greater obligations.

Touche Ross had already submitted a quite lengthy list of directors' transactions which needed to be clarified. Not all of them related to Venables. If Venables had had £5,918 worth of tickets unpaid for, then Tony Berry had £1,882 worth of tickets and accommodation which was not paid for. If there was no agreement authorising Brown's consultancy fee of £6,500 per month, then there was none for Sandy's fees of £48,000 per annum.

However, the auditors also observed that Scribes West had purchased items from abroad through Spurs' merchandising division and that Topicplace Ltd, Venables' video company, had sold *Venables on Venables* videos to Spurs for £29,235.66. The most puzzling item was a sum of £2,434 that Venables owed to Spurs. No copies of invoices could be found; Venables said it must have been club business and after this reassurance it was written off.

It was after all this had been dealt with that Mr Tracey of Touche Ross began his seminar on how directors of public companies should behave. Tracey explained the need for a Directors' Charter and the need for directors or their associates to record transactions in such a register. The Board meeting ended with Sandy being asked to monitor progress and maintain such a register. But Sugar was soon to learn that educating Venables was much more difficult than educating Rita. And there was the continuing problem with Brown.

The day before the Bank of Liechtenstein stepped in, on 1 October 1992, the Tottenham Board had a special meeting. Normally the Board meetings followed a pattern. They were held in the afternoon starting at about 1.30 in the boardroom on the top floor of the West Stand at White Hart Lane. The long boardroom table, which would be groaning with food on match days, would now have a tray containing sandwiches and several bottles of soft drinks. At one end of the room was a coffee machine and Board members would munch sandwiches, occasionally go to get a cup of coffee, while discussing the issues in a relaxed, informal atmosphere conducive to business.

The meeting of 1 October was to be different, however. It was six months since Venables had assured Sugar at Langan's that everything would be all right, but Brown was still there, nothing had changed, and Sugar was determined to do something. So that afternoon the Board met not at White Hart Lane but in Sugar's own tenth-floor boardroom at Amstrad's Brentwood offices. This was the least unusual feature of the meeting. Halfway through the meeting discussions got so heated that one of the directors was asked to leave. This, it was felt, was the only way emotions could be contained, but despite his departure the feelings were barely held in check.

It was Brown and his activities which were the cause of the emotion. Unlike at earlier Board meetings he was not present. But the Venables camp was nervous about this meeting and, almost as a diversionary tactic, had asked Jeff Fugler to make a marketing presentation. Sugar was not best pleased about this, feeling he was going over old ground and also that it took up time before the Board came to the main item on the agenda. On the table was a thick file. This was the Sandy dossier on Brown and, patting it affectionately, Sugar said, 'You don't have to read it but take my word for it, it is pretty horrific.'

Yes, said Sugar, at the time of the take-over he had been happy to let Venables run the football and Brown the commercial side. He had gone along with the removal of Freedman and Burton but now things had to change. A decision had to be arrived at on Brown, and Sugar made it clear he wanted to take charge of the merchandising division himself. It was a mess. After an initial hype about the new kit, sales were down, there was no stock control, and no-one capable of dealing with the major issues confronting the department. When the new shop had been opened in the East Stand a good deal of the stock was just stolen. There was talk about giving concessions in other shops. But if the stock at White Hart Lane could not be controlled what chance was there in someone else's premises?

What also rankled with Sugar was that everything he did was sniped at. Ever since the take-over the Spurs programme had a promotion called 'King for the Day' but this had met with derisory laughter from the Venables camp. 'I don't comment on players,' said Sugar, 'I've no expertise in that area, so why do people laugh at marketing, an area where I know what I am doing? Terry is good at the football side, he should concentrate on that, and the financial and other issues where they support football. But leave the commercial and general administration side where he has no expertise to the professionals who know.'

The best way out of this, suggested Sugar, was to appoint a highly paid executive for the commercial side of the business dealing with merchandising, executive boxes, stock control, and also a corporate lawyer who would become company secretary and deal with the many legal research issues that were not being tackled. 'I can live with Manchester City being paid £225,000 for Paul Stewart but what I cannot abide is the way stock is not being controlled and cash is just haemorrhaging out of the group. There is just no fucking control and this is no fucking way to run a public company.'

For Venables and Crystal this was like a dagger to their hearts. 'Sugar is trying to take power away from Terry' had been their refrain for some time. Nobody was more dubious about this than Crystal. In the absence of Brown Crystal was all-important to Venables and he made the case for him. Unfortunately Crystal's style had already begun to grate on Sugar. Sandy, admittedly not an impartial witness, says, 'Alan came to loathe the way he would stand up, in the middle of a Board meeting, stick his nose in the air and pontificate. He also liked to pace up and down as if he was in a courtroom lecturing a jury, and he always had an opinion. He would even give opinions on football matters. It was quite amusing in a way. He seemed star-struck on Terry.'

Berry, who at this stage was holding the balance between the two camps, had noticed that Crystal, on his part, disliked Sugar. 'Crystal thought Alan was uncouth. Alan was free with four-letter words, that is his style. Sugar does have a certain menacing manner, he does not go out of his way to be likeable, unlike Terry who, when he wants to, can be charming. With Alan you take him as you find him. I suppose some people find him a bit strong, even a bit obnoxious, but I have always found him straightforward. Crystal was a very aggressive person but he rubbed Alan the wrong way simply by continually carrying Terry's flag for everything, almost to ridiculous levels really. We all got embarrassed, even Terry. He would say things like, "Terry is everything to the club"; "I think Terry should have the authority to do this"; "I think Terry should be allowed to buy". It was relentless.'

Berry had come to this Board meeting in some trepidation. The DTI had just published a long-awaited report on Blue Arrow, criticising his actions including his land dealings with Peter de Savary. The DTI had also said they would seek to disqualify him from being a director in a public company and the DTI report was the second item on the agenda, after payment of special interim dividends. But much to Berry's relief Crystal, who had read the report, cleared Berry. Tottenham should do no more, he said, than record that such a report had been issued and, since the matters relating to Tottenham concerned events before May 1991, 'none present can form a view on the transactions concerned'. The Board agreed unanimously.

Venables has since made much of Berry's DTI problems – which saw the DTI dropping its case and Berry in turn taking action against them – and in his autobiography he tries to make the point that Berry and Brown are on the same moral and business plane. But this was clearly a view developed with hindsight. It is also a comment that looks more than a little foolish given that the DTI has moved to disqualify Venables as a director. However, on that October day in 1992 Venables had no problems endorsing Crystal's view that Berry's DTI problems need not concern Tottenham.

As it happened, the unanimous decision proved one of the few points of agreement around the Board table that afternoon. After that Sugar moved in on Brown and soon Venables and Sandy were in a slanging match. You talk of Brown getting rid of Freedman and Burton, said Venables, what about the accountant you got rid of? He was only a temporary appointment, retorted Sandy.

After many such exchanges Venables seemed prepared to let Sugar do the merchandising but he resented any implication that he had not done his job properly. Tony Berry recalls:

> Terry could not give way. For him to agree to Alan running the merchandising meant accepting he hadn't done a good job and he couldn't do that. It was not in his nature to give way, to accept that he couldn't do a job, any job. Yet it was clear that, given his football commitments, he didn't have time for anything else. That was clear from the accounts. He also did not have enough experience of the commercial and general management side of the business to know that his control was slipping.

By now the atmosphere in the room was stifling, threatening to boil over, and it was agreed that Sandy should leave the Board room, an unprecedented step for a director. 'It was felt,' says Sandy, 'that my views on Brown were known. It was for the others to decide.' Berry could hardly believe what he was hearing. As he told me:

> Sandy had to leave, tempers were really getting very hot and the argument was fierce. I was very unhappy about the tone of the discussion. Although I had been a very active non-executive director and went to the club once a week, usually on a Friday, there were things coming out I hadn't known. What saddened me was that here we had two men supreme in their spheres. Alan, in Murdoch's view, was one of the country's great entrepreneurs, and Terry was the best football coach in the country. I said, 'Surely it is not beyond our wit to draw the best from both of you.'

By the end of the long, acrimonious meeting there did seem to be a conclusion. Sugar and Venables agreed that job descriptions for a commercial manager and corporate lawyer were to be prepared. But despite this Berry left the meeting an unhappy and disturbed man. His fear was that Sugar might get fed up and just walk away: the consequences of that could be disastrous, for he knew how much Tottenham's turnaround was Sugar's money. Berry reflects:

> Alan isn't that communicative. Other than on match days and

at Board meetings he never spoke a lot. He is, though, a very open bloke, he won't say something to you and something different to me. He told me that he wasn't going to put up with it for much longer. I thought all this sniping would make Alan feel this is not worth the candle. His arrival was sudden and a surprise. He could depart just as suddenly.

Did Venables and his supporters hope that, by constantly goading Sugar, they might engineer his departure? Given that, after his sacking in 1993, Venables made great play of his ability to bring in outside shareholders he might have thought so. A month after this Board meeting, Venables met Berry and Buchler at the Langham Hotel and discussed the possibility of Sugar just walking away from Tottenham which would leave him clear to find another partner. However, as Berry was to discover, Sugar may have been fed up but he wasn't going to walk away, his mind was moving in a different direction; and any thoughts Venables might have had of goading Sugar to walk away would soon be nullified. If Sugar had been ignorant of Venables, Venables was about to misread Sugar. The football business might have been new to Sugar, but he is a proud man, and proud of the fact that he isn't a quitter.

In the autumn of 1992 Venables' problems remained hidden from the world but Sugar was involved in a very public war with his own shareholders. Amstrad, after many years of stunning success, had 'hit the buffers' and Sugar, never enamoured of the City, wanted to take it private so that he could radically cut it back into a small buccaneering type of operation. However, not all shareholders of Amstrad were convinced, and some of them voiced their feelings so openly that Sugar's very public dispute with the shareholders, including City institutions, dominated the City pages.

To Venables this must have appeared as if Sugar was fighting on two fronts: the public one with his Amstrad shareholders, the private one in the Spurs boardroom. As the differences between the two developed, Venables would use Sugar's problems with Amstrad as a weapon to counter the criticisms Sugar was making of his own management of Tottenham. The line from the Venables camp was, if you can't get on with your own shareholders, who can you get on with?

If Venables' camp was concerned that Sugar was making a bid for power, then such feelings were reciprocated in the Sugar camp. Nick Hewer had had his first taste of this a few weeks before the explosive Board meeting, on 19 September, when Manchester United came to Tottenham. All eyes were on Ryan Giggs who scored a wonderful goal, answered by one for Spurs from Andy Turner in a 1–1 draw.

But in the Tottenham boardroom the focus was on something else. For some time now Crystal had been telling Sugar about an article that *GQ* magazine wanted to run on Tottenham and how worried he was about it. It is easy to see in retrospect, with all the financial deals Brown was trying to engineer, why the Venables camp should be so nervous. But Sugar, not aware of all this, was puzzled and eventually asked Hewer to talk to Crystal.

Hewer recalls: 'In his usual Crystal style he would glide past me in a crowded room and out of the corner of his mouth say, "*GQ* want to run an article, very worrying", and then he would disappear into the crowd. On that Saturday I cornered Crystal. He said, "I'm very concerned about this article on Tottenham that *GQ* are planning. Maurice Barnfather knows this journalist and knows where he is coming from, and wants to help. I think he should be brought in to deal with this." '

The mention of Barnfather's name put Hewer on the alert. Barnfather, a former City editor of the *Mail on Sunday*, had started his own financial PR business and was a potential rival to Hewer. 'Barnfather runs a PR company, does he not?' asked Hewer. 'Nothing to do with that, nothing to do with that,' replied Crystal. 'He is just a good friend of the club, good friend.'

Over the weekend Hewer thought about it and first thing on Monday morning he rang Barnfather. Barnfather mentioned that Martin Tomlinson, the former investigative reporter for *Private Eye*, had been commissioned to do the piece. 'I know him well and if there is anything I can do to help . . .'

'Don't worry, Mr Barnfather,' said Hewer, 'if there is any help I need I shall turn to you. But you have already been very helpful.'

Hewer called Tomlinson and arranged to meet him. Soon after that he sent a memo to Sugar saying there was no need to involve 'Jonathan's friend'. When he later spoke to Sugar, Hewer said, 'Alan, you should stick to people you know, people who are loyal to you.' Sugar nodded his head and, at the next match as Crystal sauntered into the Spurs VIP room, he beckoned him over. 'Jonathan, who is this man, Barnfather, who wants to be a hero?' 'No, no, he doesn't want to be a hero at all,' protested Crystal. 'He is a well-known PR, does the Hanson PR.'

'Well, Jonathan, I think we need not bother him, let Nick handle it,' said Sugar.

Hewer believes that this episode was a planned attempt to switch the PR function to a Venables/Crystal nominee: 'I have never met Barnfather; by all accounts he is an excellent practitioner, but life would have been much simpler if they had control of communications with the press, particularly the City press.'

A few days later, when Hewer did have lunch with Tomlinson, a tough straightforward old-style Fleet Street journalist, Crystal's fears turned out to be exaggerated. Tomlinson decided not to do anything on Tottenham but eventually did an article on Amstrad and Sugar's problems with the buy-out. But during the lunch, he said to Hewer, 'Tell Sugar to watch out for the company he is keeping. He is mixing with some very odd people at Tottenham. Next time he is in the Tottenham boardroom ask him to have a good look round.'

But if Tomlinson did not pursue his interests there were others in the media curious both about Venables as chief executive and what made the Venables-Sugar regime tick. Nobody had any clue as to the nascent civil war between the two but there was some inkling of Venables' wider financial problems. Back in June, Nick Gilbert, writing in the *Independent on Sunday*, had said that 'the business suit does not always seem to fit Mr Venables as snugly as the tracksuit. His choice of associates seems colourful and his business background is, to say the least, eventful.'

In the autumn Mark Honigsbaum, writing for the *Evening Standard* colour magazine, returned to this theme: 'Tel' was a superb football coach but did he know much about business? The article, 'Tel Tales', which was to become the subject of a libel action by Venables – since settled – began with a riveting portrayal of Venables on the Tottenham training field:

> In his black Umbro sweatshirts and shorts, he shuffles across the pitch in a menacing, crab-like manner, occasionally darting forward, teeth pushed strangely against lower lip. As he moves he shouts in gnomic football speak, 'Your job is to stand up and cover with your feet. Stand up and cover!' There's a certain poignancy in watching a middle-aged man playing football and, at forty-nine, Terry Venables is more often seen in a business suit than a football kit, but he still looks good in motion.

Honigsbaum went on to describe how, after he had finished

training, he spent thirty seconds doing a quick interview with the waiting journalists, then, quickly changing and without eating, rushed to his Mercedes to drive from Mill Hill to Kensington and Scribes. Venables even joked about his two clubs, 'People are asking me, "How's your club doing?" I don't know which club they mean, Scribes or Tottenham.' As they approached the car the phone rang and Venables said to Honigsbaum, 'Come on, don't be a slow walker.'

One of the pictures accompanying the article showed Venables standing at the bar at Scribes laughing uproariously, a glass of champagne in front of him on the bar. It was clear that this was where he felt at home, with Eric Hall puffing his cigars and introducing karaoke turns while Venables took to the stage, bringing the house down singing 'That Old Black Magic'.

But much as the magic of his business deals intrigued the press, nobody could quite penetrate it. Honigsbaum had raised the question: now that Venables was more involved on the training ground, did this mean that Sugar's hands were on the Tottenham tiller?

Something similar had also been puzzling Roy Ackerman, a television producer with a company called Diverse. A long-standing Spurs fan, he worked closely with Chris Horrie, whose book *Sick as a Parrot: The Inside Story of the Spurs Fiasco* had described the events from the Scholar-Bobroff take-over of 1982 to the arrival of Sugar and Venables in the boardroom. Horrie, a self-confessed Murdoch watcher, had started off with the thesis that the Tottenham story was one of a small company being used as a pawn in a major television game, one where the stakes had been raised by Sky's right to televise Premier League matches. His book came out in the summer of 1992, just as Sky won the Premier League contract, and was an excellent basis for a television programme.

However, while writing the book Horrie had been rebuffed by Nick Hewer when he approached him for an interview with Tottenham. Horrie went away with the impression that Sugar did not want to talk to him, but in fact Hewer had been told to turn Horrie away by Venables.

'Horrie came to my office,' recalls Hewer, 'and I was taken by the idea of the book. I asked Alan and he said, "I've no objection, ask Terry". So next time I was at Spurs I went into his office and asked him. He said, "No way, I don't want anything to do with that book." "Why Terry?" I asked, genuinely surprised by the rejection. Terry said, "No, no I don't want to help him, I might decide to do a book myself".'

However, in June 1992, when Ackerman approached Hewer to make a programme looking at football as a business with Spurs as a focus, Hewer was able to persuade Venables to allow access. Ackerman, aware of the Horrie rebuff, decided to keep Horrie in the background. 'Given Horrie's rebuff I did not push him forward as the first point of contact.'

As the programme took shape two stories developed. Horrie recalls:

> There was what we called the big story, the one of how Tottenham, this little company, was a pawn in a major television game. Murdoch had not wanted Tottenham to fall to Maxwell. Murdoch's Sky had won the rights to televise Premier League and was saying, this is crucial to us, and if Sky did not succeed it would have a major impact on Murdoch. So we wanted to look at the Murdoch-Sugar deals. Then there was what we called the little story, the deals Venables had done, and while doing the programme we had a discussion whether we should concentrate on the little story, but in the end decided not to.

Horrie, however, did do some digging into the Norfina loan and puzzled long and hard how Venables had acquired the money to buy Spurs. Had Sugar by some chance financed him? Horrie put the question to Venables. This is his recollection of how Venables reacted:

> Venables laughed, a hollow, cynical laugh, and rolled his eyes and said, 'You must be joking, Alan Sugar wouldn't help me.' But he wouldn't tell us where he had got the money from. All he would say was, 'I have stretched myself to do it, really stretched myself.'

Ackerman met Venables three times: once at Spurs, twice at Scribes:

> I got the impression that these were two very odd bedfellows. When we interviewed Venables at his office in Tottenham Sugar seemed to be peering over him. He was so close he nearly got in the way of the cameraman. I thought that is a curious way to behave towards your chief executive. Then we met Venables at Scribes, once to get his permission to use stuff from 'The Manager' and on another occasion to put some more questions. On both occasions it was in the afternoon,

Scribes looked a ghostly place, this plush club where nobody was around, and Venables did not look happy. I remember him looking me in the eye and saying, 'All I want to do is rest easy in my bed.'

How easily Venables rested in bed is open to doubt for the questions Horrie and Ackerman raised about his finances certainly disturbed his entourage. On more than one occasion Crystal told Hewer that the programme wanted to 'stitch Terry up'. Hewer, in trying to pacify Crystal, spent some time ringing Ackerman and even some journalists in trying to discover whether the programme was, as Crystal feared, straying from the subject and doing a hatchet job on Venables.

The programme was due to be screened on Sunday 29 November 1992. As luck would have it, that week saw some of the ghosts from Venables' past come alive. On the Sunday Jeff Randall had had a story in the *Sunday Times* about a new boardroom split. There was mention of a stormy Board meeting although no specific details were given. From Monday 23 November Irving Scholar's book *Behind Closed Doors*, which I had helped him to write, began to be serialised in the *Daily Express*. Scholar had made it very clear that there was no love lost between him and Venables and the book reflected this view of Scholar's. The *Express* was quick to pick out what it felt were the juiciest bits. One of them was that Venables had often proposed to sell Gary Mabbutt, the Tottenham skipper.

By Tuesday, when the *Daily Express* ran another extract, Crystal was straining at the leash for a response from Spurs. Hewer was asked urgently to fax cuttings from the *Express* to Bryan Fugler, for legal advice, which was done at 5.15 that evening. Venables put out a statement saying it was strange the man who had taken the club to extinction could pass judgement on those who had saved it, and then sought to rebut Scholar's allegation that he had wanted to sell Mabbutt, but producing the sort of denial that didn't deny the thrust of the Scholar story. By that evening the Spurs Board had commented, Hewer putting out the statement, expressing dismay about the 'inaccuracy, distortion and untruth' of the *Express* extracts.

The drafting revealed Crystal's hand. One of Scholar's main points was that Venables was no businessman, what is more Sugar had never rated him as one and told Scholar so even before the take-over. The Spurs Board denied that Sugar had ever met Scholar, a strange denial since the book had never made such a claim. Then it went on to say that the two men had only ever spoken twice, both times before Sugar and Venables had started working together at Tottenham: 'accordingly, he was hardly in a position to doubt Mr Venables' entrepreneurial abilities'. The statement concluded by hoping the book did not present a 'crooked view of history'.

That day Harry Harris, whose attitude to Venables is well known, ran a prominent article in the *Mirror* giving a preview of the Ackerman programme. The programme, in trying to explain the Venables-Sugar take-over, had dramatised Venables' testimony during the Scholar libel trial when he was describing how various people, including Sheikh Zayad of Abu Dhabi, had been involved in Venables' efforts to raise money. The Harris article highlighted rather than revealed new facts, Venables having made his court appearance six months earlier, but for the Venables camp this was another example of a campaign against Venables. As the *Express* extracts continued, Crystal got even more concerned.

The next evening, just before midnight, as Hewer drove down the ramp to his underground car park, the car phone rang. It was Crystal.

'Did you see yesterday's *Daily Mirror*? I am very worried about the television programme. They are out to destroy Terry.'

'Don't worry, Jonathan,' said Hewer, 'I have been given assurances by the producer, Roy Ackerman, that it is not about Terry but about football as business using Spurs as a focus.'

'I hope your judgement is right,' said Crystal. 'If not the consequences will be very severe. There will be an explosion at next week's Board meeting if you are wrong.'

The next day Hewer rang Ackerman and, unable to reach him, decided to send a fax to Crystal with copies to Venables, Sugar, Sandy and Berry, enclosing letters from Ackerman which had formed the basis of the co-operation between Tottenham and Ackerman. Hewer concluded, 'If your fears prove to be correct, it will be monstrous . . . I will contact you as soon as I have spoken to Roy Ackerman.'

That evening Ackerman reassured Hewer that the trial scene had been exaggerated by the *Mirror*. On 27 November Hewer wrote a letter to Michael Attwell, Commissioning Editor at Channel Four, expressing the dismay felt by Tottenham's directors about the *Mirror* article and asking for assurance that the programme did not 'denigrate Mr Venables'. Indeed the programme did not. Bearing the same title as the Horrie book, 'Sick as a Parrot', it tried to prove that the Spurs take-over was part of a prearranged plan between Murdoch and Sugar to exploit the television potential of football. Despite its best efforts it failed to prove this extraordinary thesis. The effect of the programme, which did not denigrate Venables, was that he emerged as essentially a bit player in the story.

Even before the programme was broadcast Venables had tried to turn the publicity battle. On Thursday Venables gave an interview to the same paper which had been serialising the Scholar extracts, the *Daily Express*. James Lawton wrote a clever piece which portrayed Venables as the wise, magnanimous man saddened, rather than angered, by the Scholar criticism. The only flash of 'raw anger' had come when he read of the Scholar story describing how Venables had once cried in the Spurs loo bemoaning his fate. No, the only moment he had cried was when leaving Crystal Palace and that was in the car park. In any case what is wrong with tears? 'I would never feel shame, anyway, in showing how I feel. From time to time I do feel very strongly about the game. It's on the record.'

The interview showed how well Venables could manage the press. But if all this kept the world in blissful ignorance of the real situation at White Hart Lane, evidence continued to accumulate that Venables was losing his grip on Spurs ever more, and that his management style was producing curious results.

This was perhaps the most curious of the many management decisions which Venables took during his reign at Spurs and one that emphasised his failure to understand the role of stewardship a chief executive is required to provide. Sometime in late October 1992 Venables told Sandy that an invoice would arrive from Eric Hall for £20,000, plus VAT, for work he had done for Tottenham. However, said Venables, he had arranged that Hall would not have to be paid until next June. 'Next time you see Eric just thank him for that, he would like that,' said Venables. 'Fine,' said Sandy who, like most accountants, was always delighted to hear of creditors happy to delay payment.

On 17 October Spurs played Middlesbrough at home and Sandy made a special point of going up to Hall in the Oak Room and thanking him for postponing the payment of the invoice. Hall seemed very pleased. On 26 October Hall sent an invoice claiming £20,000, plus VAT, for 'Public Relations and Commercial Activities on the Club's behalf'. The invoice made it clear that the money would not have to be paid until 1 June 1993.

Nothing further was said or done about it until the time came for the payment of the invoice. By then, as it turned out, Venables was no longer chief executive. Sugar, mystified by the invoice, wrote to Venables for an explanation but did not receive an answer. Hall pressed for payment and then filed a writ. As Tottenham prepared their defences against the action they began to unearth a story behind the invoice which was extraordinary, for it was immediately clear that Hall's fee had nothing to do with public relations or commercial activities as claimed in his invoice. He had acted as an agent for Justin Edinburgh, Paul Moran and John Hendrie, who had all been playing for Spurs, in their contract negotiations with Spurs. Hall's story, which he repeated in two affidavits, was that in June 1992 Venables asked him to negotiate new contracts for Edinburgh, Moran and Hendrie.

Edinburgh had a year of his contract to run, the contracts of Moran and Hendrie had expired. 'A fee was agreed between myself and Terry Venables of £20,000, plus VAT, for my work regardless of whether I was successful in persuading the players.' Hall was successful but when it came to payment Venables pleaded poverty: the club was suffering financial problems, so could he delay the invoice? Hall, who luxuriated in the title of agent extraordinaire for Venables, readily agreed. In October, when he approached Venables, Venables again told him the club was suffering financial problems. Hall told Venables he would submit his invoice straightaway but payment could be made in June 1993.

Venables in his affidavits backed up the Hall story. He had called Hall in because the three players had rejected an initial offer he himself had made to them. In his second affidavit he added that Hall had initially wanted £10,000 per player but Venables had negotiated him down to £20,000 for all three. One curiosity about the Venables story was why he should have pleaded poverty at Tottenham and tried to delay payment of the bill. On 27 October, the day after Hall presented his invoice, Tottenham had an overdraft facility of £4m. Yet its overdraft that day was £2.2m., so a cheque for £23,500 would not have bothered the bank. Nor, at that stage, was Tottenham suffering such financial difficulties that its chief executive needed to ask a creditor to wait over six months for payment.

The greater curiosity in all this was: who was Hall acting for?

For Tottenham? Or for the players? When Tottenham asked Edinburgh, Moran and Hendrie they produced affidavits which put an entirely different twist on the story.

All three players said that Hall was supposed to be acting as their agent. Players at Tottenham fill in a form stating who their agent is and Venables was well aware that Hall acted for all three players. Hall charged Edinburgh £5,000, Moran £1,000 and Hendrie £1,000 for his services, although he only collected the money from Edinburgh who paid him in cash. None of the three players knew that Hall was acting for Tottenham, let alone being paid by the club. Also, contrary to what Venables and Hall had said, none of the players had initially refused a contract, they had never been offered one. The first and only contract they saw was the one offered through Hall.

Justin Edinburgh presented the most fluent account of what happened:

By May 1992, Mr Venables had indicated to me that he was pleased with my progress and wanted to renegotiate my original contract with Spurs...It was clear that in the renegotiations I would be represented by Mr Hall. Although Mr Venables had told me that we would sit down and discuss my new contract with Spurs, this never transpired. All negotiations were conducted through Mr Hall on my behalf. I saw Mr Hall on several occasions to discuss how he would conduct negotiations and he told me what I should expect to be offered. He said that he would try and get his fee paid by Spurs as part of the negotiation of my new contract, but that if he did not I would have to pay it. I took this to mean that if Spurs paid Mr Hall's fee, I would pay nothing. He led me to believe that it was highly probable that Spurs would pay his fee. My agreement with Mr Hall was an oral agreement in which I gave him a free hand to negotiate the best terms he could obtain for me. He did not at this stage mention how much his fee would be. I was aware that it would be usual to pay an agent a fee.

In May 1992 Mr Hall came to visit me in hospital. He told me he had negotiated the best contract available with Mr Venables and that Spurs had refused to pay his fee. He told me the terms that he had agreed with Mr Venables and, on the basis of Mr Hall's assurance, I was satisfied that they were the best terms available. I had no option but to agree to the fee which Mr Hall then told me I had to pay, being £5,000. This was the first time a figure had been mentioned . . . Mr Hall did not send me an invoice for the £5,000 but he telephoned me and asked me for the money. I paid Mr Hall in cash the sum of £5,000, eight or ten weeks later. I cannot remember him asking me to pay the fee in cash but I can think of no other reason why I would have done so, as writing a cheque would have been much easier for me. I was not given a receipt for this sum . . . I now discover that Mr Hall had done a deal with Mr Venables under which, instead of representing my interests, he actually represented the interests of Spurs, interests that conflicted directly with my own. In return for doing so, Mr Hall was to be paid a fee. I knew nothing about this, and would not have consented to it had I been told about it . . . I thought Mr Hall was representing my interests honestly, impartially and to the best of his abilities. I had no idea that he was playing both sides against each other.

Hall had demanded £20,000 from Spurs, he had got £5,000 from Edinburgh and wanted £1,000 each from Moran and Hendrie. But faced by the evidence which Tottenham presented, Hall, contrary to his first affidavit, said he had not expected to be paid by Spurs if he did not succeed in negotiating the contracts, only if he succeeded. As regards Edinburgh paying him £5,000 Hall thought Edinburgh had got this confused with other work he had done for the player. In any case the player was at liberty to pay the agent over and above what the club had paid and Hall claimed that in this case he had achieved for Edinburgh substantially more than he had been originally offered. Yes, he might have got a few dates wrong but that was because 'I do not keep detailed written records'.

Tottenham's lawyers' defence was that it was illegal under civil law for an agent to be paid by both sides, without the knowledge of all concerned, and that further this might amount to a possible breach of the Prevention of Corruption Act, 1906. Section I(1) of the Act prohibits any agent from agreeing to accept 'any gift or consideration as inducement or reward for doing or for bearing to do . . . any act in relation to his principal's affairs of business.' In simple terms this means that a football agent cannot take money from a club for negotiating a contract for a player when that player is the agent's client.

The same section of the Act contains similar provisions regarding persons who agree to give any such gift or agree to pay a fee. Venables' affidavit made it clear that he had asked Hall to convince the players to sign the contracts; he knew that Hall was their agent and had agreed to pay Hall a fee in order to get his clients to agree to the terms Venables was offering. The leading counsel Tottenham turned to advised that, 'The Hall and Venables agreement was a secret agreement under which the plaintiff [Hall] was to act for both parties in the negotiations. Accordingly the agreement is void for illegality.'

On 15 November 1993 the Tottenham evidence was presented to Master Topley and he went against Hall and dismissed the matter. His conclusion was that it was arguable that the alleged agreement in respect of which Hall was suing was illegal. Within days Hall had dropped his case and paid Spurs' costs, but it was the reflection of the whole case on Venables that was most disturbing. He may or may not have been aware of the 1906 Act, but for him not to recognise the conflict of interest was remarkable.

Chapter 19

Time-bombs at Christmas

On 5 November 1992, with the fireworks at the October Tottenham Board meeting apparently forgotten, Sugar and Venables met socially in the presence of their families. Sugar had arranged to have dinner with his family at Langan's to celebrate his wife Ann's birthday and, just before the family came, Sugar and Venables had a chat during the course of which Sugar asked about Landhurst. Its problems, receiver called in, SFO investigation, were well known and Sugar wondered how Venables might be affected. Venables confirmed that he had given a PG, a personal guarantee on the loan.

A few weeks later Sugar met Venables again at Harry's Bar. This was a one-to-one meeting meant to sort out their problems. Both men were aware that there were some tough issues to be discussed. If Sugar was to take over the commercial side then he felt he should be paid. At this stage Sugar had not received any money, after nearly eighteen months as chairman. The previous chairman, Nat Solomon, had received a fee of £40,000 at a time of acute financial difficulty for the club and Sugar felt that if he was to organise Tottenham's commercial side it was only right he should get some money for it. Venables hummed and hawed. Well, he said, I don't mind, you can have the money but in that case I want more money. In the end it was agreed that Sugar was to have a contract.

Sugar felt pleased by this chat at Harry's bar. He had raised the difficult issues, including Brown, and Venables had reassured him that everything would be all right. 'He was very amiable, very charming, agreed with everything in principle'. Then he added:

'Apart from the Harry's Bar meeting we had other one-to-one meetings and it was always the same. He would be very pleasant, very charming, but then he would go away and do things his own way. He would leave the meeting and deny what was said, what was agreed. As if he wasn't there, had never agreed to it. Perhaps he has a terrible memory but it was impossible to work in such a situation. You could not deal with the man. I have never come across anybody like him before.'

The problem, as Sugar analysed it, was that while on his own Venables was a person he could live with, once he went back to his den at Scribes his entourage filled his head with delusions of grandeur. Whatever Sugar did, Venables had to match. Sometimes this appeared childish: the 1 October Board meeting had been held at Sugar's boardroom at Amstrad. So the next Board meeting, eight days later to discuss ground safety, met at Scribes West.

Interestingly, this last did not start up as a formal Board meeting. Venables, Crystal, Sandy and the others were present – though not Sugar – and decided to formalise their discussions into a Board meeting. It was this precedent Sandy had in mind when the much disputed Tottenham Board meeting at Arsenal took place but, while for Venables and Crystal the one at Scribes was proper, advertising Venables' own club, the one at Arsenal, less convenient from their point of view, was legally controversial.

Venables' guru on the law was Crystal, and Sugar was soon convinced that many of the things that needled Venables were due to the many conversations he had had with Crystal. Venables would not hear a word said against Crystal, and felt that Sugar, on his side, was wound up by Sandy. All this meant that the spirit of goodwill generated at Langan's and Harry's Bar could not last.

On the Thursday before the 3 December 1992 Board meeting at Tottenham, Bryan Fugler arranged a meeting with a leading counsel to discuss the Ian Gray settlement. Should Tottenham capitulate, what were the chances of winning the case? Since Sugar did not have an office he took him to Venables' office – Scholar's old one. He had barely settled down to discuss with counsel when Venables, who was not at White Hart Lane, rang his secretary Penny to say he was on his way. A few minutes later Penny came in to inform Sugar that he would have to leave the office as Venables was going to hold a conference with Doug Livermore.

Sugar thought that once Venables arrived he would realise the importance of his meeting with counsel on a matter that involved having to decide whether Tottenham should pay £225,000. Sugar hoped the conference with Livermore, which was after all an internal meeting, could take place elsewhere. When Venables arrived Sugar introduced him to the counsel and told him what they were discussing. 'If you want us to move, I will move,' said Sugar. Venables did not offer the room and Sugar found himself picking up all the files and with leading counsel in tow trawling up and down White Hart Lane for a spare room. It was an extraordinary position for the chief executive of the club to put the chairman in.

Sugar was soon to discover that, although he owned the inn, there was no place for him there. He went to the VIP lounge and found it full of auditors and accountants. In the boardroom Igal Yawetz and his model maker were assembling their proposed new stand. Never, wrote Sugar later, have I been in such a ridiculous situation. Venables' response to the Sugar complaint was to say that it was Sugar who was at fault, his conference with Livermore was essential pre-match preparation. Venables had got it wrong, it was not a match day and the whole episode suggested that for Venables even to spare Sugar his room for a few minutes was too much of a concession, too much like giving up power. It seemed to show he had a possessive streak, an almost child-like need to cling to what he had.

The prejudices of both sides were reinforced at the Board meeting which followed a week later. It should have been a very pleasant one. On the field the team was now doing a lot better. Having started at the bottom of the table, as Tottenham so often did during the Venables reign, it had put a few victories together. However, a series of decisions were taken that day which would prove to be a set of ticking time-bombs.

Some of it concerned confirmation of bad news that had been expected. The advice senior counsel gave Sugar was not encouraging and it was decided that Tottenham had to pay £225,000 to Ian Gray. When Gray had filed his action Crystal had been confident it could be resisted, Sugar had wanted to fight but the fact that Tottenham were now settling on Gray's terms left a residue of bitterness in both the Sugar and Venables camps. The loans that the Scholar regime had given players had been a feature of Tottenham Board meetings since August 1991. Crystal had been dealing with the problems that had arisen. However, it now emerged they were being investigated by the Inland Revenue and there was some discussion as to whether Touche Ross should be asked to prepare a report.

But the more lethal time-bomb was one concerning Sugar's role in the merchandising division. Two weeks earlier Sandy had sacked Mike Pay and Ivy Calvino, to the intense irritation of the Venables camp. Sandy had been a bit nervous about sacking Pay, who was a large man, and had arranged for a security man to be discreetly present should he turn nasty. He didn't and Ivy Calvino just burst into tears. Sandy believed his decision was fully justified: Pay, far from helping him monitor stock control, was, he felt, hindering him. But I have kept John informed, Pay replied when Sandy gave him his P45, I am supposed to report to him, not you.

When Sandy narrated this to the Board, Venables said, 'No, no, you've got it wrong. John has not been involved in merchandising for two months now.' Venables saw the sackings as yet another instance of Sandy sticking his nose into business that did not concern him. Listening to Venables, Sandy got the impression he did not know what was going on.

Soon there was an additional complication. Both Pay and Calvino were talking of legal action and it was decided that Brown should be allowed to offer them better terms. It seems amazing that Brown still had some executive role. After the October Board decisions Sugar and Sandy should have been in charge, but Brown would not let go of the reins. However, the end-result of the Pay-Calvino saga was that Sugar did now take formal charge of the merchandising department and the Board was told that, while they waited to appoint an executive, Sandy would assist him particularly in monitoring stock. Not that this was to prove the end of the affair, only the beginning of yet more problems.

The Sugar contract was also another time-bomb. Sugar had assumed that, since Venables had agreed at Harry's Bar to his having a contract, everything was all right on that front. He soon faxed a contract to Venables at the training ground and to Crystal at his chambers. As it happened Crystal was holidaying in Mauritius, the first time he had been away since becoming a director at Tottenham. When Crystal learnt what had happened he was in no doubt that Sugar had waited until he went on holiday to give himself a contract, part of what the Venables camp would later see as a well-planned conspiracy. Sugar, far from harbouring any such thoughts, believed the contract would be faxed on to Crystal and he considered he was following standard Tottenham procedure. In any case, although Sugar signed the contract and got Sandy to sign it, no money changed hands. This still awaited formal Board approval. When that meeting took place Crystal, back from holiday, erupted.

Interestingly, the Sugar contract was based on the standard Amstrad contract which had a clause containing an instrument that could be used to destroy Sugar. It said that, should a director lose a vote of non-confidence in a Board meeting, he would lose his seat on the Board. It might have seemed an innocuous clause but in the situation of Tottenham seven months later it could prove deadly.

Quite by chance about this time the Sugar camp had stumbled on something Crystal had done and, while this was not connected with Tottenham, it was just as deadly. On the morning of the 3 December Board meeting Nick Hewer was in Court 61 of the High Court in the Strand. A Mr Edward Northcote had brought an action against Amstrad with regard to the buy-out and this was to be heard by Mr Justice Vinelott that day. Hewer was waiting with Margaret Mountfort of Herbert Smith and other Sugar lawyers when suddenly he saw Crystal rise and address the court. Hewer was surprised to see him in court. Is he representing Amstrad? he wondered. However, it soon became apparent that Crystal was before the court on another matter.

Crystal asked for a matter, in which he was due to appear before Justice Vinelott at 2pm that afternoon, to be postponed by a week. The opposing counsel, a Mr Jarvis, described the application as 'the most bizarre application made to your Lordship. This is part heard. What is left is for Mr Crystal to reply. As I understood the matter yesterday, he thought his reply would be very short.'

Justice Vinelott was not too pleased either as he had thought that Crystal was available that day or that morning. Jarvis wondered what professional commitments prevented Crystal from dealing with the matter.

Crystal explained his problem: 'My Lord, the position is I have a disciplinary matter which is part heard, which I understood is going to be at two o'clock and in fact it has been re-convened for 11.30 this morning.

Mr Justice Vinelott: 'I see.'

Mr Crystal: 'But if your Lordship directs that the matter is to go ahead today, my Lord, then I'm happy of course to stay and try and deal with that.'

Mr Justice Vinelott: 'Is this before the tribunal – a senate tribunal?'

Mr Crystal: 'My Lord, it is not a senate tribunal. My Lord, I'm representing somebody at it.'

Justice Vinelott then agreed to adjourn the matter until 4.15pm, a time which was convenient for the opposing counsel. 'I will hear Mr Crystal very briefly at 4.15 and then I will give judgement.'

Mr Crystal: 'My Lord, that course probably will be actually the worse for me, with respect, because the tribunal is not sitting in this locality and will sit almost inevitably well into the evening. It's not a tribunal that is sitting in a conventional court house.'

Mr Justice Vinelott: 'When does it sit tomorrow?'

Mr Crystal: 'My Lord, it does not sit tomorrow and, my Lord, clearly I can be here. My Lord, I said next Thursday because I understood that that would be a convenient date for everybody. I'm absolutely available at any other time.' Justice Vinelott fixed it at ten o'clock the next morning

At 6pm that evening Hewer telephoned Colin Sandy and they chatted about various matters, including the Board meeting. 'Oh, by the way, was Crystal there?' asked Hewer.

'Yeah,' replied Sandy.

'When did he get there?' asked Hewer.

'He was there from the start for the entire meeting. He did not miss anything. You know Crystal,' said Sandy.

'Really,' said Hewer. 'I find that very surprising.'

'Why?' asked Sandy.

Then Hewer told Sandy about what Crystal had said in court about the disciplinary hearing.

It would be many months before the significance of this would dawn on Sugar.

However, despite all that, and with Crystal, fast growing as his bête noire, away that Christmas, Sugar appeared more relaxed. Just before the holiday he invited a friend of his, Harvey Gilbert, to a match and on the way to the ground asked his advice on the merchandising division. Gilbert, vastly experienced in this field, offered to help and his wife suggested Tottenham appoint Kay Lyons. Perhaps, thought Sugar, it will at last be possible to get a grip on things.

Chapter 20

Dear Terry . . . Dear Alan

If Sugar felt any optimism after the Harry's Bar meeting, it had all but evaporated by the time the Christmas decorations came down. In the beginning he had accepted that Venables' style of doing business was to keep 'things confidential and secret', as Sugar put it in a memo. But in a football club this meant that Sugar, the chairman, was often the last one to know when players were on the move. In mid-January a group of serious fans asked Sugar if Gray was on loan. Sugar said, 'No way, that's not true', only to discover from Venables that it was true. Then one match day a certain Pini Souharni, an Israeli agent, stopped Venables to say he was showing a Russian player around. Yes, said Venables, he would purchase a Russian player if he could sell Durie. Worse still was the whole affair with Paul Allen and Colin Sandy, although in this case it was Venables who felt aggrieved.

Allen was due to have a testimonial. Crystal suggested Sandy help him with his tax. So after the home match against Sheffield Wednesday on 16 January Sandy had a word with Allen. Clearly there was some misunderstanding. Venables had agreed Allen would get 100%. He went away thinking he would be best advised to take only 60%. 'I have,' wrote Venables to Sugar, 'had to deal with a huge problem with the player for three days on the trot in a Cup week. Frankly, his [meaning Sandy's] behaviour is unforgivable and he cannot be left to deal with players again.'

This, as it happened, boomeranged on the players. Sugar told Sandy to keep away, whereupon Sandy refused to get involved with Eric Thorstvedt, letting Crystal handle it and the result, as Sugar put it, is 'the player is being pursued by the German authorities and nobody is doing anything other than Jonathan asking Colin what the latest status is'.

So on 21 January 1993 Sugar sat down at his desk and, turning to the Amstrad word processor by his side, began tapping out a memo. It began 'Dear Terry' and it was a bit like a lover who, rushed into marriage, was now discovering the warts on the face of his beloved one. Sugar had imagined that Venables as chief executive would be a hands-on chief executive, but he was so rarely at White Hart Lane that 'the site at Tottenham seems to have a lot of "wandering lost lambs" with no direction. This is because the top management is "transient", i.e. popping in and out, having quick brash meetings with no day-to-day direction.' He went on:

> You are paid as the Chief Executive of the company and it is my opinion, for the benefit of the company, and all of those in it, that your services should be seen as that of coaching the team in co-ordination with the other staff in the morning sessions, as you do at the moment, and then personally being on site at the ground for the afternoon sessions each day dealing with the day-to-day matters of the company . . . This is what is expected in any large company that has a £20 million turnover and makes profits of £2m. or £3m. There is no other company that I know of such a size that does not have a full-time Chief Executive on site.

Sugar was reflecting a general feeling about Venables' style of the management. It meant there was no distinct line management. Venables was now spending more time than in the first year at the training ground compared with White Hart Lane. When Mike Rollo, Tottenham's commercial manager, wanted to contact Venables he had to beard him at the Royal Garden Hotel or at Scribes. If it was a morning meeting Venables preferred the Royal Garden, if it was late evening he preferred Scribes. The compensation for Rollo at such meetings was that he did have Venables' undivided attention rather than the distracted air he wore at the training ground.

By the time Sugar wrote the memo the line management had become even more complicated. Even Brown, who in the first year of the Venables regime had spent a good deal of time at White Hart Lane, began to be less visible there as the 1992–93 season began. David Press, who had been employed by Brown as manager responsible for video production and sales, found this very disturbing. He had joined Tottenham at the end of April 1992 and rarely saw Venables at White Hart Lane and Brown for not more than two or three hours a day, and even then not every day.

Press was another interesting Venables appointment. A founder-director of Karaoke Entertainment, a company that supplied karaoke machines to pubs and clubs, he had resigned in April 1991. In April 1992 the company closed showing no assets and owing creditors, including Inland Revenue and Customs and Excise, more than £95,000.

His recruitment, actually by Brown, indicates the style of the Venables regime. An advertisement had appeared in the *Daily Telegraph* in January 1992 for the position of Senior Marketing Executive. Press was interviewed by Brown and Audrey Zolnierowics, Tottenham's Personnel Manager, on 16 January. The job he was being interviewed for was supposed to be Group Marketing Manager reporting directly to Venables. After the interview Press did not hear anything for another three months, then a 'Dear David' letter came from Brown on 27 April offering him a three-month consultancy at £4,000 per month, his job being that of the manager responsible for video production and sales. Press joined, only to be told on 1 June that, while he was now going on the staff, he would be paid £25,000 a year, a lot less than the consultancy fee, but with bonus to be agreed. By May 1993 the bonus had not been agreed and he could never pin Brown down. It was some six weeks after he joined that he met Venables for the first time and this only by going to Scribes one evening and introducing himself. Press doubts whether Venables knew anything about his bonus arrangement.

Venables' management style meant many issues which should have been solved, like the audit of Letherby and Christopher, the Chanticleer arrangements, the North Stand construction, had not been sorted out. 'I personally believe,' Sugar's memo to Venables continued, 'that you have too much to do (when you include your private affairs during the working day) and I do not want to interfere with your private matters but I go back to the fact that you are paid as the full-time executive of the company and a full-time executive means that.'

In Venables' absence Brown was the man everyone turned to, and Brown 'most certainly is not the person for everybody to report to and quite honestly I do not believe anybody other than you should be that person.'

Brown had to go. Sugar recognised that it was 'somewhat of a comfort factor' to have 'John around in your life'. Sugar was quite prepared to pay him a year's fees, £78,000 to get rid of him. He could still advise Venables on his own personal matters but not work for Tottenham: 'The recent events which have led to another bout of bickering is frankly worrying me because we have a big business and it is being run as if it is a game with two camps of people. I am certainly not interested in this style of business and I know that Colin Sandy, who has worked with me for five years, does not have that style either. I cannot put up with this any longer.'

True, Sugar was not used to sharing companies, but he had allowed Venables to take the helm of the company, treated him with utmost respect but felt he had been rewarded with contempt and a very cold shoulder. The old wounds re-emerged: he had not been consulted about Shreeves' appointment, about the Durie purchase, he often learnt of a player being bought for the club from the press:

> I am the last to be informed when you have your eyes on other players to be purchased . . . The reality is that 20% of the club belongs to you and 50% belongs to me and the reality is that when you go out and spend money on players you are spending 50% of my money and, in most cases, I know nothing about it and I think, up until now, I have been pretty damn reasonable in allowing you a completely free hand . . . I would be delighted if your dream comes true and that you prosper together with me in Tottenham but each of us must use their best talents to make that happen.

Sugar ended the memo with a plea that was almost from the heart: 'One thing is for sure, I am not going to carry on in the way we are at the moment. Either you recognise my position in the company (between ourselves – there is no need for public recognition) or I believe we should seriously sit down and resolve alternative ways which could only result in one or other of us parting from ownership of Tottenham.' Then he added in his own hand '. . . which I for one do not [and he underlined the word not] wish to do'.

The letter asked Venables not to 'discuss this matter with Jonathan Crystal'. Whether Venables accepted this request we do not know but while Sugar had typed his own letter and was aware that it had typos and mistakes, for which he apologised, Venables had his memo of 25 January 1993 typed by his secretary Penny.

Curiously it was Venables' memo that had the major error, being wrongly dated 25 January 1992 when it should have been 1993. Venables was clearly angered by Sugar's memo and wrote, 'Your memo is offensive and worse so inaccurate. You have been wound up and, unfortunately, seem to have no feel for the business.'

If Sugar hoped his memo would start a dialogue, it became something of a slanging match. It was in this memo that, for the first time, Venables articulated his anger that 'you pushed through the rights issue rather than raising finance on the properties. You knew I did not have the extra money'. As far as talk about Sugar's money being spent, Venables countered, 'It is mine as well'. He then went on to castigate Sugar for not understanding the football business which had led him to moan about Venables' absence from White Hart Lane. But he was at the training ground and that was where the 'football product' was manufactured. If Tottenham wanted to catch up with Milan that is how they would have to go, to use the stadium only on match days and move everything apart from finance to the training ground. The comparison with Milan was not quite appropriate: true it did not own the stadium at San Siro, but it had administrative offices, where its management team including the top executives were located, and this was in the centre of Milan and quite a way removed from its training ground.

If Sugar's bête noire was Brown, then Venables' was Sandy, and he had a catalogue of Sandy's alleged sins which, apart from the Paul Allen affair, ranged from management accounts never on time, Board minutes at the last moment, but above all that he was 'not prepared to remain Finance Director, he has set out to empire-build. He has upset people and I am sure winds you up.' If Sugar complained that Brown acted as if he ran the place, then Venables moaned that Sandy acted in similar fashion. 'If he is often at the ground, he is not doing what he should but involving himself across other people's jobs.' Then after emphatically denying that his working day short-changed Spurs or that he did Scribes work during his working day he came to almost the same conclusion as Sugar:

Things are capable of being worked out sensibly, and I hope they will be . . . it needs mutual recognition, understanding and respect and if you are not happy with that I will sit down with you and look at alternative ways forward. The sooner the better.

However, for any talks to succeed the two men had to agree on

223

basic facts and the memos revealed that even this was beyond them. Sugar had briefly referred to the occasion before Christmas when Venables had thrown him out of his office. Venables, justifying his action, asserted that it was a match day. As we have seen, Venables had got his facts wrong, the incident having taken place on a Thursday when no match was taking place. How could he make such a mistake? wondered Sugar, and it was for him quite alarming: 'I must frankly and honestly say, and with the greatest of respect and with no intention of being rude or disrespectful, that unfortunately your memory sometimes lapses on things which have been agreed, said, and done, and I find myself having to go over the same thing. It is impossible to put every single thing in writing.'

One of Venables' most potent weapons was the allegation that Sugar had benefited from the Sky deal and that 'your professionals' had made £¼m. 'My professionals?' thundered Sugar. 'They are our professionals', who had been paid the fees due to them. Venables had arrived at the figure of £¼m. by totting up the fees paid to Herbert Smith, Henry Ansbacher, Touche Ross, Steniford and Peat Marwick. Sugar pointed out that all these were legitimate fees, some like Peat's incurred by the previous regime. Steniford were the Registrars, Ansbacher had advised on the take-over and Rule 9, Herbert Smith on Rule 9 and other matters which Fugler could not handle, and Touche Ross, apart from the audit, was also preparing a report on the Inland Revenue investigation. 'Do you want me to ask John Brown to handle this?' asked Sugar - sarcastically: 'Again, with the greatest of respect and not wishing to be rude, you have forgotten these things and you are simply shooting from the hip.'

The temper of Sugar's memos showed also, for example, that Crystal had now really got under Sugar's skin, partly because he felt that, far from being an independent non-executive director, he was more of a hero-worshipper of Venables. Sugar ended his memo by suggesting a meeting: 10.30 on 29 January for an hour or so. This meeting could not have achieved much for, at 1.30 that afternoon, the Spurs Board met and it was back to Sugar versus Venables.

Chapter 21

Battle lines are formed

The Venables relationship with Sugar would feature in many crucial Tottenham Board meetings but the one that took place that afternoon, 29 January 1993, was the most seminal. The meeting went on for so long, almost five hours, that after three hours, at about 4.30pm, Crystal had to leave, passing his proxy to Venables.

Tony Berry, in one of his affidavits, would provide a picture of Venables and Sugar at these Board meetings. Sugar could be aggressive in getting his point across.

> He does focus his mind on profit and cost control, but to my knowledge (which simply relates to Tottenham and Tottenham plc) Mr Sugar is most professional and concerned to ensure that things are done in the right way . . . He can be overbearing at times, particularly with his assistants, but he follows advice and he does things correctly by the book. Mr Venables also listens to advice and follows advice, some of which has been wayward. Mr Venables is less aggressive than Mr Sugar, but both men are strong-willed.

Both men also had different styles of waging war. Sugar was inclined to train his guns and blast his way through, Venables followed a more hit-and-run approach, a business version of football's counter-attacking strategy, with heavy reliance on the offside tactics that Venables' teams had used so successfully on the field. As the 29 January meeting began both men were circling each other, waiting to land the first blow. Sugar got his in first.

Sugar was now fully in charge of the merchandising division, three shops and the mail order catalogue, and this was the first opportunity he had to tell the Board of the mess he claimed Venables had left behind. The report was presented by Harvey Gilbert, who had come as a special invitee to the Board. Sugar had accepted Gilbert's suggestion that he appoint Kay Lyons and she had spent a couple of weeks looking at how things were before she agreed to join. Not surprisingly Lyons was greeted with some hostility by the Venables people; however, she told Sugar she was happy to accept the job but would like someone brought in at a more senior level to assist in sorting out the division after which she could run it. Gilbert spent two days on 25 and 26 January making a more thorough survey. It was this report that Sugar and he were now presenting to the Board.

It made grim reading for the Venables-Brown management style. The division was carrying far too much stock, £1m. On a turnover of £2m. there was no proper stock control, or pricing policy in the shops; the buying department was non-existent; each area of the operation was separate from the others. The buying and selling departments were full of little empires. The warehouse did not have any heating, the upstairs floors were empty and the staff not very motivated. Gilbert, after his first visit, had told Sugar how worried he was by the fact that, on Saturdays, managers walked down Tottenham High Street often carrying £10,000 or even £20,000 in cash. Above all there was the Umbro agreement which was so badly worded that there was nothing to prevent someone from buying Umbro stock, setting up a shop in the High Road and selling it from there. As 70% of Tottenham's business was Umbro, this could be disastrous. Also Umbro received a 15% settlement discount when it was they who should have been giving Tottenham a 15% trading discount. Apart from the Umbro agreement, which Venables had inherited and could do nothing about, everything else that Gilbert said was an indictment of his management.

Venables could only sit and listen but his riposte was ready and swiftly delivered by Jonathan Crystal, who had been fuming even before the meeting began. There, sitting at the Board table, was John Ireland, a lawyer, who had just been appointed as company secretary. This followed the Board decision of 1 October and although Crystal had introduced Ireland to Tottenham – and on his first visit to White Hart Lane he had seen Tottenham beat

Liverpool 2–0 – Crystal was less than happy with the presence of another lawyer. According to Berry, Crystal felt the appointment was unnecessary, his concern being to avoid the 'appointment of an independent lawyer being employed to take-over part of the work that hitherto he had been doing. He saw this, I believe, as a further loosening of Mr Venables' control.'

Crystal waited until Gilbert had left and Sugar had approved the minutes of the previous meeting. Then as Sugar began on the agenda proper, Crystal, almost champing at the bit, began the counter-attack on Sugar. The first item provided an ideal opportunity. This concerned Sugar's contract, copies of which were now given to the Board. Crystal, at times standing up as if addressing a court, made it clear that this contract was highly improper. How come Colin Sandy had signed the contract on behalf of Tottenham without the Board's approval? Sandy replied that he had done nothing wrong. It still needed Board approval and in any case no money had been paid out. In that case, interjected Crystal, why had he said no when asked if there was an agreement? Sugar found Crystal's style sanctimonious. Why is everybody, said Sugar, holding on to their hats when Colin is supposed to have said no? What he meant, explained Sugar, was that it had not been approved by the Board or any money changed hands.

In his memo of 26 January to Venables Sugar had said, 'Have you heard the expression "what's sauce for the goose is sauce for the gander"?' So as Crystal spoke, Sugar reminded the Board about the previous September when Venables' contract had been rearranged and money paid out to him, seven weeks before the Board belatedly approved it. Also what about the contracts for Clemence and Livermore which Terry and Jonathan had entered into without any prior Board consultation? In both these cases money had been paid before the Board had formally approved.

After Crystal had finished, Venables entered the fray. Despite having agreed to the contract in Harry's Bar he now changed his mind. The fans, he said, will not understand why the chairman was being paid such a sum of money. This further infuriated Sugar. 'What about Solomon?' he demanded. 'When this club was in grave financial problems he was paid £40,000. And if there is any question of why I am being paid I am now looking after the merchandising department.'

Berry, who increasingly felt he was the peacemaker between Tottenham's warring factions, was not entirely happy about the timing of the contract or how Sugar had initiated it. But he agreed it should be approved. In the end Venables, who wanted to make sure that the contract made it clear payment was for Sugar taking charge of merchandising, proposed the resolution approving the contract, with Berry seconding it.

At this stage the Venables-Sugar match could be said to be finely balanced: 1–1. If Gilbert had scored for Sugar, then the row over the Sugar contract had been shaded in favour of Venables. But now Sugar produced the Brown file. Sugar repeated what he had said before, that he had no problems with Brown's bankruptcy but this file contained material that was too damaging. He was now going to circulate the file to Crystal, Berry and Venables and he was quite happy for them to decide whether Brown should stay or not.

Two days later Tottenham played Crystal Palace at Selhurst Park and, instead of his Rolls, Sugar brought his Range Rover. At the back of the Range Rover were copies of the Brown file and sometime during the match Crystal, Berry and Venables went there to fetch their copies. Not that anybody outside the inner circle knew what was happening. The fans celebrated a 3–1 triumph, ending a dismal sequence of one win in six matches with three successive League defeats, and that victory marked the start of a run which held out much promise for the future. Over the next few weeks the fans lustily sang about 'Venables' blue and white army', little realising the peril their beloved general was in.

Sugar's hope in showing the file to the three, particularly to Berry and Crystal, was that they would find the evidence overwhelming. He had no expectation that Crystal would act independently of Venables. However, when confronted by the facts, thought Sugar, Crystal might accept that Brown must go. But when the Board met on 25 February there was no agreement. Brown was the last item discussed, under 'Any Other Business'. Crystal had prepared some sort of response to the file which did little to convince Berry. If Brown could not provide satisfactory explanations then Berry could not see how Brown would carry on. Perhaps Brown could make a fuller response and, after that, Berry, Crystal and Venables could come to a decision.

Crystal interjected that Tottenham might have to pay Brown's costs if he had to hire solicitors and accountants to reply to the evidence accumulated in the files. Interestingly, Sugar did not press for Brown's removal at this stage. Why? Sugar was aware that such a move would bring matters to a head with Venables and might force a permanent break between them. Sugar has since explained that matters did not come to a head then because Venables kept reassuring him 'it won't happen again', and he was also aware that any precipitate action to remove Brown, which would make an open breach with Venables inevitable, might be very difficult to sell to the fans.

This was of some importance because, at this stage, the players on the field were finally producing a style of play and results that had the fans in raptures. Wretched as Tottenham's early form had been, now it was quite enthralling. Six days before the victory at Palace, Spurs had gone to Norwich and won 2–0 in the Cup. This had been followed by a Cup victory over Wimbledon, something of a bogey team for the club. How crucial this Cup run was can be seen from the way Crystal reacted to the Wimbledon triumph. As one Tottenham season-ticket holder was leaving the ground he was surprised to find Crystal standing in the car park smoking furiously and saying, 'This is the most important match in the history of the Cup.' When the season-ticket holder asked him not to be so ridiculous, Crystal said, 'You don't understand. Terry is under such pressure.' The season-ticket holder went away shaking his head in wonder, but Crystal must have felt that so long as the team did well Terry was safe.

And the team was doing well. On 7 March there was a superb win over Manchester City at Maine Road in the quarter-final, a match which was televised live on BBC-1. That victory was all the more uplifting because Spurs had been forced to play without Nick Barmby, the rising star of the side, who had been called up for England to play in a youth tournament in Australia. But Nayim had slotted so well into his place that he had scored a hat-trick. The victory took Spurs to the semi-final of the Cup where they faced Arsenal, a repeat of the 1991 semi-final. If there could also be a repeat of that triumph, then Sugar could hardly afford to rock the boat.

Sugar's patience was wearing thin, however. If Brown was not enough of a problem, by now another monster had raised its head: computerisation. This was in some ways the most curious divide between Venables and Sugar. The need for such a computer system had long been agreed by both camps. Almost a year earlier Sandy had concluded that Tottenham's stock control methods belonged to the quill and ink age, and computerisation was the only solution. The Sugar camp expected that on this issue there would be no problems with Venables. Just as he was the football expert, so Sugar was the computer expert. Yet right from the beginning there had been problems with Brown keen to offer advice and help.

In February 1992 Brown introduced a man named Haffar as a computer expert. Haffar had been associated with him in the Middle East and was, Sandy would later learn, an accountant by training. Tottenham had just taken possession of some Amstrad computers to be used to standardise word-processing operations. Sandy was not satisfied with Haffar's efforts and ordered that the job be done again. When Brown suggested that Haffar become the merchandising accountant to replace Burton, Sandy refused to accept him. Not surprisingly, when it came to computerisation Sandy relied on Amstrad people, one of whom, Richard Simmons, he persuaded for no fee, except reimbursement of car expenses and the use of a mobile telephone, to advise on the computerisation of the merchandising system, and to come in his own time.

Simmons looked at various options in the summer of 1992, including a proposal from the Foundation system which was for a complete in-house system that would cost something of the order of £175,000 to install. In addition Tottenham would have to employ a computer manager costing £25,000 a year. The Board had been discussing computerisation for some time and had even talked of paying up to £200,000. But this figure alarmed Sugar. Surely there was a cheaper way of doing it? That could only be by a bureau arrangement and that is where the fear and loathing in the Venables camp started.

It turned out that there was spare capacity on Amstrad's mainframe computer at Brentwood and the idea was a direct link to the club using Kilostream, a system somewhat similar to Wirelinks. This system was meant to provide a link with an external IBM AS400 bureau where all the relevant data would be stored. The plan was far from unusual or novel. In theory any computer bureau could have offered this service with the information only accessible to the user's terminal through the correct password. In no way legally could anyone at the computer bureau obtain access to confidential data stored on the mainframe computer. Sugar explained this at some length to Venables and Crystal.

It was intended that Tottenham would rent bureau space from Amstrad's AS400 for a figure of £25,000 p.a. but before agreeing this Sugar requested that Berry and Crystal obtain quotes from other computer bureaux to ensure that the Amstrad price was competitive. At the Board meeting on 29 October the bureau plan had been approved. The decision was meant as a temporary one to enable Sandy and Simmons to install the hardware and get the system operating. The intention was to formalise the bureau agreement between Amstrad and Tottenham after Berry and Crystal had confirmed Amstrad's competitiveness.

In his autobiography Venables has said that the minutes of this meeting do not reflect what was actually discussed about the computerisation issue, part of a wider claim of his that Sugar and Sandy were in the habit of doctoring Board minutes to suit them. Indeed he calls them 'Sugar and Sandy's minutes' as if they were not proper Board minutes.

Venables provides no evidence for such a statement, and this was also the Board meeting that retrospectively approved Venables' contract. So if Venables' logic is to be accepted, Sugar and Sandy doctored minutes selectively, on issues such as computerisation but did not alter approval of Venables' contract, when had they done so they might have caused even more damage.

At the Board meeting on 25 February 1993 it was agreed that hardware would be purchased for £75,000, the hardware comprising fifty-one end-devices, consisting of IBM computers and keyboards with title and bar-coding machines manufactured by Veriform and Codeway respectively. These had previously been used by Amstrad but, as a result of redundancies made at Amstrad, were no longer in use. In addition, several new computerised tills were purchased from a till manufacturer. The hardware bought would be needed whichever bureau was used and, being IBM, was compatible with most Intel systems. There would also be running costs of £25,000 per annum, which was to be paid to Amstrad for bureau services.

It was only after this Board decision had been taken that the Venables camp appears to have woken up to what Crystal, in an affidavit read out in court on 14 May 1993, called the 'second stage in Sugar's attempts to gain absolute control of the Company and renege on his agreement and promises to Venables'. In his own affidavit Venables would spend some time talking about the computer system, seeing it as yet another way in which Sugar duped him, although by his own admission he did not know much about computers and was clearly often not aware of what was happening or what it meant: 'Like many of my generation, I have never been trained to use computers, it was never envisaged that I should be writing information on to the system.'

In that case what kind of 'input' did he hope to have? It turned out that this was not input in deciding on a system but in making sure that whatever system there was he had control of it: 'As Chief Executive with such wide responsibilities I clearly needed to have it under my control with access to the management system via my office.'

A computer bureau would not have led to loss of control but by February/March of 1993 this is not how the Venables camp saw it. They were convinced that Sugar was trying to take the company away from them and with Brown, says Berry, prompting, all sorts of demons were easily imagined. By the time Venables came to make the affidavit he would bitterly regret that, in order to placate Sugar, he had sidelined Brown from the computerisation project which he felt led to loss of control and to the hated Sandy taking charge.

In his autobiography, however, Venables says that Brown, having been taken off the project, was put back on it, in February 1993, which came about because Simmons accidentally dropped something on a table. He also says that Sandy told him that he had been instructed by Sugar not to give him any information on the computerisation. As ever it is difficult to reconcile these various Venables versions, the more so as there are Sugar memos which show increasing frustration at Venables' inability to understand what was being proposed. What irritated Sugar was that Venables was seeking information which was already available and that, on the computerisation issue, he and Brown appeared to be keen to reinvent the wheel.

Sandy believes that this was due to a fundamental misunderstanding on the part of Venables and Crystal. The system, he feels, was beyond their comprehension. Amstrad offered a very cheap service, far cheaper than that which could be obtained elsewhere. Nor, affirms Sandy, would Tottenham's security, or the integrity of the system, be compromised. The link with Amstrad was simply one where Amstrad was employed as a computer bureau and it would be a breach of contract if it were to encroach upon the system and obtain confidential information.

Amstrad was registered as a computer bureau under the Data Protection Act. In any case, the direct link between Brentwood and White Hart Lane and Tottenham's information could be accessed only at Tottenham by using secret passwords which allowed the system to operate. Sandy was backed up by Berry who said in his affidavit, 'I believe this criticism shows a complete misunderstanding of the position by Mr Venables who, I believe, relied on advice to make the criticism but did not really understand the point being made.'

It was in order to clear up the growing misunderstandings of the computerisation issue, and to discuss the Brown affair again, that Sugar decided to have yet another one-to-one meeting with Venables. The meetings in Langan's in April and Harry's Bar in November hadn't worked but could a leisurely Sunday lunch at home in leafy Essex do the trick? Sugar hoped so and just after the victory over Manchester City the two men met. The lunch proved that Venables and Sugar could still talk to each other. Despite the slanging match they had had in their 'Dear Alan' and 'Dear Terry' memos, the lunch, as Sugar would say in an affidavit, 'was very amicable and friendly'.

Just as on the previous two face-to-face occasions, Venables was charming and agreed that, if things were going wrong, they would be put right; and when Sugar complained of certain things he promised they would not happen again. Sugar, in turn, tried to calm Venables' fears about computerisation. There was, of course, no getting away from Brown during the lunch. Sugar made it clear he had to go. He had been very patient about Brown but he could not have a man with such a disastrous financial background with the company. There need not be any loss of face, said Sugar, Venables could arrange his departure any way he liked and, of course, keep him on as his personal adviser but he couldn't be employed by Tottenham. However, the lunch was overshadowed by one other matter, Venables' demand for more money.

At their meeting at Harry's Bar he had said he wanted more money, now he put a figure on it: £400,000, a more than 75% increase on his existing salary. And there could be no strings attached to the salary. Pleasant as the afternoon was proving to be, Sugar could not agree to such a proposal. Chief executives of companies are well paid but their salary is linked to performance and, in football, the bonus structure was well established both for players and managers: so much for finishing top of the League, so much for winning the Cup, etc. But Venables was not interested in anything like that. No, no, no, he would do his best anyway, what he wanted was £400,000, no strings.

This demand of Venables, like the chorus in a ballad, kept being repeated throughout the lunch. Every time Sugar finished a topic, Venables would return to his demand for £400,000. The lunch saw no conclusive agreement but two so-called options were discussed. The first was that Venables would sack Brown, and that John Ireland would be confirmed as company secretary and become Venables' confidant. In return Venables would get a higher salary but it would have to be linked to performance and profits.

The other option was that, if there was no agreement, Sugar would buy out Venables at the price he had paid for his shares, and end his contract by making a cash settlement which would be fair. Immediately Sugar said this, Venables asked: what do you mean by a fair cash settlement for my contract?

What is interesting is that Venables did not express any surprise that, if he accepted this option, it would mean he would lose Spurs. Like the dealer he was, he wanted to know what the deal would mean in hard money terms. Well, said Sugar, in cases of executives like you, we would have to take in the fact that there are three years of your contract to go, your age and ability to get an alternative employment, so, given that you would be owed £675,000 there would be a discount on that figure. No sum was actually mentioned but in addition to the money he had paid for his shares Venables could have expected another £500,000 or so, making a total of £3½m.

But with Tottenham having a date with Arsenal at Wembley this was no time to discuss it in detail and it was agreed to leave the whole matter until the end of the season. However, it was not left there. Up to now the initiative for the meetings and attempts to find a solution had all been Sugar's. Now Venables suggested they have another meeting. So two weeks before the semi-final, on the evening of 20 March, and just after Tottenham had played away at Chelsea, the two met again. With a neat symmetry – the previous meeting having been at Sugar's home – this one was at Scribes. Venables returned to the theme of being on a parity with George Graham, who was being paid £400,000, providing a glimpse of what was perhaps driving this particular Venables demand.

George Graham earned a fortune, much more than me, said Venables. Do you know, he told Sugar, George once worked for him, he was much better than Graham. Nevertheless he was not asking as much as Graham but he wanted '£400,000 flat, no strings'. In one of his affidavits Venables denied he had suggested he was better than Graham, he merely wanted to point out what successful managers earned. But the fact that Venables compared himself to Graham and other managers suggests that, despite two years as chief executive of Tottenham, he still saw himself as a football manager. The comparison with Graham was inappropriate because Venables was supposed to be in charge of a public company. But it showed that, while he wanted the title of chief executive, as his wage demands showed, in reality he had never forsaken the dugout.

Sugar would still not commit himself on the £400,000. He was also not getting anywhere with his demand for Brown's sacking. Nevertheless, five days later, when the Tottenham Board met for their monthly meeting, the question of Venables' salary was on the agenda. But Sugar postponed discussion by saying this should not be discussed at such an open forum. The Board minutes merely noted, 'Chief executive's Service contract – Increase to salary – This item was not considered in the light of the ongoing discussion between Mr Venables and Mr Sugar'. As it happened, Venables did not attend the meeting and had given his proxy to Crystal.

The next Board meeting was scheduled for 6 May when Venables proposed to raise the issue again. What Venables could not have anticipated was that this meeting would prove the most explosive of his reign.

Chapter 22

The end game

It is one of the ironies of the Terry Venables reign at Tottenham that the defender he most admired, and the man he later made captain of England, should, quite inadvertently, have contributed to his downfall. It was Tony Adams' header that sealed Spurs' fate at Wembley and made the timing of Venables' exit a few weeks later almost inevitable.

Despite all that had happened with Sugar, and the increasing intensity of the guerrilla warfare between the two camps, Venables' mood as he approached the FA Cup semi-final against Arsenal at Wembley on 4 April could not have been more buoyant. A season that had been advertised as transitional was suddenly in full bloom. In the days leading up to the semi-final Venables visibly purred with delight as he surveyed the prospects. To him the whole occasion was an early and unexpected dividend of his stewardship of the club, both as a shrewd football judge and a shrewd businessman. What is more he was changing Tottenham. The key example of this was Nick Barmby. In him Spurs had found a wonderful player, but what is more, contrary to Spurs tradition, he was not bought from another club but was home-grown. Barmby seemed to be the apex of Venables' youth policy. Yes, said Venables, he had a lot of players on his books, stock as he called them, but most of them were youngsters and not as highly paid as some of the stars at other clubs. In the various interviews he gave before the semi-final his theme about Tottenham was a bit like Ronald Reagan's winning slogan, 'You ain't seen nothing yet'. And in case anyone missed the point, for the semi-final itself, instead of sitting in the Royal Box as the chief executive of Arsenal did, he sat in the dugout as if, rather than Clemence and Livermore, he was the real manager and the glory on the field was all due to him.

Sugar read this media outpouring about the Venables miracles with sardonic amusement, noting that in none of the interviews did Venables acknowledge his partner or the part that his money had played in the transformation. For him it was yet another example of being treated as the nutter in the boardroom. Stories in the Venables camp making fun of his lack of football knowledge were now common. Venables, himself, was fond of retelling the occasion where they were both watching a match when Barmby hit a shot that ricocheted off the cross bar. Sugar turned to Venables and said, 'There's your North Stand.' 'What do you mean?' asked Venables. 'Well, we will knock off that Barneby to an Italian club for £6m. and pay for the stand,' said Sugar.

As Venables finished the story his entourage would shake their heads in wonder, commiserating with Terry for having to put up with a man whose feel for the game of soccer was so limited, views so warped and who did not even know the name of his own player. As they laughed about Sugar, Venables and his friends sensed no danger. The match with the old enemy was billed as Arsenal's chance to avenge the defeat of 1991 and so it proved. An early penalty appeal by Spurs was turned down, Spurs could not get their attack together and by the time Barmby, who had been injured in Australia, came on as substitute he could not turn the tide. Late in the second half Arsenal had their usual winner. Merson took the free kick, for once Adams escaped Ruddock, and headed it in.

It was as Sugar left Wembley to the sounds of Arsenal celebrations that he decided that his marriage with Venables had to end. But what if Spurs had won and gone on, as in 1991, to win the Cup? A few weeks after the Venables sacking, when Sugar eventually met Scholar for the first time, that was almost the first question which Scholar asked: 'If Tottenham had won the Cup, would you still have sacked Venables?' Sugar paused and said, 'Alan Sugar has big balls, but they ain't that big.' However, in August 1993, just before the new season started, Sugar told me, 'If Tottenham had won the FA Cup the same thing would have happened. I am sure Tottenham winning the FA Cup would have made my life more difficult because the fans would have thought I am really loopy but I would still have gone ahead with it. Because the reality would have remained the same. You cannot, just because we have won the FA Cup, turn a blind eye to all the misdemeanours, the reason which led to the decision of the Board to sack him. I would then not be doing my fiduciary duties.'

Even if Tottenham had won the Cup, Venables would still, in Sugar's view, be no nearer becoming the sort of chief executive a public company needs. For all Sugar's efforts, and despite the seminar held by Mr Tracey of Touche Ross about directors' interests and how they should be kept separate from that of the company, Venables had not changed his behaviour. Invoices continued to pour into the Tottenham accounts department which appeared to relate to Venables' personal business rather than anything to do with the club. Just a month before the semi-final Venables and Sandy had exchanged their tart memos about the dance-floor which had been taken to Scribes.

Venables, of course, had claimed it was old, useless, and not Tottenham's in any case. Brown had an account at Scribes on which he allowed various parties to sign for food and drinks with Tottenham picking up the tab. One of the persons who signed in this fashion was Joe Pawlikowski, by now secretary of Scribes. Few knew that, while Pawlikowski had avoided Brown's fate of being a bankrupt, he had only done so by agreeing a voluntary arrangement with his creditors. Intriguingly among his creditors was Landhurst Leasing, to whom he owed a little over £13,000.

Tottenham had also paid for furniture and linen purchased for Scribes. Sugar had himself raised this matter of tablecloths with Venables who had complained that it was all Edward Freedman's fault. He had promised to get them cheap and had then 'done him up'. Whatever it is, said Sugar, Tottenham can't pay for them. Crystal assured him Venables would pay it back, but by June 1993 Tottenham were owed £4,000 by Scribes. Venables' elder daughter, Mrs Dobinson, who was not employed by Tottenham, continued to be a member of Tottenham's private health scheme. Venables explained that it was an oversight, she had been on it as a child and had continued even when she reached adulthood. But not even Venables could quite explain why, four days after the semi-final defeat against Arsenal, Tottenham should receive a medical bill from a Mr O. J. A. Gilmore, of Harley Street, for a consultation regarding August Bazire, Venables' father-in-law. The amount was not significant, £95, and Venables explained that it had happened because his secretary had booked the appointment. But why then was the bill addressed to Club Secretary, Tottenham Hotspur FC?

Sugar shook his head in wonder as Sandy told him about the Bazire invoice although by then he was firing off yet more memos about the merchandising department. Four months after Sugar had taken over the department neither Venables nor Brown would let go. Venables' reaction to Sugar clipping part of their empire and taking over the merchandising was to continue his successful guerrilla warfare. This had been going on for some time before the semi-final, nearly produced a spark just before the match, and reached its climax ten days after the match. Nobody had been more affected by Gilbert's arrival in the merchandising department than Tracey Venables.

When Gilbert originally surveyed the shops he had seen Tracey Venables as part of the management team that would work well together. But once Gilbert had taken charge Tracey Venables decided she did not fancy working in the shops and in February she was made International Members' secretary, a position created for her by her father. The appointment had a curious backcloth. Tracey had been given a pay rise back in September 1992. At a time when the rest of the Spurs staff were asked to accept a 5% increase, Tracey's salary was increased from £12,500 to £17,000. Venables later justified it on the grounds that Tracey had been given the increased responsibility of running the international members' department. But this did not come about until five months after the salary increase.

Gilbert's first task was to try to save the £900,000 of Umbro money that Venables' and Brown's actions had jeopardised. Umbro's importance to Tottenham could not be overstated; the club had been guaranteed payments of £925,000 for 1993 and £1m. for 1994. However, as Gilbert picked his way through the merchandising division he found that Brown was about to do a deal with Tryrare Ltd, trading as Kick Sportswear. Gilbert thought that Umbro would not only not take kindly to this, they might well terminate their arrangement with Tottenham.

What made the situation worse was that, although no deal with Kick had been signed, Brown had given them the impression that it had, and Kick had since been sold in good faith with the purchaser given a warranty that it had a contract with Tottenham. In the end Gilbert had been able to unpick it all, but as the semi-final approached and he was embroiled in further conflict with Brown and Venables he became convinced that both Brown and Venables were involved 'in a sort of power play and were making waves merely for the sake of it and where this was not in the interests of the business'.

This guerrilla warfare escalated into open war just after the semi-final, between 14 April and 16 April, with letters and memos from Brown: two memos to Gilbert, and two letters to Simon Marsh of Umbro. This was Venables, through Brown, in effect telling Sugar: keep of my turf. Brown wanted to make it clear that, when it came to products for the playing squad, 'Terry Venables had to retain absolute authority and approval over all squad products'. The merchandising department could have freedom over secondary products but even here Venables had to be consulted. In one of his memos to Gilbert there was also an attack on the new Gilbert management. Products, said Brown, must adhere to corporate image. Problem areas, he said, were the red lions on the kit badge and the club emblem over the Sportswear Shop where, he complained, the cockerel appeared to be standing on its orb resting on a blancmange.

His letters to Marsh made it clear that, when Umbro wanted squad products approved, samples had to be submitted to Roy Reyland who ran the playing kit department at the training ground and after he had tested them, the merchandising department would be consulted and then Venables would give his approval. Then and only then could Umbro begin to produce it.

Brown's letters to Marsh saw Sugar fly to his own computer. On 21 April he wrote a withering memo to Brown. He had no business writing to Umbro or for that matter any of the suppliers to the merchandising division. If anybody had to speak to Umbro it would be himself or Gilbert. Brown could make the points to him. 'If you continue to write such letters to suppliers you will force me in no uncertain terms to advise the suppliers to disregard the contents of them.'

Sugar was even more upset by the tone of the memos Brown had written to Gilbert, for instance about the cockerel being balanced on a blancmange. Had this not always been so? 'There appears to be an underlying tone of criticism being directed at the merchandising department, in most cases it is unwarranted. Will you please keep your nose out of this area in future and respectfully get on with what you are supposed to be doing. The merchandising department does not report to you or to Terry Venables, it reports to me. Neither you nor Terry will dictate any policy to that department. Any further intervention by yourself in this area, including that of communicating with suppliers to the merchandising division, will be considered by me as gross misconduct and a total disregard of my instructions.'

The next day Venables responded, complaining that Sugar had missed the point of 'John's letter'. It had been written after consultation with Venables. 'I have agreed you run the merchandising and I don't wish to interfere. But I insist on the right to approve the playing kit . . . On matters concerning playing kit I expect to be able to communicate directly with Umbro. This surely is not a difficult problem to understand. I would therefore ask you to confirm this policy to them.' As regards disciplining Brown, 'John reports to me and to my instructions. If he is to be disciplined that is up to me.'

The following day Sugar wrote to Venables denying he had missed the point. On the contrary it was Venables who suffered from poor memory:

But more upsetting is the fact that you and I have agreed this on numerous occasions and with respect, you constantly forget . . . There is need for us to professionalise the way we do business and . . . I cannot agree that anybody other than Harvey Gilbert or myself communicates with Umbro.

These memos had no sooner come off the computer than Venables was involved in another row with Sugar, this time in connection with the Fiorucci Cup, a triangular tournament held at White Hart Lane, featuring Real Madrid and Internazionale. In March Venables told Sugar about the possibility of such a tournament with each side sending their first team to play Tottenham. Spurs would keep all the gate receipts and any money received for British television coverage. But Tottenham had to provide live television coverage for transmission to Spain and Italy.

Venables contacted both ITV and Channel Four but without success. At Venables' request Sugar contacted BSkyB and spoke to David Hill who liked the idea but wanted to know the dates. However, the date of the tournament was the date Hill had contracted to broadcast the England Under-21 match live.

Nevertheless, Venables felt the tournament could still go on provided there was a television link in order to have it broadcast live to Italy and Spain. Venables suggested Sugar go back to BSkyB and tell Hill that he would be prepared to accept £20,000 instead of the £90,000 to £100,000 they would have expected for the rights to such a tournament. But Hill could not justify spending £20,000, as sending a crew would cost between £20,000 to £30,000, and Sugar conveyed this to Venables. Everything went quiet, then, ten days later, Crystal contacted Sugar and told him that Fiorucci really wanted the tournament and he would ask them to pay for the camera crew. Sugar was confident that, if Crystal could get Fiorucci to pay BSkyB's expenses, then he was sure that BSkyB would be happy to provide a television crew. BSkyB would have to promise to show the tournament at some stage, said Crystal, although it did not really matter when. Sugar confirmed that BSkyB would show the highlights at some stage and negotiated a deal whereby they would agree to provide a crew to televise the tournament on the basis that Tottenham received no payment but they would also pay nothing to BSkyB. This was a better deal than the one Crystal had suggested.

The tournament was to be held on 27 April. On the Sunday prior to that BSkyB publicised it, and the following day Venables rang Sugar and said, 'Have you seen what these bastards Sky are doing? They have screwed us.'

'What do you mean?' asked a startled Sugar.

'They are going to show the highlights on the same night the tournament is to be played,' moaned Venables. 'We never agreed to this and they should be paying Tottenham if they are going to screen it that night.'

Sugar could hardly believe what Venables was saying and tried to explain the situation to him but, recalls Sugar, Venables 'did not appear to listen to me and continued to curse'. Sugar did not like Venables' implication that he had given BSkyB something for nothing and said, 'You'd better speak to Jonathan, he knows about the whole deal'. Soon Venables was on the phone again, saying that he had spoken to Crystal and that he did not know anything about it. By this time Sugar was getting quite worked up and told Venables that he wished to speak to him and Crystal together.

Venables and Crystal were travelling that day but Venables promised to ring Sugar from the airport. When Crystal rang he asked Sugar what the problem was. Sugar repeated to Crystal what he had already told him about his negotiations with BSkyB and asked him to confirm that this was so. Crystal said, 'Yes, that's right.' Sugar then asked him to confirm this to Venables, who, Sugar assumed, was standing beside Crystal. At this stage Crystal said, 'You are not right.'

Sugar, now in considerable rage, asked to speak to Venables. When Venables came on the line Sugar told him that Crystal was confused because he had just confirmed that he was right, 'and surely you must have heard him say, "Yes that's right".' But this seemed to make no impression on Venables, who, says Sugar, 'continued to insist that BSkyB had "done us up" and "had us over".' Venables in his autobiography deals with this episode very briefly and insists that Sugar had assured Crystal that Sky would show the highlights at a later date.

For Sugar this 'sorry misunderstanding' was very nearly the last straw. A few days after this Sugar turned to his dictating machine again, and began dictating a draft letter. Sugar realised it was one of the most important letters he would ever write and consulted Herbert Smith. The letter, dated 6 May, read as follows:

Strictly Private and Confidential

THIS DOCUMENT IS SUBJECT TO CONTRACT WITHOUT PREJUDICE

Dear Terry,

It has been nearly two years since we joined together to take over Tottenham. During this period I have had enough time to consider the commercial aspects of the running of the company, and for me to form an opinion of your ability of running the non-football side of the company as well as that of the formal interface with the Premier League. My opinion of your abilities will most certainly not be shared by you and I do not in this letter intend to waste any time justifying them.

At the start of this season Tony Berry tried to diplomatically put forward to the Board that you should concentrate on the running of the football side of the company and I should take over the whole commercial side. It was once agreed that we should even employ a specialist on the subject. However, you insisted that you wished to have control of these areas and spend your time between them and the football side of the business. The merchandising division was handed over to me to control after a lot of wasted debate when it became apparent that the management you had put in place was destroying the business and causing losses, but yet it has been an area in which you still wish to try and assert your authority. Much time is still wasted over trivial matters which have no bearing on the welfare of the business and seem only to serve for you as a way to remind all concerned of the need to exert authority.

It is clear to me from this that you have the need to make sure at all times that those inside the company are constantly reminded of your position and in doing so much time has been wasted when it should be spent on the playing side of the business. Further to this, we have spoken recently about your personal salary and we are unable to agree terms with each other. You have formed a comparison with George Graham, which I reject completely. You feel that you are more talented than him and have achieved more than him. Respectfully, that is an opinion that I – and I'm sure many others – could not share. Once again I will not justify myself in this letter. I am unable to continue with matters as they are. I feel that the past two years have been enough for me to form an opinion on the way things should be run and I feel now that I have to take total executive control of the company. I therefore ask you to stand down as Chief Executive and leave the employment of the company as soon as possible. I wish for this transition to be handled in a most businesslike manner so that we are able to part as sensible people. I wish to avoid by all means bad feelings and publicity for you, myself and the company. I would like to make you the following offer which is subject to contract and without prejudice.

1. I will arrange for your shares to be purchased at the exact cost paid by you. In doing so, Stock Exchange and Take-over Panel permission must be obtained which will not be withheld but may take some time. I will enter into a contract to take up and pay for your shares once the Stock Exchange and Take-over Panel formalities have been granted – (3,542,938 shares at a total cost of £2,977,203.50).

2. The Company will pay you and/or Edennote a total of £450,000 as a full and final settlement for the balance of your personal contract as well as that of Edennote, subject to Board approval.

3. All outstanding bonuses will be paid relating to the profit of the company's financial year 1992/93 based on the current management accounts for the forecast for the balance of May 1993.

4. All parties will sign an agreement not to discuss with any external parties as well as other employees of the company the terms and conditions of this settlement. All parties will agree to a short Press Release (the words of which will be

mutually agreed by the Parties) and no further statement will ever be made to the Media or any other third party or to other employees of the company. All parties will agree to never make harmful statements against each other.

5. You will agree to assist in any legal action that the company is involved in or actions or investigations that the Government or other official bodies may wish to bring in relation to any period during your term of office as an employee of the company as long as the company gives you adequate notice and meets your reasonable expenses.

6. You or any agent working for you to Edennote will agree not to solicit, lure away or influence in any way any of the company's employees in particular but not restricted to the professional soccer players or members of the Youth and Junior playing division. No doubt you will wish to consult with your advisers on this matter. I would point out to you that the part of the offer of purchasing your shares is not an entitlement to someone who is asked to leave his employment, and it is this part of the offer which I point to you is perhaps the most valuable to you in the settlement. As you know there is little or no market in the shares and such a large block will be hard to dispose of in the market. I am sure your advisers will tell you that offering to pay fully two years of a contract which only has three years to run will also be deemed by the Courts to be a fair settlement to someone of your age who would be expected to find similar employment at a similar level of pay quite quickly. I am flexible on how the payments are made with respect to items (1) and (2) and subject to tax and legal considerations and the effect of my own financial position, it may be possible to reallocate part of these payments should you so wish.

As you can imagine, I have given this matter a lot of thought and I have made my mind up to go in this direction and I am not open to discuss any other proposal. I would kindly ask you to respond to this offer to be received at the above mentioned address by mail or fax by 5pm Monday, 10th May. If I do not receive any response I will assume your response is negative.

On the morning of 6 May, as Sugar left for the Tottenham Board meeting, he put the letter in his briefcase. At some stage he would hand the letter to Venables but he could not have imagined the circumstances which would suddenly lead him to do so.

If, on 29 January, Sugar's contract had angered Crystal, now on 6 May there were so many issues that Sugar and Sandy would later feel that Crystal was almost alight by the time the meeting started. At the previous Board meeting on 25 March there had been some discussions about the Cadbury Report which dealt with the governance of public companies and the role of non-executive directors. Sugar's views on non-executive directors were well known. He thought they were a waste of time, Amstrad did not have any although by this time, after the failure of the buy-out, they were getting some. But at the 25 March meeting both Sugar's and Berry's view was that Tottenham was too small a company for the Cadbury Report to be implemented in full and there was no need for a third non-executive director. It was decided that the Cadbury Report would be applied as far as accounting issues were concerned. However, the draft minute did not specify this. Sugar in some irritation took the minutes and added the words, 'in relation to accounting', before signing them. However, Crystal now said that that was not his recollection of the meeting. The Cadbury Report was meant to be implemented in full and Sugar was altering the minutes to suit his own position. Crystal's remarks created, according to Sugar, 'a general feeling of disquiet'. Crystal, naturally, did not see it that way. He felt he was defending the rights of the non-executive, independent director and that it was Sugar who was in a 'volcanic' mood.

But this was merely a tasty starter compared to the main, turbulent dish: computerisation. It was very nearly 4.30pm by the time the computerisation subject came up. Despite all the problems this issue had caused, Sugar and the rest of the Board were under the impression that the only matter unresolved was whether another bureau could provide a better, cheaper service than Amstrad. Berry understood this well enough but evidently the Venables camp did not. Clearly there had been some breakdown in communications for it was soon clear that the Venables camp wanted to start the computerisation debate from scratch. What now emerged was that Brown had asked Creative Project Management (CPM), a firm of consultants, to look at the whole question of how Tottenham should computerise. No exercise could have been more redundant, this assessment having been carried out many months previously by Simmons and Sandy. CPM, unaware of all this, produced a brief summary of what they thought was necessary but had done this without speaking to Sandy, the director in charge of data processing or any of the relevant staff who had been involved with deciding what data was to be placed on computers. Their letter then went on to say that the consultants would require a payment of £5,000 before undertaking a proper evaluation.

CPM's report had landed on Venables' desk on 5 May, the day before the Board meeting, and as the Board turned to discuss computerisation Venables rose, saying he would fetch the report from his office. Sandy, Berry and Sugar could only look at each other in amazement wondering what was going on. When Venables emerged with the report wonder turned to anger.

The report conceded that the idea of linking with Amstrad was a normal one of bureau processing but said 'the problem arises that the current situation is done without contract and is being done by a company controlled by a director of Tottenham Hotspur. This is at best a dubious arrangement and at worst could circumvent certain legal restrictions and regulations governing directors' actions'.

If calling in consultants was not bad enough, their comment on the possible conflict between Sugar's positions as Chairman of Tottenham and Chairman of Amstrad suggested to Sugar that they had been specifically asked to make such a comment, straying well beyond their area of enquiry. Sugar had been scrupulous about making sure that, if Amstrad was involved with Tottenham, it was at arm's length and well known to all Board members, as when they took perimeter advertising during the Southampton and Wimbledon home matches. Following Mr Tracey's seminar at the Board meeting of 5 September every piece of equipment purchased from Amstrad was duly logged and presented to the Board meeting for ratification. In the course of those two years as Chairman of Tottenham, Tottenham had only purchased hardware from Amstrad totalling £100,000. The items included IBM hardware as well as other general items such as personal computers and fax machines. Amstrad had always charged Tottenham the best trade price. Sugar also resented Venables' charge that computerisation had meant buying obsolete Amstrad stock. Surplus, not obsolete, insisted Sugar. But whatever explanations Sugar provided, Crystal now had the bit between his teeth. In his affidavit, Sandy says that Crystal 'had been ranting about the computer system', with particular emphasis on the money Sugar and Amstrad were making from Tottenham.

Money, exploded Sugar, what money? Simmons had provided

his service free, and there was to be a £25,000 p.a. bureau service fee, peanuts compared to an annual Amstrad turnover of £350m. Sugar could bear no more. At this point, as Sandy recalled later, 'Mr Sugar lost his temper. Mr Crystal had been going on and on for some fifteen minutes and although I cannot speak for Mr Sugar I suspect that this was the final straw.'

Crystal, as was his style, was on his feet and at that point was stooping forward with cup in hand to fill it with more coffee. Sugar, who was sitting at the far end of the boardroom, leapt out of his chair and ran towards Crystal screaming, 'You fucking cunt, you fucking cunt, you fucking arselicking cunt.'

By the time he finished, says Crystal, Sugar was no more than three feet away, 'totally out of control', and Crystal feared Sugar would hit him. Sugar denies he was out of control or that there was any danger of him attacking Crystal. He had never hit anyone in his life and had no intention of striking Crystal. However, he was still smouldering and, as he came back to his seat, he threw some papers in his briefcase, produced the letter he had written to Venables and flung it across the table at him. 'You'd better read this,' he said to Venables and strode out of the boardroom.

Sugar's departure meant that Berry had to take the chair and he spoke to Brown, who confirmed that Amstrad's price of £25,000 per annum was the cheapest on offer. Sugar drove home but later rang the boardroom and the next day rang Crystal at his chambers and said while he stood by everything he had said in relation to the business he realised 'that my behaviour was totally unacceptable and offensive'. Sugar made similar calls to Yawetz and Berry but, while they understood, Crystal dismissed Sugar's apology as insincere.

How did Venables react to all this? There is evidence to suggest that he found the incident frightening and bewildering. Almost eighteen months later, when his autobiography was published, he described how he put himself between Sugar and Crystal. Nobody else present in the boardroom – Sandy, Berry or Yawetz – can remember him doing that or even stirring from his seat. Sugar, asked about it, smiled and said, 'He just sat on his bum with a bemused look on his face.'

Interestingly Crystal, whose affidavit was the first public exposure of this incident, describing it in great detail including the swear words Sugar used, does not speak of any such Venables intervention. It is unlikely that Crystal would have missed such an intervention if it had taken place.

That Venables should have later fantasised about the 6 May meeting is all the more important because it was clear that, even at this stage, with the clock at one minute to midnight, Venables did not seem to grasp that the 'dream team' had been splintered and could not be put together again. Two days later Spurs travelled to Liverpool for the last Saturday of the League season. As so often during their away matches that season they conceded a lot of goals – they had let in five at Leeds, four at QPR, six at Sheffield United – now there were another six at Anfield, although the match had the feel of an end-of-season encounter and Spurs did score twice.

Venables left Anfield to go to the airport before the final whistle. When he heard on the car radio that Spurs had conceded their sixth, he immediately drove back, cancelled his appointment, and went to the Spurs dressing-room. There he told the players, 'The future's in front of you. Go away and have a good summer. Next season, we'll be going for the big prizes. Remember we're all in this together.'

It is odd that he should have told the players to go away and have a good summer because, at that stage, Spurs still had one more match at Arsenal to play; but then this story emerged on the Sunday after Sugar had sacked him and by then Venables was keen to prove that he was building something special at Spurs. It was aimed at the supporters. They were an important part of his armoury against Sugar. In 1991 the supporters and the press had helped him get Tottenham, now he needed them again if he was to thwart Sugar.

Chapter 23

Capturing the high ground

On the afternoon of 10 May, Terry Venables retired to the bar of the Royal Garden Hotel and there, overlooking the park, he conferred with two young men: Steve Davies and Bernard Kingsley. They ran the Tottenham Independent Supporters' Association (TISA), the organisation that had helped Venables win Spurs. They had been summoned by a telephone call from Crystal and now Venables wanted to know what they could do to keep him at Tottenham. Sugar had given him until the evening of 10 May to accept the offer, Venables had decided to reject it, and now he had to plan his counter-strike.

'Terry told us,' recalls Kingsley, 'of the 6 May Board meeting and how Sugar had tossed this letter to him. While we were there Terry received a fax telling him of a Board meeting on Friday [14 May] to discuss the future of the chief executive. Terry asked us what we thought the reaction of the supporters would be if he were to be sacked. We said that if that happened he would get the backing of the vast majority of the supporters.'

The next day, as we have seen, Venables went to Highbury for Spurs' last match of the season against Arsenal, and one of the strangest-ever Spurs Board meetings took place. It was then, with the Spurs directors meeting in little huddles, that Venables made it clear to Sugar that he rejected his offer. Sugar confirmed that his future would now be decided at a Board meeting on Friday. Kingsley and Davies were probably the only ones in Highbury that day, outside that group in the Arsenal boardroom, who knew what was happening. 'We didn't tell anybody and it was a strange feeling watching Spurs win at Highbury, something we haven't done for years, the supporters thinking we are building for the future and we knew it would all come to an end on Friday.'

Venables also turned to Berry, the man whose help had been crucial in winning Spurs. 'He has asked me to go,' said Venables. 'You can't win this, Terry,' said Berry. Venables was not prepared to hear such realism from Berry. 'You are backing him, aren't you, you are backing him because you think he is going to win,' said Venables. 'Face reality,' said Berry. 'I don't know Alan Sugar all that well. I am closer to you than I am to him. I am telling you what is for your own good, what is right. This Brown thing, it can't go on. You have to face up to reality. Sugar is offering you a good deal, you will get everything you want and you will still have the football, you will still be able to stay on as football manager.'

But Venables would not listen. As far as Venables was concerned now was the time to be counted, you were either for him or for Sugar, there was no halfway house. 'It disappointed me,' says Berry, 'that he wanted to go on regardless of what common sense told him.'

Venables' unmatched publicity sense told him he must organise a swift counter-strike against Sugar, a sort of PR Pearl Harbor to catch him by surprise, and he turned to David Buchler. Buchler rang his PR lady, Donna Cullen of Good Relations. She was at home ill with flu. Cullen recalls: 'The call came from David, he said something is going on with Terry. David wanted to see me. I said why don't we get Piers Pottinger involved.'

Pottinger was a director of Lowe Bell, the parent company of Good Relations, and he was well known for his City connections, Cullen being more involved in product PR. A meeting with Venables was fixed at Buchler's offices in the West End for 3pm on 12 May. Venables came with Brown and looked, recalls Cullen, the picture of misery. 'He was in a state of shock. He was flabbergasted. He could not believe it was happening. "I do not know why he is doing it," he kept saying. Maybe, he said, because Sugar did not like the way his name was being projected. Terry said he just did not know, he kept saying that.'

Venables told his newly acquired PR advisers that Sugar did not understand football and narrated the story of Barmby 'paying for' the stand. It all seemed to fit in. One reason why Pottinger had been quite keen to act for Venables, apart from the fact that it was a request from Buchler, an existing and valued client, was that he did not like Sugar. 'I knew Sugar was not very well liked, he was a temperamental man, flew off the handle, and did not have a very good relationship with the financial journalists.'

Cullen had gone to the meeting with some articles on Sugar, including one from that month's *Director* magazine, written by myself, which described how Sugar had fallen out with Gulu Lalwani, another businessman in the telecommunications field, after twenty-five years of friendship because Lalwani had hired a man who had left Sugar. The story seemed to tie in with what Venables was saying: the man was power mad, couldn't work with anyone, didn't know anything about football and all this had come out of the blue because he resented the glory Venables was getting.

Cullen and Pottinger knew they had a good story; the question was, as Cullen saw it, 'We had to capture the high ground'. That, in PR terms, meant getting the story in first and making sure that Sugar was always reacting defensively to news generated by Venables. Once the Board meeting was held on Friday and Sugar sacked Venables it would be too late. They had to get their retaliation in first. As it happened the next evening there was an ideal opportunity to do just that. It was the evening of the Football Writers dinner, the traditional eve of Cup Final dinner, to be held at the Royal Lancaster Hotel, and Cullen set to work. Nearly everyone who mattered in football would be there and Venables could not have a better showcase.

The next morning Cullen rang Peter Staunton at ITN, established that he was interested in the story and arranged for him to 'doorstep' the Royal Lancaster. Cullen had to make sure the right questions would be asked and that Venables would provide the right answers. The news of ITN's interest soon leaked out and by five o'clock that evening Nick Hewer had been rung by Sky asking about some story that was supposed to emerge from Tottenham. What is it all about, asked Sky. Hewer did not let on but rang Sugar and warned him that the story was out but they could do nothing as the Venables publicity machine rolled on.

An hour later Cullen was at Scribes to talk to Venables. By the time Crystal drove Venables to the Royal Lancaster, in what Cullen referred to as his battered Porsche, Cullen was there to make sure Staunton knew which one was Crystal's car. Staunton did a superb professional job. As Venables stepped out of the car he approached him and asked him to confirm rumours that he would be sacked by Sugar the following day. Venables, reacting with the right degree of surprise as if Staunton's presence was not something planned by his own PR, said in a voice both pained and resigned that, yes, there was to be a Tottenham Board meeting to decide his fate.

Staunton recalls:

It was quite amusing standing outside the Royal Lancaster that evening, with the football writers going in for their big night, and I was pretending we were just there to take some shots, not letting on about the scoop I had been alerted to. As they went past some of them seemed to pity me and the crew, people left out of the party . . . Venables played his part. As he stepped out of the car and saw me he reacted as if to say, 'What, you want me?' feigning surprise when, of course, it had all been arranged by his PR. And he reacted to my questions with that mixture of surprise and disbelief.

ITN was important to Venables: 'It stirred up a lot of interest in the press and the fans,' says Cullen. 'Staunton ran an excellent piece and Terry then spoke to the journalists who were already gathered there. We had achieved what we set out to, stolen Sugar's thunder.'

Venables had projected the image he desperately sought. The Spurs civil war having remained a closely guarded secret, Sugar's move to sack Venables was, for the world outside, truly 'a bolt from the blue'. This is how the BBC described it and Venables' reactions made it seem as if it was a bolt from the blue for him as well. John Cheeseman of the BBC, who was also at the dinner, got hold of Venables some time during it and asked him about Sugar's impending move. Venables replied, 'I was stopped at the door to say that people understood there was a Board meeting tomorrow morning. And that is the case. My future is to be discussed at Tottenham.'

'Your future?' responded Cheeseman. 'Can you define that more specifically?' Venables laughed, 'I think it is very specific really.' The reporter persisted, 'Why would it be in doubt?'

'Well, I don't know,' said Venables, immediately assuming an air of injured innocence which would stand him in good stead in the days and weeks ahead. 'I know as much as you. I am hoping to find out.'

Hewer had been warned almost ten days earlier by Sugar of the move to oust Venables but, keen to play by the book, the Sugar camp had not made any plans to publicise it. Now the two could only watch impotently as Venables presented himself as the saviour wronged by the man of money. In such a scenario it was vital that Venables also claimed that he was quite unable to understand why Sugar should suddenly decide to sack him. Two years later in his autobiography he would chronicle his side of the civil war that had raged in Tottenham, saying how, once the rights issue had taken place in early December 1991, he knew 'my days at Tottenham were numbered'. But now, with the world unaware of the Sugar-Venables battle, and unaware, too, that the Venables camp was orchestrating the publicity, Venables could present himself as the martyr.

Watching the ITN news were Kingsley, Davies and some of the Tottenham Independent Supporters' Association men who had been drawn into Davies' and Kingsley's confidence. They had been tipped off that Venables would be on it and it was important for Venables that their reaction was on television. Kingsley will not say by whom he was tipped off but when I asked him if it was Donna Cullen, he said, 'You can say that I couldn't possibly comment.'

At about one o'clock in the morning GMTV sent a TV crew to Davies' home and pictures were taken showing Kingsley at a terminal, Davies and Stuart Mutler, editor of *The Spur*, beside him. Davies was interviewed and his hostile reaction was broadcast at six o'clock in the morning. At 6.30 Sugar rang, waking him up. 'You shouldn't make up your mind unless you have heard both sides. Keep an open mind', he advised Davies.

'What's your side then?' asked Davies.

'I can't tell you, but keep an open mind,' replied Sugar.

'Unless you can convince us, our conclusion is that it was in the best interests of Tottenham that Terry Venables stays,' responded Davies.

Television was not the only source which Venables' publicity machine tapped. Frank Kane, then on the *Guardian* City pages and a Spurs supporter, was briefed. He met Brown that Thursday afternoon and was the first print journalist to break the story, which included a reference to problems about computerisation.

Sugar was aware that Venables could work the publicity machine well, and a few days earlier, when he had discussed it with his PR man, Hewer warned him that he could not win on the back pages. 'Remember,' said Hewer, 'that Terry has been living and drinking and travelling with these journalists for the last twenty-five years. He's probably godfather to half of their children.' But nothing could have prepared Sugar for this pre-emptive publicity strike by Venables. It meant that, instead of the Tottenham Board meeting being held in anonymity, from early on Friday morning White Hart Lane was surrounded by a crowd of supporters whose mood, initially sad and bewildered, became increasingly hostile and almost murderous to Sugar and anybody else opposing Venables.

It was there on Tottenham High Road that the size of the victory Cullen had won Venables by putting him on 'News at Ten' became evident. By 7.30 Cullen was at White Hart Lane, hoping to get there before Sugar. She just failed to beat him but drew satisfaction from the fact that he appeared livid and from the way the Venables media machine was purring. However, even if Sugar was upset, one thing reassured him. His legal advisers had warned him that Venables might try to get an injunction to stop the Board meeting. Indeed on Tuesday Herbert Smith had written to Kanter Jules Grangewoods requesting to be kept informed of any legal move, the sort of courtesy lawyers extend to each other. Melvyn Pottesman, Venables' lead solicitor, had promised to do so. By the time of the meeting no call had come from Pottesman, and Sugar and Herbert Smith breathed a sigh of relief.

Even now there was some talk of a compromise. The Board meeting of Tottenham plc had been called for 10am, the meeting of the football club for 10.30am. The previous evening Sugar had rung Douglas Alexiou, Dimitris Augustus Alexiou, to give him his full name, and invited him to join the plc Board. Alexiou had been on the Board of the plc, indeed was a former chairman and a friend of Scholar, but left soon after the Sugar-Venables take-over. Venables had been keen to get rid of him but got Sugar to break the news by telling Alexiou that he wanted to streamline the board. In the new regime Alexiou had become one of the forgotten men of Spurs. He had remained on the Board of the football club but this meant little because in two years Venables had never held a meeting of the football club Board. Even when many members of the plc Board suggested he hold a meeting, Venables postponed discussion until after the end of the season. So Alexiou would often hear of players' moves long after the world knew of it.

But he was a link with the Tottenham past, and a son-in-law of Sidney Wale, whose family had long owned Spurs. Although the Wale regime had ended in disarray, during it Tottenham had enjoyed some success and Sugar felt that, by having Alexiou back on the main plc Board and playing a more active part, he would emphasise a desire to re-establish old ties at the club. Alexiou had always liked Venables and felt that, as a man who specialised in divorce law, he could probably help bring about a more amicable parting in this messy marriage.

There was still hope on the Tottenham Board that Venables could be persuaded to accept Sugar's offer. There was talk that the final figure could go beyond what was suggested in the letter, £4m. or even higher. A couple of days earlier Sugar had spoken to Brown hoping to get him to persuade Venables to accept. Now, as Alexiou, Berry, Sugar and Sandy gathered in the boardroom there was another attempt. Brown came up to the boardroom and Berry and Alexiou spoke to him. Brown seemed to appreciate the offer was a good one and promised to try to persuade Venables to accept. As Brown went down the stairs to speak to Venables, Sugar said, 'If you can persuade him there is £50,000 in it for you.'

Sandy, Berry and the others gathered by the huge windows and watched the crowds outside the gates shouting for Venables, and the throng of pressmen. Venables may have revealed the secret of the meeting but still they felt the bloodbath could be avoided. The Tottenham Board were relying on Brown, he understands figures, he will persuade Venables to see sense. But Brown returned to say that Venables had refused.

'But I thought you said he would agree,' said Berry.

'He is his own man,' snapped Brown.

Even then Alexiou and Berry would not give up. They walked down from the boardroom to the Oak Room to talk to Venables and both men pleaded with Venables to accept Sugar's offer. For some reason Berry appears to have harboured thoughts that, even at this stage, Venables might have a role at Tottenham in a football capacity: 'I was sure that if Terry had accepted Sugar's offer he could have stayed on to look after the football side, but he wouldn't budge.' Alexiou told him, 'Terry, the offer seems a very good one. You will get your money back, pay back your loans, and you can always get a job in football, go north or abroad.' 'I don't want to work up north,' said Venables, clearly nettled at the thought of looking for work in Liverpool, Manchester or Scotland. 'I have done abroad, I don't want to go abroad again.' As Alexiou persisted in trying to change Venables' mind Venables snapped, 'Why don't you vote for me, then none of this will happen.'

Of course Alexiou did not have a vote in the plc, so he could not have influenced Venables' sacking, but he thought this was no time to raise technical points. Some time during the conversation Sugar and Crystal arrived in the Oak Room silently taking in the scene. The mediators having failed, the meetings began, first that of the plc, which considered the resolution to sack Venables as chief executive, followed by the football club which had a resolution to terminate Edennote's contract to provide Venables' services to the club.

Given the gunfire which had issued forth during previous meetings this was a peaceful, tame affair. Crystal was not the only lawyer present. Sugar had Margaret Mountfort from Herbert Smith, Venables had Martin Isaacs and Michael Salber from Kanter Jules Grangewoods and Berry had Peter Leaver, a QC he had consulted. Along with Alexiou, Yawetz was also allowed to attend the plc meeting, despite the fact that like Alexiou he was only a director of the football club. Hewer, who had been in the boardroom as the contestants were gathering, left just as Crystal and Venables entered and went to Sandy's office and started fielding the press calls.

A few preliminaries had to be finished, however, before the main bout of hostilities began. Sugar, concerned about the media publicity, presented a fax from Sky confirming that Sugar was not the source of the story. It is not clear why he should have done that unless it was meant to flush out whether Venables had been the instigator behind the leak. If so the tactic failed. Venables said nothing and did not let on that his PR had alerted the media. Crystal asked if the Stock Exchange was to be told about Venables' removal? Yes, said Sugar, that was why Nick Hewer was there to help to make the appropriate announcement.

Crystal's voice was heard more insistently when the meeting came to discuss the transfer of Ian Gray's shares to Sandy. The controversial meeting in the Arsenal boardroom had been held to approve this transfer. Crystal argued that the Arsenal meeting was improper, and until those events had been investigated the resolution should not be considered. Crystal was also unhappy that no notice of the Arsenal meeting had been given to him and Venables. 'In the past,' said Sugar, 'Board meetings that you have attended have been held without notice and since you are a barrister, Jonathan, I was just following your example.'

The resolution approving the transfer saw Sugar, Sandy and Berry voting in favour, Crystal and Venables against. It was only after this that the main bout of the morning began: Sugar proposing and Sandy seconding that Venables be sacked with immediate effect. And here Sugar, already behind in the publicity war, made a major tactical error. At the meeting Crystal asked what were the reasons for the sacking, warning that a sacking without giving reasons was unreasonable and arbitrary and the Board was entitled to hear the reasons. That such a question should have been asked now may seem strange, especially as Crystal had been at the heart of the civil war in Spurs for over a year. But the question was shrewdly put.

For Sugar the question made little sense and he saw this intervention like the many Crystal had made in the past, and Sugar replied that there was no obligation to give reasons. In any event the Board well knew what had prompted it all. To ask for the reasons now was a bit like somebody at Sarajevo, a year into the civil war, asking why the Serbs were shelling the Muslims. But in not specifying the reasons at this Board meeting Sugar had handed the Venables camp a major victory. Within twenty-four hours Venables was telling the world that he had repeatedly asked Sugar the reasons and he had not been given any. If the Board meeting of 14 May is taken in complete isolation he was right. But that also means accepting that the Venables of 14 May was an entirely different person from the Venables who, on 25 January, had written his 'Dear Alan' memo saying 'One thing I do agree is that we cannot carry on as at present'.

Even at that stage the Sugar camp was, as Sandy acknowledges, a bit naive but not spoiling for a fight: 'The decision to remove Venables was the final act. We did not want to rub the guy's nose in the mud, that is one of the reasons no formal explanation was given. We just wanted to end an intolerable situation and were not looking for a fight.'

Berry was the swing voter in this and Venables appears to have gone into the meeting still hoping he might bring Berry to his side. All eyes were on him as he explained he had consulted Leaver and was very mindful of his fiduciary responsibilities. 'I don't want to vote against Terry, nor do I want to vote against Alan. I have got nothing against Terry. I will abstain. If I am forced to make a decision I will vote for Terry's removal. On the advice of my QC I am duty bound to do so, but I will only do so if my vote is necessary to carry the resolution, otherwise I will abstain.'

Venables could not vote but pointed out that in his view the resolution could not be passed because of the agreement in the offer document. Before the meeting Martin Isaacs had written a letter to Margaret Mountfort seeking to establish that Sugar had agreed to a shareholders' agreement. But all this meant little. Venables, in boxing parlance, was about to become history at Tottenham. Sugar had the votes: 2–1, he and Sandy in favour, Crystal against and Venables, of course, unable to vote. The vote had sacked him as chief executive but there was the contract Edennote had with the football club and Venables was still a director of the football club. So the next step was to alter the articles of the football club.

Although it was now ten years since Tottenham had become a Public Limited Company it still operated under the old articles. Mountfort explained that it was normal for wholly owned subsidiaries to allow parent companies complete discretion to appoint or remove directors of the subsidiary. Crystal objected, saying this was a move that required more time for study and he did not accept the validity of the resolution. When it came to the vote Sugar, Berry and Sandy voted in favour, Crystal and Venables abstained. The football club met soon after and voted to terminate the Edennote contract. It also removed Venables and Crystal as directors of the football club. Both Venables and Crystal remained as directors of Tottenham Hotspur plc, because a director of a public company can only be removed by a vote of the shareholders in a general meeting. But this was poor consolation for Venables.

Venables appears to have been in a state of shock during the meeting. Certainly some of his recollections of the meeting and the day as published in his autobiography are bizarre. He says Sugar left the ground a few minutes after he did at 11.50, when Sugar left many hours later. He complains Sugar did not allow him to vote on the resolution, when that is the proper procedure given the resolution was about removing him. He also says Peter Leaver voted as proxy for Berry when Berry cast his own abstention. In fact he does not seem to have taken in Berry's speech that his abstention did not mean he was neutral, if his vote was crucial he would have voted in favour of Venables' sacking. This confusion led to Venables' lawyer later that afternoon to paint a picture in court that was not quite valid.

Cullen saw Venables as he emerged from the boardroom. 'He looked ashen. He seemed surprised by the vote. Even when he had gone into the boardroom he did not know what Berry would do. Berry's abstention seemed to surprise him.' However, by the time he had come back to his office he did manage a joke, 'Oh, I guess I better start looking for a job now', but the laughter that followed was hollow and the smile was thin. Once that had died down he said he wanted to see his father. 'That was almost his first reaction,' recalls Cullen, ' "I want to see my Dad".' Cullen knew what she had to do. 'We had to get Terry out of there, get him out fast. I got Penny, Terry's PA, to type out a statement and I went to the gates and I read it out standing in front of the wrought-iron gates.'

While some TISA members, like Kingsley and Davies, had been allowed in, the majority of the fans baying for Sugar were locked out. Some of them were by now burning their season tickets but with the season over this was a very symbolic gesture. Cullen's appearance created a stir. An attractive blonde woman like Donna Cullen would have been noticed at any time, but at that moment it seemed to produce near chaos. 'I had to read the statement two or three times, the pressmen kept shouting, "O yeah, blondie", and nudging each other and saying, "That's Tel's girl".'

Cullen had done her job and the high ground she had seized on the Thursday night was still occupied by Venables. When he emerged Venables was met by a media scrum and while he said nothing, maintaining he couldn't because of lawyers' advice, there was a hint that some legal action might follow. Also a smile and a joke. When someone asked, 'What next, mate', he replied, 'Dunno, mate.' Then he was sped on his way to Essex to meet Fred and as Venables' blue Mercedes, driven by Crystal, swept out of White Hart Lane it was met with an extraordinary show of emotion and support from the fans gathered there. 'Terry, Terry, Terry,' they sang, 'Good luck, Terry. We are with you, Tel. Scumbag Sugar'.

Crystal looked dazed, Venables appeared to be fighting hard to contain his tears. The *Evening Standard* saw real tears there and would headline the news 'Tel Out in Tears'. But by the time Venables saw it he had regained his composure and said with a smile, 'That's a bit over the top'. Sugar in contrast did not make an appearance before the television cameras, so the impression that this was a coup against the people's favourite by faceless money men was reinforced. Hewer braved a hostile press corps in the car park, but could give little information on the reasons for the sacking; instead he attended a hastily scheduled group of meetings. All this added to the mob's fury and by the time it came for Sugar to leave it was clear he would have no easy passage. For the baying crowd Sugar was the great villain and anybody who had helped put Terry down shared in his villainy. Berry, who had come in his Range Rover, had a rough reception and his car was dented. Alexiou encountered the hate mob in its elemental fury.

It was clear that to try to leave through the main gates was suicidal. So he decided to walk across the car park and leave by the gates behind the south stand. As he drove out of that side entrance a car in front of him stopped at the red lights. The crowd from the main gate, suddenly made aware that one of the 'villains' was escaping, rushed round. Central locking prevented them from getting to Alexiou but he was spat on, his car dented – a dent it still carries – and in the few minutes it took the light to change from red to green Alexiou feared for his life. 'Had the car not been in front of me I would have jumped the red lights. It really was frightening.'

Reports of all this had filtered back to Hewer, who was feeling increasingly beleaguered in an emptying White Hart Lane. Sugar could not leave in his car, that would be inviting disaster, let alone leave by the front door. The plan was to get him away from the back. So almost two years after he had walked out on to the ground in the company of Venables and to the cheers of the faithful, he now walked across the pitch with a steward, away from the West Stand and, his footsteps echoing in the empty stadium, made his way to the Paxton Road entrance. Hewer had driven his BMW out of the main gate to the side entrance. Sugar got in and as he drove away from White Hart Lane he could see Alexiou's car being pummelled. But with fans unable to recognise Hewer's car, Sugar was driven to safety. As they drove away Sugar said, 'I may have done the right thing by the club but will I ever be able to show my face again here?'

It was during the car journey that Hewer suggested to Sugar that they had to organise their publicity, particularly on Brown, if Venables was not to sweep all in front of him. Sugar, as is his style when absorbed in thought, said, 'Hmmm'.

But at least the deed had been done and, although he had not met the press, he had tried to explain to the staff in a hastily organised staff meeting that the removal of Venables did not affect them and that this was not a coup but the sacking of a chief executive. Sugar had been advised not to go into details about the reason for the sacking but he did mention that Terry would still have been there but for the company he kept. How much the staff understood is debatable, many of them were in tears, nearly all were confused and not even Bill Nicholson, who spoke at the staff meeting along

261

with Sugar, appeared to have realised what had happened. He told the staff that the most important relationship in a football club is that between chairman and manager, which made it appear that Venables' sacking had been the conventional manager's sacking.

In the confused and frightened atmosphere of White Hart Lane that day such sentiments were understandable and Nicholson's confusion would be shared by many of the Tottenham fans who, too, would see it in Nicholson's simplistic terms. Terry, in their eyes, was not so much chief executive as the ideal manager, building a great team and an uncaring money-mad, power-mad chairman had sacked him. Football fans are used to unsuccessful managers being sacked but how can they sack a manager when the team is doing so well? they asked. Of course it is easy to understand why the fans should have seen it as the sacking of a football manager rather than that of the chief executive of a company. The idea of a football man being the chief executive was something most of them did not understand and Sugar, unable to explain the reasons, had created a dangerous vacuum which was now filled with this simplistic notion. For Venables it was soon to prove another useful weapon.

Even as Sugar was driving away from White Hart Lane, Venables had set the wheels in motion to drive the war forward. By lunchtime he was back in central London and had conferred with his solicitors. It was agreed they should seek a court injunction to overturn the sacking. It was some time then that the drafting began of his statement in court. As he retired to drink a glass or two of champagne with his old friends Dennis and Pat Signy at the Royal Lancaster, his lawyers set to work.

At one o'clock Pottesman rang David Gold of Herbert Smith telling him they would be going for an injunction. The hearing was due for 3pm. Although this was a surprise, Gold had put Christopher Carr, the QC specialising in employment contract, on standby and he felt relaxed about Venables going to court. Any move to undo the sacking would be very difficult. In legal terms this meant demanding the specific performance of a contract of employment and lawyers recognised it almost as the first rule of law of specific performance that courts never granted such a wish.

However, what Gold, who had barely half an hour's notice of the court hearing, could not have anticipated was the venom with which Venables would mount his counter-strike. Venables, desperately keen to get back, was so economical with the truth that, a few days later, he had to apologise to the court for misleading statements.

The hearing before Mrs Justice Arden was by its very nature a rushed affair. The hearing continued until half past eight in the evening, so late that Pottesman, a strict orthodox Jew, had to leave the court before Mrs Justice Arden gave her judgement. In one of the minor ironies of the case, while Sugar is Jewish, it was the orthodox Jewish beliefs of Venables' lawyers that would often cause problems in fixing the dates for the court hearings.

Much of the evidence presented was oral evidence. The statements which Venables and Crystal made were eventually converted into affidavits although by the time the court sat they were presented as draft affidavits. The result was one of the most bizarre court hearings in modern times. Martin Mann, the QC representing Venables, assisted by Michael Gadd, relied as was only to be expected on the draft affidavits of Venables and Crystal, and the advice of Kanter Jules Grangewoods. With the judge unfamiliar with the background, and with Sugar's side caught unawares, it was as though Venables' team was playing in a game where the opposition did not know the match was on.

Mann based his case strongly on Crystal's statement, having introduced him as an independent non-executive director who was known to the judge as a barrister. Crystal's statement was a powerful defence of Venables and in his attack on Sugar he spared little, presenting almost all the points he could make with much emphasis on the Venables view of the rights issue and the computerisation. This was when Crystal described this as 'the second stage of Sugar's attempt to gain absolute control of the company and renege on his agreement and promises to Venables'.

The various Board meetings, but particularly that of 6 May with all of Sugar's colourful language, and the Arsenal Board meeting of 11 May, were additional evidence in Crystal's thesis that Sugar had a hidden agenda to get rid of Venables. To anybody coming cold to the case, as the judge did, it was a powerful performance. Yet rereading it now it appears strange. There were minor errors, for instance Crystal said he had been appointed on 8 August when he was as appointed the day before. But the most interesting feature of the Crystal statement was what it did not say. At no point did this widely advertised independent non-executive director, who had made much of Sugar's unhappiness with the Cadbury Report, mention John Brown or the problems this had caused between Sugar and Venables. Indeed Brown's name did not figure in the hearing at all.

Mann also had to rely on Venables' statement. That Venables should have alleged that Sugar had made a verbal shareholders' agreement and then reneged on it is not surprising. We have seen how valid such a claim may be. But what was a surprise was Venables' reference in his statement to the Pan Financial loan condition which had been dependent on his remaining chief executive. His statement pointed out '. . . the termination of my position as chief executive is an event of default'.

Yet the Pan Financial loan had been refinanced nine months earlier. Venables was now borrowing the money from the Bank of Liechtenstein, so what was the point of mentioning Pan Financial? The point appeared to be that Mann used this to argue that, by being sacked, Venables would suffer financial damage. Melvyn Pottesman later admitted that he did not know the Pan Financial loan had been refinanced and that the Venables draft, which had been taken to the courtroom, had been prepared in a great hurry. Pottesman in an affidavit would say that the final version of Venables' draft was settled by counsel in his chambers after consultation with Venables and Pottesman's partners. Venables read the draft in Pottesman's presence. Pottesman and his partners learnt about the refinancing on the following Monday evening, 17 May.

Venables himself, in an affidavit of 20 May, argued that his draft affidavit on which Mann had relied, had been misinterpreted and that, had he been in court and heard Mann imply he would suffer damage, he would immediately have pointed out to the court that it had been refinanced: 'I have no intention to mislead the court'. He would also say in this subsequent affidavit, 'I sincerely apologise that misleading statements were made in Court': if there had been the implication that damage would be suffered due to default provisions in the Pan Financial letter, 'that implication is false'.

His lawyers would excuse themselves by arguing that Mrs Justice Arden had noted this but not relied on it. However, Mrs Justice Arden was concerned about this and there was some debate between her and Sugar's counsel who pleaded ignorance about the Pan Financial arrangement. She also relied on other Venables evidence in coming to her decision. Sugar may have hoped that by waiting until the end of the season to sack Venables there would be little disruption. But Venables and his lawyers successfully convinced Mrs Justice Arden that the season was not over. Venables was desperately keen to be reinstated immediately. In his statement he said he worked a seven-day week, at weekends there was substantial work including staff interviews, discussion of contracts and player training. 'This weekend would be no exception and in addition work needs to be carried out this weekend in relation to a match against Enfield next Tuesday and considerable preparation needs to be made this weekend for a planned tour by the team to South Africa commencing next Wednesday on which I had intended to travel.' Mrs Justice Arden in her judgement referred to this and said, 'I do not accept therefore that the season has effectively ended.'

In fact the match at Enfield, a testimonial game in honour of Eddie Baily, was actually being played even as the court hearing was going on. It had never been planned for Tuesday. Indeed Kingsley of TISA, interviewed on the lunch-time bulletins, had spoken of a pro-Venables demonstration to be organised at the game and 2,500 fans turned up voicing their support for Venables. As far as the South African tour was concerned Venables had thought of cancelling it on Thursday and had in fact cancelled it at 8.30 on the Friday morning, almost twelve hours before Mrs Justice Arden gave her judgement.

But Mrs Justice Arden may be forgiven for concluding the season was not over. She had to rely on what Venables' counsel was saying and Mann, seemingly misinformed about Venables' precise role in the club, introduced him as chief executive, but also stated that he was manager, giving the impression that his position as football manager had not changed since he was appointed by Scholar in 1987. In the process Clemence and Livermore shared Brown's fate and became non-persons and poor Shreeves suffered a strange transformation. At one stage Mann, relying on the affidavit evidence, declared that when Peter Shreeves was sacked, Venables had taken on not only his responsibilities but his salary as well and this was the reason for the renegotiation of Venables' contract in September 1992. Of course, the real reason was Venables' need for money (as Crystal had explained to Sugar).

Venables' counsel also told the judge Venables intended to use Section 459 to buy out Sugar (did he get this idea from Brown who had used a similar devise in his business career?), Edennote was described as a company of some means and it was argued that not to undo the sacking would have an impact on the share price.

With the Sugar camp clearly caught unawares and hardly putting up any credible defence, Mrs Justice Arden, swayed by Mann's arguments, concluded that Venables and Tottenham would suffer damage if Venables remained sacked and granted the injunction. The decision meant that Venables was back and could pursue the war with Sugar from inside the city gates rather than outside.

Venables heard the news at about 9.30 that night. It was Brown, recalls Cullen, who came back to Scribes with the news and Venables cracked open a bottle of champagne. Staunton was also at Scribes and interviewed a happy Venables, television relaying it to the crowd gathered at Enfield and there was, naturally, great jubilation. The joy was particularly deeply felt by Kingsley, Davies and the other TISA supporters who had received a phone call at Enfield and had immediately left for Scribes.

The Sugar camp was stunned. Gold and Mountfort crammed into a phone box outside the law court to tell him and such was Sugar's rage that Alan Watts, standing outside, could clearly hear the four-letter words he rained on his hapless lawyers. Sugar wanted an immediate move first thing Monday morning to lift the injunction. With some difficulty his lawyers convinced him this would not be wise; better to prepare affidavits for a court action.

As it happens Gold was taking his sons, both committed Arsenal fans, to the Cup Final the next day, and he promised to talk to Sugar and arrange for Watts, who had volunteered, to go to Sugar's home on Sunday and begin the preparation of the affidavits.

Venables had won, but in footballing terms he had won a free kick, then, while the opposition protested and had not got their wall ready, he had scored. It had been a lucky victory, won with the help of misleading statements in front of a judge who clearly did not know anything about football, let alone the background. But the game was not over. However, the way the Venables goal had been scored, and Venables' and Crystal's court statements, would leave scars that would make the campaign more bitter.

Chapter 24

Bambi refuses to die

Faced by an overwhelmingly hostile reaction to his attempt to oust Venables, Sugar issued a public statement saying, 'I feel like the man who shot Bambi.' The more accurate statement might have been 'I feel like the man who has shot Bambi's mother.' Nevertheless the point was well made. Venables, irrespective of whether he should have been compared to Bambi or Bambi's mother, and despite being shot at point blank range by Sugar, was showing astonishing powers of recuperation.

The news of his sacking, and then his reinstatement by Mrs Justice Arden, had dominated the weekend media. Before the storm broke Venables had told Donna Cullen that he was worried about Sugar's influence with Murdoch and the power of the Murdoch press. But the media never works in such simplistic fashion. In one of its first broadcasts of the sacking, the Sky reporter, talking from the backdrop of White Hart Lane said, 'Terry Venables may have the support of the players and the supporters. But in the end it all comes down to money. Alan Sugar holds the financial strings at Tottenham and the other Board members have little choice but to dance to his tune and back the sacking of the chief executive.' Sky may be owned by Murdoch, but if anyone could have complained about that report it would have been Sugar.

At this level it is often the inclinations of the individual journalists or editors that matter, and here Venables had, ironically, more to fear from the *Sun*'s main rival, the *Daily Mirror*, largely because its football correspondent Harry Harris had never been an uncritical admirer of Venables. But even Harris did not have his first meeting with Sugar until a week after the sacking – when Hewer persuaded Sugar to invite him and his then sports editor to his home – and at this stage, with Venables established as the people's hero, no paper could carry anything really critical or even wanted to. In any case the true nature of the Tottenham struggle was completely obscured. This suited Venables and he also benefited from the way the media cover such events.

Most of the scenes shown were of scrums of people outside White Hart Lane or at the Enfield football ground. Venables made a few brief appearances but Sugar was not seen, so reinforcing the image of the faceless money man getting rid of a popular hero. Sugar had been forced to react when he realised that in court Venables' lawyers had made much of the loss he might suffer from the Pan Financial loan he no longer had. However, the lawyer had not mentioned that Sugar had offered to buy out Venables, and he now disclosed his 6 May offer. But even here Venables was able to turn this to his advantage by describing the offer as derisory and presenting Sugar as Scrooge.

The granting of the injunction late on Friday night meant that everyone on Saturday was agog to hear more news and conveniently Venables had the ideal stage on which to state his case. The English season's showpiece, the Cup Final, was taking place at Wembley that Saturday and Venables was already booked as a TV pundit for the game. With the twin towers as his backdrop he could hardly miss and he didn't. Arsenal's quest for a unique Cup double was almost forgotten as Venables dominated the build-up to the match.

On the way to the BBC studio he shared a lift with Roy Hattersley, the politician and journalist, who wished him all the luck and said that football should be run by footballers rather than people who just buy their way into the club. When Venables got to the studio there was Desmond Lynam, who had trailed his arrival several times during the programme. The discussion that followed was an illustration of Venables' mastery of the small screen. He managed to paint himself in all the right colours and Sugar as the evil, power-crazy moneybags who could not work with anyone and might have had a secret agenda all along to get rid of him. But his most telling point, which left even Lynam gasping, was that he had been given no reason for his sacking, despite asking for it several times. To be sacked without reason was the sort of injustice anybody could understand and Venables milked it for all it was worth.

Lynam had introduced Venables just after a feature which showed an interview with Gary Lineker preparing to play for Grampus 8 in Japan. The interview with Venables went as follows:

Lynam: Here's the man who signed Lineker twice, for Tottenham and for Barcelona. Hell of a day yesterday?

Venables: Yeah. It is a lot more relaxing where he was (motioning at the Lineker shots), wasn't it?

Lynam: Exactly. How did all this start. I mean, you and Sugar have fallen out in a very big way.

Venables: Yeah.

Lynam: Why?

Venables: Well, I think Alan bought in with me when we first started but I think he wanted more of an involvement. And I put the amount of money I put in so that I would have control of the day-to-day running of the company, the club. And he agreed with that. I mean he is now saying only one person can run a club. Well, he knew that at the beginning.

Lynam: Umm.

Venables: And if you are now saying that further down the line, ah . . . it makes me wonder whether that was the idea in the first place.

Lynam: Was it a simple falling out, though, or is there some more specific reason for it?

Venables: No.

Lynam: Is it you just do not get on or has he accused you of something?

Venables: No, nothing at all. I have asked what's the grounds, he said there's no grounds and only the fact that one person should run the club. [Then after eulogising his role in rescuing Tottenham and in the process making a profit forecast which forced Tottenham to apologise to the Stock Exchange, Venables touched the buttons the football supporters understand.] I just believe the club is the people, I have always believed that. The club is not the building, or the grass, it is supporters, the people, the players, and you are dealing with people . . . It is not something that he does. He deals with a different business and he goes back to that every Monday morning. I do that every day. That's where I put my life into my experience and I have got to this stage hoping that it doesn't slip away easily.

Lynam: You must have got on together in the first place, didn't you?

Venables (with a laugh that sounded like a sort of gurgle in the throat): Well, we didn't have . . . we . . . we didn't have to get, actually get on because we didn't work together . . . But really it wasn't us going out dancing together. It was a working relationship.

Lynam: So what's the next stage, I mean . . .?

Venables: We put an injunction in. I am back to work on Monday morning which will be for two weeks and there will be another court hearing.

Lynam: So, that is going to be when Alan Sugar will present evidence.

Venables: Correct, correct, we will both do that.

Lynam (and here Lynam seemed to be struggling to get the words out as if to imply it was monstrous that Sugar had given no reason): The evidence that he will . . . if he has got a case for sacking you he has got, presumably, to present some evidence . . .

Venables: Absolutely . . .

Lynam: Some reason for sacking you?

Venables: Yeah. OK, I mean I have asked that several times, what is the reason and there is none. I will repeat that.

Lynam: OK. We wish you the best of luck with it. You got support in football, obviously, throughout. Thank you for being so frank about it today. (Smiling) We are really here to get you to tell us whether Arsenal or Sheffield Wednesday are going to win.

Venables (laughing): I can remember that there was a game this morning (loud laughter).

Lynam: This isn't a plot to take the play away from Arsenal?

Venables (laughing quite loudly now): That's been mentioned. George [Graham] is definitely not happy.

Lynam (joining in the laughter): George isn't happy.

Lynam then introduced Clive Anderson, the chat show host, and Roy Hattersley. Anderson, an Arsenal supporter, joined in the fun by saying how it broke his heart to see Tottenham tear itself apart. As Venables verbally joshed him he added, 'I came in to bring you a cup of tea, no Sugar wasn't it?' Venables joined in the general laughter and Lynam mentioned that Anderson was a lawyer, a man whose services Venables might need. Venables said, to even greater all-round mirth, 'I am going to wait for him afterwards.'

This was a performance that even Bambi could not have bettered.

Venables' success in claiming the media high ground was confirmed in that weekend's papers. The style of most of the newspaper comment was not dissimilar to the feature in the *Mail on Sunday* written by Patrick Collins, Bob Cass and Harry Miller, called 'Mismatch of the Day'. Venables, it said, believed 'he was simply a pawn in Sugar's game, that the tycoon had the present scenario planned in detail from Day One . . . Venables was prepared to support some of Sugar's more shameless ventures'. An example of such 'shamelessness' was Sugar's support for the Sky TV deal but, said the *Mail on Sunday*, Venables 'found it difficult to stomach Sugar's indifference to football matters. The chairman, it is said, had a selective view of the transfer market: you sold them dear and bought them cheap.'

Venables told the *Mail on Sunday* that, earlier in the season, he said to Sugar that he could get £3m. for Durie. Come Christmas, Durie had not been sold and Sugar was supposed to have asked, 'What's happening? It's all my f. . . money going up the wall.' Sugar, advised by lawyers not to talk about the reasons that led to Venables' departure, could only watch all this helplessly although he did have his moments. I myself wrote a piece in the *Sunday Times* revealing Brown's record in some detail. This was the first time there had been any inkling given of his business ability to ruin companies and provided the first business angle to the story. I also mentioned that Brown and Crystal had been two of Venables' friends whom Sugar had been unable to stomach.

Venables did not like that. In his autobiography describing me as a 'friend of Irving Scholar and author of his biography' he commented that the focus had been widened to Brown and Crystal because 'If I could not be damned directly, then it would be done by association'. What my own friendship with Scholar had to do with it is hard to say unless it was to suggest that, since he and Scholar had fallen out, I would also be his enemy. In fact, less than a month earlier, just before the semi-final with Arsenal, I had written a favourable piece about how Venables had transformed Spurs. And what had spurred me to go on and look at Brown was that, with Venables claiming he did not know why he had been sacked,

271

it was the obvious journalistic exercise to find out if there was, perhaps, a reason. My piece began: 'Terry Venables says he does not know why he was sacked. We can tell him there were . . .'

On Sunday Sugar broke his silence on LBC where, interviewed by Andrew Neil, then the *Sunday Times* editor, he spoke about his relationship with Venables. While still guarded, and refusing to be drawn on Brown, he criticised Crystal. Sugar was also proposing to move against both Crystal and Brown and called a Board meeting for Monday afternoon. Crystal could not attend and Brown's contract was terminated. Venables' lawyers tried to prevent the sacking, claiming it violated the spirit of the injunction, but they must have known they were only putting down a legal marker. Sugar, in a tart letter, warned Brown that, as one of Venables' advisers, he might have to come to White Hart Lane but, when he did so, he must behave like a visitor and not attempt to instruct staff in the manner he had done when employed there.

For Venables it was, perhaps, the most uncomfortable Board meeting he had attended. There was no Crystal to support him, and at least one observer got the impression that much of what took place passed over his head. This impression was strengthened by the fact that throughout the duration of the meeting Venables sat with a cue card in front of him. On this his lawyers had written: 'This Directors' meeting has been contrived for the purpose of the litigation and on any resolutions for the purpose, I shall vote upon each resolution as I see fit as being in the best interests of the Company'.

Every time a subject came up, like Brown's sacking, he repeated this mantra. It was a performance very like the one Ronald Reagan used to give at international meetings – when he, too, read from cue cards. Venables repeated the mantra so often that afternoon that, when the Tottenham secretary came to prepare the minutes, he recorded them the first time and thereafter called them 'his comments'. The minutes of the meeting are peppered with 'he repeated his comments'.

But despite feeling isolated and uncomfortable, Venables had much to cheer on that Monday. His daughter Tracey, who had been sacked on Friday, was immediately reinstated and, most importantly from Donna Cullen's point of view, there was visible proof that Venables was back. Cullen had seen Venables' return to Spurs as an important psychological moment and wanted to make sure that the world saw Venables back at his desk. So she arranged for a Press Association photographer to be there to record the scene – Terry behind his desk on the phone, Terry holding a cup of tea – and these pictures dominated that evening's and next day's newspapers.

Cullen had every reason to feel she had won the first few days of the PR battle and that the Venables campaign was now moving on several fronts. TISA was organising the fans, writing to them not to renew their season tickets; Eric Hall was adding his own individual touch, among his efforts, says Cullen, being the so-called petticoat demonstration outside Sugar's home by the wives of the players, although in the end only Neil Ruddock's wife, Sarah, was identified as having attended. On Friday it was Sheringham who had been seen as the most vocal supporter of Venables. Now Ruddock took over. The player hero-worshipped Venables and was to become increasingly vociferous in his support for him, to the point of threatening to leave if Venables did not return.

There was tremendous popular support for the Venables campaign, fuelled by the wave of righteous indignation. With nobody outside of Venables' inner circle aware of the civil war in Spurs, and Venables keen to keep it that way, the granting of the injunction had been taken as proof that right was on Venables' side. 'When on Friday night John came back to Scribes saying we got the injunction there was,' says Cullen, 'not only great jubilation but the feeling that we couldn't have got the injunction if Terry Venables was not in the right.' Even after Brown's record was 'outed' in the *Sunday Times* this sense of moral righteousness did not leave the Venables camp. Indeed Brown made quite a joke about his record. Cullen recalls: 'John would introduce himself by saying, say, "I am the bankrupt John Brown" and make self-deprecatory jokes.' Brown felt more than a little guilty. On more than one occasion he would say, "Terry is so good to his friends". He would tell Terry, "All this is happening because of me, I'm such a burden to you".'

John did not cut much of a dash with Piers Pottinger, however. At one of his first meetings with Venables Pottinger had told him that he needed to tell him everything, he was after all dealing with a public company and once Brown's past became known he advised Venables to distance himself from him. 'But,' says Pottinger, 'Brown was always trying to get in on the act.' Pottinger confesses he didn't like Brown, and he refused to go to Scribes, but at this stage all these misgivings were more than allayed by

Venables' endearing personality. 'He would come to our offices and taxi drivers would see him in the street, toot their horns in support, shouting "Good luck, Terry". It was very exciting.'

The TISA campaign also carried sanctions. Its leaflet supporting Venables had also told supporters not to renew their season tickets until the court hearing of 25 May, and if that went against Venables, 'tell the club you won't renew until Venables is reinstated'. Their campaign with box holders had had an effect when some had written to Mike Rollo, the commercial manager, complaining about Sugar's action and saying they would not renew their boxes. Many of the rumours circulating around Tottenham found fertile ground here. So not only was the Sugar statement that Tottenham's ambitions should be realistic quoted, but also the alleged story that the reason for the split was that Venables wanted to sign Des Walker, keen to get away from an unhappy Italian experience, but Sugar had vetoed it. It is the sort of story you get when a manager, not a chief executive, is sacked, and in any event this was a subject the two men had never even discussed. If the campaign not to renew season ticket sales, meant to hurt Tottenham and therefore Sugar's pocket, was within the bounds of legitimate protest, there was a darker side to it and elements of the pro-Venables campaign went beyond what is acceptable. Nobody associated with the reinstated Venables campaign admits to illegal acts but they did happen.

On the night of 14 May the walls of Sugar's home had been daubed with graffiti, even if Sugar had been spelt as Sugare. His daughter's car was vandalised, with one of the vandals for good measure ringing the *Sun* from the car phone, a call that helped the police trace him. Above all, the Board members received death threats. One addressed to 'D. A. Alexiou, Director' read: 'Leave Spurs Now You Fucking Stooge or youre (*sic*) Dead'.

Kingsley indignantly denies that TISA had any hand in this. TISA did, however, list the business addresses of Sugar, Sandy, Berry and Alexiou and, while they emphasised that the messages must be 'polite and non-abusive', given the passion football can arouse – during the 1993–94 season a Southampton fanzine would call for the death of Ian Branfoot, the then manager – Venables' departure was bound to arouse even greater fury. Not surprising then that another message Alexiou received which advised him to support Arsenal and called him 'shitbag' was on a TISA leaflet which had a picture of Venables surrounded by four Tottenham players – Anderton, Ruddock, Sheringham and Barmby – and bore the campaign slogan: 'Don't throw away Tottenham's future – Reinstate Terry Venables'.

Cullen is keen to distance herself from any involvement in such happenings or the public demonstrations, but she acknowledges that she acted as clearing house for the media, keeping it informed of what TISA and the others were doing and in turn kept them informed about likely media interests. 'We did put Steve Davies in a couple of interview slots but TISA did its own thing, we just helped out, we didn't organise anything.'

Sugar, of course, was planning his own counter-attack. On Sunday 15 May he had sat in his dining-room and told his side of the Venables story to Alan Watts, of the Herbert Smith law firm. In between there were interruptions: calls from Kelvin Mackenzie, editor of the *Sun*; and the LBC interview with Andrew Neil. In the kitchen sat Sandy, telling his story to Gold. Sugar would continue telling the story over the next couple of days and it was on Monday in the Tottenham boardroom that he told Watts about the 'bung' allegations.

Some time that Sunday afternoon Bryan Fugler, Tottenham's lawyer, rang trying to act as middle-man. Efforts for peace would continue, Venables had dinner with a chairman of a Premier League London club who advised him to take Sugar's money. 'You will have a million in the bank and, who knows, in six months you might be England manager.' But Venables would not listen, not even when Yawetz tried to mediate.

At about six in the morning of Thursday 20 May Sugar swore his 56-page affidavit telling the story of his two years with Venables. It came complete with the allegations that would rock the soccer world to its foundations.

The Monday after this, at Herbert Smith's offices, there took place the most serious effort at peace. Venables was not present but was at the end of a telephone with Philip Green acting as a courier for his thoughts. This was very far from a friendly encounter, the Sugar camp in one room, the Venables camp in another and messages going back and forth. Sugar by now was offering £4.5m. Green relayed this to Venables but he wanted £6m. Sugar flew off the handle and said, 'No more deals'. Sugar decided there was no way he could be at peace with Venables. The man just did not know how to make a deal. Now there would be no more offers. Sugar would buy a yacht and next weekend he was in the south of France doing just that. Sugar saw the £4.5m. Venables had refused as helping to pay for the purchase of the yacht. Named the *Louisianna*, after Louise his daughter and Ann his wife, it has always been known unofficially as 'Venables' gift'. As far as Sugar was concerned, and much as he wanted to avoid a court battle, now there could be no turning back.

Philip Green drove away in his convertible Rolls from a quiet city shaking his head. As he said, 'Sugar was as good as gold, Terry had a death wish.'

What made Venables so obdurate? He bought into Tottenham on a wave of emotion. Did he cling on to it on a wave of emotion? Certainly one must question the advice he was being given. He may have won an injunction on that Friday night, yet he could hardly have imagined he would win the war. This would have involved him buying out Sugar, a difficult strategy given Sugar did not want to sell and there were not too many candidates who wanted to buy him out. Names were bandied about, particularly that of Robert Earle who was then launching Planet Hollywood in a gala opening that stopped traffic in the West End as it brought Arnold Schwarzenegger, Bruce Willis and Sylvester Stallone to London. But whether his interest was more than casual it is difficult to say. In any event, by the weekend Sugar was making it clear that even if 'the Ford Motor Company, Coca-Cola and John Paul Getty have got in a huddle behind Terry Venables nobody can force me to sell my shares. Is that clear?'

However, Venables was riding high on the support he had garnered from his public campaign. In addition he had his own plans for a come-back, including one, both audacious and breathtaking, which would come within an ace of succeeding.

Chapter 25

Venables' audacious coup

Venables was acutely aware that one area where his public image needed refurbishment was in the City of London. Piers Pottinger had been aware of this all along and, on the afternoon of Thursday 20 May, he arranged for Venables to meet Jeff Randall at Pottinger's offices, just behind the Park Lane Hilton. The meeting, recalls Pottinger, went well. Randall was too shrewd a judge to be carried away by the Venables hype but he left the meeting well disposed towards him.

In little more than twenty-four hours this impression had been erased. The next day Philip Green arranged a dinner with Randall and Venables at the Cantina, the Terence Conran restaurant just across Tower Bridge. Randall could see how popular Venables was. As they appeared at the restaurant, autograph hunters besieged Venables and he sighed, 'Oh God, this never stops.' They did find a quiet table, sharing a bottle of red wine, but for all Green's prompting and Venables' verbal skills and evident charm, the good impression he had created of a businessman who knew what he was doing was dissipated. When Pottinger heard about the dinner and its results he despaired.

With his affidavit now ready, Sugar was keen to get his story across and rang TISA. After requesting them to keep an open mind he offered to show the affidavit to them provided Venables agreed. This was a necessary precaution because at this stage the affidavits, not having been read in court, were not publicly available. Venables did agree and on Sunday 23 May, Davies, Kingsley and

James Loxley went to the offices of Kanter Jules Grangewoods and read them. But if Sugar hoped to change minds he failed. They came away even more strengthened in their belief that Venables was right. What they did not know, however, was that, even as they were reading the Sugar affidavit that Sunday, Venables was planning to launch a coup that could unseat Sugar.

The basis of the coup which Venables planned was very simple. It was the sharp legal eye of Crystal which had discovered it. Crystal had, of course, become very hot and bothered about the contract Sugar had given himself at Spurs when he took over the merchandising side. Crystal had referred to the contract in his affidavit which Mann had used when asking for an injunction, and presented it as yet more evidence of Sugar's desire to take over Tottenham and sideline Venables. Some time after this, perhaps after Venables had been sacked on 14 May, Crystal began to look at the contract again in detail. He found a clause which must have made him jump with joy. Sugar had signed a contract which had in it the weapons of his own destruction.

The contract Sugar had was a standard contract in his Amstrad empire. This required that any director who lost a vote of confidence in the Board would automatically lose his directorship and be voted off the Board. The clause, while unusual, is not rare, and some public companies even require their executives to sign undated letters of resignation the moment they join, but in this situation it could not be more devastating. Although Sugar had sacked Venables as chief executive he could not get rid of either Venables or Crystal as directors of the public company, Tottenham plc, without an extraordinary general meeting of the shareholders. Sugar was planning to do that to remove Crystal; but having signed such a contract himself, he had provided the Venables camp with a simple weapon to vote him, Sugar, off the Board. They would not even have to call a shareholders' meeting. Their strategy was to call a meeting of the Board, propose a resolution of no-confidence in Sugar and, once he lost the vote, he would automatically lose his chairmanship and be off the Board. He could still fight Venables but he would be fighting from outside. Yes, as a 48% owner of the company he could call a meeting of the shareholders, but this would take at least a month and all this time the company would be in the hands of Venables. It seemed the perfect coup and the Venables camp thought they could get the votes to make it happen.

Just as Venables could not vote on his sacking as chief executive, so this time Sugar would not be able to vote. Sandy would vote for him. Now that Alexiou was on the Board he, too, would vote for him. These votes in Sugar's favour would be cancelled out by Venables and Crystal for the motion. 2–2. And the winner for the Venables camp would come from Tony Berry.

Venables still thought that Berry could be brought on board. He needed him to complete his coup. Why the Venables camp felt Berry could be persuaded is hard to say. His action at the 14 May meeting was clear but perhaps Berry might be open to persuasion. Ever since he was ousted from Blue Arrow, and the many problems he had with the DTI, Berry had not found life easy. He was restarting in business but the DTI cast a long shadow and he had not regained his old prominence. He held a large chunk of Spurs shares; perhaps if the Venables camp organised it in such a way that a buyer was found for the shares, then everyone would be happy. Venables would be back in charge of Spurs, Berry would have the money, and Sugar, the largest shareholder, would be like the child desperately peering at a well-fortified shop window, unable to get in. All the more galling as he owned most of the shop.

On Sunday 23 May, just hours after the *Sunday Times* had led its main paper on a story about Robert Earle of Planet Hollywood offering to buy out Sugar, Berry received a call. It was from Crystal, outlining the legal possibilities. Soon Philip Green was on the line suggesting a deal whereby, if Berry sided with Venables, he could be bought out. Berry's wife was in Florida then and by the time the calls had finished it was almost one in the morning. This was just the time for the first evening cocktails and Berry rang her. After Berry had outlined the coup and said he couldn't possibly go with Venables, she said: 'We could do with the money, but you couldn't do that, you are not like that.'

'No, darling,' said Berry, 'I am not like that. Every man may have his price but there is no price on things like this.'

Early the next morning Berry rang Sugar and said, 'I have got something to discuss with you.'

'Go on, then,' said Sugar with a familiar tone of impatience in his voice.

'Can't discuss it over the phone. I must come and see you.'

'If it is that important, come over this morning.'

So Berry, after keeping a previously arranged meeting with his bank manager, drove to Brentwood. On the way he could not help but admire the extraordinary coup Venables was planning. By the time he got to Brentwood and to Sugar's tenth-floor office, Sugar was impatient to hear what it was about. On that tenth floor Sugar works in a completely open fashion. The door to his room is never closed, opposite sits his secretary, and down the corridor are Sandy and other Amshold or Amstrad executives.

But on this occasion Berry closed the door behind him and broke the news. Sugar went white. His first reaction was to take out the contract and read it again, his next a bellowed shout for Sandy who came running. Sugar gave Sandy the contract and explained the loophole Crystal had found. Sandy quickly confirmed Crystal was right. 'We are exposed,' he said. It did not take much to realise, as Sandy recalls, 'that it was a nasty situation'. Herbert Smith was consulted and it was decided to redraft the agreement, the clauses that exposed Sugar being dropped. The agreement, however, had to be put to a directors' meeting and the next one was due on the afternoon of 3 June.

But before the Board meeting could be held there would have to be a public confrontation. The date set to hear the lifting of the injunction was 25 May. Both Sugar and Venables were well aware of the contrasting public emotions they had aroused: Sugar, fury; Venables, an uncritical, adoring love. Sugar had already seen evidence of mob damage but it was at the Strand law offices on 25 May that he was to be confronted by the hate his actions had whipped up in its most elemental, primitive form. This was the first public confrontation of the two men since the sacking and it took on the style of a Victorian melodrama with Sugar the villain.

This was evident from the moment he arrived in the Strand. Alan Watts arrived with him: 'We were in two cabs and as we got out we could see the crowds milling in the road with the police holding them back. Sugar was in the front and as he walked up to the steps a builder on a scaffolding noticed him and said, "That's him". This got the crowd going and they started booing and shouting abuse. It was so vociferous that even I was shaken and they were not even shouting at me.'

Hewer had arrived early to find that most of the journalists were already waiting in the narrow corridor outside one of the smaller courts in the new building. It was hot and the court attendants would not allow anybody into the court until ten minutes before the hearing. So every time the lift opened more people poured in –

some journalists, many fans – and long before the proceedings started the courtroom was so packed that many were standing, and some even kneeling on the steps leading to the public benches. 'It was something like a celebrity event,' Hewer recalled. 'I gave up my seat to Jeff Randall. Terry entered and quietly entertained the press bench for a few minutes before taking his seat. Sugar remained huddled with his legal team.'

At the end of it, after the judge, the Vice-Chancellor, Sir Donald Nicholls, decided there was insufficient time that day to conclude the hearings, and adjourned the case. Sugar left with Hewer, flanked by two policemen. 'As we left the court room and got into the narrow corridor heading for the lifts Sugar was surrounded in the most intimidating way by fans, one of whom lent forward and persistently hissed "Judas", his lips almost touching Sugar's face. Sugar looked straight ahead and, walking very deliberately and slowly, he remained very calm in an explosive situation. When we reached the car park in front of the new building Sugar found himself surrounded by journalists who had followed him down. Looking up I noticed that Sugar's Rolls-Royce was parked at the entrance to the car park facing the crowd who were milling round the main entrance just a few yards up the Strand. I realised to use the Rolls-Royce would mean driving through that crowd, and I hurriedly signalled to Russell Cutler, Sugar's driver, to stay where he was. I went out into the Strand and discreetly hailed a black cab into the courtyard, piled Berry, Mountfort, Gold and myself into it with Sugar in the middle. Gold passed Sugar a folder to read. We pulled into the Strand and drove unnoticed through the crowd.'

Outwardly Sugar remained calm but everywhere he turned Venables seemed to trump him. Sugar had wanted a quick court hearing to lift the injunction, but the earliest date he could get was 10 June. Not only did the May Bank Holiday weekend intervene but Kanter Jules Grangewoods claimed they had other problems. May 26 and 27 were the days of Shavuot, a Jewish religious holiday on which, as a devout firm, they could not work. So why don't you instruct non-Jewish lawyers on those days, suggested Herbert Smith, a suggestion which outraged Kanter Jules Grangewoods. They had, it seemed, never heard anyone having the temerity to suggest this – and pointed out it would be against Halachah.

The delay, of course, suited Venables, the only gentile in the argument. He wanted to be given the right to buy out Sugar and, while he organised the finances, he wanted the present interim regime, whereby he remained as chief executive, to continue. In a sense he wanted to eat his cake and have it too.

All this weighed on Sugar, particularly the events in and around the courtroom. Indeed they weighed so heavily that they nearly led to a spectacular 'own goal'.

Chapter 26

The war of the affidavits

Venables had won the publicity war. Could he win the affidavit war? One of these had been provided by Mike Rollo, Tottenham's commercial manager. The first public reference to it came in the court hearings on 25 May. The next day Rollo was in Cheltenham to meet some boxholders, making sure they did not cancel their boxes. The morning papers, particularly the tabloids, worried him. They had referred to Rollo's affidavit and suggested that, if Venables won, Rollo might find his position difficult.

Rollo brooded over what he had said: while in the short term Venables' leaving would create problems and generate bad publicity, no individual, neither Venables nor Sugar, was bigger than the club and Venables' departure would not affect the club. If Sugar left, Venables would have to find a financial backer and in the long term Tottenham could be in financial difficulties. If there was a touch of the Vicar of Bray in Rollo, it was a stance common to Tottenham staff at that time. They could not be sure who would win. Rollo rang Venables. 'Terry,' he said, 'I was only telling the truth. You know I said you were a good football coach.' (Rollo had described him as 'the greatest football coach in the United Kingdom, if not the world'.)

'No, no,' said Venables with an affability that surprised Rollo. 'Your affidavit is fair. I would like you to do an affidavit for me.'

'Well, Terry,' said Rollo, 'I will have to think about that. I must consult my solicitors.'

The request put Rollo in a ticklish situation. Could he do an affidavit for both sides? He rang his solicitors who told him that, if he did, he might be in danger of becoming a laughing stock. 'They told me people might question my sincerity, that I could not make up my mind as to who to support. Then Terry's solicitor wrote to me and, trying to make me feel better, they said there was no harm in doing an affidavit for Terry.'

A date was fixed for Rollo to go to Venables' solicitors and swear his affidavit. But Rollo was not happy about it and rang Kanter Jules Grangewoods cancelling the appointment. On the morning of the meeting he received a call from John Brown.

'I hear you have cancelled the appointment,' he said, clearly displeased.

'Yes,' said Rollo, 'it's not that easy.'

'Don't give me that,' said Brown cutting in sharply. 'You just get your ass over to Kanter Jules Grangewoods, today.'

Brown then suggested a time later that day. Rollo did not know what to do. Almost in desperation he turned to John Ireland: what would the Spurs Board say if he gave an affidavit for Venables? Ireland contacted Sugar and the other directors and came back with the information that as far as the Board were concerned Rollo could go ahead and provide such an affidavit. 'This meant that I had to make the decision on my own, and I decided I couldn't provide such an affidavit. I rang up Terry's solicitors to say please don't contact me.'

This was only one skirmish in the war of the affidavits but a major battle soon developed between Sugar and Crystal. Sugar precipitated matters with a phone call made from his car to Crystal on the morning of Tuesday 1 June 1993.

In his affidavit of 10 June, Sugar described how he came to make that phone call. It is important to emphasise that he was trying to escape a charge of contempt of court and his manner was unusually contrite, but there is no denying he was exercised by Crystal. Mrs Justice Arden's decision to grant an injunction to Venables had come as a shock to Sugar. He asserted that Crystal had given a false statement and, what is more, he had been told by Gold, his lawyer, that the judge would have relied on Crystal's word, being that of a barrister.

'It seemed to me,' said Sugar in his affidavit, 'that I was fighting an unequal battle if Mr Crystal's word was to be accepted more readily (because he was a barrister) than the ordinary man's. This struck me as particularly unfair in the face of my conviction that

Mr Crystal had been misled by his loyalty to Mr Venables into making statements which I consider to be untrue.'

At this point he remembered how someone had told him of the occasion on 3 December 1992 when Crystal had told the court he had to attend a disciplinary hearing at the same time as, in fact, he had been at White Hart Lane in the Tottenham boardroom. Sugar couldn't recall who had told him the story, it was either David Hyams, Amstrad's in-house lawyer, or Nick Hewer. On 15 May Sugar telephoned Hewer who confirmed that it was he. Then Sugar telephoned Margaret Mountfort and she confirmed Hewer's version. On 17 May Sugar had spoken to Alan Watts, who told him that what Crystal had said in court that day would appear in a court transcript. Sugar asked Watts to try to obtain the transcript.

On 18 May, Crystal's first affidavit exhibiting and confirming as true his statement upon which Mrs Justice Arden had placed so much reliance was served. This increased Sugar's concern and he was convinced that the court should be alerted to the fact that, as he saw it, on a previous occasion Crystal had 'lied' to the court. Sugar's mind was filled with fear that as long as the court remained unaware of this 'the inequality in our respective positions would continue'.

The hearing of 25 May further unnerved Sugar. Two days later, on Thursday 27 May, Sugar, eager to take advantage of the Bank Holiday weekend, went to France. Although that is when he bought the yacht, 'Venables' gift', he could not get away from worries about Crystal. On 31 May Sugar returned from France. The next morning, while travelling to Amstrad's Brentwood office in his car, on an impulse, he picked up the car telephone and rang Crystal. Sugar says he told him he had met his father on numerous occasions and his mother on two or three occasions in the boardroom prior to matches and they were nice people. Then after pointing out that they were both Jewish, he suggested they talk because Crystal was being blinded by his hero-worship of Mr Venables. Sugar had something particular he wanted to tell Crystal. He didn't want to get Crystal into trouble, perhaps Crystal could take the train out to Brentwood that day and that if he did not feel comfortable talking in his office they could talk outside.

Crystal's affidavit says that Sugar rang him at home and, after saying that no doubt he was busy preparing affidavits, suggested a meeting. According to Crystal, Sugar told him he had something to show him which could affect Crystal's family and career but which did not relate to Terry Venables. Sugar denies that his telephone manner was unfriendly or menacing and he did not tell Crystal that he had something to show him, he had something to tell him. In any event it was quickly clear that Crystal could not take the train ride to Essex that day. Crystal thought he had two conferences that day but promised to get back to Sugar after he had checked with his chambers.

One of his meetings was with Venables and Brown. He was supposed to meet them at 9am at the Royal Garden Hotel. However, Sugar's call made him a little late and when he arrived he told Venables about the phone conversation. Crystal also told Venables he had no clue to what Sugar could have been referring.

Later that morning Crystal, in the presence of Venables, rang Sugar (Venables says it was about 10.30am, Crystal is precise and says he rang at 10.20). Sugar was due at White Hart Lane that afternoon for a management meeting, one that Venables would also attend, and Crystal and Sugar agreed to meet after that. Sugar would have to leave by 5.30pm, but it was agreed they would meet soon after the management meeting was over.

In preparation for his meeting with Crystal, Sugar dictated a draft affidavit for himself and faxed this draft affidavit to Herbert Smith shortly before 2pm. But by the time he met Crystal he had taken no legal advice and for the first time since the break with Venables he was rowing on his own.

Crystal arrived at White Hart Lane at 4.40pm. He met Sugar on the stairs and they went into the Dave Mackay Suite. According to Crystal's affidavit Sugar told him he was blinded by loyalty to Mr Venables. 'He said that if he produced an affidavit which he, Mr Sugar, did not like, he would swear an affidavit that I had once misled the court and that this would affect my career and my family.' It was at this stage that Sugar told Crystal about the events of 3 December 1992. Sugar also told Crystal he had two witnesses to support his allegation: Hewer and Mountfort. 'He said that these two witnesses had been in court and he had obtained a transcript of the hearing which he would exhibit to an affidavit. He would say that I had lied to the court.' Crystal says he did not speak, 'save to ask Mr Sugar if he had a copy of the transcript, to which he replied, "not on me". Mr Sugar then said, "That's it", and I went downstairs to leave. He followed and by the exit he said, "This conversation never happened".'

Sugar's recollection of the conversation in the Dave Mackay

suite is more detailed and somewhat different. He told Crystal how he had met Crystal's parents and how Crystal was, like him, Jewish, and there was no point in them doing one another any harm. But he also told him that he thought that Crystal had a severe case of hero-worship as far as Venables was concerned and that this was blinding his normal common sense. Sugar made no bones about the fact that he thought Crystal's previous affidavit was 'full of lies' and that he had 'lied' to protect Terry Venables. Sugar also expressed his fears that the judge would believe him because he was a barrister. Sugar was expecting further evidence from Crystal and warned that, if Crystal swore what he termed a 'lying' affidavit, Sugar would have no alternative but to defend himself and to prove that Crystal had told 'lies' in court earlier. It was then, says Sugar, that he told Crystal of the events of 3 December 1992 and that Herbert Smith was obtaining a transcript of that hearing.

Sugar's point is that he did not tell Crystal that if he swore an affidavit which he did not like he would put before the court the matters referred to above. He would feel compelled to take such a course, if Crystal swore a 'lying affidavit'. Secondly, he did not say he had obtained a transcript of what he had said in court on 3 December, he said he was in the process of obtaining a transcript.

Crystal returned to his car and immediately made a note on a piece of paper, writing:

'2 witnesses you lied in court to Vinelott J

4 40 evidence

Hewer/Mountfort

This conversation never happened.'

At around 5.45pm that evening Crystal went back into the building and up to Venables' office. 'He looked,' said Venables in his affidavit, 'shaken. He said, "I'm going". I said, "Hang on" but he wanted to go. We arranged to meet at the Royal Lancaster Hotel.' A few minutes later, at six o'clock that evening, Crystal made a full note of his recollection of the two telephone conversations he had with Sugar and of his meeting with Sugar, the note being made on the reverse side of the paper where he had made the earlier note in his car. It was only when Crystal arrived later that evening at the Royal Lancaster that Venables learnt what Sugar had said to him.

In his affidavit Crystal would say that, 'Following the conversation, I was left with the clear impression that if I made an affidavit which was unfavourable to Mr Sugar's case, or supportive of the

Petitioner's case, Mr Sugar would seek to discredit my professional reputation and thereby damage me and my family.'

By this time Sugar, having launched his Exocet without informing his solicitors, had begun to realise that the Exocet was threatening to turn into a boomerang. When Sugar told Alan Watts what he had done, Watts' first words were, 'You did what?' Herbert Smith moved quickly to try to repair the damage. The next day, 2 June, they wrote to Kanter Jules Grangewoods as follows:

Mr Alan Sugar has brought to our attention that he had an off the record and highly confidential conversation with Mr Jonathan Crystal yesterday afternoon, during the course of which he mentioned something which Mr Crystal may or may not have passed on to you. We wish to make it clear that the conversation took place without Mr Sugar having the benefit of legal advice and if, and in so far as, Mr Sugar may have deemed to suggest, in the course of that conversation, that Mr Crystal should refrain from filing evidence in the above case because of evidence which Mr Sugar would file concerning his [Mr Crystal's] professional conduct, that would be a misunderstanding of Mr Sugar's intention. We wish to make it plain that Mr Crystal should feel free to file whatever evidence in this matter he chooses.

We must plainly reserve on our clients' behalf their right to use whatever evidence is appropriate to this case but would repeat that there is no intention to prevent Mr Crystal from deposing to such evidence as he sees fit.

By now Sugar knew he had committed a major blunder. In trying to clear the ball he had blasted it straight at his own goal and Crystal, having been gifted a goal, could hardly fail to build on that advantage. Crystal immediately instructed his own solicitors, Messrs Burton Copeland, who wrote to Herbert Smith on 3 June, recording Crystal's version of the events which had taken place. Paragraph 4 of the letter said:

It's quite plain that your client has sought to influence the evidence that is to be given by Mr Crystal in connection with the proceedings presently before the court between Edennote Plc and Tottenham Hotspur Plc and others. The means by which Mr Sugar sought to influence Mr Crystal are viewed by us with the utmost seriousness.

Burton Copeland said that Crystal was entirely satisfied there was absolutely no justification to criticise his conduct before Justice

Vinelott on 3 December and that they would bring the matter to the attention of Venables' lawyers for any action they might wish to take. Burton Copeland's letter to Kanter Jules Grangewoods was also dated 3 June, a date that was assuming quite some significance.

It was the day when the Tottenham Board met to deal with the fall-out from Venables' failed coup against Sugar. If this did not have some of the explosive content of the 6 May meeting it was still full of suppressed anger and evident ill-will. Venables was not present, he was busy with his lawyers trying to prepare his court case, but Crystal was and he was none too happy that his coup plan had been discovered.

Sugar was like a man who had seen the tanks gather on his lawn, then managed to deflect them and he played this Board meeting like a master. Before he moved on to the most crucial item he whetted the directors' appetite. He had a most interesting titbit as starter. It was that very morning that Sugar had personally discovered the £8,750 VAT on the £50,000 given to McLintock. The Sugar camp had only realised the existence of this money when Sandy read an affidavit presented by Venables' lawyers. His first thought then had been, 'Am I going mad?' For some days after that a search had gone on for this money but nobody in Tottenham's accounts office knew anything about it. It was only that morning that Sugar had located it in Peter Barnes' safe where, according to Barnes, it had been put under Venables' instructions. The money was still wrapped in the packings in which the Midland Bank had put it on 27 August, one of the packings was dated 26 August, and the fact that it had lain there for nine months without anyone but Barnes, Venables and McLintock knowing about it came as a shock to the rest of the Board. Berry could hardly find words to describe his surprise. Alexiou wanted an explanation from Venables.

Crystal did have his moment when the payment of £10,000 to Gilbert came up. Why was this payment necessary? Was there a contract? Wasn't Gilbert a friend of Sugar and had not Sugar said he would work for free? Sugar could ride this explaining that, when Gilbert had offered to work for free, that was for a one-off consultancy, now it was ongoing. In any case Sandy and Berry confirmed that they knew Gilbert was being paid.

Everybody knew all this was minor skirmishing before the main bout, to vote on the supplemental agreement to remove the explosive clause in Sugar's contract. Sugar introduced it as if he was dealing with a minor technical matter, 'We have to deal with some of the agreements that are already in existence. It has been brought to my attention that the contract Amshold have with Tottenham with regard to me needs to be changed. The agreement was drafted from an earlier Amstrad agreement and has certain provisions which are not appropriate. Of course the agreement was looked at by Jonathan before it was signed but now it needs changes. This is a matter on which I shall not be voting but before we discuss it I would like to state that there was a very unsavoury incident whereby Tony [Berry] was approached by someone to ask if he would vote against me using a clause in the agreement to remove me as director. I would like to thank Tony for advising me of the approach.'

Crystal knew that the coup against Sugar had failed, but he kept on protesting. At the start of the meeting, when Margaret Mountfort had been invited to attend, Crystal said he took 'no position'. Now he felt it was inappropriate to consider the proposed amendments given that litigation was going on. It was improper that changes were being made to a director's contract, when a court case was going on, more so as this change would benefit Sugar. If the changes had to be made there was need for completely independent advice. Sugar confirmed Herbert Smith had advised him personally as well as Amshold but Crystal must have realised how isolated he was. Alexiou was happy to take Herbert Smith's advice, Margaret Mountfort pointed out that the court action did not concern this, and the amendments were obviously required. The motion was proposed by Alexiou, seconded by Berry, Sandy voted in favour and Crystal against.

But if this was a defeat for the Venables camp, by the time Crystal left the boardroom that evening he knew that, while Sugar may have escaped the boardroom coup, there was every chance he could get Sugar on the contempt charge.

Sugar's discussion with Crystal on 1 June amounted to a potential contempt of court: trying to influence a witness while a court hearing was going on. How serious this could be became clear when, on 4 June, Crystal filed a draft affidavit and asserted that Sugar's allegation 'about my professional conduct is entirely without foundation. Notwithstanding this, on the advice of senior leading counsel, I have reported that matter to the Professional Conduct committee of the Bar Council.'

On the basis of this, and of a Venables affidavit, Kanter Jules

Grangewoods moved in for the kill. It came on 7 June in the form of a petition served on Sugar. Its purpose was stark: at ten o'clock on 10 June an application would be presented to persuade the court to put Sugar in prison for 'his contempt in seeking to deter by threatening to discredit his professional reputation Jonathan Crystal for making an affidavit on behalf of Edennote.'

Sugar knew he had to make amends. On the night of 9 June, while England's chances of qualifying for the World Cup were dashed in a 2–0 defeat in Oslo – a defeat which had enormous significance for Venables – Sugar prepared his affidavit in answer to Crystal. In the early hours of 10 June he swore it. He admitted he had committed contempt of court and apologised 'unreservedly to this court for my contempt'.

Sugar's affidavit concluded, 'I now know that I ought not to have spoken to Mr Crystal in connection with his evidence as I in fact did. In addition, I now understand that it is not for me but for the Judge to assess the credibility of witnesses and to determine which witnesses are telling the truth.'

The Venables camp strategy with regard to the contempt was clear. In his opening address Martin Mann mentioned the contempt charges against Sugar. Although the punishment for contempt can be imprisonment it was always unlikely that, even if Sugar had been found guilty, he would have been sent to prison. However, the law requires that a contempt be purged. So what the Venables camp wanted was that, unless the Sugar contempt had been dealt with and purged, his affidavit should be set aside and not considered for the purposes of the litigation. Clearly they feared his evidence. But the judge, the Vice-Chancellor, Sir David Nicholls, brushed aside this argument, saying he would deal with the contempt at the end, and admitted Sugar's affidavit.

This was the explosive one which detailed the allegations about 'bungs' and, although it had created a stir in the press, it did nothing to dent the public support for Venables; if anything the gut feeling for him was even greater. As in May Venables was borne to the steps of the High Court on a remarkable wave of emotion and public sympathy and, as he arrived in court, the Strand was like Tottenham High Road with Venables treated as if he was returning to White Hart Lane with the championship.

But there was also an air of menace and nastiness; the desire not only to triumph over sporting opponents but to destroy them was very much in the air. The recent history of English football is often the story of hating opponents and Sugar was very much the enemy for the Tottenham supporters who had gathered there. If some of the Venables wave lapping up the Strand that day and over the next few days was genuine and spontaneous, a good bit was also organised and had its sinister side. Tottenham Independent Supporters' Association, who had given the call for the demonstrations, claimed they were peaceful and Donna Cullen insists she played no part in anything violent or untoward. But video evidence would show some of the organisers working the crowd: their faces set, their actions more suited to the political arena than a sporting one, let alone a judicial one.

After the events of 25 May the case had been transferred to a bigger court on the first floor of the old building with a raised gallery for the public. But this would cause its own problems for Sugar. Whenever he entered the court to take his seat, there would be a low hiss from the public gallery although the fans were careful not to make overt trouble. However, it was different outside the courtroom where some thirty or forty fans, unable to gain access to the court proper, lounged around on the benches in a menacing manner, smoking and reading the *Sun* which, contrary to fears which Venables had expressed to Cullen, was very pro-Venables.

The result was that the pressure on Sugar was maintained throughout the hearings by the hostile crowds, the worst manifestation of which came on the second day of the hearings. His wife Ann had come that day to show support and it was during the lunch break as they left the courtroom that they encountered the hate-filled mob at its worst. Their path to the special room set aside for their lunch was through a gauntlet of fans in the corridor, then down a set of semi-circular stairs. Sugar led the way, followed by Ann, and as he was halfway down the stairway, a fan ran to the railings overlooking the stairwell. Throwing his head back he spat down at Sugar, hitting the shoulder of his blue suit. Sugar did not react until he reached the room. Then as Ann wiped it off he said, 'Bloody hell, they are spitting at me.' The Sugar camp even made a joke about it. Gold asked Watts, 'Did they spit on you?' 'No,' replied Watts. 'Pity, I missed again,' said Gold.

The air of heavy menace returned that evening at the end of the day's hearings. Sugar and his wife, accompanied by a policeman, left the court and went down a private spiral staircase that led to the judges' car park, where his driver was waiting to whisk them home. Hewer, delayed by a journalist, followed a couple of minutes later. Reaching the car park Hewer was suddenly aware of a small group, perhaps eight men, quietly rounding a corner into the car park. He was alerted to the sinister nature of the men because they were silent, middle-aged, in a tight group moving as a team and he heard one of them say, 'Don't go round there, there is a camera on the wall.' They were clearly looking for Sugar's car and were disappointed to discover that Sugar had given them the slip. One of them said, 'He's gone but that's Berry's Range Rover.' As they moved towards it, two policemen in shirt sleeves arrived and told them that they were in a restricted area and led them back to the public yard.

Hewer found himself in the middle of this group being escorted away. 'One of them,' says Hewer, 'recognised me as part of Sugar's team and without actually being touched I found myself crowded with messages whispered from behind to the effect that, "tell Sugar and tell Berry we'll get them".' Hewer, convinced they were not ordinary fans, called the police, who told him that they were aware of that group and were keeping a close eye on their activities.

In the courtroom, however, things were not going well for Venables. For the Vice-Chancellor the crucial questions were: was there a shareholders' agreement, if not why should a court over-turn a decision about the contract of its chief executive taken by the Board of a company, something courts are loath to do? There was also Venables' desire to buy out Sugar, but did he have the money?

When Mann said Venables wanted to be given an opportunity to buy out Sugar, the Vice-Chancellor intervened, 'Very well . . . I do not think that you should be given an opportunity simply on the basis of: "Now I will go away and see if I can find some money." You have to have some reasonable ground for believing that this is a serious possibility. That is why I asked if there is any evidence. I am asking whether this is an achievable course.' Mann replied, 'My instructions – there is no evidence – are that this is a course that is achievable. For the purposes of the petition, evidence will have to be filed to that effect. That is something that we fully accept. We have no evidence at the moment. We are not aware as to how the mechanism of such a purchase would be put together.'

The Vice-Chancellor laid little store by the shareholders' agree-ment that Venables alleged existed and which would make Tottenham more of a partnership. Tottenham was a public company and he ruled that it was no business of the court to over-

293

turn the decision of the Board of Tottenham. It was after this on the last day of the hearings, 15 June, that he dealt with Sugar's contempt. And here the behaviour of the fans helped Sugar.

The Vice-Chancellor said:

In considering this matter I have very much in mind that over the last few days some of the behaviour of some of the supporters of Tottenham Hotspur towards Mr Sugar has been disgraceful. Their behaviour in court while the court was sitting was exemplary. Elsewhere this has not been so. Even within the precincts of the court Mr Sugar has been subject to physical intimidation and abuse and threats. This behaviour was itself a contempt of court.

He went on to say that he did not hold Venables responsible for any of this but in his view, 'Mr Sugar has been sufficiently scarred by this vilification and abuse and threatening behaviour for it to be inappropriate for me to take any further action over Mr Sugar's own admitted contempt.'

However, despite the victory, it was Sugar, menaced by the crowds, who had to be smuggled out of the side exit. Hewer could not afford the risk of running the gauntlet of hate and anger that shook even the reporters at the scene. Venables emerged from the front door looking the victor. As the crush barriers and the police held back the crowds Venables made a grandstand exit, arm raised, a smile playing on his lips; the *Independent* photograph even suggested a twinkle in his eye. The Sky journalist, contrasting the two exits, said of Venables' front door exit, 'He has nothing to fear.' Certainly his demeanour was that of a man who might have lost a match but this was only the first leg, the return leg was still to come. Accompanied by Donna Cullen he murmured, 'Don't worry, we will sort it out', before being whisked off in a taxi, prompting the Sky journalist to say he had gone to a secret location to plan his strategy.

Venables seemed to have several options. Apart from the plan to buy out Sugar there were still very grave doubts whether Tottenham as a team could still hold together. Sheringham warned it might fall apart and there was the continuing problem with Ruddock who had made his allegiance to Venables very plain. The supporters still pledged their loyalty to Venables and were eager to refute Sugar's suggestion that their support for Venables was a nine-day wonder that would vanish once Tottenham began winning.

But in reality the defeat for Venables was quite total. Venables

had come to court on a wing and prayer. Although Venables'
Section 459 case had not yet been heard, talk of getting someone to
buy out Sugar soon evaporated. Less than forty-eight hours after
the High Court defeat a spokesman for Robert Earle made it clear
he was not interested in investing in Spurs. Venables' failure to win
had put paid to any hoped-for Earle investment. On the evening of
Friday 14 May Venables' legal advisers, in seeking an injunction,
had hit a speculative 35-yarder and it had gone in off the far post.
Now Sugar, more deliberate in method, was coming back.

Sugar would later liken himself to the tortoise and Venables to
the hare, 'The hare gets off to a splendid start but who wins the
race? The tortoise. That is what I am doing. And I have got a very
thick shell.'

And although Sugar had missed out on Glenn Hoddle, his first
choice, he would soon get Ossie Ardiles, another immensely
popular former Spurs player, as manager. This to an extent
mollified the fans. Sugar had also begun to exploit Venables'
Achilles heel: lack of money. Creditors had constantly circled
Scribes: the landlord had been a persistent thorn; now the man
who supplied champagne, and the milkman, were threatening
court action; and then there were legal costs to consider. Sugar
began to aim at this soft underbelly.

This would inevitably result in further court action and Sugar
warned Venables that if he persisted in fighting him, there might
be more revelations about Venables' management style. Yet even at
this stage, with all the bitterness that had emerged during the
court battle, an honourable compromise might have been worked
out had the Football Association listened to Rick Parry, the chief
executive of the Premier League. Just hours before the court
assembled at the Strand, England had played USA in Foxboro, an
American football stadium in Massachusetts. To the amazement
even of the Americans, they beat England 2–0. The defeat was,
rightly, seen as deeply humiliating. England had already been
beaten by Norway (in Norway) during a World Cup qualifying
match; it was by no means certain they would return to the US for
the World Cup and there were calls to replace Graham Taylor,
widely ridiculed as 'the turnip'.

Rick Parry wondered whether this might not be a good time for
the FA to bang the heads of Sugar and Venables together, make
Venables give up his quest to own Tottenham, arrange an amicable
parting between the two men and, as part of the compromise,

appoint him England manager. Sugar would be free of Venables, England would have a first-class football brain to try to get them to America for the World Cup. But the FA, being the organisation it is, bureaucratic, rule-bound, sniffed at the idea. Peter Swales, then head of the FA international committee and Taylor's boss, would not hear of it.

Chapter 27

The battle to save Edennote

Terry Venables had lost his Spurs. Would he now lose Edennote, the strange company that Larry Gillick had bequeathed him? On 17 June there was a meeting at Herbert Smith of Sugar's top lawyers. The decision was to ask Venables for security of costs. In plain language, Sugar was saying: Terry, show us the colour of your money. David Gold's estimate was that the legal bill Edennote would have to pay Sugar was already running at about £231,000, then there would be the costs of the Section 459 action, which was due to come up sometime in November and could last five weeks or longer. To start an action does not require much money but to defend it can cost a lot and Sugar's lawyers feared that, although they might win at the end of the day, it would be a pyrrhic victory if it turned out that Edennote had little or no money. Under Section 726 of the Companies Act, 1985, a limited company involved in litigation which has had costs ordered against it, as Edennote had, could be forced to give sufficient security in order to meet those costs, and Herbert Smith set after Edennote.

The next day Herbert Smith carried out a search in Companies House. What they found shocked them. Edennote had never filed any accounts. It should have done so by 5 October 1992 but all Companies House had were the articles of association, the various changes which had taken it from a Larry Gillick company to a Terry Venables one, and lists of charges. A draft set of accounts of the company had been provided by Pottesman but this was even more dispiriting. Liabilities exceeded assets by £427,000 and in any case Pottesman had said the financing shown in the draft accounts had changed which, he said, made the position complex.

Since Venables wanted to buy Sugar's shares and Edennote's only asset was Venables' shares in Tottenham, in Gold's mind the inescapable conclusion was that Edennote was probably insolvent.

Gold was not the only person to come to this conclusion. On the day the hearings before the Vice-Chancellor had started, the estate agents, Savoy Stewart, had presented a petition to wind up the company. They were not demanding tens of thousands of pounds of legal costs. Savoy Stewart's bill amounted to £3,818.75. But it had been outstanding since 16 August 1991 and, despite repeated correspondence, had not been paid.

This bill was settled and appears to have been part of the pattern for such Venables action: a creditor presents a bill, it is ignored for a long time, creditor moves to take court action either for bankruptcy, winding up or whatever, and then the bill is settled almost on the steps of the court. But there is also the publicity angle. The *Mail on Sunday* reported on 27 June that the bill had been settled 'last week' which would make it sometime between 20 and 26 June. In fact the bank giro credit of £4,510 was not sent from Edennote for almost another two weeks, on 7 July. There was a further twist. Venables was later to say that this was something that had been inflicted on him; but the bill was for the valuation of White Hart Lane which Savoy Stewart had done, work that had been commissioned by Tony Berry in April 1991 when Venables was planning the Spurs take-over. Since this would have helped Tottenham raise money, Venables had been under the impression Tottenham would pay, but he never clarified why Tottenham should pay for something he had incurred before he became chief executive. That a bill of such a small amount, in the context of the big money to buy Spurs, should only have been settled two years after the take-over was extraordinary.

The security of costs litigation sent Venables and his advisers into a frenzy of action. Their first requirement was to gain time, their biggest problem was Landhurst Leasing. The receivers were claiming £1.4m. which represented the return of the loan of £1m. plus interest. Venables did not want to pay anything like that. But he knew he had to settle with Landhurst. Receivers in such a situation like to settle, they prefer money to court action, and, with his hands full trying to fight Sugar, the last thing Venables needed was a second-front war with the Landhurst receivers.

Initially David Buchler acted as his adviser in trying to reach a settlement but on 22 July 1993 these negotiations broke down and Brown took over. We shall see how Brown fared but just then the breakdown of talks could not have come at a worse moment, the date of the breakdown being crucial.

The day the Landhurst negotiations broke down was also the day when the very last glimmer of hope Venables had of buying out Sugar and retaking Spurs died. At this stage, Venables, at least in the public mind, was steadfast in his desire to regain control of Spurs. The only doubt about it had emerged when the *Daily Mirror* revealed he had had discussions with David Kohler, chairman of Luton, about buying the club. Kohler had approached Venables, and in July 1993 they had a couple of meetings. After the *Mirror* story emerged Venables claimed he was acting as an agent, but this was never made clear to Kohler who had, and still has, the impression that it was Venables who wanted the club. Venables sued the *Mirror* and this story would have further twists and turns.

The Luton interlude apart, Venables' problem seemed to be in getting a credible businessman who had the money to buy out Sugar. Now there appeared another businessman who could be a potential financier and, conveniently, he was a man who, like Venables, had fallen out with Sugar, and this after a twenty-five-year friendship. He was Gulu Lalwani. He had featured prominently in my article in the *Director* magazine which Donna Cullen had shown to Venables at their first meeting in Buchler's offices back in May. Sometime towards the end of June Venables had rung Lalwani at his Hong Kong headquarters.

Lalwani was not a complete stranger to Venables. 'I had met Terry twice before, on both occasions through Alan Sugar. Alan had taken me to Terry's club just below Barkers, I think sometime in the summer of 1992, and I had also seen Terry at the wedding of Simon, Alan's son, in September of that year.' (The wedding took place on the same day that Spurs played Ipswich where a freak fifty-yard goal by Cundy saw Spurs draw the match.) 'Terry,' recalls Lalwani, 'arrived late and at that stage I was under the impression that Alan and Terry were getting on fine. After all you don't invite a man to your son's wedding if he is not a friend.'

Lalwani recalls his conversation with Venables when he rang him in Hong Kong in June: 'Terry's first words were, "I hear you've fallen out with Alan Sugar. Well, I have a business proposition to make which will interest you." I was going to London and we decided to meet in my offices at Wembley.'

At 4pm on 21 July, Venables arrived accompanied by a friend whom Lalwani believes was Bobby Keetch. 'What he said was "Tottenham is a great business, if you buy out Sugar and become chairman I can make money for you. Alan interferes too much, you will be a better chairman and it will be a good investment for you." ' Lalwani was interested but wanted to make sure the deal could be done with the blessing of Alan Sugar. He had no intention of making a hostile bid. And if Sugar was not likely to sell, wondered Lalwani, would Venables sell him his shares? The question seemed to surprise Venables. 'I hadn't thought of that. I came here to try and get you to buy out Sugar,' he said.

However, after a few minutes, and with Lalwani stressing the need for the whole affair to be resolved amicably, Venables said, 'Well, you have put a thought into my head. I hadn't thought of selling but if you want to buy my shares I may be willing to sell at the right price.'

The next morning, 22 July, Lalwani rang Sugar on his car phone. The two had not spoken to each other since their parting in January and initially Sugar was frosty. But the moment he heard that Venables had met Lalwani he perked up. 'What did he say?' asked Sugar all agog. After Lalwani had explained, Sugar said, 'I am not a fucking seller and you can tell Terry Venables that.'

'What if I want to buy Terry's shares, will I get a seat on the Board?'

'You can buy the shares,' said Sugar, 'I can't stop you buying them. But I will not make you director', words that made buying the Venables 23% stake very unattractive. For such a large holding Lalwani would be no different from a small-time investor. 'And another thing,' said Sugar, 'you can tell Terry Venables from me I am going to grind his fucking face in the dirt.'

Twenty minutes later Sugar rang Lalwani. He had reached his office and was clearly much taken by the suggestion that Venables might be prepared to sell. This was the first time any such idea had come from Venables and Sugar asked Lalwani, 'It might be very useful in the court case, would you be prepared to say that in an affidavit?' Something about the conversation made Lalwani pause and wonder. 'Alan,' he asked, 'are you by any chance taping this conversation?'

'Yes, I am,' said Sugar with an honesty that made Lalwani sit up, 'and I shall send you a copy of the tape.' Sugar duly did that.

Sugar was keen that Venables' willingness to sell his shares be broadcast to the world and he persuaded Lalwani to speak to Nick Hewer. Within five minutes Hewer had rung and, says Lalwani, 'pleaded with me to speak to the *Evening Standard* and the Press Association. I really didn't have time, I was due to go to Frankfurt, but he said they can talk to you in the car and I spoke briefly to the journalists concerned.'

By the time Lalwani was flying out to Frankfurt the *Evening Standard* was on the streets of London with the news that Venables might sell his shares. Apart from the Luton story this was the first hint the public had that he might disengage, and in some ways the first break in the so far impregnable Venables position – that his heart belonged to Tottenham, he would never leave, and would come back and displace Sugar.

Sugar's quick PR work in releasing the Lalwani intervention, almost the first time Sugar had been ahead in the game, could have been potentially very awkward for Venables. It came just four days before he was due to appear on TV's 'Sport in Question', a discussion programme chaired by Ian St John and with Jimmy Greaves as a regular panellist. This would be his first major chance on television to explain his case since the Cup Final 'Grandstand' six weeks earlier. What is more Greaves had made it clear that in the Sugar-Venables battle he favoured Sugar.

However, Venables has an empathy with the small screen that is almost magnetic and despite the news that he might sell he went to the television confrontation comforted that, in the same studio a week earlier, Sugar had given perhaps his most wretched, wooden performance of this whole affair. It is something that still makes some people in the Sugar camp cringe with embarrassment. Hewer explains:

We felt badly let down. Alan had been approached some weeks before and agreed to go on to discuss the relationship between business and football and nothing else. I was tipped off by a journalist that the Tottenham Independent Supporters' Association would form a significant part of the audience and I rang Sugar in Hong Kong and we agreed to pull out. I told the producer why we were taking this action – we were not prepared to be conned. However, Jimmy Greaves talked Alan round saying that the original agreement would stand and he would not be quizzed about Venables or Spurs. When we got to the studio and saw the monitor in the hospitality suite, we realised that people we knew as TISA supporters were filing in to the studio. I knew then that we were in trouble. Alan was in an awkward situation. Instead of confronting the audience and saying he was unable to answer specific questions on the situation he froze knowing that one of his lawyers [Alan Watts] was with me in the gallery watching the situation. You see, Sugar cannot behave like a politician in a tight corner; he is candid to his bootstraps, he can't fudge.

One of the hostile questions Sugar tried to parry was from a supporter asking whether, had he been at Arsenal, Sugar would have sacked George Graham. Sugar's answer should have been that Venables was not football manager at Tottenham but chief executive and the comparable person at Arsenal was Ken Friar, a fine football executive but whose sacking could hardly be expected to raise the storm that Venables' departure had done. But Sugar, hot, bothered, blinded by the lights, did not say that and the situation was lost. He later told Hewer, 'I couldn't see the audience, Nick.' Greaves, who had been supportive of Sugar, tried to help him but Hewer concedes that 'the overall episode was perhaps the lowest point we ever reached.'

The Sugar camp were also upset that Venables was on the following week – something they knew only when they reached the studio – and Venables was given the chance to wind up the debate, as it were.

Venables worried about Greaves. Before the show he discussed tactics with Cullen. She advised, 'If Jimmy Greaves is very pro-Spurs, why don't you make a joke about Greaves being appointed the PR for Tottenham?' Venables not only made that crack but when someone raised the question of his becoming England manager he appeared both dignified and self-deprecatory: he couldn't discuss a job that someone else already had and as for another job, the way things were he would be grateful for a job as a hod carrier. The remark went down well with the audience.

Sugar, or rather Hewer, did strike back, to an extent. Hewer had negotiated tickets for the Venables show and this helped him introduce some vociferous and hard-questioning Spurs supporters who were not Venables fans. Brown was also in the audience and for the first time the spotlight was thrown on him. He looked suitably

(Above) Paul Gascoigne, Venables and Gary Lineker celebrate Tottenham's victory in the FA Cup, beating Nottingham Forest 2-1. *(Below)* Alan Sugar and Terry Venables announce their purchase of Spurs at a press conference on 21 June 1991.

(*Above*) Sugar and Venables celebrate their take-over of Tottenham, after which Venables was made chief executive. (*Below*) The sale of Paul Gascoigne to Lazio was one of the strains in the relationship of Venables and Sugar. Others directly concerned were Jonathan Crystal, a Tottenham director, and Gino Santin (*both on right*), who played an important role in the final arrangements.

(Above) After the dismissal of Venables by the Tottenham Board, he was driven away, palpably moved, by Jonathan Crystal, as *(below)* Tottenham fans, outraged, turned out in force to back him.

(Above) Outside the High Court, support for Venables, vilification for Sugar.

(Left) Venables, having lost his case, still tries to look a winner.

(Left) Venables announces the selling of his Tottenham shares, in the company of his lawyers and accountants, and Eric Hall in the background.

(Below) Venables, looking every inch the businessman, pictured just after the first *Panorama* programme, 9 October 1993.

(Above) Jimmy Armfield, the former Blackpool and England captain, and a true philosopher of the game, met Venables when acting as head-hunter for the FA. *(Below)* Venables appointed England coach, 28 January 1994.

FOUNDED IN 1863

THE FOOTBALL

(Above) Venables, his old ebullient self, May 1994.

(Below) training with his England team, and John Scales, 1995.

(Above) Who'd be a coach? The agony of England 0, Norway 0, on 12 October 1995.
(Below) Venables with David Davies of the FA.

ashen-faced and, when questioned, was at times incoherent.

Greaves went in to bat for Sugar and gave Venables such a roasting that, at the commercial break, Terry threatened to walk out there and then. Faced with an empty seat for the second half, the producers promised to ease off, and so a suitably soothed Venables returned looking chipper for the second part of the programme.

Despite this, the two programmes in successive weeks were a great television victory over Sugar for Venables. His popularity seemed undiminished. Brown's presence suggested that Venables' business associations might be questioned but the allegations of Tottenham paying for Scribes purchases did not appear to have damaged his reputation irreparably. When they had surfaced during the June hearings Brown had dismissed them to Cullen saying they had all been paid for, sometimes in cash, and the feeling in the Venables camp was that, if this is all Sugar can produce, we have nothing to fear.

As if to emphasise that he still occupied the moral high ground, Venables told the press on the day of his television hearing that he was launching a £1m. wrongful dismissal action against Tottenham. Some of the press reporting suggested he already had launched it but, in fact, this was Venables milking the publicity long before he acted. The writ was not issued until 17 August and not served on Sugar's lawyers until 24 August, almost a month after the press announcements. But who cares about such niceties? Hype and publicity were still Venables' great assets.

But as things turned out, that performance on 26 July was the high point of Venables' popularity in his battle against Sugar. Never again would he appear so deserving of public sympathy, quite so much the popular hero fighting a faceless moneybags who could not even explain why he had sacked Venables. Sugar, the tortoise, was at last starting to catch up with Venables, the hare.

The tide began to turn three days later, on the morning of 29 July at the Royal Courts of Justice in front of Justice Harman, as he began to hear the security of costs case in the courts. Venables' lawyers, harried by Sugar's lawyers, Herbert Smith, had tried to get more time for their client but they couldn't delay any further. So it was that, on 29 July, far from the crowds that had gathered in May and June, and with hardly any reporters present, Judge Harman began to hear the case. In front of him was an affidavit which Venables had sworn on 23 July as his evidence in reply to Sugar. Harman described this affidavit as 'totally inaccurate in

every possible foot'. One of the country's senior judges on company matters not only doubted the truth of Venables' affidavit but
gave his counsel, Alan Stenfield, a rough ride. At one stage Justice
Harman even rebuked Venables' counsel for presenting papers
that were not properly punched and which he could not easily file.

What had particularly irritated Justice Harman was the action of
Venables' lawyers just before the court was to sit on the morning
of 29 July. A few minutes before ten o'clock they came with a second Venables affidavit which also included a letter from
Edennote's accountant containing draft accounts for 31 March
1993. Harman had spent many hours the previous evening reading
the evidence that Venables had filed, after pleading for more time,
on 23 July. To be confronted by fresh evidence, as Harman said at
the eleventh hour and fifty-ninth minute, was just too much and
he very nearly did not allow it. As he told Venables' counsel, 'It is
grossly unfair to the Court as a public matter to load evidence at
10.30 or ten o'clock, when I sit extra early to accommodate you.'
Harman even thought the evidence had been, 'carefully arranged
so as to arrive at ten o'clock on the morning of the hearing'.

The real problem was that Venables did not have a very strong
case. He was trying to show his company as solvent and that he
had money. And his room for manoeuvre was limited. Edennote
had no assets other than the Tottenham shares, but the majority of
the shares were pledged to the Bank of Liechtenstein and some
against the interest-free loan Yawetz had given. That left Venables
with 1,292,938 shares he could still play with.

Despite this in his 23 July affidavit Venables argued that
Edennote was a healthy, strong company, which could meet any
costs. However, he could only argue that as a result of some questionable accounting. For instance, Edennote had made an
operating loss of £398,769 for the year ended 31 March 1993, which
would seem to back up Sugar's lawyers' argument that Edennote
was in a precarious financial position. Not so, said Venables, look
at the consolidated profit and loss account which shows a profit of
£290,000. This was done by taking Edennote's share of
Tottenham's profits, as if it belonged to Edennote. Statement of
Standard Accounting Practice, SSAP 1, did allow a company which
had 20% or more of another to consolidate that company's profits
into its own, but such consolidation is only possible if the company
exercised significant influence. And, of course, as at the accounting
date, 31 March, Venables was chief executive of Tottenham and

able to exercise control. However, by the time the Edennote accounts had come to be signed off, on 23 July, Venables was no more than a non-executive director. He may have owned 20% of Tottenham but he had no control over the company, indeed was fighting the major shareholder, Sugar. In such circumstances to take in Tottenham's profits was stretching even accounting imagination.

The new evidence, contained in Venables' draft affidavit, that Harman was presented with on the morning of 29 July amused him even less. In these draft accounts Edennote's loss of £398,769 had become a profit of £41,094 although there was no explanation how this had happened. (When the audited accounts were eventually filed in Companies House on 19 December, this draft profit had reduced to £14,830 and there was a deficit on the balance sheet of £371,439.) Also, whereas in 1992 the investment in Tottenham had been shown as fixed assets, now they were shown as current assets meaning they were on a par with cash or debtors. This was, of course, a hint that Venables may have been thinking of selling the shares.

Further, Venables' latest affidavit contradicted facts which he had presented in his 23 July affidavit. In that he had said that the amount owed by Edennote to him was £1.473m. Six days later this latest affidavit was saying Edennote owed him £1.223m.

The reason for the change was that, in the 23 July affidavit, Venables had added up what Edennote owed to everybody and claimed it was all owed to him. So even the £250,000 Edennote owed to Yawetz was described as owing to Venables and his other companies. Harman was furious about this. How did he include the £250,000 owed by Edennote to Yawetz as money due to him when Yawetz was not a member of his family? asked Harman. The fact that Venables gave no explanation, and his cavalier treatment of facts did little to lighten Harman's mood.

In this second affidavit Venables, in a last attempt to avoid the awarding of security of costs, was prepared to swear that he would 'subordinate', meaning postpone, payment of money that Edennote owed him until all other creditors, including costs which Sugar and Tottenham had won, were met. Harman was not to be persuaded and awarded Sugar security of costs of £300,000. Venables could have had no illusions about the effect of the judgement.

But even as the judgement was being given a greater danger was looming. The Edennote accounting papers were about to emerge and they had the potential to devastate Venables. Indeed the day before Justice Harman had upbraided Venables and his legal advisers, a meeting had taken place at the offices of the *Daily Mirror* which would have resonance for months afterwards.

This meeting was between Peter Hounam, who headed the then Mirror investigation unit, and his freelance colleague Tony Yorke, with Nick Hewer and Alan Watts, representing Sugar. Ever since Jeff Randall and I had revealed in the *Sunday Times* of 29 May the Sugar bung allegations and the Inland Revenue investigation into football clubs (a story which was reproduced the next day in the *Sun* under the tag 'exclusive') journalists had been scouring the country for more such allegations of corruption in football stories. Details of Brown's business dealings were also being scrutinised.

Tony Yorke was one of the busiest workers in this field. He had discovered a number of Brown ventures. He would regularly keep in touch with Hewer and tell him of his discoveries, such as the Independent Balloon Company. However, now he appeared to have come across even more sensational papers, relating to Edennote. These papers promised to solve the great mystery of the Venables saga, the relationship between Edennote and Landhurst and perhaps explain how Venables had financed his purchase of Spurs. Until then, apart from a little-noticed Nick Gilbert story in March 1993, Venables had kept his connections with Landhurst a closely guarded secret. The discovery of the Edennote papers was like a gold strike, their appearance a sensation for any journalist covering the story.

The Edennote papers consisted of handwritten accounting schedules and working papers used to prepare accounts. The papers and how they got into the public domain have been the subject of court affidavits in two court cases and a police investigation which led to the conclusion that no crime had been committed. Venables, relying on information from Yorke, would make sensational allegations in court and in his autobiography.

According to a Venables affidavit filed in court, Yorke told him how these papers came into his hands. This is how the Yorke version went: that Gillian Theobalds, the wife of Richard Theobalds who had worked with Brown at Scribes, had 'admitted stealing copies of the confidential internal accounting records of the company from the company's office at or about the time of her leaving the company's employ in mid-1992.' A year later her husband Richard had offered 'a major national tabloid newspaper these stolen copies for £10,000. A figure of £8,000 was eventually agreed between the two parties.' Richard and Gillian Theobalds have vehemently denied any wrongdoing (see below, page 313).

It seems that the newspaper, the *Daily Mirror*, was prepared to pay £2,000 and approached Hewer to see if Sugar would pay the balance. It was this that led to the meeting between Hewer, Watts, Yorke and Hounam. According to Venables they reported back to Tony Berry, who had once employed Gillian Theobalds, and her husband then confirmed that 'a deal was then done' and 'copy documents were handed to Mr Tony Berry'.

By the time Venables made these disclosures in court, Yorke himself would file an affidavit in support of Venables although he did not go into such details, no doubt feeling that he should keep faith with journalism's conventions and not discuss sources. Venables' decision to bring these matters to court resulted in affidavits by Hewer, Watts, Berry and Mr and Mrs Theobalds. The Theobalds affidavits were not used in the court action and it is not known what they say, but from what Hewer, Watts and Berry testified it is possible to paint a more complete picture.

According to Hewer, Yorke had telephoned him, some time in mid-July 1993, and told him he had papers which proved that Landhurst Leasing had lent money to Edennote. The papers would cost money, would Sugar pay? Hewer was noncommittal but with Herbert Smith keen to find out about Landhurst Leasing, and how it affected Edennote, it was obviously of great interest. Hewer arranged to meet Hounam and Yorke and took along Alan Watts.

They met at 8.30 on the morning of 28 July at the offices of the *Daily Mirror*. Hounam explained that the *Mirror* intended to publish an article about Venables and Brown's financial activities, Watts glanced at the documents briefly and asked whether they had been properly obtained. Yorke explained that he thought they had been posted to someone by Edennote's auditors. When Watts also asked whether they had been got legally, Yorke could not assure them on this. Watts took Hewer to one side, and told him that, since it was not clear how these documents had been obtained it would be wholly inappropriate to obtain them. The two men, in the time-honoured phrase of Fleet Street, made their excuses and left.

Hewer and Watts insist that this is the only discussion they had with Yorke about the documents, and Hewer adamantly denies ever reporting back to Berry or discussing these documents with him. Berry has said that he did not know about the *Daily Mirror* meeting. Gillian Theobalds was employed in one of his companies but he did not know her then although he might have met her at one of the social functions. He had met Richard Theobalds but denies doing any deal about the papers or sending Edennote's accounts to Messrs Reid Minty, the solicitors acting for Arthur Andersen, Edennote's receivers.

In the hardback edition of his autobiography Venables repeated the false information that Berry had paid £20,000 to Theobalds to get the papers, which prompted Berry to issue a libel writ. The paperback edition removed these passages and, shortly after-wards, lawyers acting for Venables, the publishers and the *Mail on Sunday*, who had serialised the book, apologised in open court to Berry and agreed to pay damages and costs estimated at £350,000.

But by then the Edennote papers had long entered the public domain. The *Daily Mirror* were the first to use them, in August 1993, and I did a story in the *Sunday Times*. Venables could no longer conceal the mysteries of his company. His secrets, which he had guarded so zealously for so long, were now about to be revealed to the public, and a new face of Venables, far removed from the cheeky chappie always ready with a smile and a quip, was about to emerge. Until now Venables had kept his private face well hidden from the public; now, as revelations rocked him, he found it increasingly difficult.

But even as his secrets began to tumble out, Venables performed one clever shimmy, probably the cleverest he would execute, which the public would not know for a long time. This was in rela-tion to his shares. It was aimed at preventing Sugar and Tottenham from getting their legal costs back and benefited Venables person-ally to the tune of half a million pounds.

Yamichi, acting as brokers, had started hawking the Tottenham shares round the City and eventually sold them. Just before the sale Venables claimed that he had also lent Edennote money. How come? It turned out Venables was saying that the million-pound loan from Landhurst which, as we have seen, had gone through Edennote's books, was not a loan to Edennote, or even to Venables Ventures Capital, as he had sometimes claimed, but to himself. In other words he had borrowed the money and lent it to Edennote. This meant he was a secured creditor of Edennote. And as a secured creditor he had a claim on Edennote's assets, which were the million-plus shares of Tottenham not already pledged to the Bank of Liechtenstein or Igal Yawetz.

And, on 24 August 1993, just before the sale of the shares he pledged the remaining unpledged shares to himself, some £1.2m. worth. The same day his lawyers, Kanter Jules Grangewoods also took a charge on some of the unpledged shares, £450,000 worth. The charges were actually registered on 10 September, 1993. It meant some of the money from the sale would come to him and his lawyers.

Venables got just under £3m. in total from the sale of the shares, £2,984,624.30 to be precise. Through September and October there were regular sums of money doled out to various people. Venables was the first to claim his share. On 13 September Venables took £435,986.30 as part payment for the loan he claimed he had made to Edennote. On 15 September Edennote itself was paid £278,200. On 17 September the bulk of the money, £2,059,731.51 went to the Bank of Liechtenstein to repay their loan, and on the 22 September, £13,600 went to pay the bank's lawyers for their fees and costs of early redemption. Five days later, fees of £587 regarding the Chubb guarantee were paid. On 6 October Ansbacher's £20,000 fees were paid and, on 26 October, £175,000 went to Kanter Jules Grangewoods. They were paid a further, smaller sum on 26 October.

By then Venables had every reason to feel he had executed a neat manoeuvre, outflanking Sugar. Sugar did not know about it for months and, by the time he did, the story had moved on.

Chapter 28

The pictures on the wall and the screen

Even before Venables sold his Tottenham shares he knew that his business past, and particularly that of Brown, was about to broadcast to the nation at prime time. The story which Jeff Randall and I had published led to a lot of interest both in newspapers and television, and three television programmes appeared to be very keen to develop the stories: *Panorama* on BBC-1, *Dispatches* on Channel 4, and *World in Action* on ITV. *World in Action*, however, soon took a different path, and provided the twist in this tale of three programmes. But by June *Panorama* and *Dispatches* were in head to head confrontation.

Both programme makers had approached Hewer, as had *World in Action*. He was non-committal but *Panorama* got the impression that if Hewer helped anyone, he would help *Dispatches*. After all, he had come to know them when they made 'Sick as a Parrot'. *Panorama* saw themselves as outsiders and concentrated on Venables' business activities. *Dispatches* were keener to tell the story of the Venables-Sugar split. Both programmes saw Venables' repeated declarations that he did not know why he was sacked as a challenge to be taken up.

One matter which both programmes were soon investigating was the payment to Gino Santin of £200,000. Venables knew he had to do something to draw the sting of these revelations and was particularly worried by *Panorama*. He faced up to the programme in much the same way that he did to Sugar's calling of the 14 May Board meeting to sack him, with a PR offensive.

However, this time Donna Cullen could not help. For a start, this was not her sort of public relations, and in any event by this time the old Brown strategy was hobbling Venables: unpaid bills. Good Relations were owed £11,000. They had billed Venables personally. Brown told Cullen it should be billed to Edennote but even after that had been done, it was not paid. Within months Good Relations, fed up with waiting, issued a writ demanding payment, but at this stage they were still talking and when Venables asked for help Cullen held a breakfast meeting directing him to John Stonborough who worked in the same building. Stonborough had worked for the investigative TV and radio journalist, Roger Cook, and, as a sort of a poacher turned gamekeeper, specialised in companies dealing with investigative journalists. Before Cullen pointed.Venables in his direction she did warn Stonborough to make sure he got his money up front. Stonborough no doubt did, and prepared a media offensive.

So 14 August 1993, the opening day of the season, saw a Venables pre-emptive strike. While the media attention was taken by Venables' comments to the *Sun* – his allegation that Sugar wanted to drive him out of football and his confession to a feeling of emptiness about missing the start of a soccer season for the first time in thirty-five years – the more interesting story was in the *Guardian*'s City pages. Venables told Frank Kane that he would ask Michael Heseltine, Secretary of State at the DTI, to investigate Spurs. Venables also informed Kane he had taken advice from leading counsel and wanted Heseltine to look into the transfer of Gascoigne to Lazio. 'Sugar says I am a bad businessman', Kane reported Venables as saying, 'but I was able to push up the price for Gazza to £6.5m. Santin played a part in this and, of course, he had to be paid.'

This was the first time Santin's name had been mentioned and also the first time Venables had alleged that there was a dirty tricks campaign against him in the tabloid press. But if Venables hoped to blunt *Panorama* with it, the ploy did not work, and while the DTI eventually launched an investigation, it was not Tottenham they probed but Venables himself.

However, Venables did begin to benefit from the media race. *Panorama* and *Dispatches*, both driven by their desire to tell the story first and better than their rival, created an unstoppable momentum which, as can often occur in such media rivalry, led to several happenings. One of these was that Venables suddenly found information which would provide him with more ammunition to allege dirty tricks. Hugh Dehn, one of the producers of *Dispatches*, says, 'It was a no-holds-barred fight with *Panorama*, it got very, very, dirty but we got Venables, Sugar, Santin, Brown – everyone who was in the story – on tape, *Panorama* didn't.'

So why did Venables speak to *Dispatches* and not *Panorama*? Was it because he was provided with a tape which suggested that *Panorama* had paid Theobalds money for information, particularly the Edennote papers? This is one subject which Dehn will not comment on or even discuss. All he would say was that 'Venables talked to us because he knew we had played it straight, we were not paying anybody for our information. *Panorama* was.' *Panorama* bitterly contests this suggestion and argues that in the long term their programme has had much greater impact.

There is other evidence to suggest that Venables was somehow informed of Theobalds' involvement with *Panorama*. Soon after the programme he began to talk about a tape that would prove his allegations of dirty tricks. The allegations centred on the Edennote papers which were central to *Panorama*'s approach. *Dispatches* claim they also had them ('they came in a brown envelope', says Dehn, 'at that stage we were getting lots of brown envelopes') but didn't use them on the programme. Nor, unlike *Panorama*, did they focus on the Landhurst Leasing aspect of Venables' business deals. *Dispatches* see this as conscious decision, while *Panorama* would argue that *Dispatches* were beaten by the boys from the BBC. *Panorama* insiders have told me, '*Panorama* transmitted first and this forced *Dispatches* to rethink its whole programme.'

As the deadline for *Panorama* neared, Venables gave clear indications that he knew *Panorama* had Theobalds' papers and tried to exploit this to his advantage. He insisted on stringent conditions before he would speak to *Panorama*. They would have to give him details of the programme, including a list of sources, and he wanted to know whether the BBC had paid their sources and how much. *Panorama* refused and Venables did not appear.

Venables was also sufficiently concerned about *Panorama* to hire Mark Stephens of Stephens Innocent, a lawyer whom Crystal had organised for him. Stephens was told that *Panorama* was in possession of Edennote papers, papers stolen from Venables' accountants Crouch Chapman, and on 14 September he wrote to *Panorama* threatening them with the 1968 Theft Act and criminal proceedings. A day later Crouch Chapman wrote to *Panorama* demanding the return of the Edennote papers. These papers, however, had not come from Crouch Chapman.

Panorama had got them from Gillian Theobalds, who had done some work for Brown. Much of the work had been done at her home, Brown had not paid her, and he had never asked for the return of the papers. She felt the retention of the papers was payment for her work. In any event *Panorama* had followed what they call their own Standard Operating Procedure which means they had photocopied the documents, so at most theirs was a copyright infringement – a charge also made by Mark Stephens.

Meanwhile the war between *Panorama* and *Dispatches* went on unabated and, to Dehn's great joy, Venables consented to an interview. 'We did all three of them one after the other at Scribes. They were all very nervous.' It was here, at Scribes, that the fax showing that Lazio had always agreed to pay £5.5m. was shown to Venables and his amazement recorded.

Having got Venables, Dehn now used this to get Sugar: 'We had been talking to Hewer for a long time and he had given the impression Sugar might talk. But he kept saying no. When we got Venables I rang Hewer and told him, "We've got Venables." He said, "Leave it with me." ' In order to persuade Sugar, Dehn had given Hewer details of how Venables and his entourage had performed under the cameras. Hewer summarised this information, along with Dehn's comments, in a confidential four-page memo to Sugar dated 14 September 1993. Hewer sought to give Sugar comfort by saying that he, Hewer, could get a list of the detailed questions *Dispatches* would ask and even get access to their edit suite. 'I was desperate,' says Hewer, 'for Sugar to do the interview and may have over-egged the situation somewhat. He sounded dismayed: "Alan won't go for it." There was then a short silence, and Sugar came on the line. He said, "Fine, what's that got to do with me – getting Venables to talk? I'm not fucking helping your programme." I said, "If you don't talk to us you are fucking round the twist." This seemed to rock him back. He said, "I'll call you back." Within ten minutes he had rung. "All right, my office. Ten o'clock tomorrow." '

Dehn noticed the contrast between the two men. 'When we went to Scribes, Terry was very charming and very pleasant. Help yourself to drinks, he said. We were an hour and a half in Sugar's offices in Brentwood and we didn't even get a cup of tea. Sugar was his gruff self, but when the cameras started he was charming and made some superb imitations of Terry, quite funny really. I think it was his best television programme.'

In getting Venables on tape Dehn also secured Santin. 'Terry was obviously close to Santin and told us he would talk to Gino. Santin came one afternoon and we were very worried he would walk out. We interviewed him in a room where we placed the cameras in such a way he would have had to jump over the cameras to get away. He threatened to but did not.'

If getting Venables and Sugar was a plus for *Dispatches* they were, however, about to lose the race to be first. *Dispatches* normally went out on Wednesday night, *Panorama* on Monday night, but *Dispatches* in great secrecy decided to bring their programme forward to Sunday 19 September. *Panorama* had been planned for the previous Monday but had been gazumped by Jane Corbin's programme on the Israeli-Arab peace deal. To wait for the following Monday meant losing out to *Dispatches*, so they brought their programme forward to Thursday 16 September, the sort of move only done in extreme emergency. The last time it had been done was during the Falklands conflict. But it did mean that *Panorama*, normally a fifty-minute programme, was restricted to half an hour. Also certain legal constraints meant some incompleteness, since the original story of Venables and Brown and their business deal could not be told.

But even then it had gone much further than any other programme. It not only revealed many new things but threw a spotlight on Venables, his business methods and those of John Brown, which amounted to a powerful indictment of Venables the businessman and severely questioned his judgement. The programme alleged that he had broken the law with the Landhurst deal. *Panorama* claimed it would, for the first time, reveal why Sugar had to sack Venables and, judging by the next morning's papers, it was clear *Panorama* had scored a major hit.

The effect of the *Panorama* programme was summed up by John Sadler, the *Sun* columnist who is billed as the journalist who 'gives it to you straight'. Sadler wrote:

Football fans throughout the country feel cheated this morning. Disillusioned, dismayed, led up the garden path and seriously let down. And all by one man, Terry Venables, whom they'd come to respect, admire, worship as a hero . . . Not only the supporters of Tottenham Hotspur feel misled and duped by the disturbing allegations that now surround

Venables' dismissal by Alan Sugar ... Whether or not Venables has ever acted illegally as Spurs manager or chief executive is a matter for examination elsewhere. What has hurt football people is the feeling that Venables, with cheering hordes following in his footsteps, was not exactly straight with his disciples. The feeling is that the Pied Piper continued to play a happy tune, knowing all along that somebody was going to blow the whistle.

The *Daily Mail* was convinced this meant one thing. 'Goodbye England' was the headline on its article saying that Venables was facing up to the 'reality that any faint chance he had of becoming manager of the England team has disappeared'. The article, relying on senior FA sources, said that Venables would not be short-listed if Taylor failed to take England to the World Cup. One official was quoted as saying, 'He is under investigation by the FA and that says it all.' This was not an isolated opinion. Rob Shepherd and Nick Craven's article in *Today* was headlined 'Tel dream destroyed', and said, 'Terry Venables has lost all hope of ever becoming England manager.' They also reported that the BBC were planning to drop him as their football expert.

That morning the press gathered outside his mews house in West London. Dehn was also there with a camera crew and noticed how nervous Venables was. 'He looked ghastly. Before we interviewed I sat with him in his kitchen and he told me he had lost a million on his pubs. I wondered how a football manager comes across so much money. When we got the cameras rolling he denied any wrongdoing, whenever we presented a document he said he had not seen it. But he was sweating, we had to stop the cameras every now and again and mop his brow.'

Venables was quick to counter-attack and it was in *Today*, where he had just started writing an exclusive football column, that he sought to retrieve his reputation. In a long interview with Alex Montgomery, Venables attacked the *Panorama* programme as ill-informed: 'They have set me up, stitched me up, call it what you like ... Whether they have ruined me, only time will tell that.'

That *Panorama* was a blow to his solar plexus was undoubted. For him *Panorama* was the *Panorama* of Richard Dimbleby, and the fact that it had broadcast a special programme just to try to expose him left him bewildered and shaken. This may explain why, at one stage in the *Today* interview, he said he couldn't explain the impact and likened himself to the innocent victim of an IRA bomb outrage. So keen was he to fight back that he made the first of his many curious charges.

Paul Riviere had been interviewed on the programme, the first time anyone from Venables' own inner circle had broken cover. It showed him emerging from a building in the City and getting into a taxi. Venables, without naming Riviere (but the reference to the former business associate makes it clear who he was talking about), told Montgomery, 'They filmed a former business associate of mine outside the offices of Alan Sugar's lawyers – was that a mistake maybe they thought we wouldn't spot?' In fact Riviere had been photographed emerging from Lloyd's which is more than a mile away from the offices of Herbert Smith near Liverpool Street. But Venables, in his eagerness to suggest Sugar was the cause of all his problems, was not sensitive to such niceties.

Venables' counter-attack was backed up by Stephens, although he was not to remain his lawyer for long. He went as quickly as he had arrived. 'I was never told not to act. The assignment had come suddenly, it went suddenly. The phone calls stopped being returned. It was clear that my services were no longer required. He did not say anything nor did anyone contact me. It was all a bit bemusing.'

To add to Stephens' worries, when he submitted his bill of £5,000 in October, it was not paid and he had to issue a writ. Probably Venables felt he did not need Stephens any more; he had, as it were, served his purpose. Venables had told Montgomery that he knew the programme had been based on 'stolen' documents. Soon he was claiming he had a tape to prove it.

On the Saturday after *Panorama*, but with the *Dispatches* programme still to come, some of the Sunday papers, particularly the tabloids, got a call from Eric Hall about a press conference Venables wanted to hold. Simon Greenberg of the *Mail on Sunday* recalls: 'He asked us to come to the Royal Garden. When we got there Venables was not there and Hall was sounding very mysterious. It seemed Venables was at Scribes, but Hall said we couldn't go there. In the end we did go to Scribes.'

Then they were told of the tape which would clear Venables' name. Bob Harris in the *Sunday Mirror* quoted him as saying, 'It was sent to me and the tape identifies who is involved . . . It backs up everything I have said about the missing papers . . . It helps me and tells how the documents went missing.' Greenberg also reported Venables as saying he had a tape but, while Harris had been told that Venables had not yet informed the police, Greenberg quoted him as saying, 'It is being dealt with by the appropriate authorities and shows who has been involved in trafficking the documents. That's all I can say.'

According to Greenberg the tape contained a telephone conversation identifying both parties with details of documents stolen, who they were going to and how much was being paid for them. Greenberg made it clear that there was no suggestion *Panorama* was involved with the alleged theft. It is now clear, as Tony Yorke himself has said, that this was a tape of a conversation between Yorke and Richard Theobalds. How Venables got hold of this tape and whether, as Yorke was to believe, it was through Channel Four, is impossible to say. Nothing more has since been heard about the tape.

Some days after the *Panorama* broadcast, another character entered the story. This was Detective Inspector Ray Needham, who visited *Panorama* and told them he was investigating the theft of Edennote documents, following a complaint to Chelsea police by Venables and Brown. Now it turned out the theft was not from Crouch Chapman as alleged in their letter – since Crouch Chapman are based in the City it would have been a City police matter – but from Edennote's offices in Exhibition Road. *Panorama* explained their position, Needham went away satisfied and eventually concluded that if there was a theft it was of photocopy paper worth twenty pence. (Needham also interviewed the Theobalds and Scotland Yard concluded that no crime had been committed even in regard to the photocopying paper.)

However, before he left he said something that shook *Panorama*. He remarked that he had looked at the Landhurst deal and he was sure Venables had done nothing wrong. That Needham 'clearance' would prove crucial for Venables.

Interestingly, Venables had a much different view of *Dispatches* and soon after the programme he told Dehn he found it fair. He has since changed his mind on this and, when he came to write his autobiography, he treated it on a par with *Panorama*. However, from the beginning *Panorama* was the monster he had to slay. He began with the announcement that you almost expect in such circumstances. He told the press and anybody who would listen that he was issuing writs against the programme and would repeat this several times in the weeks and months ahead.

Panorama waited but no writ arrived. After some time, as

Venables kept repeating he was suing *Panorama*, the programme itself employed legal researchers to search the High Courts and find out whether a writ had been issued. Venables could have issued a writ, which would cost £50, but not served it. More than a year later *Panorama* could still find no writ.

It is interesting to speculate why for a year Venables kept saying he was suing, for it created the impression of a wronged man seeking justice. He needed that impression, for the wounds inflicted by *Panorama* not only stung him deeply, but seemed to make him a non-person in football. In October 1993, BBC's *On the Line* programme examined the state of English football just before the England-Holland match. The great and good of English soccer were there, but no Venables.

Nothing seemed to be going right for Venables. He had filed his wrongful dismissal case and on 15 October his lawyers even won a judgement in his favour because, by then, Sugar's lawyers had not presented a defence. But this was technical point-scoring. Sugar's lawyers had asked for time, advised Venables' lawyers about it and their insistence on going for a judgement in default meant that it only delayed Venables' case by another three months.

Venables was now sunk in such gloom that when, in early November, Frank Kane went to meet him at Scribes, he presented a picture of a man in despair. Venables confessed he was 'totally pissed off' with football.

Kane's concluding picture could not have been more bleak – Venables sitting in the empty dining-room at Scribes waving his arm at the wall on which hung pictures of his glorious past. These pictures, wrote Kane, are the only ones 'listening to him'.

Just over a week later, on 17 November, England played San Marino in the last qualifying match of the World Cup campaign. They won the match, but failed to qualify, and suddenly Venables' life was transformed. Soon more than the pictures on the wall would be listening to him.

Chapter 29

Of plots and conspiracies

On Saturday 9 October 1993, Terry Venables gave an exclusive interview to Jeff Powell. The *Daily Mail* clearly saw this as a major scoop. It was billed as Venables' fight to clear his name, 'the other side of the *Panorama* picture', and took up nearly three pages: the back page and two pages inside. It could not have made a better case of presenting just the image Venables wanted. His photograph, dominating the back page, showed him in the pose of the sober-suited businessman, complete with reading glasses, poring over what the *Mail* called 'evidence'. In contrast the photograph of Sugar on another page showed him looking rather goggle-eyed.

The big bold headlines further emphasised all this. 'I think it's a plot,' shouted the headline on the back page with the subheading, 'Venables calls in police to probe smear suspicions'. The headline on the inside going over two pages was: 'Venables: I want it all in the open'. The article not only touched all the right buttons but also used the buzz words Venables has repeated so often since: police, smear, plot, fight and two phrases he has used whenever allegations about him have surfaced: 'I am convinced there is a conspiracy against me', and 'The tide is beginning to turn and some people out there are getting worried about what is coming out'. For the unwary the article, and not least its presentation, made a very powerful case in favour of Venables. Concentrating on the Gascoigne deal it reprinted extracts from Tottenham Board minutes and Sugar's own letters which showed that Sugar and the Tottenham Board were well aware of the Gascoigne deal, Santin's

319

role in it, and the payment made to him.

However, a more careful reading of the article showed that the Venables defence was more papier-mâché than really watertight. There was the claim 'a writ is now ready to be served on *Panorama*'. A year later, when his autobiography was published, Venables freely confessed he had not served the writ, waiting, it seems, for the right moment to strike. Then there was an attempt to discredit the Allen and Overy letter sent the day before Sugar and Venables took over Spurs, the one that said Lazio were prepared to pay £5.5m. According to the *Daily Mail* Venables had instituted a 'legal investigation' into the document, claiming it was not authentic. Venables knew it was important to cast doubts on the document, for, as he told Powell, 'Of course the intention of the letter, which was fed to *Panorama*, was to make it appear that I had lined my pockets through Santin. The truth is that I ploughed a great deal of my own money into Tottenham and, thank heavens, I never took so much as a bag of crisps out of the social club, never mind a dodgy penny.'

Yet more than a year later, when Venables' writ against *Panorama* finally emerged, all this talk of doubts about the authenticity of the fax had vanished. As for the 'legal investigation', if it produced any conclusion Venables has never revealed it.

Just as interesting, given Venables' fears of a conspiracy against him, was this paragraph in Jeff Powell's article:

The *Daily Mail* publishes the Venables case on some key issues here. One other national daily [Powell was referring to the *Daily Express*] has just published Santin's documented evidence against the Gascoigne allegations. A leading Sunday newspaper, having been given full co-operation to explain Venables' private files, is preparing to exonerate his personal business affairs which were criticised on television.

This seemed to make the *Mail* article part of a trilogy. The curious thing about it is that newspapers, particularly tabloid newspapers, rarely give credit to other newspapers, the more so when they are claiming exclusive rights as the *Mail* was. And for the *Mail* actually to draw attention to an article published the previous day in its rival, the *Daily Express*, was very unusual. For it further to draw attention to an unnamed Sunday paper – presumably not its sister paper the *Mail on Sunday* – seemed to suggest that the *Mail* article was part of a carefully planned media offensive by Venables. As it happens the heavyweight article in the 'leading Sunday newspaper' that was presumably meant to discuss business deals such as Landhurst – a principal concern of *Panorama* – never saw the light of the day. *Panorama*'s producers kept tabs on Sunday papers for weeks and finally gave up two months after Powell's piece. In that time no Sunday newspaper, leading or otherwise, produced anything remotely like a Venables refutation of these allegations.

All this mattered little to Venables. He has always worked on the principle that if the public's attention span is notoriously short then the football public can barely remember what happened the day before yesterday. The *Mail*'s piece had served his purpose admirably and he followed the technique he had mastered so well as a soccer manager. A bad defeat? Well, it can be explained by the referee not giving us a penalty and not noticing their winger was offside when the ball for their goal was crossed. Venables, like all managers, knew journalists gathered for a quick post-match comment are content with such explanations: they provide the necessary headlines for the next day, few bother to investigate whether the complaints about the referee are justified and the match itself is soon forgotten. Unfortunately for Venables neither *Panorama* nor the serious allegations it had made could be wished away quite so easily.

Even as the *Mail* was splashing its exclusive it had missed a far bigger story. The DTI had called on *Panorama* to look at the evidence it had accumulated on Venables. In early October Gaye Burn, a DTI investigator, along with a colleague, spent a day with Mark Killick and Martin Bashir going through the *Panorama* files and even looking at material, particularly in relation to Landhurst, that had not been transmitted. After a cup of coffee the investigators said, 'Right, we have looked at Venables, now let us look at Brown.' Much to Bashir and Killick's surprise they seemed to know all about Brown, even more than the two BBC men.

Following this visit, and less than a month after the *Daily Mail* exclusive, on 3 November, the Department of Trade launched two Section 447 inquiries into Scribes and Edennote. A Section 447 investigation enables the DTI to look at a company's records and is a confidential fact-finding operation. They had already appointed Graham Richard Horne, Stephen Parkinson and Amin Rahman as investigators from the companies investigations division of the DTI. Soon the trio was collecting evidence and Gavin Hans Hamilton and Geoffrey Van-Hay were summoned to help them unravel Scribes.

But if the *Mail* article had no mention of a DTI investigation it had intriguing information which would prove useful for Venables. This was that Venables had called in the police, who were looking into theft of documents and of a tape. This was clearly a reference to Needham, although Powell did not mention his name. Powell had mentioned that 'officers are investigating a tape recording'. This made one journalist, Tony Yorke, immediately twig what it was about.

Yorke suspected that a tape he had made with Theobalds, and which had been made available to *Dispatches* when he was working on their Venables programme, had somehow found its way to Venables. Yorke was not best pleased but, far from damaging Venables, this worked to his profit and in perhaps the most unexpected by-product of the *Panorama-Dispatches* rivalry, Venables was now to find in Yorke an ally.

This aspect of the Venables story has something of a John le Carré feel to it, although one wonders if even he could do justice to it. Yorke's involvement in this story began as an investigator working for the *Daily Mirror* and probing Brown's business interests. During this he struck up a relationship with Nick Hewer. In his work with Hounam and with *Dispatches* he could not have been more diligent in searching out sources and people who might throw light on Brown and Venables. He located Theobalds, visited him at his home, and then made contact with other Venables and Brown business associates, including Paul Riviere.

Sometime in the autumn of 1993 things began to change. Yorke, from being the man on the outside looking in at Venables and Brown, now became the insider. He told Hewer that he was going to visit Scribes to meet Brown and Venables. Hewer wished him well and jokingly warned him that he would be 'seduced' by them but Yorke was confident this would not be the case. Before Yorke went to Scribes he had been investigating yet another Brown venture, Five Star Batteries, which, he suggested to Hewer, might be explosive. When Yorke had first met Brown on what he described as 'civil terms', Five Star Batteries did come into the conversation. But Yorke never did a story on Five Star Batteries. Whether this marked conversion on the road to Scribes is not clear. Venables' autobiography gives no clue but it does say that Yorke 'now realises how he had been used'. This realisation made him write more favourable articles about Venables. Nevertheless even after Yorke had entered the bunker, as Scribes was now called by Venables and his associates, he kept his line to Hewer open by assuring him that he was doing all this to help expose Venables when the time was right.

The Yorke conversion was significant. He had a wealth of taped material and he also provided an insight into a breed of journalist Venables knew nothing about. For Venables one of the most disquieting things about the television exposés about him, in particular *Panorama*, was that they were made by journalists who were not part of his usual football circle. The football writers might sometimes write unfavourably about him but he could tackle them. *Panorama* confronted him with an entirely different breed, current affairs reporters whose mission was to investigate and expose. In the early days of this, confronted by investigating journalists, the Venables entourage reacted with third-rate farce. Yorke was different. He saw himself as much of an investigator as the best of *Panorama* and the moment he walked down the steps of Scribes, Venables felt he had somebody who could help him with information to tackle the activities of these journalists who were taking an extraordinary interest in his business affairs.

One of Venables' first tasks was to confront a man whom Yorke's investigations had brought out: Paul Riviere. Since the Venables-Sugar split, Riviere had constantly rebuffed media attempts to get him to talk. 'Yorke was the first person who showed me things which suggested that companies I had been involved in may have broken the law. I felt I needed to distance myself and agreed to be interviewed by *Panorama* to set the record straight. Both before and after the programme I received anonymous calls which warned me not to get involved.' Some weeks after the *Panorama* programme, Riviere received an urgent phone call from Venables. Riviere, by now bankrupt, took a couple of days to respond and Venables' first words were an angry, 'Fucking hell, Paul, why did you do *Panorama*?' Venables, in his fury, believed *Panorama* had paid Riviere £10,000 when they had merely paid £1,000 to cover his expenses. Riviere was eager to set the record straight and the two men met at The Goat in Kensington in the first of three meetings. It was a heavy confrontation.

Riviere explained that, on *Panorama*, he had refrained from any comment on Venables and done it to highlight his concern about Brown and his business dealings. All this should have been obvious to Venables, for it was exactly what Riviere had told him back in the summer of 1991. But Venables could not understand why Riviere felt he had to distance himself from Brown. Riviere offered to bring along the Theobalds letters which he had first shown Venables in 1991. A few days later the two men met again and Venables took away the letters for photocopying. There was a final brief meeting when Venables returned the letters and promised to set up a three-way meeting with Brown to sort it all out. Riviere waited for the call for weeks but it never came. And as he waited he could not help but reflect on something very curious Venables had said. This was that he had got transcripts of Riviere's interviews with Yorke. Yorke had taped not only Riviere but also conversations with Dadak, Riviere's lawyer, and his partner. Venables assured Riviere he had not brought a tape recorder to the meeting. Riviere was not worried, he had nothing to hide, but this was the first indication from Venables that a Yorke factor had come into play.

By now Venables was also working on his autobiography. He had acquired a literary agent, Jonathan Harris, who was offering the autobiography round the publishers: his starting price being some £200,000. If the story provided by Guy Nathan in *Barcelona to Bedlam* is correct then, sometime in July 1993, Harris had secured an offer from the Penguin Group, through their hardback subsidiary, Michael Joseph. Soon after this Nathan, a long-standing Spurs supporter who felt Venables had been wronged by Sugar, approached Harris. Through the summer and early autumn Nathan discussed with Harris the idea of writing a Venables book. Nathan says that it soon became clear that Venables wanted a quarter of a million pounds for it. Nathan wanted to write a quickie about his divorce with Sugar, with the 'full monte', as he puts it, left until Venables' future became clear. The deal broke down and, in the end, Nathan published a book which was the story of Venables versus Sugar up to January 1994. Nathan's book, having begun by describing how much he had respected Venables when he had sent him a message as he lay in hospital thinking he was dying of cancer, ends with a 'Dear Terry' letter which expresses his disillusionment with Venables.

Venables and Harris spent time selecting a co-writer from a shortlist of Pete Davies, Dave Hill, Giles Smith and Neil Hanson. Hill recalls meeting Venables and finding him a likeable grizzly bear with one of those incredible Popeye walks common in football men. But he did not take to Harris and in any case was rejected in favour of Pete Davies who was prepared to break his vow never to write ghosted books, just for Venables. However, Davies was outraged by the way Harris treated him and by the fee, £15,000. Harris returned to Hill and offered him the same deal promising him that, if sales went beyond a certain figure, he could earn more, between £20,000 and £25,000. But neither Harris nor Venables would tell Hill how much Michael Joseph was paying Venables. Hill had heard it was between £150,000 and £200,000 and told Harris and Venables that they stood to make a quarter of a million. If only, they replied. But, says Hill, 'when invited to disabuse me, they declined'. Hill concluded a partnership of equals was an impossibility, and Hanson got the job.

The provisional title Harris had drawn up was 'Raped of a Dream', which indicates how Venables felt about Sugar's actions, though it could also have been a reference to Venables' feeling that the Tottenham affair was going to prevent him from getting the England job. This did seem the case on 23 November when, following the San Marino match, which extinguished the slim England hopes of qualifying for the World Cup, Graham Taylor resigned. Venables did not appear to have a realistic chance of being summoned to Lancaster Gate, and it seemed likely the FA would skip a generation and go for a younger man.

Ray Wilkins, still with Queens Park Rangers, and Glenn Hoddle, player-manager at Chelsea, were among those mentioned in the media, but the initial favourite was Howard Wilkinson of Leeds, although there was also considerable backing for Kevin Keegan, whose managership of Newcastle was being widely praised. Keegan also received the support of Jimmy Armfield, the former England captain turned media expert. Venables was ranked twelfth, with odds of 25–1 being offered by William Hill. Graham Sharp of William Hill recalls, 'Venables would have been one of the favourites had we taken away the financial baggage, but with all that we felt he was out of the running for the job.'

Within a month all this had changed and Venables had become the firm favourite. Why? There are a number of reasons, not least that the FA changed the selection system. In the immediate aftermath of Taylor's departure there were media calls for a wholesale clear-out of the FA leaders: Sir Bert Millichip, the chairman, Graham Kelly, the chief executive, and Peter Swales, chairman of the international committee.

To add to the FA's problems it also scored quite a few own goals. There was talk of a major in-depth look at football but it turned out this was an FA committee looking into how vice-presidential posts are decided and one that would take years to report. Swales did eventually leave, being replaced by Noel White, former chairman of Liverpool, but Kelly and Millichip had no desire to go. England had won the right to hold the 1996 European championships, the first international football competition in the UK since the World Cup of 1966, and they were determined to see that through.

Kelly, trying to deflect criticism, decided to appoint a head hunter. The chosen man was Jimmy Armfield. Kelly had known him for a long time and saw him as someone who would assess what the professionals in the game were thinking. Millichip, too, had his own agenda and, keen to shake up the FA's press office, turned to David Davies, an experienced BBC journalist. Inside Lancaster Gate Davies' appointment was seen as Millichip balancing Armfield's appointment by Kelly. However, it was Armfield's recruitment that was to prove crucial to Venables.

The FA were very aware of the 1977 fiasco when, in the wake of Don Revie electing to go to the United Arab Emirates, they had turned down the people's favourite, Brian Clough. Subsequent England failures had been ascribed to that decision.

Initially Armfield's appointment did not suggest that Venables would get the job. But the longer the race went on the odds on Venables changed. On 25 November William Hill cut him to 14–1 and the next day to 10–1. At this stage Wilkinson was still favourite but, as the Armfield mission gathered pace, so Venables attracted support. The most significant movement came on 14 December when, between 10.27am and 1.26pm, William Hill took nine separate bets of £100 for Terry Venables to become England manager – in Eltham, Feltham, Richmond (twice), Kingston, Twickenham, Pitfield Street N1 (twice) and City Road. The odds were cut from 7–1 to 6–1, although at this time Keegan was still favourite at 5–2.

The next day the papers were full of reports that Armfield had indeed gone for Venables and by 17 December Venables was down to 4–1. On that day he was made favourite at 5–2 and Sharp told the press, 'We know all about Mr Venables' well-publicised non-footballing problems but with so many leading fancies apparently stressing their reluctance to be associated with the job and with the continued support from the punters we have been left with no opinion but to promote him as favourite.' He displaced Keegan, who went out to 3–1. By 20 December the book on the England job had been closed. Venables was such a hot favourite that William Hill could not risk taking any more money.

It is almost tempting to say that Venables' rise to unstoppable favourite had been reflected on Armfield's milometer. He had driven some 2,000 miles up and down the country, a football man talking to football people, and their unanimous opinion was that for all the allegations of failed business ventures, Venables was the man for England. George Graham was one of the first to say so, although had Graham made the call a year later – when he was embroiled in his own difficulties – it might not have carried the weight it did.

In strict theory the Premier League inquiry into the Sheringham transfer, which had not yet reported (it still has not), might have been a barrier. But by this time the Premier League's bungs inquiry was being overshadowed by another twist to the story which had begun to put a different complexion on the whole question and in many ways helped Venables' cause.

Ever since the original allegations by Sugar, the general picture that had been built up was of Sugar trying to clean up the sport, where Venables was one of the shady characters in his path. Now a new story emerged which suggested that wrong-doing at Spurs had not started with Venables: there had been breaches of football regulations long before he took over, indeed in some ways Venables was the man trying to clean up the Augean stables and it was Sugar who had tried to stop him.

On 13 December, the day before William Hill took the nine separate bets on Venables, *World in Action* ran a prime-time programme describing how Tottenham, over a number of years, had provided interest-free loans to several players including Ossie Ardiles. The loans were declared to the Inland Revenue but not to the football authorities, which was clearly a breach of the football rules. The *World in Action* revelations would prove as big a bombshell as the bung allegations, except that they would detonate in the faces of Sugar and Spurs.

In many ways the Tottenham loans story deserves a study of its own, and is not properly part of this story. However, in the way the Venables story has unfolded it needs to be understood. There is no doubt that Venables considers the story crucial, since he devotes to it almost ten pages of his autobiography.

But, first, we need to step back and consider what happened and why. Football clubs seeking to give loans to players is not new. They can arise in all sorts of situations. At Tottenham the loans situation had arisen when Ossie Ardiles and Ricky Villa arrived from Argentina in 1978. The then Board of Sidney Wale and Arthur Richardson had entered into an arrangement for salaries, bonuses and expenses, including return fares to Argentina once a year. Some of these payments were guaranteed to be tax free. At one stage the details were done on scraps of paper but after consulting counsel a scheme was devised which was felt to be more tax efficient.

This has since become known as the O'Leary scheme for it was about this time that Arsenal was trying something similar with David O'Leary. On 1 August 1979 O'Leary, then entering a new contract, told Arsenal that, as well as his basic wages, he wanted an additional sum of £28,985 in, as the legal jargon has it, 'a tax efficient manner'. In order to give it tax free to O'Leary, Hambros Channel Island Trust Corporation Ltd set up a trust of which O'Leary was the beneficiary and Arsenal lent the trust £266,000 free of interest and repayable on demand. The money was invested in a deposit account at a Jersey bank. The interest from it, less the trustee's fee, was equal to the sum O'Leary wanted and as O'Leary was an Irish national not domiciled in the UK, it was argued that this money was not subject to UK tax. When the taxman asked for his share, O'Leary's advisers argued that this money was not from his Arsenal employment but from the deposit account opened by the trust – a quite remarkable argument. When the case finally came to court in December 1990 Justice Vinelott held that O'Leary had to pay tax.

With Ardiles and Villa, Tottenham did something similar. Scholar and Bobroff inherited the scheme when they took over the club. It was soon clear that, as with O'Leary, the Inland Revenue would not accept it. There was a Special Office investigation which led to a settlement. However, since Ardiles had been given an undertaking that this would be tax free, Tottenham agreed to pay the tax, along with tax on certain other benefits that had been promised as tax free to Ardiles. Although this meant the matter had proved more expensive than Spurs thought, it should have ended there.

However, by this time Tottenham was a public company and Bobroff, as chairman of the public company, was worried about the profits forecast and refused to write the amount off. He preferred to show it as an Ardiles loan. Over the years other bits were added to this notional loan, namely all the benefits the old Board had contracted to give Ardiles free of tax, and so the Ardiles loan figure grew and grew until it finally reached £106,000, a figure which came to haunt Spurs when the TV programme *World in Action* decided to focus on this issue.

But if the Ardiles loan was in part a Tottenham foul-up, the Scholar regime also gave interest-free loans to players which arose not from any muddle but as a deliberate decision. Throughout the 1980s football clubs were struggling to provide more tax-free income to their players. The yuppie culture was growing, soon the City would be talking in terms of golden hellos to attract people but English football found itself – and still does – in a peculiar situation. Unlike the continent, where players can often receive the equivalent of $1m. or more on signing for a new club, in this country the signing-on fee has to be spread over the period of the contract. Under this regulation no player can receive a truly large lump sum on joining a new club and players in the third or fourth year are still receiving their signing-on fee as if they have just signed for the club. The regulation particularly hits players moving from the north to the more expensive south who often need a large cash sum to put down a deposit on a new home. To get around this, clubs started by adjusting the transfer fee, adding, say, another £50,000 or £100,000 to the transfer fee which would be paid by the buying club but passed on to the player as if it was the selling club providing an ex-gratia 'thank you' fee. So if the transfer fee was £500,000, the buying club would pay £550,000 knowing that £50,000 was to go to the player. In 1982, when Nottingham Forest sold Peter Shilton to Southampton, they paid £75,000 to Shilton and tried to argue that this was an ex-gratia payment, the first £30,000 of which would be tax-free. In 1991 the House of Lords held that the payment was no such thing and could not escape tax.

The problem grew so intense that, in 1988, the Inland Revenue decided to declare an amnesty agreeing to forgive clubs which had indulged in such practices but warning that, in future, it would come down hard on anybody who transgressed in this fashion. Scholar was keen to avoid such complications but knew that an incoming player still needed a large dollop of cash. For instance, in 1988, when Scholar signed Gascoigne, he was staggered to learn that Gascoigne had been paid a mere £12,000 a year at Newcastle. On that money it was impossible for him to have saved enough to put down a deposit on a house in the then booming south-east. This is where the interest-free loans came in.

It was explained to the players that the loan was repayable if the player requested a transfer and would be repayable on his leaving the club. The loan arrangements were disclosed to the Inland Revenue but not to the football authorities, partly because the loans were made by the public company not the football club, and Scholar was advised that, while the football club was subject to FA rules, this was not the case with the public company. This may sound like splitting hairs, as the public company's principal activity was football, but Scholar, like many in football, felt that the rules about disclosure were antiquated. But whatever Scholar may have felt about the football rules, there is no doubt that he did breach them, although it could be argued that the breach was a failure to disclose rather than anything very sinister.

The loans to Paul Allen, Mitchell Thomas and Chris Fairclough came into a somewhat different category. The transfer fees for these players were fixed by the tribunal and failure to disclose loans may have affected their valuation. Colin Sandy in his memo of 27 November 1992 had no doubt that, 'Through the working practices, or lack of them, of Derek Peter [for a time the Bobroff-Scholar regime's finance director] and the dominance of Irving Scholar, who had scant regard for financial controls . . . I doubt that there is any area where some errors in procedure have not been made, either deliberately or by default.'

But if Scholar created the loans pool then Venables, both as manager and then chief executive, continued to swim in it. Paul Stewart's loan was signed by Venables in June 1988 and, even after he became chief executive, three players, Fenwick, Walsh and Nayim, were given interest-free loans which were non-repayable. In the case of Fenwick this was an alteration to an existing interest-free loan which had been repayable; the Nayim loan was authorised by Jonathan Crystal on 21 October 1992, two months after the Premier League was formed. Venables, in his autobiography, does not mention these examples, nor does he mention that he himself received an interest-free loan, although since he was not a player it did not conflict with FA regulations.

Venables does not mention these examples, possibly because it could detract from his thesis that, on the loans issue, he was the crime buster; and that Sugar stopped him from pursuing the supposed 'villains', Scholar and the old Tottenham Board. Venables presses his case with a mangled version of a legal Opinion given by Elizabeth Gloster, which the learned QC herself would scarcely recognise. It is worth dwelling on this Opinion for it seems a revealing insight into how Venables' mind works. This is how that particular paragraph in Venables' book reads:

A legal opinion from lawyer Elizabeth Gloster in autumn 1992 advised us that we should sue all the directors at the time of Scholar's previous irregular dealings – Scholar himself and his co-directors, Bobroff, Alexiou, Berry and Gray. 'Prior to July 1991 . . . some payments were falsely characterised as "loans" in order to evade payments of tax,' said Gloster, 'but in reality, such "loans" were understood both by the company and the recipient to be non-repayable.' A total of over £2 million was claimable, in Gloster's opinion, including £400,000 in written-off 'loans' to players, £200,000 in irregular repayments to Paul Gascoigne and Chris Waddle, £260,000 to Gray, and £500,000 in payments on account to the Inland Revenue. She went on to warn us that if we did not sue, we would lay ourselves open to legal action. 'The board itself will run the risk of action at the suit of the company's shareholders, if no steps are taken to recover losses caused by such directors.'

As presented in Venables' autobiography it seems very clear. Unfortunately this version of Gloster's Opinion bears little relation to the original Opinion. For a start there is nothing in Gloster's Opinion to substantiate Venables' assertion that she felt £2m. was claimable. It would be strange if she had mentioned the Venables figure of £260,000 to Ian Gray since this, as we have seen, was an out-of-court settlement for wrongful dismissal to a former chief executive, not a loan to a player. But in any event there are no figures in the Opinion. Nor does Gloster's Opinion mention any of the individuals cited by Venables. The Opinion does not name Tottenham, Sugar, Venables, Scholar, or anybody connected with the company. The Opinion is addressed to Claire plc, whose majority shareholders are described as A and B, who are said to have bought the shares in July 1991 from X and Y.

The quotation from the Opinion in Venables' version, which makes out that Gloster held that the loans were made to evade tax and were falsely characterised as loans, is not Gloster's Opinion but part of a larger sentence where she is restating information given to her as part of her brief. She was not asked to examine the legality of the loans or anything like that. Her task was, as her next sentence makes clear, to advise the Board as to what action should be taken, 'in the event it transpires that members of the Board at the time the payments were made knew of, and/or sanctioned, the payments'.

This line Venables does not quote. But perhaps more worrying is the use Venables makes of a sentence in Gloster's Opinion which leaves the reader with the impression that she warned the present Board that if they did not sue Scholar and company they would be in trouble: 'The board itself will run the risk of action at the suit of the company's shareholders, if no steps are taken to recover losses caused by such directors.'

Now you would expect to see such a complete sentence somewhere in the Gloster Opinion. You will search in vain. This quote had been cobbled together by Venables from a sentence of nine lines which is hedged with qualifications and lawyers' caution into a grim warning. The entire sentence reads as follows: 'However, if the present board forms the view, on advice, that a clear prima facie case of breach of fiduciary duty lies against certain directors and they are worth suing, the board itself will run the risk of action at the suit of the company's shareholders if no steps are taken to recover losses from such directors – in the absence, that is, of a resolution of the company in general meeting absolving such directors from liability or taking the decision not to sue them.'

Venables had made this sound like a grim warning by taking the middle three lines of the sentence, 28 words plucked out from an 84-word sentence, stripped of its qualifying phrases, and presenting it as a complete sentence. For good measure he has even then misquoted Gloster. Gloster had also made the point that a person who was a director at the relevant time but who had no knowledge of any wrongdoing nor should have known of any wrongdoing, would not be liable for the unauthorised misapplication of the company's funds simply by virtue of the fact that he was a director at the relevant time.

Venables would have given a more accurate flavour of the Gloster Opinion had he quoted the final paragraph which read: 'In order to advise specifically in relation to the liability in any individual action, I would clearly need much more information than that contained in my present instructions; for example as to the manner in which "the improper" [note the use of the inverted commas by Gloster here] payments were made and the extent to which information in relation thereto was available to board members generally and to the individual director in particular.'

But again this paragraph would hardly advance the Venables thesis, which was to argue that Sugar disregarded legal opinion to sue Scholar and company. Immediately after he misquotes her he says that, when the issue of suing was raised at a Board meeting, both he and Crystal said 'We've got to sue them' but Sugar blocked legal action. Tottenham Board minutes for September 1992 do not record any such call and it would have been startling had such a call been made, given that the real Gloster Opinion, as opposed to the incorrect one Venables presents, contains no such advice.

One explanation is that Venables was thinking of something entirely different when he referred to the Gloster Opinion in his book. He certainly appears to be in the wrong season. For some reason Venables says the Opinion was given in the autumn of 1992. In reality it was dated 11 August 1992 and, while the month of August may be many things and it is often a month of war, it has never before been described as autumn.

The fact is that the loans issue came up soon after the Sugar-Venables take-over, because Sugar was anxious to find out whether the amounts would be repayable. When Sugar asked Venables he was told the loans were not repayable. After that, various people at Tottenham – including Brown, Sandy and Crystal – started investigating the loans saga with, at one stage, Brown saying Sandy could not understand the complexities of the issue, which was a bit odd given that Brown has no professional qualifications while Sandy is a tax expert. Legal opinion was also sought. In October 1991 Sandy, Brown, Crystal and Bryan Fugler went to see Anthony Grabiner and he urged full disclosure to the football authorities, advising Sugar and Venables to seek a private meeting rather than write any letters. Venables was meant to liaise with the players.

After that a series of meetings took place and central to them was Jonathan Crystal who presented the legal report to every Board meeting and, as a barrister, was a natural to co-ordinate the issue. Crystal took special interest in the Ardiles issue, which by now also involved money withheld from his testimonial. The Waddle loan had not been mentioned to Grabiner but Fugler hoped to tackle this with Crystal. Fugler's subsequent attendance notes, dated 22 July 1992 and 4 August 1992 – seven days before Gloster gave her Opinion – indicated the position that Crystal took on both occasions.

On 22 July, by which time Spurs were facing an Inland Revenue investigation, Fugler spoke for twelve minutes to Crystal, who told him he did not want too many people to know about the investigation. On 4 August Fugler spent eighteen minutes discussing it with Crystal. According to Fugler's notes, 'He did not see there was any point in mentioning anything to the Football League and felt that we had no duty to say anything to the Premier League.'

Fugler also records that he told Crystal, 'Peter Leaver thought we might have a duty to the FA which Jonathan said we did not'. However, in his autobiography Venables says that Leaver, retained as a counsel by Tottenham on this issue, advised Tottenham not to disclose, the reason being that, as from June 1992, Tottenham had resigned from the Football League to become part of the Premier League. For good measure Venables then ridicules this alleged legal advice by Leaver. How Venables reaches such a conclusion is impossible to fathom from what he writes.

There is another interesting implication of Venables' questionable reporting on this issue. He spends much time trying to castigate Sugar for not pursuing Scholar and Co., so that the reader is left with an impression that Venables regards not reporting to the football authorities as being of little consequence, a surprising position for a man employed by the FA to take.

This issue might not have mattered, and indeed may not have occurred, had *World in Action* not latched on to the loans story. They had become interested in the Tottenham story soon after the bungs allegations first surfaced. Philip Clothier met Nick Hewer several times through the months of June, August and September 1993. At these meetings there was no mention of the loans issue. *World in Action* appeared to be investigating alleged wrongdoing in football with several prominent managers mentioned as possible suspects, and for a period Clothier based himself in the Midlands where, he told Hewer, he was investigating Venables and his connections with travel agencies.

Soon after I wrote the story of the Inland Revenue investigation of football clubs for the *Sunday Times*, Clothier had also rung me wanting Scholar's telephone number and then rang Scholar in Monte Carlo. It may be assumed, given the version Venables provides, that Clothier's first instinct would be to question Scholar about the loans, but this conversation, sometime in July, was about a travel invoice relating to Venables that had been allegedly presented to Spurs from a Midlands travel agency in connection with a European trip when Venables was chief executive. Did Scholar know anything about the invoice? Since the invoice was after Scholar's time he did not and the matter ended there.

After that, as *Panorama* and *Dispatches* indulged in a race, *World in Action* seemed to be following its own course, although just as *Panorama* was being broadcast, the *Guardian* reported that *World in Action* had a profile on Venables, ready to be broadcast in two weeks' time. But when *World in Action* turned to football it was for a programme on Brian Clough.

Suddenly, in November, *World in Action* returned to Tottenham, but their questions now related to loans given to Ossie Ardiles when he was a Tottenham player. By this time Tottenham had been fined £25,000 by the FA for making what was held to be an illegal approach to West Bromwich Albion and this provided *World in Action* with powerful ammunition.

World in Action would later say that, in trying to stop them, Sugar scored an own goal. Faced with dishonour for the man he had appointed to soothe fans after the Venables sacking, Sugar decided to pre-empt the programme by releasing the entire Tottenham file on loans. Sugar also gave a television interview to *World in Action*, where he had his own cameras present as well, but, although he made a robust presentation of his case, he did not succeed in discrediting the programme. If *Panorama* was a headache for Venables, then *World in Action* left Sugar with a sore head.

The FA appointed a commission to look into the affairs and this put Tottenham in the dock. From then on the Tottenham loans saga became embroiled with the Venables story in a sort of macabre dance; every time something happened to Venables, the loans issue would figure in the media as if to balance the presentation. For Venables the Tottenham loans issue was like his equaliser: if Sugar had scored with the bungs allegations, Venables got back with a sweet and unexpected free kick of his own, even if it meant putting the boot into Spurs, the club he professed to love. Coming as it did just as he was going for the England job it was an important morale booster for a man who hates to be behind in anything. It meant he could now try to get the England job content that he was level.

The week before Christmas 1993 Venables met Jimmy Armfield at the Royal Lancaster Hotel. They met again on Christmas Eve. At this second meeting, which took place partly in Venables' car, Venables was convinced he would get the England job. The only doubts were the non-footballing ones. Venables says he told Armfield he had seen the police, the Serious Fraud Office, the Inland Revenue,

Customs and Excise and the DTI. 'If there was anything to find they would have found it. For some extraordinary reason people keep making allegations about me to these bodies, which then have to investigate them, though they turn out to be false.'

This is one of those Venables statements that tells us a lot less than it appears to. The reference to the police is classic. He had called them in to investigate alleged theft of documents from his company. They had found there was no crime committed and had gone away, so why should that prove that Venables had been cleared of any wrongdoing? As far as the DTI was concerned, they had just begun their investigation and, given the glacial pace at which it works, there would be no question of being cleared, certainly not quite so soon. However, such distinctions did not matter to Armfield or the FA who really did not want to delve too deep and put a lot of store by Venables' assurances, the more so as he repeated them when he was interviewed by the FA on 5 January 1994.

In theory this meeting should have been with the international committee which normally appoints the England manager. But Venables was meeting a special committee consisting of Millichip, Kelly and two members of the international committee, Noel White and Ian Stott of Oldham, with Armfield present as the head hunter. Venables went to the interview with some cards he could play. Wales wanted him, and Alun Evans had even come up to Scribes to offer him the job. Nigeria were also interested. The Welsh FA couldn't wait until England decided and Venables couldn't pass up the chance of being interviewed by England but, even so, Venables could present himself as a man in demand with various other options. It certainly impressed the FA for, when Kelly was asked why the hurry in choosing Venables, he mentioned the fear he might be tempted by other offers.

The meeting was held at the League's commercial offices just off London's Edgware Road and, despite newspaper certainty that the job was his – that morning the *Daily Telegraph* reported that Venables would be offered the job that day – Venables was so nervous he almost drove his wife Yvette to distraction. His nerves could hardly have been eased when he arrived at the League's offices to find the FA were not quite ready. So he spent twenty-five minutes in the offices of Lee Walker, the large, amiable official in charge of broadcasting who put him through something like a mock interview.

During this Kelly poked his head around the door. Walker recalls, 'Kelly and the FA had been having a meeting with Rick Parry earlier in our offices. Kelly came in and said to me, "Is it all right if Terry sits with you, we are slightly delayed." I said, "Yes, we are having a good old chat." He said to Terry, "Is it OK if Rick stays in because he has been here for a meeting and we'd like him to sit in on our meeting?" Terry said, "Yes, I am not bothered".'

Venables does not mention Parry's presence at the meeting in his autobiography but his meeting with the FA, which had delayed the Venables interview, was crucial. While Venables chatted with Walker, Parry, in charge of the bungs affair, was telling the FA that although the inquiry into the Sheringham transfer was still far from concluded, nothing would emerge to prevent Venables from getting a job in football. If he were to be appointed as chairman of the finance committee, that would be different, but the FA was appointing him for his football skills, not his business nous.

Bolstered by this vote of confidence the interview went well for Venables, the only drama being a woman threatening to jump out of an adjoining building. Ian Stott joked, 'Terry, you are so desperate to get the job you have got your wife to jump off the window' and this banter set the tone for the meeting with the tricky aspects, such as his financial dealings, smoothed over. Venables refused to back down on his wrongful dismissal court action against Sugar but, as if in compensation, he determined not to haggle over money. He accepted the £130,000 Kelly offered him.

In one of his interviews with Armfield he had already rejected the job on a caretaker basis, and although the interview finished without a specific job offer Armfield, who saw him to the lift, seemed pleased. The next day both the *Sun* and the *Daily Mail* were convinced that Venables would be given the job; the only doubt seemed to be that Millichip, who in the past had spoken about Venables' 'funny' reputation, had to be convinced. Noel White was also unconvinced and was to remain sceptical for some time. Partly to allay fears about Venables' financial deals it was decided to consult the international committee and amend the job title they would offer Venables. He would not be described as manager, as past managers had been, but as coach.

But try as the FA might to distance itself from Venables' business affairs, Venables had no desire to stop his extra-football activities. Just over a week after his FA interview, on 12 January, Herbert Smith discovered how Venables, by setting himself up as a preferential creditor, had used the sale of the Tottenham shares to pay himself and Kanter Jules Grangewoods, leaving Edennote with no money to pay Tottenham's legal bills. Sugar was furious at what he felt were unfair preferences, the more so as Herbert Smith had tried to find out about Edennote's creditors and been fobbed off by Venables' lawyers. He could only thwart Venables and recover Tottenham's legal costs if he moved to wind up Edennote within six months of the assignment. Sugar just made the deadline.

These were not the only business worries for Venables. There were the negotiations with the Landhurst Leasing receivers and problems with Scribes West. Here Venables faced a claim of £130,000 from Vincent Isaacs, who had brought a winding-up action against the company. Scribes' accounts were also dreadfully late and the DTI were threatening to strike the company off if accounts were not filed, while Recall City was in the process of being wound up. However, for the moment all this remained a secret and by the second week of January it had become clear that the FA were getting ready to appoint Venables.

One man who watched these developments with a keen eye was Ian Hargreaves, then deputy editor of the *Financial Times*. He had been very impressed by the *Panorama* programme and, as a former Head of BBC News and Current Affairs, he knew both Killick and Bashir. But if the FA were appointing Venables, did that not mean *Panorama* had made a mistake? In early January he rang Killick asking, 'Are you sure you got it right?' Killick and Bashir offered to write an article on the subject, taking the story further since they made the *Panorama* programme, and by Wednesday 12 January they were ready.

Here Venables' luck intervened. The *Financial Times* was not only insistent that the article be legally vetted but that one of their own reporters should check out with Charlie Dyer about the Landhurst loan. The article had been meant for Friday or Saturday, but the FT's checking meant it was not ready, and it was then that Yorke stepped in.

Tony Yorke had confided to Hewer that he saw his mission as one of infiltrating Venables' bunker and bringing him down. He kept in regular touch with Hewer who, warned that Yorke was in the habit of recording all his conversations, had by now begun to take his own precautions. In almost thirty years of public relations he had never had any reason to use a tape-recorder; now he decided to invest in one. So when Yorke rang him he, too, recorded his calls.

The Yorke conversations with Hewer are fascinating. They reveal how Venables was determined to pursue his wrongful dismissal case against Sugar. There was no question of letting bygones be bygones and, as Venables neared the England job, Scribes, too, was no longer looking like a beleaguered bunker. Yorke told Hewer that Venables was 'riding high again. And also it's amazing how many people are now flocking into Scribes . . . all the hangers-on are there, all the journos, yeah, they're all coming back in now. Now he's going to take over the helm. So the door is open there. I just cannot for the life of me believe that he's going to be given the job. I know he is.'

In fact Yorke could not wait for Venables to get the England job, 'And all I'm waiting for is for Mr V to become England manager . . . I'm dotting a few i's and crossing a few t's at the moment, I've established contact with three people who've been very helpful to me on this one. Believe you me, we, the *Mirror*, are not going to mess up like we did the first Venables story, we're going to go with it and go, I mean this is the one to get him booted out of the England job.'

But before he booted Venables out he wanted first to help install him as manager and this meant clearing up any doubts regarding the £1m. loan he had got from Landhurst, the gravest of the charges made by *Panorama*. On Sunday 16 January Yorke, in a *Sunday Mirror* back-page lead headlined 'Cops Clear Tel in £1m. TV Loan Row', reported: 'Terry Venables was last night given the go-ahead to take over as England boss after a top cop sensationally cleared him of a £1m. TV loan row. This latest disclosure removes the final barrier to the FA naming Venables as their man this week. Ray Needham, a detective inspector with the Metropolitan Police, spearheaded a probe – instigated by the former Spurs chief executive – into Tel's business empire. And last night he told the *Sunday Mirror*, "I'm satisfied that Mr Venables has not been up to any mischief. He has been accused of improperly obtaining a £1m. loan. That simply isn't true." ' Yorke quoted a relieved Venables as saying, 'The loan I obtained from Landhurst was perfectly legal and above board. It has just taken a long time for people to start believing me.' Both Needham's comments and Venables' remarks were reprinted in bold at the top of the story.

Just before this story was published Yorke rang Hewer to warn him what he was doing but at the same time reassuring him that it did not mean anything. 'I'm doing it for the *Sunday Mirror* and it will probably be on the back page, but just to let you know, I mean, don't read anything into it because things are going to be happening later in the year to Mr V and if he's installed as England manager, all the better.'

Yorke went on to tell Hewer that once Venables was installed as manager and had got his feet under the table, 'things would go bang' and that this would result in both Venables and Brown being nailed. As Yorke put it, 'So I mean he'll get his feet under the table then bang, ha ha.' When Hewer asked what sort of direction the bang would come from Yorke said, 'The Revenue, I think', and Yorke claimed to have noticed when he talked to Venables about the Revenue that 'the old worry lines, stress lines appeared on his forehead.'

The Yorke story was soon discredited. Scotland Yard denied it, Needham had no involvement in the Landhurst investigation, which had been subject to a Serious Fraud Office investigation, and the following Sunday, the *People*, the *Sunday Mirror*'s sister paper, which did run a story about Venables' problems with the Revenue, poured even more buckets of cold water on Yorke. But it did not matter. Yorke had set the agenda and for Venables it was beautifully timed.

On the previous Thursday Millichip, while breakfasting in Hotel Belle Vue in Berne, had met Jon Marshall, a British journalist. Asked about the Venables' appointment Millichip said, 'I think there are many who would like to see Venables as England manager but he has this funny reputation.'

Within hours of Yorke's story hitting the streets Millichip had been converted. That Sunday afternoon he was interviewed by television reporters in the lobby of the hotel and declared that, now that he had got the all-clear from a top cop, he was happy with the choice of Venables. The next day Killick and Bashir finally ran their piece in the *FT*, an article in a quite different class from Yorke's, but its timing meant that, instead of setting the agenda, it seemed only a reaction to Yorke.

Nevertheless it did have an impact. The draw for the European championships was due to be held on Saturday 22 January in Manchester and the FA had wanted to announce Venables as the next manager on Thursday 20 January. The *FT* article made the FA pause, then on the Tuesday Sugar and the loans issue emerged.

That day Sugar was meeting the lawyers acting for the Premier League's bung inquiry. Just before the meeting news broke that

Tottenham were seeking to wind up Edennote. Instead of being seen as a justified response to something Venables had done, this was seen as Sugar hounding Venables. To the Premier League Sugar confirmed what he had always said, that if Venables stuck to what he knew, football, he could be a winner for England. However, he added a rider that considerably upset the FA. This was that if the FA were planning to appoint Venables then they should also clear Tottenham of any wrongdoing over the loans issue as Venables had been involved both as chief executive and manager. For Sugar this seemed a very fair deal and, if the FA did not see it that way, he hinted that there could be legal action.

Kelly reacted furiously to Sugar's proposal. There is little love lost between the two men, they could not be more different, and Kelly saw Sugar as the party pooper. Sugar's implied threat led Kelly to cancel the Wembley coronation and issue a threat of his own: that he was not afraid to take on Herbert Smith, he had taken them on before and won both for the FA and the League. This public spat was sufficiently worrying for Rick Parry to ask me to convey a message to Sugar, since I was going to Tottenham that evening to watch them play Aston Villa: would Sugar please phone Parry who would arrange a meeting with Kelly to cool things down. The two men did meet and tempers did cool, but some newspapers began speculating that Venables might be appointed on a caretaker basis.

Tuesday had also seen Venables come to a settlement with Isaacs on the steps of the court. Instead of the £130,000 he claimed, Isaacs received a little over a third, £50,000, and agreed to a confidential clause in the settlement. By Sunday the appointment still seemed in doubt and there was speculation about a possible DTI investigation, with an insolvency lawyer warning that, if the FA went ahead, a DTI investigation could lead to the FA ending up with egg on their faces.

The FA did try to find out what the DTI were planning. To Rick Parry the DTI gave the guarded answer they always give, that they could not discuss individual cases, but they did go through the parameters of a DTI investigation. They also warned Parry that appointing Venables could be premature. The mills of the DTI grind very slowly but they do grind exceedingly small, and they had only just begun to grind. The FA seemed unable to appreciate the complexities involved. Simplistic stories like Yorke's, which seemed to support Venables' claims that he had been wrongly accused, were easier to understand. One FA councillor, well versed in the affairs of the City, understood this clearly and wrote to Millichip warning him against any hasty decision on Venables, but Millichip did not respond.

The FA were committed. The interventions by the *Financial Times* and by Sugar had postponed the event, not cancelled it. Even the fact that people like Roy Hattersley writing in the *Daily Mail*, who having supported Venables the day after he was sacked by Sugar, now felt he was not suitable, cut no ice. On Tuesday 25 January Venables was rung by the FA to be told he had got the job and on the afternoon of 28 January he was at last crowned at Wembley, the event having been postponed by a day because of the death of Sir Matt Busby.

However, even now the FA seemed to be fearful that something would emerge at the last minute to thwart their plans. The invitation summoning the press to Wembley did not name Venables, only that there would be press statements from Kelly, Millichip and the new England coach. To heighten the mystery Venables arrived six minutes late and then had to undergo the usual media scrutiny, a posse of photographers asking him to turn every which way on the Wembley turf, so much so that he was heard to mutter, 'This is a nightmare. Is this a wind-up or what?' Nick Townsend in the *Mail* thought he had the same stern expression as when going into the law courts in the summer, and Michael Calvin in the *Daily Telegraph* was not the only one to notice how nervous Venables looked.

That Venables' appointment marked a new beginning was very much the theme of the press conference that day at Wembley. David Davies, who was also making his debut as the FA's head of public relations, in introducing Terry Venables to the media said that although England were not going to the World Cup, the FA were determined to put the misery of the recent Taylor years behind them. Davies pictured it as the dawn of a new era for England.

Venables was certainly quick to put his own distinctive management stamp on the job and revealingly it was in the area of press relations. For nearly two decades, ever since Ron Greenwood, it had been the practice of the England manager to hold a separate morning press conference following a night of international football. Venables immediately abandoned this. Journalists might have been expected to be upset by this but so skilfully did Venables present it that the journalists left wondering why they had not thought of it before. Venables flattered them by explaining that this was the practice on the Continent. If the new Venables style meant that journalists saw less of Venables than of Taylor, what they saw was more controlled.

Under Venables, press conferences for matches can often go on until midnight as he first deals with the dailies and then withdraws to the small bar above the main banqueting room at Wembley to hold a separate press conference for the Sundays, but once that is done, he collects his video of the match and heads home. Where Graham Taylor tended to be long-winded, Venables rations his output, at least in the formal arena, and is held in some awe by the journalists.

Right from that first day Venables also emphasised another trait that set him apart from most managers – he would be much more of a video manager. A Sunday paper had decided that it would make a superb front-page picture to catch a glimpse of Venables watching his first match as manager and assumed his first task the next day, a Saturday, would be to go to a match. But when the Sunday paper's reporter asked Venables which match he would be at he said he wouldn't, he had other engagements. Since then Venables has been pictured often enough at matches but he remains the video manager, happiest when studying matches on video in the privacy of his home. On the Saturday before his first game, against Denmark, he preferred the BBC studio at Shepherd's Bush rather than nearby Loftus Road. His physical presence there would have meant a solitary match; instead he could watch three games being transmitted to the studio. And just before he went on his 1994 summer holidays much was made of the heavy case load of videos Venables would be taking with him.

Millichip had spoken of Venables coming to the FA with clean hands, and the FA refused to be drawn on any let-out clause should the financial complications prove too much. But it was stressed he was the coach, not the manager, and privately Kelly made no secret of the fact that Venables had been told to disengage himself from his business affairs including the running of Scribes.

In retrospect the most interesting aspect at the press conference was the Venables c.v. which was circulated to the media. This ignored his two years as chief executive of Spurs. The c.v. went from 1991 to 1994 as if the years between did not exist. When Kelly was asked about this two-year gap he seemed surprised, saying he had not seen the c.v. It was as if the FA were hoping that, having appointed Venables, despite the doubts about his financial deals, the financial baggage that Venables brought to the job would just go away. The unspoken message was, now that Venables was the England football man, the media should concentrate on his football.

In June 1991 Kate Muir in *The Times* may have hailed Venables as 'football's renaissance man, the Leonardo da Vinci of the League', the man who could swap tracksuits for suits, dugouts for boardrooms, with remarkable ease. And it was not even four years since Venables had declared in *Son of Fred* that he would be a more complete football chairman than people like Doug Ellis, Ken Bates, Ron Noades or Irving Scholar.

But now the FA, the guardian of the English game, was telling everyone to forget about the Leonardo da Vinci of the League and Venables the businessman. Forget it ever happened, forget that period of his life ever existed. No Communist apparatchik in Stalinist Russia could have more ruthlessly expunged inconvenient historical facts.

But unfortunately for Venables and the FA the past cannot be so easily wished away.

Chapter 30

Football and writs

We don't want to know about Venables' business life, the FA had in effect said. But even as they dithered over appointing him, Venables himself could not be separated from his business – past and present. On 10 January the VAT office in Dorset House on the South Bank – the one that looks after central London – had issued a VAT assessment to Edennote. They had found the invoice which Brown, on behalf of Edennote, had sent to Landhurst, detailing the sale of furniture, fixtures and fittings of the four pubs as part of the £1m. loan. The invoice was for £1,050,000 and had promised that a VAT invoice would follow. The assessment notice was to collect the VAT which came to £183,750. After adding interest of £21,241.14, it totalled £204,991.14.

This was not the only Landhurst headache Venables had. There were also the much larger sums of money the receiver wanted as repayment for the loan. Venables had initially offered to pay a mere £150,000 against an outstanding loan of £1.4m. After several months of negotiations he, or rather Brown, offered more money. In the end Venables agreed a down payment of £400,000 plus £60,000 a year for five years, beginning in January 1995. 'Mr Venables,' noted the receivers in a report to members of the Landhurst syndicate, 'is personally responsible for the remaining payments.' Venables had also promised to grant Landhurst a second charge over one of his properties. But less than a month after he got the England job, on 24 February 1994, the receivers expressed their unhappiness over the way Venables had failed to provide this mortgage. 'This he has so far failed to provide despite a number of reminders. If the charge is not forthcoming, it may be necessary to terminate the agreement and initiate bankruptcy proceedings against Mr Venables.'

Faced by this threat Venables settled. But perhaps his legendary charm, or Brown's great business acumen, meant that he ended up paying substantially less than the sum he had originally agreed. The receivers, finally, accepted £568,000, although in order to pay it he got another loan of £100,000 from ANZ Bank through yet another of his companies.

While he denies he committed any wrongdoing in getting the Landhurst loan, Venables has never denied that he took a loan of £1m. For instance, he did not deny it to Tony Yorke in that seminal article which 'cleared' Venables over the Landhurst loan and helped him get the England job. Venables had told Yorke: 'I took out a straightforward loan, which has since been fully repaid.' Given that the article appeared on 16 January it seems strange that on 24 February, nearly five weeks later, the Landhurst receivers were warning of instituting bankruptcy proceedings against Venables. And it is impossible to reconcile Venables' claim that he had fully repaid the £1m. loan plus interest with a repayment of £568,000 unless, when Venables tells the press he has fully repaid something, he really means just about 40% of what he has borrowed.

Of course from the purely financial point of view, the tactic was brilliant, even if it meant that every creditor had to pursue Venables through the courts. Venables has since claimed that the creditors only emerged out of the woodwork after his split with Sugar; twelve out of his fifteen creditor actions, it seems, were due to his battle with Sugar. The implication is that Sugar was somehow orchestrating it. The truth is that Venables had a long history of battling with his creditors and the lawyers who worked for Venables were well aware of them. On 15 July 1992 – almost a year before his split with Sugar – Jonathan Ebsworth had written to his colleague Bryan Fugler about Venables' method of delaying with creditors pursuing Scribes. Ebsworth could just about accept it when it concerned claims against their client which related to the period before Venables took over Scribes. But there were many claims for the period since Venables took control and here, even when there was no defence against such claims, Venables had instructed Ebsworth and Fugler to put in a defence which

Ebsworth saw as nothing other than a means of improving Scribes' cash flow: 'I am concerned, however, that we are being instructed on Summonses relating to matters that arise during Terry's involvement where no real Defence has arisen as far as I am aware. I think this puts us in an invidious position and involves us in incurring costs without being paid.'

By January 1994, as Venables got to Lancaster Gate, this strategy of giving his creditors the runaround had produced the predictable result: a whole army of creditors unable to secure their money began to issue writs. From now on threats of court action, or even bankruptcy, would begin to punctuate his England career – and they started even before he had sent out the team for his first match.

On 9 February, less than two weeks after his Wembley coronation, and exactly a month before the opening match against Denmark, NatWest issued a writ demanding £66,000 regarding guarantees he had given to Recall City. A spokesman for NatWest said, 'The writ is against Mr Venables personally. We understand from his solicitors that he will make a counter claim against us for a similar amount. We are awaiting details.'

Two of his former lawyers were also seeking money. Finers had acted for him many years ago, soon after he had joined Spurs, and their invoice for £8,000 was two years old. In March David Swede, managing partner of Finers, said, 'We issued a writ against Terry Venables for £8,000 about a couple of months ago.' Mark Stephens, the lawyer Venables had used briefly, was still bemused by his treatment and not a little aggrieved that his bill had not béen paid. And also waiting to be paid was Lowe Bell. Piers Pottinger said, 'I always sound sombre whenever I hear the name Venables. Despite a public statement that he has paid us he has made no attempt to pay us.' He proposed to take Venables to court in May when England were due to meet Greece at Wembley.

Then, on the Friday before the first match, on 9 March against Denmark at Wembley, came the heaviest blow. Venables was served with invoices from Bryan Fugler asking for £312,000. Venables immediately retaliated with a writ alleging negligence in Fugler's legal duties. The writ arrived at Fugler's offices after Fugler had sent his bill but it was dated a few days previously. A spokesman for Venables said, 'We had been considering a claim for negligence for some time and I understand it is a valid claim.' Fugler, having acted for Venables for a number of years, refused to discuss details of the bills but said, 'The writ will be defended and the fees that I am owed will be pursued.'

The fight between Venables and Bryan Fugler was like a family parting. Not only had Fugler been close to Venables, and received much legal work from Tottenham when Venables was chief executive, but he was first cousin to Eric Hall. There was another consequence. Bryan's brother Jeff was claiming nearly £20,000 for marketing work he had done for Scribes back in 1992. Bryan advised Jeff to lay off, confident he could get Terry to pay him, but now that Bryan had fallen out with Terry, Jeff was free to pursue his claim and, although the amount was tiny compared to what Bryan was claiming, it was one of those small things that could produce a mighty noise.

The demand for money was not all one way, however. Venables himself was seeking £144,000 from Kirby. This was a legacy of Transatlantic Inns relating to the joint and several guarantees that he along with Kirby and other Transatlantic directors had given to the NatWest. For Venables this was an important action for it showed that people owed him money as well. In his autobiography he makes a lot of this action against Kirby, saying Kirby and Wright had left him to pay off the creditors and the bank which cost Venables £500,000. And so exemplary was his conduct, he says, that the Official Receiver complimented him and his associates. However, while he did pay the money, some of the payments to creditors were to Grand Met and Inntrepreneur Estates, the landlords, so that he could back some of the pubs originally leased by Transatlantic Inns and run them through his own companies. Like most of Venables' business ventures nothing was simple; the deal to get hold of Macey's was particularly difficult and, at one stage, was held up by the fact that a lawyer who previously acted on the deal for Venables had not been paid and would not release information until his bill had been met.

If this was a sombre background against which Venables had to prepare for his first England match he showed little concern, helped by the fact that the chasing he was receiving from the creditors was not much known about – certainly not the secretive Landhurst affairs. Even if snippets of it emerged the football public did not seem to want to know. They were enthralled that he was not Taylor, which was emphasised by his choice of team. It included three uncapped players – Anderton, Le Saux and Le Tissier – but, in the biggest break with the sterile Taylor regime,

Peter Beardsley, the man Taylor had discarded, came in while Carlton Palmer, the man Taylor had chosen for the crucial qualifying match against Holland, was dropped. Altogether 72,000 people came to Wembley to see England win 1–0 and left happy that England gave the impression it had new ideas. The FA could not have been more delighted. At a Council meeting the following day Millichip pointed to the victories by the Under-21 and the senior England sides as evidence that, now Venables was in charge, everything was right in the English football garden.

However, less than twenty-four hours later, after Venables had proved what an inspirational football coach he could be, yet another of his business ventures led to much head-shaking at a meeting of the Premier League clubs, resulting in a complaint to the FA. Kelly had to write to Venables. This latest Venables venture was to do with phone lines which could rival the Premier League clubs' own lucrative club call lines. The Venables alternative, sponsored by the Professional Footballers Association – calls were charged at 48p per minute at peak time and 36p per minute off peak – claimed that the telephone interviews hosted by Terry Venables offered fans the chance to hear their favourite players and be able to 'influence decisions'. Callers ringing the number heard Venables say, 'Hello, this is Terry Venables here, presenting the new exciting PFA Players chatline.' He promised a unique three-way chat and, in the one with Vinny Jones, Venables, charmingly, confessed he had not met him much at the professional level but they had sung a song together. The advertisements made much of the fact that the profits would go to the game but it turned out that this would be after providing a fee for Venables, the players being interviewed and Newton Wells, who ran the line and whose managing director was Bobby Keetch. Graham Kelly came to Venables' rescue saying, 'It was Venables' commitment which he had entered into when he was out of work. He had mentioned this to us when we interviewed him. But I have written to him to drop it as it is causing a conflict with the clubs.'

Venables in his business affairs was now like one of those comic fire fighters so common in silent movies, rushing from fire to fire with a bucket. However, at Scribes he was at last able to file accounts. He had prevented Scribes from being struck off for not filing proper accounts. On 19 April 1994, Scribes' accounts for the year ending August 1990 were finally signed by Ernst & Young. The auditors explained that they had to wait so long because, although audit work was complete in October 1990, they were not sure Scribes was solvent and could not get any information from Venables.

Much of the explanation, as ever, came from Brown, and his reaction to suggestions that Scribes might be broke was: but it is backed by Terry Venables. How dare you suggest anything is wrong. Ernst & Young qualified the accounts but did not audit Scribes again and Crouch Chapman took over as auditors. Having waited for nearly four years for the 1990 accounts, Venables seemed to be in a rush to catch up and Crouch Chapman submitted three years of accounts in almost as many months, filing the August 1993 accounts by September 1994. In six months four sets of annual accounts had been filed.

In qualifying the accounts Ernst & Young said, 'We are unable to form an opinion as to whether the accounts give a true and fair view of the state of the company's affairs at 31 August 1990 or of its loss or source and application of funds for the period then ended or whether the accounts have been properly prepared in accordance with the Companies Act 1985.' Since then Crouch Chapman have been preparing the audit report and they have certified that Scribes West's accounts were 'prepared on a going concern basis', provided it continued to be backed by Venables. The accounts for August 1993 revealed how much the company depended on Venables. It had £158 in the bank, liabilities exceeded assets by £362,376 and Venables and other directors and shareholders were owed £465,072.11.

But perhaps the most interesting information on Scribes was never filed in Companies House. We have seen the drama of Brown resigning as director of Scribes after his bankruptcy was disclosed. However, nowhere in Companies House was there any mention that he had ever been a director. Scribes Board minutes said Fred Venables had become a director following Brown's resignation in September 1991, but the documents filed with Companies House stated he became a director the same day as his son, in April 1991.

Venables' desire to keep Scribes going was all the more urgent, not only because he saw it as his court – once he had become England coach journalists eager for titbits from the England coach gathered round at every opportunity – but he knew that Sugar was all but ready to kill off Edennote. Sugar was trying to reverse what he saw as an illegal Venables move to declare himself a secured creditor of Edennote and get his hands on the money from the sale of Spurs shares. To stop it he had to wind up Edennote. Venables' lawyers sought to postpone the action, although at times their efforts were quite hilarious. In one exchange of letters with Herbert Smith they argued they could not respond because Herbert Smith had not included the enclosures mentioned in their letters. Yet some of these enclosures were actually copies of Venables' own affidavits which his lawyers would be expected to have.

But even as they sought time, Venables must have known that his chances of saving Edennote were slim. On 5 March, four days before the match against Denmark, Venables had executed yet another neat legal move which, if made on a football field, would have produced gasps of astonishment. He transferred all his shares in Edennote to Terence Venables Holding Ltd.

Like so many of Venables' manoeuvres this one only emerged later when the case came to court, and then quite accidentally. While making her arguments, Venables' counsel, Miss S. Proudman, let it be known that the shares in Edennote were now held by another company. Herbert Smith immediately did a company search and discovered it was Terence Venables Holdings Ltd. It did not take Sugar's lawyers long to work out why. Edennote's shares were partly paid and J. Crow, acting for Sugar, told the court that 'If in fact a company is wound up the first thing the liquidator is going to do is to make call on the unpaid capital which would have been £37,500.' However, if Venables had transferred his shares to a company with a £2 issued share capital and no assets, then there was nothing the liquidator could do. By this move Venables saved himself £37,500 and quite legally.

But what could Venables do to save Edennote? He could argue, as he did in yet another affidavit, sworn within hours of the end of the match against Denmark, that if Edennote was wound up then his claim against Tottenham would be stifled. The wrongful dismissal case was paramount for him and he would not give it up. He had made that clear to Graham Kelly at the FA and has reiterated it since. Yet Venables must have recognised this was a poor defence; he needed something else, a second front against Tottenham and Sugar. And this is where Tony Yorke began to come in very useful.

By now Yorke, whatever his earlier desire to boot out Venables, had told him of the plans to buy Edennote papers and of the alleged roles of Hewer, Watts, Berry and the Theobalds. Yorke, himself, submitted an affidavit in support of this and in April 1994 Venables swore yet another affidavit in connection with the Edennote hearings. Venables' lawyers argued that the actions of the Sugar camp were an abuse of the process of the court and justified the winding-up petition being dismissed.

The affidavit, particularly the revelation that Yorke had now definitely switched sides, would cause enormous consternation in the Sugar camp and, as we have seen, Hewer, Watts and Berry filed affidavits denying the allegations. Theobalds also provided affidavits but they were never filed in court. In a sense this was Venables' first stab at trying to prove the conspiracy theory, the one he had talked to Powell about back in October 1993. However, even before the judge could rule on it, it had an airing in a Sunday tabloid.

The court hearing on Edennote was scheduled for the week beginning 9 May 1994. In the weeks leading up to it, Yorke wrote a major series for the *People*, the title of which – 'The Fall and Rise of Terry Venables' – gives its flavour. The final piece on Sunday 8 May dealt with what the paper headlined: 'Dirty tricks cost Venners two dream jobs', and the article itself previewed the evidence that would come up before the court.

This alleged that Theobalds had offered the Edennote papers to a prominent White Hart Lane figure for £25,000 and that use of the papers by *Panorama* resulted in severe damage to Venables. Venables was quoted as saying, 'The allegations damaged me severely and led me to lose lucrative jobs with Grampus and Real Madrid. It cost me £3m. and that's how much I will be claiming from *Panorama* when I issue my writ.' (Yorke did not ask and Venables did not explain why a writ on *Panorama* 'ready to be served' on 9 October 1993, as Jeff Powell had reported, had not yet been issued by 8 May 1994.)

The article was written in the accepted tabloid style and was very artful. Although it mentioned a taped interview with Gill Theobalds, nowhere did Yorke mention his own involvement and the investigative role he had played in locating people like Theobalds and the Edennote documentation. It was as if Tony Yorke of the *People* was exposing the work of Tony Yorke of the *Daily Mirror*. As far as *People* readers were concerned this was presented as an exposé of the dark deeds of the Sugar camp. And while Yorke drew on the 'evidence lodged with the High Court' he did not mention that this was in the main an affidavit he had him-self supplied in favour of Venables.

Miss Proudman tried hard to use the Yorke allegations to get more time for Venables and delay the death of Edennote. But the judge made it clear that this latest Venables evidence was not rele-vant, that he had had enough time to produce his evidence, and decided to ignore it. The case revolved around whether, in wind-ing up Edennote, Venables' claim against Tottenham and the legal precedents surrounding it would be thwarted. And he decided that Edennote deserved to be wound up.

In the weeks leading up to the dirty tricks article Yorke had focused on other aspects of Venables' career, trying to demonstrate that there had been misdeeds in Tottenham for a long time, long before Venables took over, and if anything Venables had sought to unmask them. So Yorke made allegations against Scholar and Roach, with his major target the Tottenham loans saga. Having, through much of 1993, been the investigative scourge of Venables, Yorke had now turned his guns on Tottenham and in particular the transfer of Mitchell Thomas from Luton to Tottenham in the sum-mer of 1987. And, as with the dirty tricks story, Venables and Yorke formed a formidable partnership.

Sometime in mid-April 1994 Eric Hall rang David Kohler, chair-man of Luton Town, and asked him whether he would speak to Brown. Brown, Hall told Kohler, was acting for Terry Venables. On 11 April Brown came to see Kohler and told him that when Tottenham bought Mitchell Thomas in 1987 they gave him a loan of £25,000 but did not disclose it to the tribunal who set Thomas' transfer fee. Kohler could not accept what he felt were unsub-stantiated allegations but Brown said Yorke had the proof. The result of the conversation was that Yorke came to visit Kohler and told him that he was investigating the circumstances in which Mitchell Thomas had been transferred to Tottenham from Luton. As it happened Thomas by then had returned to Luton.

And, just as his article alleging dirty tricks against Venables coincided with the court case, so Yorke's investigations into the Tottenham loans affair was superbly timed, coming just as the FA investigation of the loans affair was reaching a climax.

Tottenham felt clemency was due to them. They had co-operated with the investigation, provided all the evidence and at worst the crime was a minor one of non-disclosure. However, the loans saga, as featured by Yorke, was of a different dimension. Yorke detailed loans to players whose prices were determined by the transfer tribunal. Such loans could have resulted in a case of manipulation of the transfer market and it could be argued that this was more than a mere technical offence. Venables' interest in helping Yorke highlight it was obvious, but did he do more? There is some evidence to suggest that he and Brown gave evidence against Tottenham. Venables has never disclosed this but when Sugar kept insisting that Tottenham were being charged as a result of the evidence they had themselves submitted, Kelly said there were other sources. However, he would not say who or what they were, although there is some evidence to suggest they came from the Venables camp.

Now, just as Venables' appointment had become intertwined with the Tottenham loans saga, so the death of Edennote was overshadowed by the more lingering death that seemed to await Tottenham at the hands of the FA. On 9 May, even as Mr Justice Rattee rose after giving judgement, across London in Lancaster Gate the FA made moves which effectively ensured that the next day's headlines would be not Venables but Sugar, not Edennote's demise but Tottenham's likely peril.

That afternoon the FA announced that Tottenham would be charged with misconduct for making loans to players between 1985 and 1989. The FA held a press conference and the charges were hastily biked to Tottenham. Sugar was convinced that the FA had deliberately timed this to put the winding up of Edennote in the shade. David Davies, who was responsible for it, denied this, saying the timing was coincidental, and that he wasn't even aware what was happening to Edennote.

In some ways what the FA had done was to take the evidence Tottenham had presented to the FA, plus any contributions Venables and Brown might have made, had the papers reviewed by their lawyers, Freshfields, and presented the case back to Tottenham saying: answer it. For the second year in succession, just days before Cup Final, it meant that Spurs were centre-stage not because of their football but for what had happened in the boardroom.

In also meant that the Sugar-Venables situation had now been reversed. Venables luxuriated in the glow of the man with the magical touch. Two days after the Cup Final, albeit in front of a poor crowd (but the weather was wretched) England routed Greece 5–0, a triumph that led the tabloid press to declare that it was a grotesque injustice that Greece was going to the World Cup but not England. In some ways a better test came five days later when Norway, who had thwarted England, came to Wembley and earned a 0–0 draw, although England did have an apparently good goal disallowed. But despite this draw, the fact remained that, under Venables, England had not conceded a goal, they had played with a style and verve lacking under Taylor and, of course, Venables was making all the right noises, talking of Christmas tree formations where Shearer played as the lone striker supported by quickly breaking midfield players. English football, so long moribund, seemed to have rediscovered some imagination.

In contrast Sugar was under grave threat. Tottenham, who had just avoided relegation on the field, faced relegation by the mandarins of the FA. On 14 June, just days before the first World Cup match, the FA's five-man commission met at Wembley for a day-long hearing. The Sugar camp felt pleased with their effort and confident that the commission would take into account that it was Tottenham who had provided much of the material, that there had been no breach of the laws of the land – in sharp contrast to Swindon where the chairman responsible had been jailed – and that improper conduct amounted to failure to disclose to the FA. Tottenham could have contested some of the charges but the commission gave Sugar the impression that if he pleaded guilty it could be resolved that day and this would be of benefit to Tottenham. But after the day-long hearing, when the commission announced its judgement, it turned out that Spurs would be fined £600,000, have 12 points deducted and be booted out of the FA Cup. The sentences stunned the world of soccer and were widely seen as relegation by a slow painful process.

Sugar decided to fight and, in the appeal, discarded their QC and made the arguments himself. This time the fine was doubled to £1.5m., the points deduction reduced to 6, but the ban on the FA Cup stayed. The fine was six times higher than the highest ever fine, £250,000, awarded against an oil company for discharging oil and polluting the atmosphere. The FA made it clear this was the end of the road but Sugar refused to accept it. However, few thought his chances were good, the advice from the game was to accept the bitter pill, and when, on his way to the press conference to talk about the FA decision, Sugar stumbled and nearly fell, everyone saw it as symbolic and got ready to write Tottenham's obituary.

Sugar, determined to get a fair hearing for Tottenham, began to engage in a prolonged correspondence with Kelly. The letters between the two read like a thriller. Sugar, keeping the threat of legal action up his sleeve, presented his arguments as to why Tottenham should have a proper independent hearing. Kelly prevaricated, not knowing how to respond to Sugar and taking days, even weeks, to reply. But every time Kelly responded, Sugar promptly wrote back, often within hours, and in the end Kelly was overwhelmed. The FA finally decided that the Tottenham matter would go to arbitration where an independent set of three arbitrators not connected with football would decide whether the award was just. The arbitrators eventually cancelled all the points penalty, returned Tottenham to the Cup but reconfirmed the £1.5m. fine. Sugar, confounding the pundits, had won a great victory and, at the next home game, received a standing ovation.

As Sugar was having his public examination of Tottenham's past by the FA, the FA's most prominent employee was, very much more privately, being examined by the DTI. The DTI had visited *Panorama* within weeks of the programme. Their initial interest in Venables had been aroused by the Official Receiver for Transatlantic, and *Panorama* made them act. The DTI's mills had begun to grind, slowly but surely. In January 1994 they had called Mark Killick, the *Panorama* producer, back for another chat. They had secured a copy of the Landhurst lease but it did not look anything like the Landhurst lease shown on *Panorama*. Was it not the same? Killick confessed that *Panorama* had seen the lease but did not have a copy. They were allowed to read it out into a tape recorder and, since television requires visual evidence, they had then done a graphic representation of the lease. Hence the original lease which the DTI had, and the one on *Panorama*, looked different although they were the same lease, word for word.

Soon after this the DTI inspectors had extended their enquiries into Venables. Section 447 investigations had been launched into Venables' role in Landhurst in February 1994 and in March Venables' stewardship of Tottenham began to be investigated. DTI inspectors were also interested in the way Venables had taken a charge over Edennote's assets, just before he sold his shares in Tottenham. They had been present in Mr Justice Rattee's court on 12 May 1994, when the judge, in deciding to wind up Edennote, said he took into consideration the argument by Sugar's lawyers that Venables' action of taking a charge over Edennote's assets – the discovery of which had lead to Sugar bringing the winding-up petition in the first place – was an 'improper preference – a proposition which should be investigated, irrespective of the outcome of the company's [meaning Edennote's] claim against Tottenham Ltd, and which can only be properly investigated in the context of a winding-up order'. As Mr Justice Rattee spoke of a proper investigation the DTI inspectors could be seen to glance at each other and take notes.

By June the DTI were ready to quiz Venables himself. So, just about the time Sugar went to Wembley to face the FA commission, Venables with his lawyer went to Victoria Street, headquarters of the DTI. So while Sugar and Tottenham faced their ordeal amidst intense media speculation, Venables was grilled for three days by Horne and Parkinson. Venables did not sound convincing. He often could not remember and when a lease or document was put before him with what seemed his signature, nearly always denied that it was indeed his signature.

The DTI examination was an ordeal. However, Venables managed to keep this secret, publicly still presenting an open, smiling face, always ready with a joke and a laugh. With the DTI he could do nothing, but he could try to do something to save his wrongful dismissal case against Tottenham.

This was in two parts, reflecting the fact that his contract split his salary between a payment to himself and one to Edennote. Since the payment to Edennote was much the larger amount, Edennote's winding up put this action in jeopardy. Now it was up to the liquidator to pursue the action. But here there was another problem. Some months earlier Sugar had moved for security of costs in the wrongful dismissal action, in a manner similar to the one that had ultimately destroyed Edennote and, in effect, saying show us you have the money to pay the legal bills to pursue this case. The case had been adjourned until the fate of Edennote was decided. Now that Edennote had been put into receivership Sugar's lawyers resumed the security of costs case. It was due to be heard on 29 July. It was clear that there was no way the liquidator, Stephen Ryman of Rothmans Plantell, could show that Edennote had the money to avoid a security of costs judgement against it. And if that succeeded then Venables' wrongful dismissal case would fail.

The only alternative was for Venables to buy out the wrongful dismissal action from the Receiver and pursue it on his own. This was discussed at a meeting in June which Brown held with Ryman in the company of Nick Trainer of Bowden Trainer and a representative of Crouch Chapman. Ryman took advice and agreed; on 28 July the deal was signed. It cost Venables £7,000 plus 10% of any proceeds he might recover from Tottenham. The previous day Herbert Smith had been informed this was happening but could do nothing. Now they had once again to put aside the security of costs application, and start an action to remove the Receiver and set aside the assignment. Sugar's lawyers told the Receiver that they would be prepared to pay Edennote's liquidator £50,000 for buying the wrongful dismissal action which would work out much cheaper than fighting Venables in court. For the first time since the series of court actions had begun the previous summer, Sugar did not feel entirely confident he would succeed.

About this time there was one other action Venables was involved in which did not receive any publicity. In May 1994 Jeff Fugler had presented a winding-up petition. On 25 July a compromise was reached where Venables' lawyers, Bowden Trainer, were paid £10,000 by Venables to be kept in an interest-bearing account pending a settlement with Fugler who had until 30 August to bring an action. Jeff Fugler was claiming just under £20,000, and Venables felt no fears about it. It would prove a ticking time-bomb.

But with the outside world largely unaware of all this and concentrating instead on the problems Sugar had with the FA on the loans issue, it was Venables who looked the picture of health and happiness as he headed for America to comment on the World Cup for the BBC. In April Robert Phillips in the *Daily Telegraph* had written how four weeks into his job Venables had so transformed Lancaster Gate that everybody was in stitches. One insider said they had not laughed like this in years. Phillips saw him as Sergeant Bilko and Lancaster Gate as Fort Baxter, full of mischief and fun, and on the screen a sun-tanned Venables radiated that same feeling.

But unknown to Venables an old adversary was gearing up: *Panorama*. In March Killick had been shown a Landhurst lease. He believed it was the one he had seen when making his first programme. But it wasn't. Then he thought that he and Bashir had made a mistake in their first programme. With Venables constantly telling the press he was suing *Panorama* – although no writ had emerged – Killick was sensitive to any mistakes. But it turned out that this was a second lease and that there was even more to

Venables' business dealings than *Panorama* had shown in the first programme. Killick began to think in terms of a second *Panorama*. In April Stephen Illidge of Landhurst was contacted and, by the end of June, Bashir, who had been working on another programme, rejoined.

Venables returned from America and, as the new football season began, it seemed that everything was still working out right. To Venables' delight Sugar appeared to be losing ground even on such matters as bung allegations. Back in October 1993 Sugar had made a complaint to the Metropolitan Police's Fraud Squad about possible misappropriation of funds in relation to the Sheringham transfer. The Fraud Squad had interviewed several people including Sugar, Sandy and Venables. The Criminal Prosecution Service (CPS) were sent the papers in May but now, in August 1994, they concluded that there was insufficient evidence for convicting anyone and the case was dropped.

Sugar also had little support from the press when it emerged that he had banned Venables from White Hart Lane. Many found it petty and even Jimmy Greaves, who was quite critical of Venables' football selections, urged Sugar not to indulge in verbal broadsides against Venables.

Venables, himself, was preparing to fire his own very considerable broadside at Sugar. His magnum opus, his autobiography, was now almost ready. Sometime during the summer it had been shown to Graham Kelly who, according to Tony Yorke, in another *People* exclusive, had asked for major alterations to passages about Sugar but approved Venables' allegations of dirty tricks orchestrated by the Sugar camp. As Yorke put it, 'Terry Venables is renewing his war with Alan Sugar – with the full backing of the FA bosses.'

Venables had used a co-writer to write his book, but as the book was being finished, Venables did his own research. He asked Gulu Lalwani for help, although one piece of Venables' research did lead to a curious result. Earlier in the year, on Good Friday, Venables had invited Philip Clarke of Diverse Productions for lunch at the Carlton Tower. Clarke recalled in an interview with me in September 1994: 'We hadn't had any contact since our *Dispatches* programme the previous September. It was a very pleasant lunch until the end when Terry tried to get me to admit that we had made mistakes in our programme and I refused to do so. We hadn't made mistakes. Indeed after the programme Terry had told us it was a very fair one.'

During the lunch Venables was also keen to get a copy of the fax that Lazio's lawyers had sent Tottenham's lawyers the day before his take-over of Spurs confirming the price of £5.5m. they were ready to pay for Gascoigne. In September when Venables' book emerged it surprised Clarke to find that not only was there no mention of this lunch but that Venables had said the following in his book: 'As the wall of lies begins to crumble, however, more and more information is forthcoming to . . . our lawyers. *Dispatches*, for example, having realised how seriously astray they were in the programme vilifying me, based on evidence they now know to have been false, have agreed to open their files to us and have made statements to our lawyers.'

At that stage Clarke did not know who Venables' lawyers were: 'As to opening our files we don't have any files to open. From the time the programme went out until the lunch on Good Friday I had no contact with Terry and I am dumbfounded by the version in the book, it bears no relation to anything that passed between us. He tried to get me to admit we were wrong but I did not.'

Clarke also denies Venables' assertion in the book that Santin was suing them. 'We have had no legal action from Santin at all so I do not know where Terry got that from.' Clarke wrote to the publishers suggesting they make changes before the edition was reprinted but when the paperback emerged it had the same allegations against *Dispatches*.

This was not the only remarkable statement in Venables' book. He confidently asserted that Luton were planning to sue Tottenham over the Mitchell Thomas loan. Kohler wanted money from Tottenham but he had no intention of suing and has launched no such action. But if Clarke and Kohler were surprised by the book, the man who felt the Venables treatment the worst was his old friend Paul Riviere.

Riviere had had no contact with Venables for almost a year, since their meetings in The Goat just after the first *Panorama* programme in October 1993. In September 1994, as Venables prepared for his first international of the 1994–95 season against the USA, Riviere suddenly heard from Venables. Quite out of the blue he received a message to call him. Riviere, who had just got back from America, did so and on Sunday 4 September, three days before England played USA, Venables took time off from the England training camp at Bisham Abbey to meet Riviere at the Carlton Tower.

Riviere told me in an interview: 'Terry was concerned to know I had been talking to you. He knew you were writing a book and he wanted to know why is this Mihir Bose writing about me. There have been books by Harry Harris, and *Panorama*. What is there to say? Then he spoke about his book. I asked him what he had said about me. He said, "I have given you a wrap on the knuckles, but you must remember I wrote it after *Panorama* when I was angry with you for *Panorama*." '

Venables also told Riviere that he was no longer close to Crystal, and that Brown made mistakes. He added he didn't expect to make much money, not expecting to sell more than 30,000 copies. As the two men parted Venables punched Riviere playfully on the arm, the two men had said bygones should be bygones, and Riviere saw the gesture as if to suggest 'let's put the past behind us'. But the gesture did not entirely reassure Riviere. He had asked to be shown a copy of what Venables had written but Venables had said he couldn't as the book wasn't finished.

After his conversation on the Sunday, Riviere wondered if Venables had carried a hidden tape recorder: 'Terry had mentioned how he had asked a journalist to take off his jacket. I did not know whether he was taping me. Terry told me, be careful what you tell Mihir Bose. I said, "What do you mean?" He said, "Be careful, Paul", and I wondered if he had taped any of our previous meetings with him at The Goat after the first *Panorama*. I asked him, "Are you taping our conversation?" He said, "Not now". That made me think he might have in the past, but he assured me he had not. Not that I was worried, because I had already spoken the truth. He had told me that Yorke taped everyone.' Riviere was keen to find out if the book was being serialised but Venables denied it was. However, as Riviere observed, 'When he said he was not interested in serialisation I immediately knew he had other plans.'

Far from not being interested in serialisation the *Mail on Sunday* began publishing extracts from the book the following Sunday and it seems odd that Venables did not know about the deal a mere seven days before the paper printed extracts from his book. However, the serialisation was kept such a secret that even on Friday various sections of the paper did not know it was being serialised.

When Riviere saw the book he could hardly believe his eyes. He felt Venables had traduced their relationship, converting fifteen years of friendship during which Venables had often said that Riviere was the nicest man he had ever met into a situation where Riviere was a hopeless misfit who needed to be rescued, 'The Manager' was more the work of Brown and, far from being his partner at Scribes, Venables employed him there. 'In the book he makes it out I was in need of help and he helped me and I then shopped him to *Panorama*. The fact is that I was running a very successful financial services company when I joined up with Terry to do "The Manager". It was as much my creation as his. But what really hurt was that he dragged my divorce into it. Terry has made it personal and I would not stoop that low, although I could. We were business partners for fifteen years and he has reduced it to a mockery.'

The extracts also drew a fierce response from Sugar who lambasted it as 'Hans Christian Andersen's fairy tales'. The publishers drew a cordon around the book, making it one of the most tightly controlled books since the Thatcher memoirs. This is not as uncommon as it may seem, with publishers paranoid about leaks, although it meant that review copies to newspapers, normally sent out some three or four weeks before publication, did not arrive until four days before the book was launched at Scribes on 22 September. The guests for the launch party were carefully screened as well. A *Sunday Times* request for me to be invited, representing my sports editor, met with the response: we will come back to you. The specialist publicity agent hired by the publishers never came back.

The book launch had two unusual aspects. Every guest was required to buy a copy and Venables adopted the pose that, despite it being his autobiography, he hadn't written it. Kevin Mitchell of the *Observer* was at Scribes that night and stayed to watch Venables help clear the promotional cardboard cut-outs of himself that had been sprinkled about the place. Mitchell asked Venables if he was pleased with the book.

'Yes,' replied Venables, 'what I've read of, I think it is great.'

Mitchell commented, 'This is an interesting new concept of the genre. Perhaps he was being flip. But the making of this ghost blockbluster, *à la* the Ian Botham confessions and, bless her, Naomi Campbell, candid non-novelist of our time, confirms that auto is not what it was.'

However, whether he had been joking or not, Venables could not escape the legal responsibilities and within days of the book being published both Sugar and Berry, outraged by the allegations it contained, were training legal writs on him. On the Thursday afternoon of his launch Venables had signed copies at Selfridges amidst much media interest, with Irving Scholar's wife in the queue to get an inscribed copy. The following Thursday when he was up in Leeds at Dillons bookshop, amongst the callers was a writ server from Herbert Smith presenting two writs, one from Sugar, and one from Berry. Sugar made it clear he wanted to go for Venables personally. Soon Clifford Chance, acting for Michael Joseph, the publishers, had written to Herbert Smith and the battle was joined.

Sugar, invited by the *Sunday Times*, also reviewed the book, much against the wishes of his lawyers, who felt it might harm his libel action. Venables' response was immediate. He gave a long interview to Joe Lovejoy, the paper's football correspondent. Ostensibly this was meant to be a scene-setter for the match against Romania but in essence it was an answer to Sugar rubbishing his book, with Venables arguing there was a vendetta against him.

The interview revealed two traits about Venables. It indicated that Venables would never let any attack go unanswered. Also that he always wanted to stake out the moral high ground, however spuriously. So he castigated Sugar for bringing Venables' father, Fred, ill in hospital, into the argument. How could Sugar stoop so low? asked Venables. I can never forgive him for that. Yet what heinous thing had Sugar said? All Sugar had done, in his review of the Venables book, was point to the passage where Venables narrated how, as part of the deal that took him as an apprentice to Chelsea, his dad got a part-time scouting job that paid him more than Venables earned then. Sugar had wondered if such a thing could be done now. A thrust at Venables to be sure, but one arising from what Venables had himself said. Yet the way the Venables interview read it was as if Sugar had dragged a sick man – and how was Sugar to know he was sick? – into an argument.

As it happened the Romanian match saw Venables for the first time come under attack in the footballing press, even from some of the friendly tabloid writers. Until Romania came to Wembley, Venables had been able, with some justification, to present a pleasant face of English football, recovering from the disappointments of Taylor. Romania shattered it, not only scoring a goal – the first a Venables England team had conceded – but indicating that in terms of skill England were still in the second division. Also

Venables' tactics, with both Wright and Le Tissier played out of position, were questioned. Against USA he could recall Barnes, written off as a has-been, and not hear a whimper of protest. Now even John Sadler spoke of sleaze, albeit in the footballing sense.

The larger question of financial sleaze was soon on the agenda again. *Panorama* was all but ready to proceed with its second programme. By September Killick and Bashir had finished, Bashir even travelling to Hove to watch the Official Receiver grill Brown before he decided whether he could release him from bankruptcy. Soon Killick and Bashir were making a more significant journey to see Noel White, chairman of the international committee of the FA. White explained that Venables was well nigh invulnerable. He could withstand press allegations, even disqualification as director by the DTI or criminal charges against Brown. However, if there were criminal charges against Venables himself, the FA might look again.

On 31 October the second *Panorama* programme was screened. The week before there had been hectic activity. On the Tuesday *Panorama* wrote to Venables, requesting an interview. *Panorama* were going through the motions and he, not surprisingly, refused. On Thursday Venables at last issued a writ, on the first *Panorama* broadcast thirteen months earlier, a tactic which the programme makers saw as a diversion to stop their second programme. Venables let it be known he had issued an earlier writ but it had lapsed; in fact *Panorama* had never received a writ. Originally the *Panorama* programme for 31 October was meant to be on O. J. Simpson. It was only on the Friday that *Panorama* announced that they were switching from the American sports legend to an English one.

The result was a barrage of publicity, some of it generated by *Panorama*, some the usual Venables counter-strike against an event he feared. On the Friday evening preceding the programme Joe Lovejoy of the *Sunday Times* received the call to come to Scribes where Venables tried to defend what he feared *Panorama* might prove. Venables told Lovejoy that *Panorama* had got hold of the three cheques Landhurst had issued to Edennote but it had been a mistake and as soon as he realised it he had had them corrected.

The most interesting publicity battle was fought in the pages of the *Independent*. Ian Hargreaves, now editor of the *Independent*, ran a prominent article previewing the programme. But in the news pages his reporter, Steve Boggan, went to Scribes and appeared to present Venables' case. *Panorama* II turned out to be a complex programme but probably the most complete television account of Venables the businessman. Centred on the Landhurst loan, it detailed the intricacies but also made the telling point that Venables had been less than open with the FA about business skeletons in his cupboard.

Venables' response was on two levels: that he had done nothing wrong and that the documents they had were forgeries. A handwriting expert consulted by the *Mirror* suggested the signatures were genuine. *Panorama* had ended up pointing out that the SFO had called for the DTI papers. Venables made available to the *Independent* the witness statement he had given the SFO when they had called him as a witness in their general investigation into Landhurst. This, he claimed, proved his innocence against the charges made by *Panorama*; however, being called as a witness and being investigated are two very different things. Also what *Panorama* were alleging was wrongdoing in relation to Transatlantic Inns, a company of which Venables had been a director. The SFO had not investigated this company. They had called Venables as a witness in connection with Landhurst, a company from whom he had borrowed money. If, as *Panorama* alleged, he had unlawfully used assets of Transatlantic to borrow from Landhurst, then this would be a matter for a Transatlantic investigation, not a Landhurst one.

What was significant was that, compared to the first *Panorama* programme which seemed to devastate Venables, this one did not seem to dent his sangfroid. He even joked about it, 'Not even serial killers get two *Panoramas*, I am only a football manager.' And the night it was screened, far from watching it behind drawn curtains, he went to QPR to see them play Liverpool, sitting next to his old friend Rodney Marsh. The next morning he flew out to Barcelona to act as TV commentator on the Barcelona-Manchester United game.

The second *Panorama* made less of an impact than the first, partly because Venables' allies presented it, quite wrongly, as a rerun of old material, partly because other soccer news intervened. Thus, three hours before the programme was broadcast Sugar summoned Ardiles to his home and sacked him. The *Sun* led with that story, relegating Venables. But the real reason Venables could maintain such an impressive public front was because Graham Kelly had publicly backed him, saying the programme had not proved he was not a good football coach. Kelly's and the FA's response indicated that the FA, having got into bed with Venables, could not let go of him unless he was charged.

The DTI had referred to the SFO eleven matters which ranged from the allegations in the way he had used the pubs to borrow £1m. from Landhurst to alleged misstatements he had made when taking over Tottenham. In November 1994, within days of the *Panorama* programme, there was a fractious meeting between the DTI and the SFO at the SFO's offices. A senior DTI civil servant, Martin Roberts, realising the SFO would not act, told George Staple, the SFO's director, that it might be necessary for him to brief ministers and even the private office at No. 10. According to an article by David Hellier in the *Independent* in January 1996, on 3 November 1994 the SFO wrote a letter to the Attorney General's chambers warning him that they might have to delay their announcement of not proceeding against Venables in order to give DTI time to go to the ministers.

But in the end the SFO made the announcement that it was not launching a criminal proceeding against Venables. In any event, the amount involved was small compared to the fraud allegations the SFO investigated, and within weeks of receiving the papers from the DTI, the SFO returned them. As the *Sunday Times* reported on 24 March 1996, the SFO were not convinced that a successful criminal prosecution could be undertaken as it felt there was insufficient evidence or 'credible witnesses' to support it.

Venables, understandably, presented this as a great victory and it helped him to sideline *Panorama*. Also, soon after this, *Panorama* announced its settlement with Santin, admitting its libel, which strengthened the impression that, as Venables had been saying, much of this was smears and slurs.

Yet if publicly Venables gave the impression that *Panorama* did not matter, privately it concerned him greatly. The first *Panorama* had made him call in Detective Inspector Ray Needham and speak of a conspiracy. Now on 11 November 1994, less than two weeks after the second, Brown went back to Needham and filed an allegation of conspiracy. On 22 November Peter Rose, crime correspondent of the *Daily Mail*, reported this saying the conspiracy was to get him the sack and make him unemployable so that he could no longer finance any civil action. However, if this was the original complaint, at some stage it became a complaint of a conspiracy to pervert the course of justice but when the metamorphosis in the charge took place is not clear.

Rose's article said that detectives were to question Venables about his claim that day indicating that either Venables or Brown was the source, assuming the detectives were not. In any event little was heard of this and the story made such little impact that, when the *Sunday Times* reported on Venables and his problems in July 1995, more than six months later, they claimed to have broken the conspiracy story.

That Venables believes in conspiracy theory, and that the conspiracy is orchestrated by Sugar, cannot be doubted. But the fact is that Sugar was not his only enemy, even if the most high-profile one. There were by now any number of people worried about Venables.

On 30 January 1995, Kate Hoey, the Labour MP for Vauxhall with a particular interest in sports – having been an education officer at Arsenal in charge of youth players – initiated a debate in the House of Commons on corruption in football. In a wide-ranging speech, Hoey suggested to the government that it was time an independent commission looked into football. Hoey wondered why, after fifteen months, the Premier League inquiry had not yet reported, and, speaking of Venables, she said, 'The evidence in front of the Commission on Terry Venables is, I believe, damning.' She was referring to Venables' involvement with Eric Hall which might possibly have breached the Prevention of Corruption Act. Hoey stressed she was speaking of his football activities, not his business dealings, and many welcomed what she said. Venables, not surprisingly, did not, and tried to rubbish Hoey as an MP who used the cloak of parliament to make charges. Hoey's actions were much more worthy than that. But Venables had his supporters who took up this refrain and, mixing it with a dose of sexism, made their dislike of Hoey very plain.

Hoey's speech had come just a day after the *Mail on Sunday* had highlighted Venables' DTI problem. Until then nobody in the print media had done any original work on Venables and the DTI. Now the *Mail on Sunday* did. On 29 January 1995 the leading article on its business pages revealed how worried the Venables camp was about the DTI and the dangers the investigation held for him. The article mentioned that Ian Burton, of Burton Copeland, the lawyer who had accompanied Venables to the DTI grilling in June, had two weeks previously, in mid-January, written to the DTI. Venables, Burton had said, was quite prepared to come and talk to the DTI and help them in their investigations. The DTI reply was chilling. Venables could come and talk but anything he said might be used as evidence in a future prosecution.

The DTI investigation into Venables under Section 447, which gave them powers to obtain business documentation, was now being widened with the DTI investigating possible criminal offences under Section 47 of the Financial Services Act 1986. The statement Venables had made in the Spurs share offer document had come under scrutiny. The SFO had decided not to prosecute Venables but the DTI was, at that time, looking into the possibility of a criminal investigation.

'Venables gets DTI warning on deals,' the *Mail* had headlined its piece. A week later Venables, as it were, struck back. If the *Mail on Sunday* article was an anti-Venables piece, then this one, on the front page of the *Sunday Times*, was definitely pro-Venables. 'Venables victim of £100,000 blackmail plot', it shouted. It seemed that in the days leading up to the Romania match, in October 1994, Venables got a call at the hotel adjoining the England training camp at Bisham Abbey. The message was to ring a mobile number. When he did a man with an Irish accent answered who, it seems, had got hold of the DTI report on him. Venables, said the article, initially dismissed the caller as a crank but three weeks later the man rang Venables again, this time at Scribes, giving details of the DTI file which indicated he had seen it. The caller demanded a meeting in London, Venables stalled, and Burton was told of the threats, which were also reported to the police.

On the advice of Scotland Yard a meeting was arranged at Dirty Dicks, the City of London pub where Venables went, accompanied by Brown. The caller met them, seemed to have precise details of Venables' DTI file and the meeting ended with the man giving Venables and Brown an Irish telephone number. The man, according to the *Sunday Times,* hinted he might need persuasion if he was not to publicise the file. The caller eventually demanded £100,000 and the police took over. Scotland Yard organised a sting operation with their Irish counterpart and a meeting was arranged at the Burlington, a smart Dublin hotel, on 19 December. The policemen entered the lobby carrying a notebook computer and a case with £100,000 in notes. The notebook computer was necessary because the information the man had was on disk. It turned out to be authentic, 200 pages of the 400-page DTI report. A thirty-two-year-old man from County Kildare was arrested and the next day

Scotland Yard in London arrested a woman, a temporary typist who had been sent by an agency to work in the Treasury Solicitor's office. The man and the woman were brother and sister. The woman had come across a disc containing Venables' DTI file and copied it.

The *Sunday Times* reported Venables' shock and dismay and his demand that the government hold an inquiry. 'Many of my private papers have gone missing, and some very strange things have happened. I am sick of suddenly being the centre of attraction when all I want to do is get on with the football.' The article did much to negate the *Mail on Sunday* revelations and painted a picture of Venables as the victim of plots.

Three weeks later he did have a chance to concentrate on football but this, his first overseas foray, proved ill-fated. On 28 February 1995 England went to Dublin to play Ireland – the match lasted twenty-seven minutes as English soccer fans rioted and forced the abandonment of the match – the first time an England international had been cancelled in this fashion.

The same day back in Victoria Street the DTI convened a meeting about Venables. Chaired by Treasury solicitor Gervina Jones it pondered the question: what should the DTI do? Horne, Parkinson and their team had done a good job, but Jones, aware that this was a high-profile case, knew the DTI could not afford to get it wrong, and so she now decided that another set of investigators would go over the ground again. Robin Tarvin and Roger Dixon, two ex-coppers, were assigned. They had to convert the interviews of Horne and Parkinson into sworn witness statements. Tarvin's choice was interesting. A lifelong Chelsea supporter, he went to Stamford Bridge every Saturday and had seen Venables make his Chelsea debut.

Venables returned from Dublin making all the right noises about hooligans in football. In Victoria Street Tarvin was making somewhat different noises. Occasionally outsiders caught a whiff of the tension within Venables. As Venables completed his first year as England coach Brough Scott, in the *Sunday Telegraph*, wrote a warm, sympathetic piece about Venables, but he noted, 'There are moments when his face has a lined and lived-in look from rather deeper hurts than away defeats. But on the soccer front he is still on his own.'

As the 1994–95 season ended this was how English football saw Venables: perhaps a bit of a lad, a bit wide, but peerless when he dons the tracksuit. Not even the end-of-summer tournament featuring Brazil, Sweden and Japan when Venables lost his first match, a defeat at the hands of Brazil, and did not exactly shine against Sweden or Japan, dented this. Venables, the refrain went, was reshaping English football and the hope was the DTI and the others would just leave him alone.

Yet the past was continually catching up both with Venables and some of his closest companions. On 9 May 1995 the Disciplinary Tribunal of the Council of the Inns of Court, with His Honour Judge A. Hallgarten, QC in the chair, sat to hear the charge of professional misconduct that Sugar had brought against Jonathan Crystal. This related to that day back in December 1992 when Crystal had persuaded the judge to grant an adjournment in a case he was involved in, claiming that he was representing somebody at a part-heard hearing before a disciplinary tribunal. Crystal did not tell the judge the real reason – that he wanted to attend a Tottenham Board meeting, which he duly did. When in June 1993, in the middle of his court battle with Venables, Sugar had threatened Crystal with exposure on this matter Crystal had given evidence which led to a charge of contempt of court.

Now, in front of his fellow barristers, Crystal finally came clean and confessed he had been lying all along. None of the statements he had made to the judge on 3 December 1992 were true. This is what the Disciplinary Tribunal said:

'Mr Crystal admitted the following charge of professional misconduct:

Charge

Professional misconduct, by knowingly misleading a court. . .'

The tribunal concluded that: 'This conduct was contrary to paragraph 202 of the Code of Conduct of the bar of England and Wales, and hence professional misconduct by virtue of paragraph 802.1 of the Code.'

Crystal's counsel, Mr Swift QC, made a plea of mitigation and it was 'ordered that Mr Jonathan Crystal be suspended from practice as barrister and from enjoyment of all rights and privileges as member of the Honourable Society of Middle Temple and be prohibited from holding himself out as being a barrister without disclosing his suspension for one month.' The Treasurer of the Middle Temple pronounced the sentence on 17 May and the suspension came into effect from that date.

About a month later, two CID officers from Brighton, after making a prior arrangement, came to London to see Jeff Fugler to find out if he could give evidence regarding a case they were investigating. What they discovered in Fugler's possession was to have a dramatic impact on Venables.

Chapter 31

The policemen and the judge

On 6 September England played Colombia at Wembley. They were not England's first choice – they would have preferred Argentina but they wanted much more money. Venables wanted Croatia but that fell victim to the Balkan wars. Nevertheless Colombia was still an attractive fixture, a creative South American side which played the sort of football that Venables wanted to test England.

How much the match told Venables remains debatable. It finished 0–0 with Venables making the usual noises of England learning and getting themselves geared for the championships. The most memorable moment of the match was the Colombian goalkeeper saving a shot while doing a back flip, which so caught the nation's attention that some tabloid newspapers immediately asked goalkeepers to demonstrate if they could emulate it, despite warnings from coaches that that could ruin a player's career.

On the morning of the match, there was a phone call to Graham Kelly from a police officer regarding some new evidence he had found which greatly concerned him. The caller was the officer from Brighton CID who, along with his colleague, had in June called on Jeff Fugler who was a possible witness.

In the course of the conversation with Jeff Fugler, Fugler, trying to find some documents, discovered he still had copies of the Silver Rose and First Wave invoices and the handwritten Brown note with details of the Sheringham transfer which he had inadvertently picked up in Brown's office on 27 August 1992, the day of Sheringham's transfer. Fugler now told the officers the story that he would later tell the court, that these invoices to raise £50,000 from Tottenham were in connection with the Sheringham transfer.

They were struck by the fact that the Silver Rose invoice was raised two days before the Sheringham transfer, had the same mis-leading wording as the First Wave invoice, and the invoices were addressed to Brown. The officers were aware that there had been bung allegations regarding the Sheringham transfer and these invoices suggested that something here needed to be investigated. These Silver Rose papers were not relevant to the Brighton CID officers' case but, since it seemed to shed some light on the un-resolved Sheringham transfer, the officers felt they should put a call through to the highest authorities in charge of English football. Hence the call to Kelly.

Kelly's surprise on receiving such a call on the morning of the international can be imagined. At this stage it seems there was nothing that threatened the bond between Venables and the FA, and if he had off-the-field problems they were being contained. There were court cases pending but the FA had helped deal with what it felt was the most explosive. The Berry libel action was listed for hearing on 2 October, the week preceding the Norway match, but Venables had assured the FA it would not interfere with preparations for the match.

Venables, by threatening to resign, had also persuaded the FA, almost unprecedentedly, to intervene with the judge and put back the major libel action brought by Sugar. Sugar had wanted it to coincide with Berry's action but, as a result of Millichip writing to the judge, it had been put back to October 1996, well after the European championships. Interestingly the FA had not intervened in the one case where it could be said to have maximum influence. This was the one brought by Venables against Paul Kirby, an FA councillor. Here were two men from Lancaster Gate fighting each other, Venables was pursuing Kirby, but the FA took no action.

There is also some evidence to suggest that the FA was trying to monitor the DTI investigation into Venables. By the summer the DTI had commenced their investigation by assigning a prosecu-tion file number – 1005/94 – to Venables, but no decision had been reached on whether any offence had been committed. On 13 July 1995, Tarvin had written to interview a potential witness regarding Venables. In the letter Tarvin made it clear that the DTI were in-vestigating an allegation that Venables may have committed an offence under Section 47 of the 1986 Financial Services Act in that he 'may have made a misleading, false or deceptive statement in an Offer Document'. Whether the FA knew the details of the case is not known, but it was suggested to one DTI investigator that he might want to keep the FA informed about how it was proceeding. The investigator replied that if he investigated an employee of Unigate he did not keep the Unigate managing director informed, so why should the FA be different?

But if the FA was unable to pierce DTI secrecy it could always pretend that all this was extraneous to football. Now suddenly a policeman was raising questions about strange invoices and dodgy dealings on the Sheringham transfer, a deal which went to the heart of football. It could not be considered extraneous to football and the Premier League inquiry into the case had still to report.

But apart from surprise and, it seems, a sort of inarticulate worry, Kelly had nothing to offer. The Brighton CID officers put the phone down extremely disappointed. The officers had thought Kelly might be concerned. The guardians of the English game did not seem to want to know anything or even be curious as to what light it might or might not throw on the past activities of their coach.

About this time I had become aware that some new information throwing light on the Sheringham transfer had emerged. I began my investigations and spoke to the police officers. As serving officers they pointed out that they had to act within their guidelines and I carried on making further enquiries.

For the next few weeks I investigated the mystery of Silver Rose. One of my early calls was to Jeff Fugler but he refused to be interviewed, let alone see me. I was not surprised. I had often tried to talk to Bryan Fugler but he had just as consistently refused to talk. On one occasion we agreed to meet but he cancelled at the last minute. If the Fuglers, Jeff and Bryan, had a story to tell they were not going to tell me.

This still left me with plenty to work on. At that stage, in all the court affidavits and the various evidence on the Sheringham transfer, there had been mention of only one First Wave invoice for £50,000 plus VAT. The fact that First Wave had issued another invoice without VAT was news, the existence of a Silver Rose invoice, dated two days earlier with the same wording, was quite incredible. It further complicated a transfer which still remains mysterious. Tottenham's then accountants confirmed that Tottenham had only ever paid on one First Wave invoice, the £50,000 plus VAT – the VAT was of course subsequently returned – and had not seen either the First Wave invoice without VAT or the Silver Rose invoice. McLintock confirmed to me that only one invoice was raised but in any case he could not help any more because he did not deal with the administration. Invoices and such other matters were the province of his partner Graham Smith. He also told me that Smith had given up the sports management business and left the country to go and live in America.

I was very puzzled by the reaction of Bernard Berrick, from whose Monte Carlo fax number the Silver Rose invoice was said to have been sent to Brown at Tottenham. When I first rang him he was curious and informed me that Jeffrey Silver of Silver Rose was the father-in-law of his son Steven. While he did not want to say much about Jeffrey Silver – 'He is after all an in-law,' said Berrick – his manner seemed to imply his business practices might be worth looking into and he mentioned that Silver had featured in *Private Eye*. He promised to ring me if he found out more. A few days later when I rang him he sounded very upset, saying that according to his source on the *Daily Telegraph*, I did not work there and was some sort of imposter.

Even more intriguing was the reaction from the Venables camp. Venables' statement in court, when Sugar had made the allegations, said he had no part in drawing up the terms of the invoice. I decided to contact Brown, his name having featured with all three invoices. His version of what had happened in the transfer was little known. I left messages on his answer phone and sent a fax requesting an interview.

I did not hear from Brown but the next day, Friday 29 September, the day before the article was to be published, the *Daily Telegraph* received a fax from Clifford Chance, the lawyers acting for Venables' publishers, warning that my article on the Sheringham transfer might be a contempt of court. On the Monday the libel action brought by Tony Berry against Venables' autobiography was due to be heard, and the lawyers were threatening us with the Attorney-General. The libel action was about allegations that had nothing to do with the Sheringham transfer and we decided to ignore the threat.

However, that Friday evening, sometime after 5pm, David Davies of the FA rang the *Daily Telegraph*. He wanted to speak to

David Welch, the sports editor. Welch was not there and I took the call. Davies said he had heard I was planning a Sheringham article: 'You must be careful what you print. I understand that new information has come into the inquiry on this.' What sort of new information, who had told him? I asked. Davies did not know what the new information was but as for his source he said, 'You know where this information is coming from', meaning the Venables camp. 'I just thought I would mark your cards because something new might be coming up.' The impression I got was that the Venables camp had asked Davies to fire a warning shot across my bows. But since Davies could not tell me what the new information was we decided we had no reason to alter our plans to publish.

Two hours after this conversation Jeff Fugler was presenting his witness statement in the case he had brought against Scribes West. Although previous witness statements had not mentioned the Silver Rose material, he had had a change of lawyers who felt that since credibility would be a major issue in the case everything should be mentioned. So he included the invoices and narrated the story of his meeting in Brown's office on 27 August 1992.

The witness statements were sent to Venables' lawyers at about 7pm that Friday. The fact that these invoices were to be part of the court case had been intimated to them two days earlier on 27 September, when the list of documents exchanged. Fugler's witness statement gave the explanation of why the documents were part of the case.

I was, of course, totally unaware of this and only came to know about the coincidence after the court case started in November – the exact details of the remarkable coincidence of timing of which Venables' lawyers would make so much did not become known until 7 December, more than two months later.

Venables clearly did not see it that way. He saw it as yet another conspiracy. On the Monday after my story was published Brown was in touch with Denton Hall, lawyers for the Premier League inquiry, asserting that the documents were forgeries and that they should get in touch with Jeff Fugler and his lawyers. The implication was that Fugler had supplied me, when he and his lawyers could truthfully assert that they were not my source.

Apart from the *News of the World* reprinting parts of my story, 'Spurs, Teddy and the knickers shop', there was little follow-up and Venables made no public comment on the story. However, just then Venables did have a lot on his mind.

On the Monday following my revelations in Saturday's *Daily Telegraph* Venables had a particularly busy day. In the morning he announced his squad for the Norway-England match, England's first away trip since Dublin. Then, in the afternoon, there was the High Court where the libel action brought by Berry was due to be heard. Venables had by now removed the offending passages from the paperback edition of his autobiography and there had been intensive efforts to settle the case. His publishers, the *Mail on Sunday* which had serialised the book, and Clifford Chance were keen. But for Venables to accept defeat at the hands of Berry was an anathema and he resisted.

Just before the case was due to begin at 2pm Venables, himself, appeared and conferred with his lawyers. This, it seems, was when he was finally persuaded he could not hope to contest the action. He had to surrender and when the court convened a statement was read in open court spelling this out.

Timothy Cassel, QC for Berry, described how Venables had alleged that Berry paid £20,000 for documents stolen from Edennote. Berry was 'not only incensed, but deeply embarrassed and upset by the unjust accusation of theft'. Cassell went on, 'The defendants, having carefully examined the evidence, and in particular Mr Berry's account of his role in the matter, have concluded that the information on which they based the section of Mr Venables' book which is at issue, was quite simply unreliable.'

Lord Williams, the QC who had acted for Scholar in his successful libel action against the *Daily Mail*, and given Venables such an uncomfortable time in the witness box, was now appearing for Venables. He said, 'on behalf of all the defendants I accept all my learned friend has said'. Venables, he conceded, accepted he was given wrong information and, on Venables' and the other defendants' behalf, he apologised to Berry. In the usual style of such actions it was said that Venables, his publishers and the *Mail on Sunday* had agreed to pay 'substantial' damages. This, it seems, amounted to £350,000. In addition to this there would be legal costs on Venables' side making a total bill of upwards of £500,000. No defeat could be more comprehensive and as Berry said, 'It is a complete apology and you cannot do better than that.'

Venables did not hear these words, having slipped away before the case was settled. So while Berry spoke to the press and wondered why the FA had not intervened to settle a matter that should never have come to court, Venables retired to mount a counter-strike. Characteristically this took the form of a press statement. Like the football manager whose post-match press conference can be more important than the match, Venables' press statement tried to reclaim the ground he had lost so comprehensively in court. It would have been entirely understandable had his statement expressed disappointment, but Venables sought to transform his complete apology into a realistic compromise. It was a bit like the famous story about Michael Grade's father – a fervent Charlton supporter – who with his team losing 6–0 at half-time predicted a draw. When the match finished 6–0 he said, 'Well, we got a draw in the second half'.

So Venables seized on the fact that he, himself, did not have to pay a penny to Berry and took much delight in that. He reiterated that the Edennote papers had been stolen and distributed to the media but conceded that 'certain evidence provided to us had proved unreliable'. The implication of his statement was that he could hardly be responsible for wrong information given to him.

However, in his desire to convert a defeat into a draw, Venables went even further than Michael Grade's father would ever have done. Lord Williams, while apologising on Venables' behalf to Berry, had protested that Venables had acted in 'entire good faith'. Berry's counsel made no comment on that, he did not need to, his client had won everything he wanted. But Venables in his press statement used that part of his own counsel's statement and claimed that 'Mr Berry has fully accepted that I acted with honesty and in good faith'. In reality, Williams, as Venables' counsel, was trying to mitigate Venables' role, which was, after all, what he was paid to do.

Venables' behaviour revealed that trait of his character, that he could not accept defeat, he had to dress it in the fashion he liked. He knew how the papers would treat it and he wanted the comfort that this misleading press statement gave him. The *Sun* the next day ran the headline across its back page of one word: 'Humiliated'. The article began: 'Terry Venables has climbed down and said sorry over a libel case which cost £500,000 in damages and legal bills.'

The Venables statement may also have been designed as a straw for the FA to clutch at. The FA statement said, 'We note that it was accepted that Mr Venables had acted in entirely good faith.' The FA seems to have accepted Venables' line that this was not a defeat, but a tactical retreat, which helped keep his powder dry for the libel battle with Sugar.

Yet behind the scenes something else seems to have been going on with the first signs that Venables was worried about his future with England once the European championships were over in June 1996. At this stage there had been little or no speculation about what might happen to Venables once the championships were over. His contract ran out then and the assumption was that the whole question would be looked at after that. That was how England, historically, did things. It had refused, for instance, to give a commitment to Bobby Robson, England's most successful manager after Alf Ramsey, about a new contract when he took England to the semi-finals of the World Cup in 1990.

However, just a week after the defeat in the High Court, and on the eve of the Norway match, suddenly a new contract for Venables took centre stage. On Sunday 8 October, as Venables prepared to take England to Norway, the *Sunday Telegraph* reported that he had turned down a job offer from Inter Milan, worth £1.5m. tax free. Colin Malam, then working with Venables on a football book, revealed that three weeks previously, while on holiday in Spain with Yvette, a representative of Inter Milan approached him and said, 'For any money would you be able to leave now?' Venables rejected the approach explaining, 'I happen to believe in loyalty and honouring contracts.'

Within days Inter denied any such offer. Venables insisted there had been an offer, saying, 'It often happens that there are two sides to every story. I will deal with the Milan thing when the time is right'. The *Sun* asked its readers: 'So who the hell is telling the truth?' And 65% of *Sun* readers who called the 'You the Jury' vote-line believed Inter's version of the story. Inter did appoint an Englishman but it was Roy Hodgson. Colin Malam has since said that Venables could not defend himself by naming the middleman who had approached him because he had promised not to do so. As Malam presented things, it was Venables' critics who were in the wrong with Venables, keeping his word, as the man of honour.

However, to many the whole episode seemed like the classic ploy of the football manager who, worried about a new contract, lets it be known that he is in demand elsewhere. In one of his chats with journalists, during the Oslo trip, Venables had made it clear he wanted his future settled. 'It is no good to me coming out of that tournament with a week left on my contract to sort myself out. I would think it made sense for the future to be sorted out for me and for the FA.'

On the face of it the ploy worked. In Oslo he had discussions with Millichip and Kelly about a new contract and Millichip publicly expressed his keenness to keep Venables as coach for the World Cup. Two days after the match, on 13 October, the *Sun* reported, 'Terry Venables' job as England coach is guaranteed until after the 1998 World Cup.' The next day its sister paper *The Times* predicted, 'The future of Terry Venables as England coach should be secured by Christmas. He has convinced Sir Bert Millichip, the chairman of the Football Association, that he is the man to take England to the 1998 World Cup finals.'

But was this the whole story? How much of this was newspaper hype? A lot, as we shall see. Three months later – within four days of Venables quitting – Venables, himself, put a very different gloss on all this. On 14 January 1996 Malam revealed in the *Sunday Telegraph* that, even at Oslo, as journalists were speculating about a new contract and the *Sun* was telling us we had another three years of Tel, Venables was preparing to quit. 'I know that,' wrote Malam, 'because he had told me before the match of his intention to quit.'

According to Malam, 'It was after fending off questions about Inter at a pre-match press conference in Oslo that Venables told me of his intention not to continue as England coach following the European championships. "There are one or two things I'm not happy about," he said, though without explaining exactly what they were.'

For a journalist to sit on such an explosive story for three months is unusual but Malam explained he was prevented from using the story by the *Daily Mirror* running yet 'another avalanche of so-called exclusives' on Venables' business affairs. Venables told Malam that to reveal it now would look like he was running away. The explanation sounds odd. Although the *Mirror* did attack Venables at the time of the Oslo match, putting a Norse noose round his head and with Nigel Clarke, who had always supported him, writing an open letter asking the Inter president to offer Venables a job, this was on football matters. The *Mirror* exclusives on his business deals came almost a month later and in any event the rest of the press did not share the *Mirror*'s footballing criticism of Venables. The draw with Norway was boring, but everybody seemed to feel Venables was making a fair stab working with the material he had. The only doubt was whether the Christmas tree formation, which meant a lone striker in Alan Shearer – whose goal supply for England had dried up – could really work.

So why did Venables tell Malam he wanted to go and, more intriguingly, what were the one or two things he was 'not happy' about?

Could he have been worried about a bankruptcy petition filed by his former lawyers? He had no sooner returned from Oslo than he had to deal with it. On the afternoon of Friday 13 October, he just managed to avert a petition from Finers, his former lawyers, seeking to make him bankrupt. The petition was due to be heard at 10.30 the following Tuesday, 17 November. The Finers bill, now nearly three years old, had, after adding costs, risen to £10,000. At about 4pm on Friday Finers heard a cheque was on its way. However, given the way Venables had been coping with creditors ever since he came under Brown's influence, why should this relatively minor matter make him want to quit?

Could it be the DTI? Venables had plenty of reason to be worried about the DTI. Tarvin and Dixon had completed their gathering of the witness statements. Their prosecution file was ready. Now it was up to Gervina Jones and the Treasury solicitors to decide what kind of action to launch against Venables.

There is some evidence to suggest the 'one or two things' Venables was unhappy about might have included Silver Rose. It was certainly weighing on Venables' mind. He was well aware that Fugler's Silver Rose allegations had set the clock. The case was due to begin on 8 November and once the hearings began Fugler's witness statement would become a court document. Brown seemed most agitated by it. Soon after my own article appeared Brown had returned to Needham. There had been no action on the conspiracy case since the allegations were made the previous November. Surely, said Brown, this proved a conspiracy and Needham set to work. What Brown was saying, in effect, was that any article that raised questions about Venables must be the work of conspirators and, of course, that suggested Sugar. Criminal conspiracies are notoriously difficult to prove but the interesting question that was not asked was: what if the information was true?

On the evening of 17 October, three days after *The Times* had 'given' the England job to him until the 1998 World Cup finals, Venables rang David Welch. He told Welch he felt the *Telegraph* was being got at, there was another side to the story and he offered to show documents to present his case. Welch was happy to hear his case but emphasised that, as I was the investigating journalist, I would be the one to look at it. Welch rang me to prepare myself for a visit to Scribes, probably accompanied by Welch or his deputy Keith Perry, but no call came.

On the same day that Venables rang Welch to suggest a meeting on Silver Rose, Joe Pawlikowski – by now secretary of Scribes West, and who had been a director of Five Star Batteries for one day – was questioned and released on police bail. The next morning, 18 October, police officers went to Brown's home, seized a quantity of papers and took him to Holborn police station. After questioning, he also was released on police bail. The police had for some time been investigating Five Star Batteries.

One result of this was that another of Venables' business problems began to unravel. Brown had been negotiating with Customs and Excise about back VAT. Scribes had always had problems in this field and Customs had finally sent in bailiff officers armed with a warrant to levy distress. Customs have powers to issue warrants for non-payment and in some ways their powers are greater than those of the Inland Revenue. Something like £160,000 was due and, when the bailiffs arrived, a certain sum was paid to them in cash. Brown then negotiated a deal whereby Scribes West made what is called a 'time to pay' arrangement, a deal crucial to Scribes whose accounts to April 1994 showed that total liabilities exceeded total assets by £204,384. Scribes missed one of these payments although subsequently this was made up.

The police questioning does not appear to have derailed Brown for long. He was soon busy again on Venables' behalf. Back in 1993 Venables had launched two libel writs against the *Daily Mirror*. One was in relation to Harry Harris' article on Venables' talks with Kohler to buy Luton, the other was on Peter Hounam's article, based on Tony Yorke's research, which had first revealed the Edennote-Landhurst connection. Nothing had happened on the Harris-Luton writ and for a long time nothing much happened on the Hounam article either. But suddenly now Venables activated the writ on the Hounam article. This soon involved a third party. Venables' lawyers served a subpoena on Diverse to produce documents and, almost a year after Venables had said in his autobiography that Diverse were opening their files, Diverse did open their files to Venables. It was a shrewd Venables move. As we have seen Yorke, then working for the *Daily Mirror*, had also been involved in the Diverse production and Venables must have felt this would yield material he could employ. It might even help prove his conspiracy theory.

On 24 October Brown, accompanied by solicitors from John Bowden Trainer, went to visit Diverse's offices in Hammersmith and took away almost 1,000 pages of documents relating to Diverse's Venables programme.

In retrospect 24 October is another one of those crucial days for Venables. The Venables camp was determined to prove that the Silver Rose invoice was a forgery. That day his lawyers went to court asking for originals of the invoices from Fugler's lawyers so that they could test them for authenticity. Fugler only had copies and, while his solicitors did give them to Venables' lawyers, since they were not original the tests on them proved a waste of money.

This was also the day Needham, and an assistant, came to see Welch at the offices of the *Daily Telegraph* in Canary Wharf. Needham was investigating whether the Silver Rose invoice was a forgery as part of Venables' conspiracy allegations. The visit was a curious one. Normally, when police officers come to a newspaper, they follow a procedure, first a letter to the editor, then a request to see information a newspaper has and which the newspaper may or may not release. Newspapers asked by police for photographs of demonstrations, for instance, always ask the police to go to court and get an order to produce such photographs. Of course in certain cases, such as child-molesting, the newspaper which has done the investigation will willingly help the police, but there is a fine line for a newspaper between helping the police and becoming a policeman's nark. Needham, however, did not follow this procedure. He rang Welch and said he wanted to have an informal chat.

Needham brought copies of the Silver Rose and First Wave invoices. He also had another invoice which had a signature tippexed out and he showed this to Welch, suggesting that it proved they were all forgeries. Welch pointed out that, because yet another invoice had tippex marks, this did not mean forgeries. In any case the Silver Rose and First Wave invoices had been faxed, it was surely difficult to forge a fax? Also, asked Welch, could not the existence of the Silver Rose invoice, two days before the First Wave invoice, mean Silver Rose was a trial run for the subsequent First Wave invoice? As Welch made this point Needham became very thoughtful and said, 'Now that you put it that way, it could, I suppose.'

Needham also told Welch that he had been misquoted in the Venables book about clearing him in connection with the Landhurst loan and that, with his retirement not far away, he had been asked by his superiors to spend his remaining time in the force clearing up the Silver Rose affair. Welch got the impression that this was an easy-going investigation. He gave the two officers tea and as they left, came out and told his colleagues, 'I have just had a very strange conversation with this policeman.' But Needham's enquiries were more urgent than he had given Welch to understand. On 26 October he was seen at Scribes, probably questioning Brown further about aspects of his investigation.

As it happened the next day, Friday 27 October, the House of Commons was due to debate sport. Kate Hoey was preparing her speech. At this stage I had never spoken to Kate Hoey, although I was aware of her speeches in the House. Hoey had come across the second article I had done on the Sheringham transfer, the follow-up to the Silver Rose one. This quoted Parry as seeing the discovery of the Silver Rose and First Wave invoices as significant. Not having seen the Silver Rose article she was intrigued but could not quite follow its significance. She rang the *Telegraph* and I suggested she look up my original Silver Rose article.

Hoey and her colleague, Patrick Cheney, who has a long association with sports administrators having worked for Denis Howell, Labour's legendary Minister of Sport, had followed various aspects of the Sheringham transfer, in addition to other football stories. They were well aware of the DTI investigation into Venables and I found them both knowledgeable about various aspects of football and sharing a healthy distrust of the propaganda doled out by the football authorities.

In her speech Hoey, as in January, made several well-argued points about sport in general and football in particular, calling again for an independent inquiry into 'our national game, particularly the allegations of corruptions, bungs, alleged match fixing and greed'. Then, referring to the Sheringham transfer, she said, 'Terry Venables has not been cleared and new evidence has recently come to light'. She went through some aspects of my Silver Rose article, mentioning the various invoices, the coincidence of their dates and the fact that they all had the same wording. 'It may be difficult,' concluded Hoey, 'for the Premier League to accept that it does not have the power to get to the bottom of this matter. It cannot subpoena witnesses and it took over a year for it to get Brian Clough to turn up. Nobody is on oath and that makes it difficult to elicit evidence. Much of the story came out afterwards when people in the media asked questions.'

Hoey also referred to the DTI investigating Venables, prefacing it with, 'I do not think that there is any secret about the fact'. Then, after talking of the Section 47 investigation, she said, 'I understand that other matters are being investigated and there may soon be some developments. I do not want to go into the business side of these issues because I am interested only in what is happening in football. However, such matters leave a big question mark over who is in charge of football, who is our national coach. We are soon going into the European championships and we must get to the bottom of this.'

Although barely a dozen MPs attended the debate and the press galleries were nearly empty, Hoey's speech created an enormous wave. Papers which had ignored the Silver Rose story turned to it. The *Sun* dealt with it at length, crediting the *Daily Telegraph*. Venables' immediate response was to say the invoices were forgeries and that Hoey had been naive to accept them at face value. He now claimed that he had insisted the Premier League look into the invoices. But certain questions went unanswered: when had he insisted on an inquiry, and who had made it, he or Brown? And was such a request made after the invoices had entered the public domain through the *Daily Telegraph*? In *Venables' England*, published in April 1996, Venables makes it clear that he sent Brown to the Premier League on the Monday following the *Telegraph* article.

As Hoey was speaking Venables' grandson Sam was having a party to celebrate his sixth birthday. Venables had agreed to an exclusive article for the *News of the World* on the danger of drugs for young footballers. But Hoey's speech resulted in the first part of the article being about Hoey. Venables linked her to a small number of people who were out to destroy his reputation and his life. Hoey's speech gave him a splendid chance to rehash his conspiracy theory.

Difficult as it must have been even for a believer in conspiracy theory to link Hoey's speech to drugs, the *News of the World* somehow contrived to do that. So having complained that such attacks were turning Venables' family's life into a nightmare, the article went on to discuss drugs and how Venables feared for his grandson Sam who, according to Venables, had a wonderful left foot. At this stage the reader almost expected to be told something was wrong with Sam, or even that it had been caused by Hoey, but Granddad Venables was worried about the general condition of the world in which kids were growing up. There were drugs available and unlike his Dagenham days, kids were no longer able to play street football.

The article had a prominent photograph of Venables and his family, Yvette, daughter Nancy and son-in-law Paul, complete with party hats, celebrating Sam's birthday. The way the story was presented, coupled with the headline, 'Kate Hoey is making my family's life a nightmare – Terry Venables lashes out at "cowardly and wicked" Labour MP', gave the impression that somehow Hoey's raising of the Sheringham transfer and the DTI investigations was blighting Sam's life even before he had properly begun it.

But if for *News of the World* readers Venables was seen worrying about Sam's future, privately he must have been worried about his own future with England. Despite confident predictions in the press, Lancaster Gate was not really offering the sort of contract that Venables wanted. A year's extension maybe, or a conditional one, conditional on European championship success and nothing to be signed until June 1996. Even this was tentative, offered in chats with Kelly, with the full international committee, that decides on such issues, still to be involved. Millichip may have favoured a longer contract, but he, himself, was due to retire after the championships and few in the FA shared their chairman's view. As Venables has since revealed, even Kelly's offer of a year's extension was 'not a concrete offer', and in any case quickly withdrawn. Venables now clutched at the hope that the conspiracy theory could be proved, which in essence meant proving that Alan Sugar or people around him constantly fed the press information harmful to him.

On 30 October Needham arrived at the offices of Diverse. He intimated that he had documents related to the programme and was keen to talk to a researcher who had worked on the Diverse programme, now more than two years old. Needham also contacted the researcher who, by this time, was in Manchester and asked her to come to the Chelsea police to help with his enquiries. She, in some anxiety, contacted Diverse and this brought in the Channel Four lawyers. They were intrigued to know how Needham got the documents. On 2 November in a conversation with Channel Four lawyers Needham explained he had received them from Brown but insisted he was legally entitled to have them. Since these documents had been given to Venables' lawyers in a discovery process – whereby the documents remain secret and are not given to a third party until the case comes to court – Channel Four's lawyers wrote to Venables' lawyers asking for clarification that there had been no possible contempt of court. I, in trying to check the story, put some questions to Nick Trainer, Venables' lawyer, and he immediately faxed Channel Four's lawyers accusing them of slander. This resulted in acrimonious exchanges with both sets of lawyers threatening to involve the Law Society.

Needham also went to the House of Commons. Some three months previously Patrick Cheney had contacted Needham, intrigued to discover how he had cleared Venables over the Landhurst loan, as quoted in Venables' autobiography. Needham told him he had been misquoted. Following Hoey's speech, Cheney agreed to meet Needham and his assistant on a confidential basis. It was emphasised that Cheney was not being interviewed as a witness in Needham's investigation. The appointment was for 11am on 7 November. Exactly twenty-four hours earlier Peter Rose, crime correspondent of the *Daily Mail*, rang Cheney and asked him whether Needham was going to interview him. Cheney could not work out how Rose could have known since he, himself, had not told a soul.

Needham came with his assistant. Cheney recalls:

We met in the tea room of the House of Commons. Curious place, curious meeting. It was like *Sweeney* all over. Throughout our meeting Needham's sergeant kept his gaze fixed at me, and, whenever Needham said anything he said, 'Yes, guv', 'No, guv'. Needham was very interested to know where Kate Hoey had got her information. Had she been in touch with Mihir Bose? He asked how people got their information and who was talking to whom. Were we in touch with the Sugar camp? I said we were not spokesmen for the Sugar camp and we had no direct contact. They had not asked us to do anything and our concern was with the wider aspects of football. I said I wanted to clear something up. I said to him, 'You have often been seen at Scribes. I am also very puzzled that you asked me to keep the meeting confidential but Peter Rose knew about it. Is Rose one of your contacts?' As I spoke about Needham going frequently to Scribes, and Rose knowing of our meeting, he gulped. I could see his Adam's apple going up and down. Then there was a silence. Needham and his sergeant looked at one another and the sergeant said, 'I think we know this Rose, don't we, guv? Someone must have said something but it wasn't us.' Needham said, 'No, no, we don't know anything about this.' I also wanted to know how Needham had got involved with Venables. He explained he had been called in to investigate the theft of documents from Venables' company Edennote. His investigation showed that, at most, there was theft of photocopying paper worth 20p. But how, in the course of it, I wondered, had he cleared Venables of any wrongdoing in relation to the loan from Landhurst? Needham said he had to look into it but he had been mis-quoted in Venables' book. However, his superiors had told him it was not worth bothering about. Then Needham explained how this enquiry had restarted following the Silver Rose article when Venables had renewed the charge.

Cheney emerged from his chat with Needham extremely puzzled and told Kate Hoey, 'I have met this copper and had a very strange conversation, very strange.'

The next day, 8 November, was the day set for the start of Jeff Fugler's case. Only two days earlier, on the afternoon of 6 November, had I become aware of the date. Fugler's lawyer, Ash Karim, rang the *Telegraph* and left a message for me. Karim, acting for the Pakistani cricketer Javed Miandad, had once collected sub-stantial damages from the *Telegraph* and, when I made contact, he regaled me with the story. He had got in touch with me because he wanted to see some recent cuttings of mine relating to Brown.

I was intrigued that the case was coming to court at all. Yet in this case, in a virtually unknown court – even taxi-drivers had to be told about Central London County Courts where courtrooms were so small witnesses sat next to the press and public – there would virtually be a parade of the Venables 'family': Terry himself, Brown, Eric Hall, Joe Pawlikowski, Yvette, and Ted Buxton, the England scout, were all listed as potential witnesses. And all to fight over an alleged debt of just under £20,000. The case meant Venables would take the witness stand for the first time since he had appeared in the libel action brought by Scholar more than three and a half years before. He and his lawyers had been involved in many cases since then, many of them much more important, there had been plenty of writs and Venables had, occasionally, attended court, but never taken the stand.

I thought Venables' decision to fight suggested he felt he had a very good chance of success. But Karim, too, was confident of winning. A flamboyant character, he interspersed his conversation with stories about Javed Miandad and other Pakistani cricketers. He had also acted for Sarfraz Nawaz when his barrister on that case was Jonathan Crystal, whom Karim knew very well. Karim was also close to Bryan Fugler, while one of Venables' witnesses was Eric Hall, first cousin of Bryan and Jeff. This made the case all the more of a family quarrel and when Eric Hall gave evidence in support of Venables' case, his aunt, Jeff Fugler's mother, sat in court watching their nephew trying to defeat her son.

Karim predicted that Jeff Fugler would win. I warned the office of the case and, on the day of the hearing, the *Daily Telegraph* had, besides myself, an experienced court reporter and a photographer ready to snap Venables, Brown and Fugler as they arrived. I was relieved to find no other newspapers had got wind of the case.

Meanwhile, just as we were waiting for the court to sit, across London in the offices of Herbert Smith, at about 10.30 that morning, Needham was meeting Colin Sandy with Alan Watts also present. Needham wanted to know about the Sheringham transfer. Sandy suggested he ask his fellow officers at Holborn, SO6, and read the statement Sandy had given them. However, there was one question Sandy had not dealt with and which Needham was keen to ask. Had Sandy seen Fugler on 27 August 1992 at White Hart Lane? Sandy said he had not seen Fugler. The significance of this question and answer would become clear only as the court case started.

The opening arguments of counsels on both sides took nearly all day and Fugler did not get to the stand. Also a problem emerged, at least for the press and the public. I had assumed that once Fugler took the stand his witness statement would then be available for public examination. Fugler's lawyers had assured me of that. Then we would know what he was saying. In modern court practice not all the evidence is read out in court. Much of it is presented in witness statements which the judge reads – this is to save court time and prevent surprises – but once the witness takes the stand and confirms it is his statement it becomes a court document which can be reported.

However, the practice at County Courts is different. Here the judge needed to give his assent before witness statements could be made available to the public. Late on the afternoon of 8 November

Arthur Wynn Davies, the *Daily Telegraph*'s lawyer, found this out and we had to ask Fugler's counsel to intervene on our behalf and ask the judge to rule on this. Venables' lawyers said they would have to consult.

As a result of this there was a lot of hustle and bustle between me and the Fugler lawyers, in particular Karim's son, Imran, who was also working on the case. Notes were passed between us about what action we should take to get a copy of the witness statement. This would hardly be worth pointing out except that, a few weeks later, when Venables returned to his long-standing belief that there was a conspiracy against him, his lawyers saw my exchanging notes as evidence of my involvement in the case. A ridiculous charge, but it highlighted the state of mind of the Venables camp. At this stage, however, conspiracy had not been publicly aired and we were more concerned with getting hold of the witness state-ment. The *Telegraph*, seeing this as an important principle of the ability to report court cases fully, hired a counsel and the next day he came to argue our case. The Venables camp initially sought a short adjournment, then opposed the *Telegraph*'s application, argu-ing that the witness statement should not be open for public inspection. When it was suggested that, in that case, Fugler could just read his statement from the witness box, this was also opposed by Venables' counsel who pointed out that the judge had earlier ruled that witnesses would not have to read their statements. There was an interesting argument about when the statement would be open for inspection: would it be when the witness took the stand or after cross-examination? The judge, who had been making witty references to Silver Rose and the naughty knickers company, felt that if it was after cross-examination it would be like putting the cart before the horse. Then in an aside he added: 'I could use a ruder expression.' He ruled that witness statements would be avail-able as soon as the witness had taken the stand and confirmed he stood by his statement. It was an important victory for freedom of press and the proper reporting of court cases.

By mid-afternoon Venables had come to court, although only for a short time to see what was going on. The day was dominated by Fugler in the witness stand. His statement proved to be, as Karim had promised, explosive. With an agency man present all the papers had it but the *Daily Telegraph*'s coverage was the most com-prehensive, complete with a front page photograph of Venables looking far from happy.

For Venables it must have been like his worst nightmare, allegations of 'financial impropriety', not only in relation to the Sheringham transfer, but also in asking Fugler to over-invoice Tottenham to offset fees from Scribes. Fugler also alleged that Crystal had assured him of getting him lots of work from Tottenham if he did work for Scribes West.

The Venables camp knew they had to defuse the Silver Rose issue. On the opening day, as Fugler's counsel Shane Dougall took the judge through the documents, Venables' counsel Michael Jefferis rose to say, 'On Silver Rose both sides are agreed it is a forgery.' Dougall immediately rose to correct him, 'We have not agreed to anything of the sort.' Jefferis tried his best to discredit Silver Rose and Fugler when Fugler took the stand. But under cross-examination Fugler, very truthfully, denied he had fed me the invoices, explaining how he had acquired them and then given them to Brighton CID officers. Despite all his efforts Jefferis could not shake Fugler. At the end of the three days allotted to the case it was far from over, Venables was yet to enter the witness box, and the case was adjourned. This left Venables to cope with the problems created by Fugler's testimony.

By Saturday other papers were trying to catch up with the *Daily Telegraph*. The *Daily Mail* reported an unnamed member of the international committee of the FA expressing concern about Venables' constant embroilment in litigation. The committee man was quoted as saying, 'It is one thing after another. There always seems to be something else coming up. It does worry us.' Neil Harman, who broke the story, speculated that unless Venables 'clears himself of all allegations he will not be kept on for the next World Cup campaign'.

That weekend Venables was with England preparing for Switzerland's visit to Wembley the following Wednesday. He knew he had to organise a counter-strike. It came on the Saturday. Predictably it was a press statement, but not from Venables. It came from David Davies, who was sitting next to Venables at the press conference. He not only backed Venables but said, 'Within recent days Terry has made the FA aware of evidence of a concerted and organised campaign to discredit him. We have also heard of a police investigation into such a campaign. We will clearly be seeking to keep abreast of all developments in this investigation.'

At this stage few outside a very small circle knew that Venables had lodged a criminal conspiracy complaint or that Needham was investigating it. Although some of the Sunday papers reported that the original complaint was a year old the way it was presented made it seem like a major new development. Nobody mentioned Sugar or Tottenham but it was clear who was meant to be the arch conspirator.

Venables, who had told the press on Saturday, 'I think anyone with half a brain knows what's going on', had every reason to be satisfied with the way the Sunday papers converted what looked like a very tricky situation for him into such a blazing counterattack. This was the righteous man calling in the police to set matters right. For the Sunday papers the story had all the magic words required: Scotland Yard, cops called in, criminal conspiracy, and they had a field day. 'Venables calls in Scotland Yard,' thundered the *Sunday Telegraph* where at least one journalist fantasised that Needham's informal call on Welch was some sort of raid on its sister paper. Some newspapers also saw arrests imminent. Alan Hubbard in the *Observer* suggested that papers would shortly be sent to the Crown Prosecution Service and four people could be charged with conspiracy to pervert the course of justice.

Yet Venables, in his eagerness to push the idea of conspiracy, had got one tiny detail wrong. He said he had lodged the complaint, when it had been Brown. The next day I established that not only was Brown's complaint a year old but that the FA had known about it for a year. Davies conceded the point but said, 'Only recently did we become aware that it is an on-going investigation.' I also highlighted Needham's investigations and his pattern of visits to media offices which had written or broadcast critical items about Venables.

While the football press was as pro-Venables as ever, not everyone took such a sycophantic attitude. Michael Parkinson, in his inimitable style combining wit with shrewdness, suggested Venables should step down while he cleared his name. And co-inciding with England's match against Switzerland Harry Harris, in the *Daily Mirror*, ran a whole series focusing on Venables, in particular his role as Tottenham's chief executive and his tendency to blur private and business spending. It was hard-hitting and ended with details of a taped conversation between David Webb and David Dent, the Football League chief executive, about the alleged bung Webb had received from Venables. Webb claimed that the payment was for scouting work which Venables offered in compensation for not making him manager of Tottenham.

Outwardly Venables seemed to brush aside the *Daily Mirror*'s attack, fortified by the fact that on the field, in perhaps their best performance under Venables, England beat Switzerland and Steve Stone emerged as a great find. Even more gratifyingly Sheringham scored an electrifying goal. But no sooner was the match over than Venables' actions betrayed worry that his pet conspiracy theory was coming apart.

On the afternoon of Thursday 16 November, he rang Welch again. This time, in contrast to the earlier conversation, he sounded deflated. Talking about the Silver Rose invoice he asked Welch, 'Did I sign it?' I had made the point in one of my articles that Venables had not followed up on his offer to Welch to show the *Daily Telegraph* his own evidence which would contradict my Silver Rose article of 30 September. Venables told Welch, 'I am sorry you feel I did not follow up on that but I knew Needham was coming to see you and he had the evidence.' It suggested a close and rather curious connection between Needham and Venables.

Scotland Yard had now begun to look at Needham's investigation. Alan Sugar had complained and the Yard was not pleased to receive shoals of press calls on the Saturday night about it. Davies' announcement had caught them by surprise. For one thing it inconvenienced Needham, who was holding a family party that weekend, and had to be disturbed in order to answer press enquiries. More significantly, there were doubts higher up in the Yard about the way Needham was carrying on the investigation.

In a sense the high profile which Venables and the FA had given it, in order to deflect the Fugler sleaze allegations, had put the spotlight on Needham and his activities. So within days of the FA and Venables blazing it across the papers, Peter Brant, commander of the operational crime unit in Central London, was asked to look at what Needham had done and determine whether this was still a criminal matter. By Friday 17 November, I had established that such a review was on and when I tried to speak to Needham he referred me to Brant.

While Brant decided the fate of Venables' conspiracy theory, the DTI were deciding what they should do with Venables the businessman. It had been a long and lengthy debate. The decision was to take a civil trial to disqualify him as director which would be before a Chancery judge. He might not be impressed by talk of Le Saux's hamstring, or Shearer and the Christmas tree. It was now up to Jonathan Evans, the DTI minister, to sanction the disqualification.

Now in a curious way, although totally unrelated, Brant and the DTI seemed to be marching in step. By Wednesday 22 November Brant had decided that, whatever Needham's investigations had revealed, it was not a criminal matter. It was best left to civil authorities. The conspiracy investigation was over.

But Venables refused to accept that. He even found a conspiracy in the fact that I revealed Brant's decision in the *Daily Telegraph* even before he had received the letter. 'How can this be?' he asked, suggesting another deeply laid plot. The explanation is more prosaic. Not only had I been following the story with interest but, ever since I had established that Brant was reviewing it, I would ring the press officer every day, often more than once a day, to find out what was happening. Earlier that Wednesday I spoke to him and again expressed my interest. The moment Brant had reached a decision and logged it with the press office, I got a call to ring the press officer. When I did he read out a simple press statement. Any other journalist could have got the same information. None made the call.

The very day that Brant decided there was no criminal conspiracy case for Needham to investigate the DTI decided to act on Venables. Jonathan Evans had by now decided that the DTI should commence proceedings against Venables and move to disqualify him as a director. It was almost his last act as DTI minister – the following week he moved to the Lord Chancellor's department. So, on Wednesday 22 November, the DTI wrote what is known as a 'ten-day letter' to Venables, the ten days meant to correct mistakes such as the DTI getting the wrong Jones, the father instead of the son, or some such mistaken identity. The ten days can also be used by directors of public companies to organise their affairs before they fight an action.

It is not clear when exactly Venables received the letter but that weekend, two Sunday tabloids, the *News of the World* and the *Sunday Express*, reported a new Venables claim. This was that the signature on the First Wave invoice on which Tottenham had paid £50,000 plus VAT was not his but had been forged. 'It's definitely not my signature on that invoice.' The *News of the World* brought in an expert and showed him the McLintock invoice and compared it to the signature Venables now claimed was his genuine one. The expert was convinced the signatures did not match.

If Venables hoped that would be the end of the matter, he was disappointed. The main reason for the expert's opinion was that the signature Venables claimed was genuine was a signature he had started using recently. In this version he spelled out 'Terry Venables' in full when signing his name. On the McLintock invoice he had signed as 'TF Venables' with T and F clearly visible, which had been his signature historically.

All these Sunday tabloid articles did was to give Harry Harris one of his easier targets. He produced some thirty Venables signatures, many of them affidavits signed before solicitors, showing he had always signed TF Venables, exactly the way he had signed the McLintock invoice. In two and a half years, ever since the invoice had come into the public domain, he had said a lot about the Sheringham transfer but nothing about his signature on the invoice not being genuine. Now suddenly, four days after the DTI had decided to bring charges against them, this had become a burning issue. Why? This was not the first time Venables had claimed forgery. He had done it in October 1994 when *Panorama* had produced Landhurst leases which bore his signature. And then, too, Harris, using the expert witness Michael Handy, had persuasively questioned Venables' claim.

On 30 November, four days after the tabloids had helped raise the spectre of yet another Venables signature being forged, I had a front-page story in the *Daily Telegraph* revealing that the DTI had sent the ten-day letter and they were going for disqualification. Later it emerged that the DTI had framed nineteen charges in relation to four companies: Scribes West, Edennote, Tottenham Hotspur plc and Tottenham Hotspur Football and Athletic Club Ltd, based on Tarvin's 400-page report. In addition there was a 118-page affidavit that Graham Horne had prepared.

The FA's reaction was predictable. They continued to pretend that, contrary to the popular football song, there was in fact not one but two Terry Venables. Venables the businessman had nothing to do with Venables the football coach. This was despite the fact that when the alleged offences were committed his business was football, being in charge of Tottenham which is nothing if not a football club. If the FA affected unconcern, there was more than a touch of bravado in Venables' response. Venables seemed to feel that he had been vindicated by the fact that the DTI was going for a civil action not a criminal one. His line seemed to be: after nearly two years of investigation is this all you can produce? He also dismissed the charges as technical and complained yet again about press leaks. This made the DTI, already paranoid, even more paranoid and they had yet another leaks inquiry. Their chief press officer even warned me about trying to talk to the investigators.

Venables' dismissal of the charges against him as technical was interesting. Just over ten days earlier, with mounting speculation about a possible DTI prosecution, Venables was asked how he reacted to a possible fifteen-year ban as a director. He said, 'Though it is now clearly accepted that the source of virtually all the allegations is the same small group it disappoints me the media continue to cover reports as though this source is honest and reliable.' This did not amount to a denial of any DTI action, or even an assertion of his innocence, but by providing such a response Venables helped the paper to use this headline: 'Tel furious over 15-year ban slur.' The newspaper may not have meant to suggest it, but the implication of the headline was that talk of DTI action was propaganda being put out by Venables' enemies. And even when the DTI ten-day letter was publicly revealed that attitude persisted. So on the morning I wrote my front-page story in the *Daily Telegraph* about the DTI action a radio presenter saw it as yet more mud being thrown at Venables. If anything, that suggestion was a slur was on how the DTI had done its job. Far from throwing mud it was making serious allegations. Interestingly, a few days later, when I revealed that Brown, too, was being charged, but that he would face criminal prosecution, there was no response from the Venables camp.

Venables now seemed to pin his hopes on a victory in the Fugler case and he was supremely confident. Shortly before the revelation of the DTI action, Paul Riviere had two meetings with Venables. Riviere was still angry about Venables' book and wanted a retraction. In the summer there had been considerable exchange of legal letters and Riviere had decided that he would stay any legal action until various investigations into Venables and Brown were complete because of the considerable cost of litigation.

The two men met at the Carlton Tower and, as he had two years earlier, Venables promised to arrange a meeting with Brown to sort things out. This time he kept his word and, ten days after this meeting, the three met, again at the Carlton Tower. Both Venables and Brown exuded an arrogant confidence. Venables sensationally claimed that not all Berry's costs had been paid by his publishers, a claim which came as a surprise to Berry's lawyers. The duo were confident they would win against Fugler. Brown dismissed the police investigation into Five Star Batteries as a trumped-up charge. As Venables had always said, he did not understand why Riviere was so against Brown. Riviere had wanted a meeting with Brown for two years in order for him to confirm to Venables that he, Riviere, knew nothing of what was going on in companies such as the Independent Balloon Co. Brown told Venables in Riviere's presence that this was indeed the case. Riviere insisted on an apology for the remarks in the book. As they parted, Brown suggested it might be possible for Riviere to get an apology from Venables, if Riviere helped Venables over his *Panorama* libel action. He did not specify what help was needed. Riviere made it clear he could only tell the truth about his dealings with *Panorama*. Venables assured him that he would hear from his lawyer by the beginning of December but the deadline came and went and Riviere heard nothing.

And, despite his public show of confidence to Riviere, Venables decided that for the second round of Fugler he had to try something different. The first three days of hearings had not gone well. We are 3–0 up, claimed Shane Dougall, particularly after the mauling Brown had taken in the witness box when the judge warned him for evading the questions about his disastrous business record. So, with the police having abandoned the conspiracy investigation, Venables decided to use the Fugler trial to revive the conspiracy charge. He had tried it before, using Yorke's evidence, when attempting to save Edennote in May 1994. It had not worked. Now he would use not friendly journalists but journalists he saw as his enemies to save his own reputation.

The two journalists he chose were myself and Harry Harris. On Friday 1 December, a process server arrived with subpoenas for me and Harris at 1 Canada Square, Canary Wharf, where the offices of both the *Daily Telegraph* and the *Daily Mirror* are located. The process server was unable to serve subpoenas on us as we were not there. I took service at about 3pm on Monday 4 December, at the offices of Bindman & Partners, the lawyers the *Daily Telegraph* had appointed for me. It was a 'subpoena duces tecum', which means 'come to court with certain documents'. I was asked to produce the Silver Rose and First Wave invoices and any other documents relevant to the case. Harris was asked for other documents pertaining to the articles he had written. We were clearly going to resist and the hearing was set for Monday 11 November, the day before the Fugler case was to restart.

Our hearing revealed that Venables was changing jockeys in

mid-race. Michael Jefferis, who had not exactly shone on the first part of the hearing, was now relegated to junior with David Farrer taking over. A QC, he had the bearing and the style of a silk, more significantly he was a man hardened in criminal practice. Given the case involved a £20,000 debt in a county court the employment of a QC was unusual, Farrer was clearly unfamiliar with the surroundings of the Central London County Court, and it must have cost Venables as much money, if not more, than the money Fugler was claiming. It showed how much Venables was investing in a victory and Farrer was there to push the conspiracy theory. The police may have discarded it; could Venables get a judge, in a civil action, to accept it?

In trying to convince the judge that Harris and I should take the witness stand Farrer conceded that, contrary to what the subpoena said, the Venables camp was not interested in the documents we had. They already had them and they were part of the court record. What they wanted to know was, who had given us the information? Although he did not mention Sugar at our hearing, in a few days it was clear that Sugar was the man Venables was targeting. Farrer also made an interesting admission.

Journalists are protected from disclosing sources by Section 10 of the Contempt of Court Act 1981. It requires something major like national interest to override it. This was, probably, the decisive factor in the Sarah Tisdall affair, the Ministry of Defence official who had leaked to the *Guardian*. Her identity was disclosed and she was jailed. In this connection Farrer emphasised that the Venables camp was not suggesting that anybody had done anything criminal, so there was no question of imprisonment. So if we disclosed our source that person, unlike Sarah Tisdall, could not be jailed. Given that, only a few days earlier, Venables was pursuing a criminal complaint against alleged conspirators this was a significant admission. However, for all Farrer's silken skills, the Recorder, Mr David Williams, was not convinced and dismissed the petition, granting costs to Harris and myself.

This was not the only blow for Venables. That evening Karim informed Venables' lawyers that they would be introducing new evidence to prove that Fugler was telling the truth when he said he was at Tottenham on 27 August 1992. This would come in the form of Tottenham security logs which had been subpoenaed from Tottenham.

Next day the Fugler case resumed, although with Venables busy with England – that night they played Portugal and were fortunate to get a draw – it was the rest of the Venables clan who filled the stage. There was Frank McLintock, who admitted the Sheringham invoice was not properly worded, and had broken the then FA ban on use of agents in transfers. His plea was that this was outdated law, a curious reason to justify breaking it. Yvette looked striking in red but did not impress with her words, more so as she left the witness box complaining, 'I came to talk about the ten thousand and nobody asked me about it.'

Fugler's counsel Dougall was eager to try to prove that Brown had committed contempt of court. The *People* of 3 December, in trying to discredit Fugler, had quoted from McLintock's witness statement, which at the time was privileged. How did they get hold of it? The article quoted a 'close friend' of Brown. Was this close friend Brown himself? asked Dougall. Brown claimed he did not know who this 'close friend' was and he denied he was the source. And despite the production of the log Brown continued to deny that he had seen Fugler on 27 August 1992.

The log proved decisive and its production was a trump card for Fugler. Farrer did his best to discredit it, even got special leave to bring Fugler back to the witness stand to cross-examine him on it. However, during the cross-examination, Farrer, in trying to trap Fugler, trapped himself. Fugler, in answer to a question, showed he had read the log more thoroughly than Farrer. The judge was impressed. As he said afterwards, the log may not have been entirely satisfactory, but it did prove that Fugler was telling the truth when he said he was at White Hart Lane on the day of the Sheringham transfer and had met Brown.

The next day Ted Buxton, the England scout, took the stand in support of Brown's claim that Fugler was not there that day. Buxton had not seen him, also Buxton was not shown on the log as coming in and out of the ground. But that still did not mean Fugler was not there and all Buxton's testimony did was present a bizarre picture of English pubs. In the course of cross-examination Buxton claimed he never visited pubs, because he only drank wine. For the real wine we had to wait for Venables, and he took the stand immediately after Buxton.

Hours after England had earned a draw with a polished Portuguese side, and just about the time that Venables' predecessors had held press conferences to talk football, Venables came to court to talk business. The ground-floor courtroom – the case had moved from the basement to the ground floor between November and December – could hardly accommodate everyone and some of the journalists sat on the floor. The excitement even seemed to be conveyed to the men on the scaffolding outside the courtroom. Venables had often said he was waiting for his day in court 'My time will come,' he had said. It came just before 11am on 13 December.

Venables, looking dapper, was in his element from the beginning. He had come without his glasses but the judge lent him a pair and the court adjourned while his clerk went to fetch them. The judge then joked about the pair being sold at Sotheby's the next week. Even Dougall seemed overawed, suggesting that Venables had a brother when he meant Jeff Fugler had a brother. '1–0 to you, Mr Venables,' said Dougall. 'If you score in the second half it will be 1–1,' responded Venables, which was exactly what had happened in the Portugal match. And there were other Venables cracks, so familiar to football journalists who had covered his press conferences over the years. When Dougall tried to hurry him along with, 'We haven't got all day, Mr Venables,' Venables replied, 'I am not going anywhere.' Everyone laughed.

However, the laughter punctuated the serious point Venables wanted to make: use the witness box to advertise his conspiracy theory. He suggested that there was a link between Tottenham and Fugler, 'because of the amount of information coming from Tottenham. Unless he found them in the street. I don't know where else it could have come from.' There was also a plaintive note admitting that people thought him 'a shady character' and the whole thing was so unfair. When he spoke of his paranoia the judge remarked that even paranoids have enemies.

But he was forced on the back foot when asked to resolve the contradictions between his autobiography and his witness statement in relation to the Sheringham story about the cash payment to McLintock. We know what he said in his autobiography, how he had asked for the money to be paid to McLintock, and then discovered a few days later that McLintock had been paid in cash. But in his second witness statement he claimed he only knew of the cash payment from a television programme, some four months after he had left Tottenham. Dougall pressed him on this and he grudgingly admitted his autobiography was inaccurate on this point. It was to prove a damaging admission.

By the time he took the witness stand he had had the summons, along with supporting affidavits, from the DTI detailing their case against him. The DTI had issued this on 11 December, summoning him to court on 12 February 1996. However, news of the summons was not yet publicly known and in the witness box Venables continued to insist that the DTI was prosecuting him only over technical offences. He said: '*Panorama* accused me of criminal proceedings. I was shady, I was dishonest, robbing the banks, and all these wild allegations which, as you know, the DTI pursued with me and they have cleared me of criminal proceedings; cleared me of dishonesty. They say, there might be technical breaches. Where does *Panorama* stand today on that, after these allegations?' The question was disingenuous to say the least but such was the beguiling performance of Venables that by lunch-time, as he left the stand, the journalists were unanimous that he had charmed the judge and would win the case.

This impression was strengthened in the afternoon when Farrer introduced the conspiracy theory. In response to Dougall's point, Farrer made it clear he saw Sugar as the conspirator, the man who was the third party behind it all and had been stoking the Fugler action, feeding him with all sorts of information including, possibly, the Silver Rose invoice.

Here Sugar had, unwittingly, provided Venables with a weapon. After the first part of the Fugler hearings in November, Sugar had got Herbert Smith to write to Karim. The letter said that, since court references had been made to Tottenham's affairs, and given they were not involved in the case, Tottenham needed copies of witness statements. Also would the resumed hearing have other references to Tottenham? If so Tottenham might move the trial judge and intervene in the matter. It was rather a huffy, peremptory letter of the sort an overlord might write to a subordinate. Worse still a copy was sent to John Bowden Trainer.

Karim took exception to the tone and the fact that Herbert Smith had suggested that they only knew of this case through media coverage. On 3 November, five days before the trial began, the Karims had contacted Herbert Smith. They were researching into Brown, could the Sugar camp help? The Sugar camp decided that the Pridie Brewster report on Brown would be made available. So on receiving Herbert Smith's letter Karim wrote an indignant reply, mentioning all this. As Herbert Smith had sent a copy to John Bowden Trainer, so Karim's reply had to be sent to them and the Venables camp seized on this, crying conspiracy.

Yet even here Venables had a holed ship. The Sugar camp had

helped Fugler, but the earliest contact with Herbert Smith was 3 November, long after Silver Rose had entered the picture, so how could that invoice have been supplied by Sugar? Despite this, Farrer pushed the conspiracy as best he could, and, impressed by his summing-up and the way the judge had joked and feted Venables, I was convinced Venables would win. Only one man disagreed. Ash Karim.

He accurately predicted that the judge would rule in favour of Fugler but would not give him all his claims. He would not get his disbursements. Fugler, as per advertising practice, had levied a mark-up and Karim said the judge would discount that. I bet £10 that he was wrong and that Venables would win.

The next morning Shane Dougall, in a methodical summing-up, did much to make a powerful case for Fugler. Then in the afternoon, as Mr Recorder Williams began his judgement, it became clear that all the journalists had hopelessly misread the judge's banter with Venables as acceptance of this case. The court was nowhere as full; most of the Venables clan, apart from Brown, who was always in attendance, had left. Mr Recorder Williams began reading his judgement at 2pm and for Venables and his supporters it proved devastating.

Mr Recorder Williams first ruled out any conspiracy, or third-party involvement in the case. He accepted that Fugler was telling the truth when he claimed he had picked up the Silver Rose and other invoices from Brown's office in Tottenham on 27 August 1992, much as he had described them in his witness statement. The judge did not know what to make of Silver Rose and he offered two explanations. It could be an April Fool's day-type joke. It could have been created to stir things for one or other of the parties, presumably for the defendants. However, he concluded, 'It is not for me to decide on that document which appears to be a concoction of some sort, and I think the least added by me to the remarks I have made the better, because it may be for other bodies to look at the documents and make adjudication on them in other respects.'

The judge did not like the way he felt Fugler had used the Silver Rose document and commented on its appearance in my article in the *Daily Telegraph* within hours of the production of Fugler's witness statement. 'I find the proximity of these events to be more than coincidental.' He saw it as subtle pressure by Fugler on Venables to settle.

But while this was a mark against Fugler, this paled when compared to the scorn with which he treated the testimony of the entire Venables clan. Brown's evasiveness and his disregard for creditors did not impress him and he said he would treat his evidence with 'more than a pinch of salt, more likely a fistful or handful, with what he has told the court'. Of Yvette Venables he said, 'She did her best to be of assistance to her husband, to the defendant company with which he is associated and to the court, in that order of priority. She was more than keen to give evidence on matters which were not raised by counsel, even her own counsel.' Eric Hall was summarily dismissed. 'I found that he made up for lack of substance in his evidence by entertainment value . . . I cannot accept that his evidence should be given much weight, if any.'

But what about Venables? Here, for all the apparent bonhomie with which he had treated Venables in the witness box, his appraisal of him was cool and judicial. He was not impressed by the fact that, in the witness box, Venables had contradicted himself:

> Unfortunately for him and the defendant company, his evidence under oath was found to contradict what he had said not only in the liquidation proceedings [which Fugler had brought earlier in an effort to get his money] but also in his published autobiography. I refer to the reference in his autobiography to his knowledge at the time, or shortly after, of the payment in cash to Mr McLintock. He tried to rectify the situation by saying that what he meant was something quite different relating to an overpayment to Mr McLintock which included VAT. There were other items. I find his denial on oath in the liquidation proceedings of receipt of the plaintiffs' invoice [the crucial Fugler invoice which had asked for the money due to Fugler] as being rather wanton. Had a diligent search been made, the invoice in question would have been recovered. That was one of the main planks of the grounds for resisting the winding-up petition. It is for those reasons that I do not accept his evidence as entirely reliable, to put it at its most charitable.

The judgement meant that, for the second time in two and a half years, a judge had cast doubts on Venables' ability to tell the truth. Justice Harman had said his affidavit was 'inaccurate in every possible foot', now Mr Recorder Williams, in a different court and different case, had called his evidence 'wanton'. Any other man might have been tempted to take stock, ask searching questions of himself. But Venables, always the counter-attacker, attacked. For some time his lawyers huffed and puffed saying Mr Recorder Williams had been misreported. He had not said Venables' evidence was 'wanton', he had said it was 'wanting'. Their protests died down when the transcript of the approved judgement showed the word used by Mr Recorder Williams was indeed 'wanton'.

The judgement had, however, given Venables a few straws to clutch and he clutched them fervently. The judge, as Karim had predicted, had not given Fugler everything. This prompted Venables to issue a press release saying he was 'significantly vindicated'. It must be the first time a man, whose evidence the judge had disbelieved, can claim to be vindicated. Then he quoted the judgement so selectively that he made it appear the judge had damned the Silver Rose invoice when, as we have seen, he had merely puzzled about what it might mean.

But, in perhaps the most characteristic Venables move, on a par with the one he had played after his defeat in the Berry case, he used words said in court by his own counsel and tried to suggest they had deeper significance or wider acceptance than they had. With Berry it was the claim everybody accepted that he acted in good faith. Now it was his use of Farrer's remarks after Mr Recorder Williams had given his judgement. As is usual after a judgement, the argument was about costs and Farrer tried hard to convince Mr Recorder Williams that Venables should not have to pay Fugler's costs. In his submission he referred to Fugler's use of the Silver Rose invoices and labelled them as blackmail.

In his press statement Venables quoted this, commenting 'the judge did not disagree'. This suggested Farrer's comments had some sort of judicial sanction, which was nonsense. Just because the judge did not disagree, or rather made no pronouncements, it did not mean he agreed. He did not have to comment on everything which Farrer said, or for that matter Dougall. If Venables' logic is accepted, then any comment by counsel of either side, with which a judge does not disagree, can be said to have his approval.

Mr Recorder Williams gave Fugler only half his costs and this meant that, despite winning, Fugler would be out of pocket. Venables commented this should be a warning to other creditors who pursued him. The implication was if you tangle with Venables then, like Landhurst, be prepared to accept 50% or so of what you are owed, otherwise you might lose out.

As it happened, the day after the judgement Venables was making an out-of-court settlement with another creditor, the two-year-old bill of Mark Stephens for the work he and his firm had done at the time of the first *Panorama* back in September 1993. Like Finers, Stephens Innocent had threatened bankruptcy, and finally got paid, although what percentage of their fees was paid was not disclosed.

By the weekend Venables had made further efforts to try to undo the damage Mr Recorder Williams had inflicted. Now he gave the impression he was leading a righteous crusade summed up in the *Sunday Telegraph*, whose Ronald Atkin had been in court and wrote a sympathetic piece, with the headline 'Venables: Why I battle on'. As ever, his weapons were the press release, aimed at the Sunday papers. In the past such press releases, as we have seen, had targeted Sugar and Kate Hoey. Now he mentioned me, clearly nettled by my article in that Saturday's *Daily Telegraph*, which concentrated on the implications for the Sheringham case of the judgement. I had suggested further lines of enquiry for the Premier League inquiry. Silver Rose still bugged him and Venables' lawyer followed this up with a letter to the *Daily Telegraph* protesting about my article and using such selective quotations from Mr Recorder Williams' judgement that it was almost misleading.

Having said under oath in the witness box that his autobiography was inaccurate with regard to the cash payment to McLintock, Venables now changed his mind. He told Ronald Atkin, no, his book was accurate. It was his witness statement that was not accurate. What he had meant to say in his witness statement was that he had only seen the full invoice, on which McLintock was paid, on *Panorama*, screened four months after he had left Tottenham. He had, of course, known about the cash payment for a long time, as detailed in his autobiography. However, in his witness statement he had ended up saying he had known about the cash payment only as a result of *Panorama*. 'This,' Venables told Atkin, 'is not what I meant to say.' But how could this be a lie? he wailed. Venables did not seem to realise that these words of self-justification, far from restoring his tarnished credibility, only undermined it further.

How much his position had been undermined by the judgement became evident that weekend. On the Saturday, after paying a visit to his father, he drove up to Birmingham to attend the draw for the European championships. That morning Noel White had been reported in the *Daily Mail* as saying that there were certain matters about Venables' contract that must be considered. Venables arrived in Birmingham and met Kelly, the meeting taking place in Venables' room at the Hyatt Regency. The *Mail on Sunday* which gave, perhaps, the best version of this meeting wrote, 'Venables confirmed that he would not seek a new contract after the European championships.'

Venables' supporters would later picture this meeting as the one where he told Kelly he was resigning. That is absurd. Not to seek a contract, which has not been offered, is not resignation. Venables had every intention of fulfilling his contract until the European championships. What he wanted was FA reassurance that he would have a contract after the championships were over. He wanted the reassurance now, six months before the championships, and based purely on his performance as coach in friendly matches. Kelly and Millichip may have been willing to extend his contract on that basis, but they could not speak for the entire FA. Venables has since strenuously denied he was trying to steamroller the FA but it is hard to see what else it was. He was behaving like football managers down the ages: as the expiry of his contract approaches, he seeks an extension.

However, to consider this the international committee would have to discuss it. Then it would have to establish a procedure, perhaps appoint a small committee to consider a new contract for Venables. None of this had happened. Noel White, as chairman of the international committee, would be at the heart of it. He had been reading press reports of how Venables had been offered a contract by Kelly and in Birmingham he sought a meeting with Kelly and Millichip to discuss matters. The meeting was fixed for Sunday morning and it was decided that, after the three had met, Venables would join them.

Nothing of this leaked out to the press, despite the fact that journalists were swarming all over the place. On that Saturday night Venables, along with Kelly, Millichip and White, joined a whole host of others to attend the gala dinner. However, Venables was clearly worried about what the morning would bring and retired early.

On the Sunday morning, 17 December, Millichip, Kelly and White met in the Jackson suite. Venables joined them later. For a time it could have been any Sunday morning gathering of four middle-aged or elderly men sitting and drinking coffee. But at some stage Venables' anger welled up. It was directed at White who Venables saw as his main stumbling block to an extension. He asked White: did he, and the international committee, want him to carry on after the European championships? White, a silver-haired, soft-spoken man, was quite clear. He had no problems about giving Venables an extension. But he could only do that on the basis of his performance in the European championships.

This was an eminently logical position. The FA had stood by him, saying he was the best football man, that the FA judged him solely on his football. Venables knew the score when he had taken the contract, back in January 1994. To give him an extension in December 1995, when England had not kicked a ball in anger, and all that had changed was that his off-the-field business problems had considerably worsened since his appointment, would mean the FA was, in effect, saying to the DTI, and even the law courts: we don't care what you say or think of Terry Venables the businessman, we believe in him so much we will give him a new contract. The FA officials had certainly given the impression they would like to cock a snook at those whom they felt were his enemies. Soon after the first part of the Fugler hearings, when the FA held a new lottery-style third-round FA Cup draw at prime television viewing time in front of an invited audience, Venables featured prominently.

Venables left the meeting disappointed and angry. However, that afternoon, as the draw took place and the media concentrated on England being placed in a group that included Scotland, Holland and Switzerland, he gave nothing away. He played his part in building up the media hype for the championships.

But Venables knew he had to do something. What were his options? Kelly wanted him to stay. Venables had got very close to the FA officials like David Davies, who had said he had two close friends in football, one of them being Venables. The FA officials were convinced that all Venables' problems centred on his conflict with Sugar. If only Sugar's libel action and Venables' own action against Sugar for wrongful dismissal could be settled it would be all right. It is ironic that they should have taken such an attitude, given that Kelly had approved Venables' book before publication. The libel problems at least should have been foreseen by the FA.

Perhaps the FA felt that, having contributed to creating part of the problems with Sugar, they should try to solve it. They had got Venables and Sugar to talk to a mediator. Since November Charles

Woodhouse of Farrer & Co, the Queen's solicitors, had been busy trying to bring Sugar and Venables together. By the time the Birmingham meeting took place Woodhouse had met both Venables and Sugar but the chasm was wide. Venables, who had refused Sugar's offer in May 1993, now insisted he would not give up his wrongful dismissal case.

On 21 December Venables had another meeting with Kelly although, given that Kelly's office is on the second floor and Venables' office on the third floor of Lancaster Gate, it was not quite as formal as the word 'meeting' suggests. Kelly clearly wanted Venables to have a new contract. The question was how could the stumbling block of the international committee be removed? Kelly could try to push matters in the FA. But Venables had his own agenda to try to get the result he wanted and this, as ever, involved the press.

Two days after this meeting Rob Shepherd, in an exclusive article in the *Daily Mail*, reported it, saying Venables had opened talks with Kelly about a two-year extension to his contract. Talks would resume in the new year. Shepherd made it sound rather grander than it was. Venables told Shepherd he wanted a quick decision. No, he wasn't trying to pressurise the FA, only people with 'closed minds' would think that. He was trying to broaden the FA's horizons, be more continental, where coaches knew before a major championship what their future would be. In any case it was all for the greater glory of England. If he knew what was happening he could focus on the job. On the other hand if England went to the European championships with uncertainty about his future it could distract him and his players to the detriment of England's chances. It says much for Venables' ability to beguile and charm that, although this was little more than a plea for a new contract, it was presented as being for the greater good of the English soccer nation. The *Daily Mail* was so impressed it devoted its whole back page to the messiah's call.

Yet in another part of the press Venables was playing a somewhat different tune. Colin Malam of the *Sunday Telegraph* had hinted on 3 December that Venables might not seek an extension to his contract. On 31 December he wrote, 'Terry Venables will spend the first week of 1996 holidaying in the sun and mulling over the offer of a new contract from the Football Association designed to take him beyond next summer's finals of the European championships. It is not certain, however, the England coach will accept it.'

Malam has since said that Venables got him to rewrite the story three times before he would let him publish it. Malam, quixotically, sees it as proof of Venables' honourable behaviour. Given that there was no FA offer, as Venables would later confess to Joe Lovejoy of the *Sunday Times*, what Venables was attempting here was neat. He knew Kelly and Millichip wanted him to stay, so by saying he was considering an offer but might reject it he was sending signals via the press to White and the international committee; give me an extension now, before the championships, otherwise I shall start looking for another job.

One place he could have looked for a job is the Middle East where Venables went for his holiday. He went to Oman, staying at the prestigious Al-Bastan hotel. So prestigious is the hotel that guests are regarded as virtually state guests of Oman. The top floor of the hotel is reserved for the Sultan and a double-room can cost £800 a night. When Oman's English football coaches heard Venables was at the Al-Bastan they wondered about his visit, was he a guest of the Sultan? Whether he did go there to look for another job we don't know; his friends in the press scoffed at such ideas and Fred Venables would later boast to the *People* that 'Terry paid every penny of what the holiday cost. And that isn't cheap at £800 a day.' Yet at this stage he still had to pay the £11,000-odd which the judge had ordered him to pay Fugler.

He returned from holiday in the second week of January, bronzed and ready to have another chat with Kelly. The day before that he spoke with some of his tabloid reporter friends. He rehearsed his tactic. He would go in and tell Kelly that unless he was backed he would not be available after the European championships. It seems Venables did not want this conversation to be reported. But it was and, to his fury, Venables found himself in the meeting with Kelly with his negotiating position already exposed in the press. Venables was not best pleased although he had not started with a great position, in any event. Kelly did not have a contract to offer him and Venables had to decide on how to cope with the situation.

His response shows his brilliant ability to manage the media to his best advantage, even when he has nothing to manage it with. Venables had met Kelly in the morning. At 4pm on 10 January the FA called a sudden press conference to announce that Venables was quitting to concentrate on his legal battles, in particular the libel battle against Sugar looming in October. England would then be involved in qualifying for the 1998 World Cup to be held in France, and Venables felt it would not be right if he was tied up.

The press coverage was exactly as Venables would have wanted. Everybody said Venables was 'resigning', when all he was doing was saying he did not want an extension to his contract. But since no extension was being offered he was like an American Presidential candidate who, unsure that he can get the nomination of his party for the White House, announces he does not want to run. The press would see that as a defeat, but with Venables the announcement was presented as a Venables victory, certainly a moral one.

Also much was made of Venables clearing his name. Martin Thorpe in the *Guardian* warned, 'The FA may have lost a coach but his enemies have gained a greater foe. Terry Venables is out to prove his innocence and anyone in the way had better watch out.'

But given that the major legal fight which Venables and his friends had highlighted was the Sugar libel fight, where Sugar claimed Venables had libelled him, this would be more a case of Sugar trying to clear his name. True, Venables had libel cases against *Panorama* and the *Daily Mirror* and his wrongful dismissal case against Sugar, but no date has been set for them and they may not come up in 1996 or even 1997. So eager were the press to believe the Venables version that hardly anybody asked: if the Sugar libel case was now so urgent that Venables was 'quitting', why was this not seen as a problem when, at Venables' insistence, the FA persuaded a judge to postpone it to October 1996, clashing with the World Cup qualifying dates.

As always with Venables what was significant was what hardly anybody mentioned: the case brought by the DTI, where he had a court date of 12 February, little over a month away and long before the Sugar case in October. This should have been seen as the one where Venables cleared his name. The DTI is seeking to ban him as a company director yet, since the age of seventeen, Venables has managed companies and been a director. Nothing could be a greater stain on the reputation of a man who has been a director all his adult life.

However, when 12 February dawned Venables' lawyer presented a letter from Kelly saying for the sake of England's chances in the European championships the case should be postponed until they were over. The judge agreed and it was put back to July 1996. Ironically Venables was back in court the following week pursuing Paul Kirby for money. The FA clearly felt this battle between the two Lancaster Gate men would not derail England's chances.

And for a man supposedly giving up England to concentrate on his legal battles Venables' supporters were quick to try to get him the FA's technical director job, a new position for which the FA had been interviewing candidates far and wide. Jeff Powell, who had worked so hard to get him the England coach's job, now argued he should be made technical director. Venables had rejected such a suggestion back in October. Powell explained that was because he thought he would get an extension to his contract. Now that was not going to happen, he would, said Powell, love to be the technical director. Malam also wanted him as technical director, in harness with Bryan Robson as coach.

Venables and his supporters seem to find no contradiction in all of this. As the FA, quite rightly, took their time to appoint a successor, a delicate job given that some of the candidates were in the middle of their club seasons, the clamour to 'Save Our Tel', as the *News of the World* called its campaign, grew. The paper provided readers with a coupon to cut out and send to Kelly. By the end of February the paper had collected some 25,000 yes replies and ceremoniously presented it to the FA. Although Venables kept saying he would not change his mind, he also said, 'I wouldn't dismiss out of hand any effort being made by others on my behalf.'

So what did all this add up to? We had to wait for Richard Littlejohn to bring his experience of industrial reporting to cut through the waffle and the hype. Writing in the *Daily Mail* on 12 February he said, 'Call me cynical but I covered industrial relations for ten years. This looked like a classic negotiating ploy, giving notice of strike action to force the employer's hand.'

What had gone wrong for Venables was that the employer's hand could not be forced. But in contrast to the strike leaders, who in such circumstances usually get a bad press, Venables won the press war.

The weekend of his so-called 'resignation' saw him brief the press and lay into Noel White. Taking their lead from Venables, the Sundays roasted the FA. Even Gary Lineker called them old farts, borrowing the words of his friend Will Carling. White was cruelly mocked as Mr Wobbly when he had, in fact, stood fast. And the whole thing was presented as a story of Venables, the man of honour, being betrayed by faceless, cowardly men at Lancaster Gate.

Nothing could illustrate better Venables' ability to manipulate the media. He had transformed an everyday story of a man, beset by legal problems and bills, worried that his contract, his principal source of income, was expiring and seeking an extension, into a morality play. But that in a way summed up Venables' life. He may not have got what he wanted from the FA and judges may question his evidence, calling it inaccurate, not entirely reliable, even wanton, but at least on the back pages of newspapers he could present himself as a man of honour.

Alan Sugar once said Venables deserves an Emmy. On this basis he deserved the Booker Prize for sheer improvisation and inventiveness.

Postscript

Which is the real Terry Venables?

In June 1991, days after he took over Tottenham in partnership with Sugar, *The Times* described Venables as a renaissance man, the Leonardo da Vinci of the League. In December 1995, three days after Recorder Williams had branded Venables' testimony in court as 'wanton' and 'not entirely reliable', Patrick Collins in the *Mail on Sunday* likened him wittily to an Essex car salesman whose vocation is to supply used Jags and Mercs to the glitterati of Billericay. 'Your Honour, it was running like a dream when it left our premises. Why it should choose to blow up on reaching Basildon I really cannot say.'

So which is the real Venables? Venables' supporters would have us believe that *The Times'* portrayal truly represents their man. The Collins one, they would argue, is the result of the innuendoes, slurs and calumny that have been heaped on their man ever since May 1993 when he fell out with Sugar. To them, Venables did not have a problem until he broke with Sugar and since then all his problems can be traced to the conspiracy hatched by Sugar.

Venables certainly sees the world in such simplistic fashion. A few weeks before Recorder Williams gave his devastating judgement, Venables, in an interview with Alex Montgomery of the *News of the World*, saw his life as having been broken in half by Sugar. 'I had reached the age of fifty [in January 1993] without a problem. Since then I'm supposed to have done everything, and I mean everything, wrong.' How can that be? asked Venables. 'If I

413

was such a bad businessman, surely it would have come out long ago.'

But far from there being a conspiracy, as he believes, the fact that Venables cannot understand why this world has turned upside down since he fell out with Sugar is perhaps the most telling thing about him, his life and our modern football times. If Venables reached fifty without a problem it is because the world of football of which he was presented as the master – or in his lawyer's words 'an English institution' – asked little of him, certainly nothing very searching, and accepted whatever he did at his own estimation. Venables was allowed to write his own script and no editor blue-pencilled it, or not by any significant amount. The world he operated in was undemanding and Venables quickly grasped the levers that would make him king, or at least give the appearance that he was royalty.

Coming to manhood at a time when class divisions were dissolving – albeit he feels that the working class is still put upon – Venables made the most of the first of the great post-war revolutions. Popular culture was being revolutionised: music through the Beatles and the Rolling Stones, the literary world with the angry young men, the great masses not only well fed and well clothed but able to launch consumer booms; and in sports the iron chains that had kept the professional and amateur apart were dissolving with the professional losing a lot of his subservient cloth-cap image.

Venables, with his opportunism, his easy charm and his seemingly endless optimism and self-confidence, was the ideal man of football to become the man-of-the-world, the man who could cross any barrier. On the training ground he might be a footballer, not very different from the rest, but off it his ambitions could soar. He could be anything: singer, song-writer, novelist, businessman. Unlike his contemporaries his horizons did not seem limited, helped by the fact that, as he freely confessed, he is a restless soul who cannot sit still. To say that all this added up to a renaissance figure is somewhat overegging it, but he was different. However, what he gained in diversity and glamour he lost in grandeur. His great friend Bobby Moore, coming from the same working-class background, had a nobility of bearing and spirit that Venables has never been able to match.

But then Moore never could, and never desired to, compete for the back-page sports attention that has been so crucial to Venables.

414

From very early on in his career Venables understood the dawning of the age of the media, perhaps even better than the people in the media themselves. He was comfortable with them, seemed to know their pressures and requirements and was always willing to deal with them. Alf Ramsey, the most successful England manager, hardly ever spoke to the press. In contrast, Venables possesses almost a trained public relations man's feel for the press, unerringly targeting the important Sunday press with a well-timed press release on Saturday afternoons – an instrument he has used relentlessly since his problems with Sugar emerged into the open.

The post-Ramsey English football world is dominated by the post-match press conference and Venables quickly worked out how to exploit this to his advantage. This, by the very nature of things, is perhaps the most undemanding type of press conference; the journalists are under intense deadline pressure, with often no more than a few minutes in which to get some reaction from the manager on the match that has just taken place. For many managers, even experienced ones, this press conference can be unnerving. Ramsey never held one and towards the end of his career Brian Clough used to ignore it. But Venables understood that it was the ideal launch pad for self-promotion. He realised early on that if he provided the right quip, or a couple of pithy remarks, he could dominate the next day's papers and shape the way the match and his role as manager were perceived. A poor performance by his team could be converted into a debate about a bad refereeing decision. The arguments and the controversy would last barely twenty-four hours; soon there would be another match and another opportunity to mould the back pages and thus football opinion.

This worked very well until May 1993 because nobody bothered to go back and check what he had said or done. If he said he was no longer involved with the Chris McCann agency then that must be true. Nobody went back two years later and checked the records at Companies House. But his partnership with Sugar to buy Tottenham took him into a different league and, when that fell apart, the scrutiny, the examination, the enquiry which he had managed to avoid until the age of fifty, began. Then it began to emerge that there was an enormous gulf between the cultivated self-image Venables had projected and the truth. So when he took over Tottenham nobody could penetrate, or perhaps even wanted to, how he financed the take-over. Now that it has been done, it is clear that things are not quite as they seem.

This does not mean that Venables should never have aimed as high as he did, but the fact that he cannot now acknowledge that he overreached himself, that the problems he had to cope with are largely of his own making – and if he escaped lightly earlier it was because nobody looked hard at them – is very revealing of the man.

As a footballer he was good but hardly exceptional, as his record of two England caps shows. As a manager his record is at best middle of the second grade. No Premier League table of the successful post-war managers would include Venables.

Such a table would include Bill Nicholson, Sir Matt Busby, Brian Clough, Bob Paisley, Kenny Dalglish, Alex Ferguson, George Graham, men who won championships and, barring Dalglish, European trophies. Even Howard Kendall, who won two championships, an FA Cup and a European Cup Winners Cup, could lay claim to a more successful record than Venables. True, Venables had success with Barcelona in Spain, but Venables is not unique in being an English manager who succeeds abroad. What was remarkable about that triumph was the speed with which Venables made himself sufficiently fluent in Spanish to be able to strike the proper public chord with the Spanish press and media. It was as much a triumph of public relations as of his soccer skills.

The post-May 1993 reporting of Venables has revealed what may be called the darker side of his character. This shows he is very far from the 'cheekie chappie' public image he has cultivated, more a figure of intrigue with dark, unfathomable secrets. The Venables that emerges is the Venables of little charity, certainly not for former friends and associates he has fallen out with, virtually no compassion for those who disagree with him, and a highly developed sense of paranoia about anybody who crosses him. If you are not with him you must be his enemy seems to be the Venables motto.

Of course all this may not matter should Venables, as England coach and contrary to expectations, go on to win the European championships. The nation, or at least the footballing nation, hungry for success, will indeed then hail him as a messiah.

But even if such an event occurs, Venables' life does not suggest any other conclusion than that he is no messiah. He is a clever, charming man but very far removed from his hype, which has suggested that he could reach out of the dug-out and become something of a football wonderman. It is this belief that produces the recurring images of Venables the messiah.

The fact that so many people believed he could be a messiah and that the FA should have made him England coach without due diligence – in this they rather copied Alan Sugar's behaviour in joining up with Venables to buy Spurs – is a reflection of the curious world of football we have in England.

When Venables first came into prominence at Chelsea, the world around him was changing faster than football was – he made his Chelsea debut when the maximum wage still prevailed and George Eastham's transfer revolution was yet to come. By the time Venables reached out to become part-owner of Spurs the football world was changing more quickly than the wider one, and within a year the oldest league in the world had split, with a rich faction, the Premier League, breaking away. Nevertheless football on the whole is still governed by people who would not be out of place in the *ancien régime* and who fondly look back to the days when a Stanley Matthews or a Stan Mortensen would travel to match days carrying their boots over their shoulders on the same bus that carried the supporters.

But football still allows its supporters to believe that fantasies can come true, as indeed they have for Blackburn. In 1991, when Venables was bidding for Spurs, Blackburn made a £2m. offer for Lineker, and the first reaction at White Hart Lane was stupefaction. But Blackburn did get its Father Christmas in Jack Walker, and every football fan and supporter hopes for such a messiah who can suddenly transform everything, if not with money, then through magic on the field of play. The Tottenham supporters saw Venables in this way, helped by the fact that – with his *Hazell* novels, his karaoke singing, his rapport with people and the media, as well as his reputation as trainer and coach – he seemed so different from the normal, faceless men of a football Board. But in the modern football world to whose heights as owner Venables aspired – and which has come to recognise that it is a multi-million pound industry and subject to the laws of commerce – he now seems a rather dated figure, a sort of football version of Osborne's Archie Rice, or of 'Del boy'.

APPENDIXES

Dates and major events in Terry Venables' life

1943   Born Dagenham, 6 January.

1958   Joined Chelsea FC as an apprentice.

1960   Signed as a professional. Played 202 League games for Chelsea, scoring 26 goals.

1963   Chelsea gain promotion to Division One.

1964   England caps against Belgium and Holland (he had previously been capped for England at schoolboy, youth, amateur and Under-23 levels).

1965   Chelsea win the League Cup.

1966   Transferred to Tottenham Hotspur FC for £80,000. Played 115 League games for Tottenham, scoring 19 goals.

1967   Tottenham win FA Cup.

1969   Transferred to Queens Park Rangers FC for £70,000. Played 179 games for QPR, scoring 19 goals.

1974   Transferred to Crystal Palace for £70,000. Played 14 League games for Crystal Palace.

1976   Appointed manager of Crystal Palace in June.

1977   Crystal Palace promoted to Division Two.

1978   Crystal Palace finish ninth in Division Two.

1979   Crystal Palace finish top of Division Two and are promoted to Division One.

1980   Crystal Palace finish thirteenth in Division One. Venables resigns in October and takes over at Queens Park Rangers.

1981   QPR finish eighth in Division Two.

1982   QPR finish fifth in Division Two and lose in Cup Final to Tottenham Hotspur.

1983   QPR finish top of Division Two.

1984   QPR finish fifth in Division One. Venables resigns in May and takes over at Barcelona.

1985   Barcelona win first Spanish League title in eleven years.

1986   Venables signs Gary Lineker and Mark Hughes for £5.3m. Barcelona finish second in Spanish League, but lose European Cup Final to Steaua Bucharest.

1987   Barcelona finish second in Spanish League. Venables sacked in September and appointed manager of Tottenham Hotspur in October.

1988   Venables signs Paul Gascoigne for £2m. Tottenham finish thirteenth in Division One.

1989   Venables sells Chris Waddle to Marseille for £4.25m. and re-signs Gary Lineker. Tottenham finish sixth in Division One.
April 28: Transatlantic Inns incorporated. Venables is director, with Paul Kirby and Colin Wright.
August 7: Death of Myrtle, Venables' mother.

1990   Tottenham finish third in Division One. *Son of Fred*, Fred Venables' biography of Terry, published.

1991   March: Venables and Larry Gillick launch unsuccessful bid for Tottenham.
April 5: Transatlantic Inns accounts for 31 March 1990 show loss of £91,750.
April 11: Venables and Riviere take over Scribes West.
April 14: Tottenham beat Arsenal 3–1 in FA Cup semi-final.
May 18: Tottenham win FA Cup, beating Nottingham Forest 2–1.
May 20: Tottenham finish tenth in Division One.
June 21: Sugar and Venables win control of Tottenham. £500,000 unsecured loan given by Landhurst to Edennote. Venables becomes chief executive of Tottenham.
June 28: Venables resigns from Transatlantic Inns.

1992   June 1: Venables pays £144,359.64 to NatWest, Romford, to clear bank overdraft of Transatlantic Inns.
August 27: Teddy Sheringham transferred to Tottenham from Nottingham Forest.
August 28: Venables defaults on Norfina loan.
September 7: Venables renegotiates his Tottenham contract.
October 2: Bank of Liechtenstein replaces Norfina as lender to Edennote.

1993   January 30: Venables serves statutory demand on Kirby for £36,089.76.

February 3: Transatlantic Inns wound up.

May 13: ITN leak the news of Venables' sacking.

May 14: Venables is sacked as chief executive after a Board meeting at Tottenham. That evening he is reinstated on the strength of a temporary injunction. A month later he is defeated after a three-day High Court hearing.

July 22: Gulu Lalwani offers to buy Venables' shares.

July 29: Hearing of Edennote security of costs case.

August 14: Venables says he will ask DTI to investigate Tottenham Hotspur FC.

August 24: Venables and his then lawyers, Kanter Jules Grangewoods, take a charge on his Tottenham shares not yet pledged. Venables sells his Tottenham shares.

September 16: The first *Panorama* programme on Venables' business dealings.

September 19: *Dispatches* programme.

October 9: Venables alleges a conspiracy against him and says he is calling in the police to investigate the theft of documents from Edennote.

October 10: Sugar alleges possible misappropriation of funds relating to the Sheringham transfer to the Holborn fraud squad.

October 15: Venables brings his wrongful dismissal case.

November 3: DTI start investigation into Scribes West and Edennote.

November 17: England beat San Marino 7–1 but fail to qualify for the World Cup.

November 18: Graham Taylor resigns as England manager.

December 13: *World in Action* programme about interest-free loans given by Tottenham.

1994   January 5: FA interviews Venables.

January 16: *Sunday Mirror* claims police have cleared Venables of any wrongdoing over the £1m. loan from Landhurst.

January 17: Police decide no crime has been committed in relation to Venables' allegations of theft of documents from Edennote.

January 25: FA confirms to Venables the job of England coach. The public announcement is made on January 28.

February 9: NatWest issue a writ demanding £66,000 regarding Recall City.

February 23: Venables serves statutory demands on Paul Kirby claiming £144,259.44.

March 3: Bryan Fugler, Venables' former lawyer, demands payments totalling £312,000. Venables counter-sues for negligence.

March 9: Venables begins his England reign with 1–0 victory over Denmark at Wembley.

May: Jeff Fugler presents the winding-up petition. Papers on Sugar's allegations about the Sheringham transfer submitted to Crown Prosecution Service.

May 9: Court hearing on Edennote begins.

May 12: Edennote is wound up. FA charge Tottenham with misconduct over loans to players.

May 17: England defeat Greece 5–0 at Wembley.

May 22: England draw 0–0 with Norway at Wembley.

June: DTI Inspectors Horne and Parkinson question Venables.

June 14: FA Commission meets at Wembley to hear the Tottenham loans case.

July 25: Compromise on Jeff Fugler's winding-up petition.

July 28: Venables buys from Edennote's, then Receivers, the right to pursue his wrongful dismissal action against Tottenham.

August 12: Venables begins action by writ against Kirby. The Crown Prosecution Service decides, because of lack of evidence, not to pursue allegations regarding the Sheringham transfer.

September 7: England defeat USA 2–0 at Wembley.

September 22: Venables' *The Autobiography* is launched at Scribes West.

October 12: England draw 1–1 with Romania at Wembley.

October 31: The second *Panorama* programme.

November 11: Venables alleges criminal conspiracy and complains to Chelsea CID.

November 16: England defeat Nigeria 1–0 at Wembley.

December 19: Scotland Yard and the Garda combine on an operation in Dublin to arrest a man in connection with an alleged plot to blackmail Venables. Later, no charges are brought.

1995   January 30: Kate Hoey, MP, initiates House of Commons debate on corruption in football.

February 28: England's friendly match with Republic of Ireland is abandoned because of crowd riots. DTI hold crucial meeting to discuss Venables' business affairs.

March 29: England draw 0–0 with Uruguay at Wembley.

June 3: England defeat Japan 2–1 at Wembley.

June 8: England draw 3–3 with Sweden at Leeds.

June 11: England lose 1–3 to Brazil at Wembley.

July: Alan Sugar lifts White Hart Lane ban on Venables after plea by Sir Bert Millichip.

September 6: England draw 0–0 with Colombia at Wembley.

September 29: Jeff Fugler files his witness statement with regard to his action against Venables.

September 30: *Daily Telegraph* reveals the existence of Silver Rose and another First Wave invoice with regard to Sheringham transfer.

October 6: Venables loses the Tony Berry libel case.

October 8: Venables claims Internazionale offered him a job but the Italians deny it. He announces he would like his future as England coach clarified before European Championship finals, but rules himself out as a candidate for the job of England's new technical supremo.

October 11: England draw 0–0 with Norway in Oslo.

October 13: Venables settles Finers' debt, warding off their bankruptcy petition.

November 8–10: Jeff Fugler's case begins at Central London County Court.

November 12: FA reports that police are investigating Venables' conspiracy claims.

November 15: England defeat Switzerland 3–1 at Wembley.

November 22: Peter Brant decides Needham should drop his investigations into Venables' conspiracy allegations. DTI decides to start a civil action against Venables to disqualify him as a director and send him a 'ten-day letter'.

December 11: At the Central London County Court Mihir Bose and Harry Harris successfully defeat an attempt by Venables' lawyers to make them disclose their sources of evidence in Jeff Fugler case. In Paris the draw is made for the qualifying groups for the 1998 World Cup.

December 12: England draw 1–1 with Portugal at Wembley.

December 13: Venables takes witness stand in Fugler case.

December 14: Judgement in the Fugler case goes against Venables.

December 17: Venables meets Millichip, Kelly and White in Birmingham regarding his future as England coach. England drawn with Holland, Scotland and Switzerland for the European Finals.

1996   January: Venables goes on holiday to Oman.

January 10: Venables meets FA at Lancaster Gate, who announce that Venables is not offering himself for another contract as England coach after Euro '96.

February 12: First hearing in the DTI case to disqualify Venables. FA writes to Venables' lawyers, saying the case should be postponed until July.

February 19: Venables' case against Paul Kirby begins in the High Court.

March 7: Mr Justice Carnwath gives judgement in favour of

Venables, awarding him £36,089.91 and half his costs.
April: Venables publishes *Venables' England*.
May 2: Glenn Hoddle appointed England coach, to take over from Terry Venables after the European championships.

VENABLES' ENGLAND RECORD UP TO END APRIL 1996

Played 16: Won 7; Drawn 8; Lost 1; Goals for, 21; Goals against, 10.

Terry Venables: companies record to 1 April 1996

This is not an exhaustive list of Terry Venables' companies, but they are the important ones to have figured in his life.

Terence Venables Limited (Company No. 00682709)
Date of incorporation: 7 February 1961 – the oldest Venables company.
Sole director: Terry Venables.
Abbreviated accounts for 30 April 1994 approved by the Board on 22 February 1995.
Accounts show liabilities exceeded assets by £40,806.
The company is a subsidiary of Terence Venables Holdings Limited.

Chris McCann Management Limited
Date of incorporation: 1 November 1979.
This company ceased to trade on 25 April 1982. Dissolved 16 August 1994. Throughout its existence the company was beneficially owned by Terence Venables Limited.

Elite Gold Card Limited (Company No. 2487621)
Date of incorporation: 2 April 1990.
Directors: Terry Venables, Paul Riviere.
The company never traded.
Dissolved: 6 July 1993.

Transatlantic Inns Limited (Company No. 02377348)
Date of incorporation: 28 April 1989.
Terry Venables was one of four directors. The company was wound up on 3 February 1993 on a petition by Westminster Council for failure to pay rates.

Glenhope Management Limited (Company No. 2510422)
Date of incorporation: 11 June 1990.
This company was dissolved on or about 22 June 1993 and struck off the Register. Following a petition by HM Customs & Excise, a creditor of the company, it was restored to the Register on 6 October 1993 and is now being wound up.

Elite Europe Company Limited (Company No. 2487623)
Date of incorporation: 3 April 1990.
The company was struck off the Register on 3 November 1992 and dissolved by notice in the *London Gazette* on 10 November 1992.

Venables Venture Capital Limited (Company No. 2440896)
Date of incorporation: 5 March 1990.
No accounts were ever filed by this company.
The company was dissolved on 21 March 1995.

Edennote Limited PLC (Company No. 02588359)
Date of incorporation: 5 March 1991.
Company used by Terry Venables to buy Spurs. Now in liquidation.

Depthsubmit Limited (Company No. 02708543)
Date of incorporation: 22 April 1992.
Sole Director: Jakub Pawlikowski.
The company is a wholly owned subsidiary of Terence Venables Holdings Limited.
Accounts for 30 April 1994, signed by the auditors on 24 February 1995, show liabilities exceeded assets by £10,711.
A winding-up petition was presented on 25 November 1994.

Recall City Limited (Company No. 02528680)
Date of incorporation: 7 August 1990.
First and last accounts filed for period ended 31 August 1991.
Accounts signed by Terry Venables and fellow director, Jakub Pawlikowski, on 28 May 1993 show assets of £2, matched by issued share capital of £2.
The company was wound up on 26 January 1995.

Terence Venables Holdings Limited (Company No. 02782786)
Date of incorporation: 22 January 1993, under the name of Jezeco Number I Limited.
Changed its name on 13 April 1993.
Sole director: Terry Venables.
Accounts for 30 April 1994, approved 23 December 1994, show liabilities

exceeded assets, including fixed assets, by £12,400.

The company is shown as 100% owner of Terry Venables Limited, Edennote Limited and Depthsubmit Limited and 71% owner of Scribes West Limited.

Thurston Barnett Limited (Company No. 2654722)
Date of incorporation: 16 October 1991.
Directors: Jakub Pawlikowski and Terry Venables.
The company was dissolved on 7 March 1995.

Scribes West Limited (Company No. 02289013)
Date of incorporation: 23 August 1988.
Sole director: Terry Venables.
Latest accounts, for year ending 30 April 1994, signed by Terry Venables on 22 February 1995, show liabilities exceeded assets by £204,384. The cash at bank and in hand is £155.